# The New Egypt: From Chaos to the Strong State (2014-2016)

Dr. Yassin El-Ayouty, Esq.

ISBN: 1537045962
ISBN-13: 978-1537045962

# DEDICATION

To all those in Egypt and around the world who stood by the New Egypt transitioning from the chaos of the years 2011 to 2013 to the Strong State which has emerged as of 2014. May its progress and development continue.

# CONTENTS

Dr. Yassin El-Ayouty, Esq.

# ACKNOWLEDGMENTS

Among my limitations are online matters. So it is with appreciation that I acknowledge the professional assistance and advice of Mr. Raymond Chan. Without his contribution as webmaster of our organization SUNSGLOW – Global Training in the Rule of Law, this volume would not have seen the light of day. Errors which may be found in this book are entirely my responsibility.

# 1 APRIL 2014

## THE COPTIC QUESTION: PROTECTING MINORITIES DURING PERIODS OF UPHEAVALS

April 10, 2014

In my view, the most effective presentation of a case, is one that begins with the conclusions. Most education in U.S. law schools, especially in Year One, the horrible year, begins by briefing cases, not by study guides. Invariably I do the opposite. Begin by defining the terms and the issues, then go to the 60-page case and you will quickly find the holding.

The same here tonight in studying "the Coptic Question" in Egypt. It is vastly complex, and I hope that, through the principle of "start with the conclusions," the details, which follow, shall be made clearer.

When I began my research on this question, I was fortunate to have among the resources brought to me by my friends from Cairo in Arabic, especially Mr. Wagdy Rizk of the U.N., a seminal report dated November 1972. The significance of that report is that it was drafted by a blue-ribbon committee called **Al-Etaiffi Committee.** It was made up of members of the Egyptian House of Representatives, Muslims and Copts. The Committee was instructed by Parliament, and guided by a decree issued by the **late**

**President Anwar Sadat,** to investigate terrible events of communal clashes in a town called **El-Khankah** in the **Province** of **Qalyubiyah** north of **Cairo.**

The central event was an attack by Muslims on Nov. 6, 1972 against the Headquarters of the **Holy Bible Society,** a Coptic organization, which was used as a Church without a government license. The building was torched by a group which started from a mosque called **Al-Ashraf mosque.** Six days later, in a show of coptic solidarity, a large group of Coptic Clergy and Coptic civilians, travelled from various places to **El-Khankah** and held prayers at the attacked site. Counter Muslim demonstrations approached the site; a Copt is said to have fired a weapon in the air to ward off the approaching angry mob. The result was torching his and his neighbor's homes. There were no human casualties. End of **El-Khankah** episode of 42 years ago.

Studying this incident of communal clashes, one finds in it a typical example of the Coptic question which reveals, in a repetitive though more severe fashion, conclusions which I am now able to present:

The two issues involved in the Coptic Question are: Licensing to build churches, and the right to advocate and teach Christian orthodoxy;

The Muslim/Coptic confrontation incidents are usually described by the authorities, not as a "sectarian conflict," but as threats to "national unity;"

Institutional responses to these incidents, from 1970s till the present, aim at containment, not at eradication of root causes;

These responses, whether effectual or ineffectual, involve the entirety of institutional Egypt. This means from the top of the pyramid, Presidential decrees, through parliamentary committees of investigations, through the provincial levels (Governors, rural leaderships...etc), all the while guided by an advisory and reconciliation combination of **Al-Azhar,** the citadel of mainstream Islamic learning, and the **Coptic Church;**

The legal systems which impact upon the Coptic Question have their roots in the **Ottoman system** since 1517. It is called the **Millet system:** namely each religious community, in matters of marriage, divorce, wills and charitable contributions, is governed by its own internal **Canon Law** and **Sharia Law** and **Mosaic Law** based on the Old Testament;

After the collapse of the old Parliamentary system, the rise of dictatorship in Egypt caused the concomitant rise of sectarianism. The monolithic ruler, from **Nasser** in 1952 to the fall of **Mubarak** in 2011, tried at to govern through "Divide and Rule;"

Islamism in Egypt, a country which historically is secular, was bolstered unofficially by **Wahhabi** extremism, the radicalization of the **Muslim Brotherhood,** the rise of the religious state in the Middle East such as **Saudi Arabia** in 1932; **Pakistan** in 1947, **Israel** in 1948, and the **post-Shah** Iran in 1979;

The aggression against Coptic churches and establishments was met by laws which were unenforced, especially as regards the principle of equality before the law;

There is hope that Egypt, which got rid of Mubarak through a direct and solid amalgam of Muslims and Copts, promises to deal with the transgressions against the Copts through a robust legal and security system. This is the dividend accruing from the victory in **June 30, 2013** of secular Egypt over the **Muslim Brotherhood** which had promised a reign of anti-Coptic terror because of Coptic support of the ouster of Morsi; and

The term Egypt means **"the land of the Copts."** The roots of the Copts in Egypt could be traced religiously to the establishment of the first Christian Church only 200 years after **Christ.** However, civilizationally, these roots go back 5000 years to Ancient Egypt where the **ankh,** the key-like cross symbolizing enduring life, was described by the great Chicago University historian, **Breasted,** as the direct predecessor of the **Cross.** The Arab roots go back to the year 640 A.D. when Egypt came under Muslim control. That was during the reign of Omar, the 2nd Caliph after Muhammad.

These are 10 basic conclusions of my presentation which now goes into the area of forensic analysis of the on-again, off-again eruptions of the Coptic crisis in the largest demographically Arab country Egypt whose best description was offered by the **great late Shenouda,** the **Pope** of **Alexandria.** In a dialogue, two years before his death, that highly learned leader told me that **"Egypt is not a country in which we live. It is a country that lives in us."** Now let us see how this country, whose map I am now holding in my hand, lives in the heart of all Egyptians, both Christians and Muslims.

There are five areas that are worthy of probing. These are: **(a)** The demographics and the geography; **(b)** The anti-Coptic ideology; **(c)** The broad expanse of the anti-coptic attacks; **(d)** Containment: the historic, legal, and religious frameworks; and **(e)** What can be done?

## (A)  The Demographics and the Geography:

As in the case of Lebanon, there has not been a census determining the exact percentage of the number of Christians in egypt. We say "Christians," because, in Egypt, there are Copts (orthodox); Catholics; and Anglicans. The rank and file of Egyptian Muslims lump all of those denominations together as "Copts." In my case, having been raised in a Coptic neighborhood in eastern Egypt, and belonging to a family which historically has been the administrative link between minorities and the seats of powers, I have always been interested in, let us say for ease of reference, "the Coptic Question."

The percentage of Christians is generally considered to be anywhere from 10% to 15% of a population which now numbers approximately 90 million.

The geography of Coptic residence is not limited to one area of this country of nearly one million square kilometers. The Christian population lives all over Egypt with the villages, especially in southern Egypt, housing Copts and Muslims side by side. This factor is important in two ways: The absence of a Coptic region makes security a very local issue, but with national repercussions; and the Copts, being generally better educated, have a better understanding of the outside world than most of their Muslim neighbors. In the job market, in a country with 40% illiteracy, the recruiter, if a Muslim, would generally be inclined to favor a Muslim applicant, especially that no Copt is called Muhammad, and no Muslim is called Guirgis (George).

In this regard, we exclude the composition of the Egyptian Cabinet, which invariably and by tradition, has included 2 Copts, neither of them occupies **"sovereign portfolios"** such as Defense, Foreign Affairs or Justice. No Copt has ever been a President of Egypt. This is although Copts have always been in the forefront of national movements for independence and national defense.

When the British granted Egypt self-rule in 1922, the Declaration of that status contained 4 reservations, including the right of Great Britain to intervene for the protection of minorities (i.e. largely the Copts).

## (B) The Anti-Coptic Ideology:

Never in the history of Egypt has there been a horrific scene of what nowadays is called ethnic/religious cleansing, or generalized inter-communal hatred like what we see between Muslims and Christians in **Nigeria** or in the **Central African Republic.** Or what we have witnessed in the case of **Serbia vs. Bosnia Herzegovina,** or are witnessing now in **Syria, Iraq and Pakistan** between **Sunnis and Shiis.**

Nonetheless, since the 1970s, after the death of Nasser, an anti-Coptic ideology has been fueled by several factors. Foremost amongst these is the transformation of the **Muslim Brotherhood** from religious advocacy **(DAWA)** to the politics of power through force and coercion. The Coptic issue was a ready-made Islamist instrument for recruitment and mass appeal. The veil of moderation fell with the Islamists ascending to power in 2012, after the fall of Mubarak. That ascendancy was through the defective mechanism of the Ballot Box, and the **"hate -the Copts"** ideology became structured, propagandizing the following mythology:

The Copts are the enemies of an Islamic State, not only in Egypt, but anywhere. Their opposition to a **Caliphate** is fueled by their desire to oppose **Sharia,** especially as a principal source of legislation;

The Copts, in their quest for a secular Egypt see in the gradual and surreptitious conversion of the young Muslims, a path towards arresting that islamization;

Copts converting to Islam are only seeking to benefit from the liberal divorce practices of the Muslims because the Coptic Church does not permit religious sanctification of divorce of Coptic spouses;

The Copts, especially those who have immigrated from Egypt, are actively seeking to invite foreign intervention in Egypt through raising the cry of human rights violations, thus weakening the State and, with it, the right of the majority, namely the Muslims, to exercise a dominant nationalistic role.

There are other aspects of that anti-Coptic mythology beyond the enumeration herein presented. Ironically, each one of the enumerated four aspects has a small kernel of factual validity. The ideology of the recently assertive Muslim Brotherhood, and its more virulent allies, like the **Salafis,** became the oxygen keeping that anti-Coptism, not only alive, but entrenched. Translation: **Attack the Copts!!**

Although January 7, the Orthodox Christmas was made a national holiday by Mubarak, and although the Arab Spring in Egypt was a Muslim/Coptic product, yet the national upheaval was later hijacked by a Muslim Brotherhood who at first condemned the rebellion then belatedly joined it and unsuccessfully tried to co-opt it.

Protecting the Copts became difficult for the new Egypt to maintain. As of June 2012, **Shafik,** the military general, though supported by the Copts, lost his presidential bid to **Morsi,** the candidate of the **Muslim Brotherhood.** During the turbulence from November 2012 to June 2013, the security of the Egyptian street became a thing of the past.

The Ministry of Interior which controls the Police became the enemy, due to the killing of nearly 900 Egyptian demonstrators and to a prior record of torture. The only institutions which remained standing in a bureaucratic Egypt of 5000 years were: **the army and the judiciary.** To the Copts, the Islamist rule by Morsi from June 2012 to July 2013, was a year of terror. Its gradual evaporation caused by the armed forces, which are based on compulsory draft of both Muslims and Copts, (Coptic generals were in the forefront of the leadership of the war of 1973 under **Sadat**), gave the Copts the hope of a light at the end of the tunnel. Their support for **General El-Sisi,** and of the post-Islamic **Constitution of 2014,** was a natural. Yet a structural damage to Egypt's national unity had already occurred: Brotherhood versus the State; Brotherhood versus the Copts; moderate Islam, the bedrock of Coptic security, versus terrorism. Too many splits; precious little cures. An **El-Sisi** presidency in Egypt, a near certainty, shall be an early Christmas for the Christians in historic Egypt. It shall represent security wedded to, secularity.

## (C) The Broad Expanse of Anti-Coptic Attacks

Translating the above into a saga of anti-Coptic attacks has been lucidly expressed by the large volume of official Coptic material provided to me by the **Secretary-General of the Council of Egyptian Churches.** I was also provided by a large amount of photos to document those sad events which are available for the audience to review, but not to take away after this formal event.

**Pastor Dr. Bishoy Hilmy,** has provided us with an important document dated **September 5, 2013,** two months after unseating **Morsi** who is now on trial, but three months before the present Government declaring the Brotherhood in December 2013 a terrorist organization. It is an official letter signed by **Pastor Al-Biady,** the **Head of the Anglican Church; Patriarch Ishak,** the leader of the **Catholic Copts;** and above all, by the **Pope of Alexandria, His Eminence Pope Tawadros the Second,** who presides over the Coptic Orthodox community.

The letter is addressed to **Field Marshall El-Sisi** and copied to **General Taher Abdullah,** who leads the Corps of Engineers of the nearly one-million armed forces. This Corps has been active in rebuilding, at the cost of the State, Christian establishments damaged by the marauding hooligans affiliated with, or paid by, or Islamically misled by the Brotherhood in Egypt, and by **Hamas and Qatar** outside of Egypt.

The document reminds El-Sisi of an agreement reached with **El-Sisi** at a meeting in which El-Sisi asked for a comprehensive list of Coptic establishments damaged on August 14, 2013. On that date, the army and the resurrected security forces stormed the militarized sit-ins by the Brotherhood at two locations, **Rabaa** and **Al-Nahda.** After 6 weeks of appealing to the occupants of those armed enclaves to peacefully disband, official Egypt was striking back to assert the legitimacy of its Second Revolution of July 3, 2013 which the Brotherhood and most of the West, together with Turkey and Qatar and Gaza, dubbed as **"a coup."**

The letter covered Churches, schools and other Christian facilities either burnt or damaged in whole or in part after August 14, 2013 by arson, molotov cocktails, and firing of various types of armaments. It also documented theft, pillage and desecration in whole or in part. The high-level signatories of this document requested action on El-Sisi's resolute decision to rebuild and or compensate the Christian Churches and citizens.

It ended with the following phrase: **"We pray for you to be blessed and to attain full success. We ask the same for our beloved Egypt to enjoy security and prosperity. We cherish you and our brave armed forces which constitute Egypt's shield."**

We note here that that language by the Christian religious hierarchy reflects both anguish and resilience. It reflects the historic official line which proclaims that **"Egypt is not Iraq. The Egyptian Society has different characteristics. It is unified in the sense that there are no minorities. The Egyptian people, by its own nature, is integrated. Its Muslims and Christians occupy the same neighborhoods everywhere."**

But official lines and the facts on the ground in post-Mubarak Egypt suffer from a disconnect. The reports which I have from the **St. Mark Cathedral, thanks to the help of several Coptic friends,** both clerical and laity, shows that in nearly all the Egyptian provinces which number 27, destructive attacks and desecration and theft, were perpetrated. By comparison with Revolutionary Egypt, the reign of Mubarak looked in the rear view mirror to the Copts who brought it down, to have been a relatively golden age in regard to security which in this context trumps other values.

## (D) Containment: The Historic, Legal and Religious Frameworks:

It is axiomatic to say that we live in an age of rage. Law in Egypt suffers at present from an enforcement deficit, has nearly ceased to be a solution. Obviously this affects not only the Copts, but also other important sectors of life in Egypt. It also suffers nearly everywhere from erroneous re-interpretation. Even in an iconic democratic system such as in the U.S., America has refused to apply an important international convention, such as the U.N. Convention on Civil and Political Rights, to situations outside U.S. borders. Prior to this, there was even greater anomalies: discarding the Geneva Conventions of 1949 by the Bush Jr. administration as obsolete in the context of the war on terror, and the abstaining thus far from acceding to the Rome Convention of 1998 which created the International Criminal Court.

In the specific case of Egypt, there is a legal framework in existence since Ottoman times, which should have prevented anti-Coptic aggression. During the reign of **Sultan Abdel-Meguid the First,** an important Ottoman decree was promulgated in February 1856 which regulated the issue of construction of places of worship for all faiths throughout the Empire including Egypt. It went by the name of **"The Hamayooni Line."** And during the great age of **Muhammad Ali,** the founder of modern Egypt, from **1805 to 1849,** all Ottoman decrees issued with adverse effects on the Copts were rescinded. The Copts were allowed to build new churches, to carry arms, to join the armed forces, and to attain Cabinet ministerial ranks. More importantly, during the reign of **Said,** one of **Muhammad Ali's** sons (1854-1863), the tax imposed on the Copts, known by its Islamic term as **"geziah"** which was in force since the year 640, was eliminated and replaced by military service. Therefore we have here a solid legal and historical foundation on which security for Egyptian minorities, whether Copts or Shiis can be rejuvenated.

We also have in Islamic jurisprudence, a non-recognition of the term **"infidel,"** total equality between Muslims and non-Muslims, and the co-existence between Sharia and legislated law. **Muhammad** had married a **Coptic** woman, **Mary,** and the second Caliph after Muhammad, **Omar** had ordered the whipping of the son of his General Amre who conquered Egypt who had whipped a Coptic lad. In this regard, Omar famously said:

**"Since when have you enslaved human beings whose mothers have given them freedom through birth."** The Quran glorifies Mary and the immaculate conception 43 times, the only woman so mentioned by name in the **Quran,** and glorified **Jesus** as the word of God more than 30 times. This is not all for that solid Islamic foundation in cosmopolitan Egypt for the protection of minorities during periods of upheavals.

The great declaration of **Al-Azhar** dated **August 19, 2011,** and endorsed by the **Coptic Church** states the following in its 4th, from among eleven principles:

**"Full respect to the view of the others, which implicates the necessity of avoiding declaring others to be apostates and traitors; and the abuse of religion for the purposes of sowing divisiveness and hatred among the citizens. Sectarian conflict and racist advocacy are criminally injurious to the homeland."**

**Moreover, the preamble of the post-Islamic Constitution of 2014 states that "Egypt is the birthplace of faith -all faith- and that the Egyptians have embraced the Virgin Mary and her son and offered thousands of martyrs in defense of the Church of Christ"**

Its **94th Article** proclaims that **"the Rule of Law is the Basis of Governing the State."**

The first lines of the great history book on **"The Flight of the Holy Family to Egypt,"** is introduced by **Egyptian Bishop Mataous**. It starts by this phrase: **"The flight to Egypt is one of the most important historic events which took place over the soil of our dear Egypt over its long history."**

One of today's great Coptic scholars in the U.S., **Francis Basili,** the son of a luminary from among the clergymen of the Coptic Church, states the following in **"Sawt Biladi" (The Voice of my Homeland)**, the issue of February 2014:

**"The conflict between the brethren of Egypt, Muslims and Copts developed only when the Muslim Brotherhood and their affiliations ignited the powder keg of religious militancy as of the 1970s."**

**(E) What Can Be Done?**

Now is the time to start anew in the new Egypt. The upheavals of the Arab

Spring should be followed by the return to Egypt's roots, especially as regards the Coptic question. I believe that we now have a clean slate in the country which is the engine which pulls the entire Arab train behind it.

Let us start with the process of re-education, to remind Egypt of its true identity. In doing so, we do not need new laws, we need enforcement. We have enough laws except for strengthening the judiciary and its independence, and of teaching the cops that the age of torturing suspects is over.

Both **Al-Azhar** and the **Church** in Egypt have a history of mutual respect, collaboration, and the compulsive need for containment, especially in the area of tormenting the Christians in other Arab Spring countries such as **Libya and Syria.**

By education, the teaching of Islamic law should be cleansed from the aberrations of archaic interpretations of how Islam should deal with non-Muslims. Militant Islam at least in Egypt, I believe, is on the ropes. I do not expect the **Muslim Brotherhood** will have the chance of a comeback. The mosques are now being sequestered by the Government to prevent the pulpit from again becoming a free zone for hate speech. Inter-faith events should be institutionalized. Trials of religious malfeasants should be televised. Compensation for the Copts should be legislated. University education and curricula should stress what the Egyptians so far mouth, but do not practice: **"Faith is for God; the homeland is for all."**

A final word about what not to do, and then what also should be done: First: any foreign intervention or internationalization of the Coptic question is immensely counter-productive. The ethos of the Arab Spring is that reform and restoration are a home industry. We must look upon these restorative values, especially in the critical area of education, as a cottage industry. The rural areas must become the center; the capital is the periphery. The individual and the local communities are the main actors.

Since we are dealing with faith, an area which is not negotiable, let Egypt, with its unique history of Muslim/Coptic co-existence, show other Arab and Muslim countries the way. **Al-Azhar** which gave my father the way of culturally rearing me, is the focus of teaching Islamic moderation. This is why Al-Azhar is in the cross-hairs of the **Muslim Brotherhood.** Its influence in Sunni and Shii learning is phenomenal It was established in the year 975 A.D., together with Cairo, by Shiis. Under **Article 7 of the 2014** post-Islamic Constitution, Al Azhar's independence was restored. Al-Azhar/Cathedral intertwining, through joint educational programs, is a must.

The issues of the laws governing church construction without too much red-tape should be reviewed. The public and private information systems should not muzzle up the events affecting communal relationships. The Coptic community should feel that its impact on legislation, diplomacy, education, social services is assured. Interfaith events should be multiplied and the basics of interpretation of Islamic law **(ijtihad)** should find their way to the textbooks as of the primary school.

The State, all over the world, has been overstretched, thus weakened. Now, individual and communal action have their chance. In that spirit, I am launching this summer in southern Egypt, where Muslims and Copts live together, a pilot project to uplift the level of University education. Thanks-

Dr. Yassin El-Ayouty, Esq.

# 2 JULY 2014

## Journalism of the Absurd: Thomas Friedman Fantasizes About "ISIS and SISI"!!

Wednesday, July 2, 2014

In an **op-ed** article in the **New York Times** of June 25, 2014, **Thomas Friedman** writes about **"ISIS and SISI."** That play on words, for which Friedman is known, shows how low on fact and high on fiction that editorialist can be bracketed. There is nothing in that Friedman column that I find either constructive or conducive to objective understanding of today's turbulent Middle East.

To describe, as Friedman does, **ISIS and SISI** as **"the two dominant Arab governing models: ISIS and SISI"** strikes me as simply outlandish. **ISIS** is a terrorist and murderous cabal; **SISI** is an Egyptian president whose ascendancy to power was propelled by the victory of secularists over the Islamists. **ISIS** is a Sunni transient phenomenon with some roots in Syrian and Iraqi sectarianism; **SISI** is a feature of post-revolutionary Egypt whose cosmopolitanism is rooted in a history of 5000 years.

Where does **Friedman** find in this reverse of name-spelling **"Arab governing models?"** Unless he is a seer or a tarot card reader, the **"governing model's"** thesis is to be found only in the zone of fantasy.

13

The plain logic is that ISIS is on a huge collision course with SISI through the Egyptian/Gulf new axis of stability.

I can understand Friedman's chagrin over the imprisonment in Egypt of three of **Al Jazeera** journalists. Freedom of the press is an essential ingredient of progress towards democracy. But Friedman does not seem to grasp the following basic facts about the Egyptian Revolution.

It is a work in progress; it embodies the aspirations of the majority of its 90 million inhabitants for dignity and development; it is committed to secularism as the vehicle for the protection of its Coptic minority and for the preservation of its cosmopolitanism; it is the target of Islamic jihadi terrorism; it is opposed to any hint of foreign interference in its internal affairs; it is surrounded by unstable neighbors to the east (the Gaza mess); to the south (the troubled Sudan), and to the west (the Libyan State of militias).

Taking these factors into account, one should feel the pain of an Egyptian society trying to find its way out of 60 years of dictatorship. In the process, the Egyptian judicial over-reaction in the case of **Al Jazeera** can at least be comprehended, if not condoned. The entire Egyptian judicial process is now under review.

This brings me to discussing the nature of **Al Jazeera** as a TV channel or channels which is totally funded by **Qatar -the mouse that roars.** Though patterned along the lines of the **BBC, Al Jazeera** cannot be weaned away from Qatari influence, and Qatar has been one of the primary supporters of a terrorist organization called the **"Muslim Brotherhood."** The guru of **Al Jazeera** is **Sheikh Youssef Al-Qaradawi,** an Egyptian with a Qatari passport, who has been the oracle of sectarianism in the Muslim world in terms of the persecution of the Shia. That explains in part why **Egypt** and **Qatar** today maintain no diplomatic relations, especially after the revelations about Qatari support for **Hamas.**

Thus talking about the right of **Al Jazeera** to freely function on Egyptian soil is like allowing a Cuban information medium to function openly in Miami with Castro's funding while Cuba is under U.S. sanctions. It should also be noted here that the U.S., after **9/11,** has claimed for security reasons the right to subject **Guantanamo** inmates to undetermined periods of incarceration without either being charged or be transferred to civilian U.S. courts.

Without any regard to balanced editorial analysis, Mr. Friedman pontificates as follows: **"The Arab World needs to finally puncture the twin myths of the military State (SISI) or the Islamic State (ISIS) that will bring prosperity, stability and dignity."** Words of superficial gold, but substance of rusty junk. The **SISI** era has just begun; so judging it after only one month of existence as a **"military State"** is nothing but animus without reason. By the same token, Friedman's anticipation of the longevity of ISIS as an **"Islamic State"** is nothing but ignorance and unthinking alarmism. **ISIS** is a bubble which shall be **"punctured,"** not only by the Arab world, but also by the weight of its murderous overreach.

Friedman offers no credible facts or analysis as to **"Why two Arab governing models are doomed."** I am on board with him as regards **ISIS,** but must rebut his non-warranted prediction as regards the **El-Sisi** regime. From the Egyptian street, I marshal my rebuttal:

- There is no sectarianism in Egypt. The fight against the **Muslim Brotherhood** is not sectarianism by any stretch of imagination;
- Egypt's present economic decline is, by all measures, a temporary paralysis due to the marginalization of the population in Sinai and Nubia, the high rate of unemployment, and the need for more time to have the development projects produce their intended results;
- Egypt's preoccupation with containing its internal Islamic terrorism, which is largely imported from Gaza, undoubtedly has its retarding effects, which is also the case of several other countries facing the same dilemma. Both **Nigeria** and **Algeria** are prime examples;
- Emulating President El-Sisi example of forgoing a part of his salary and other property for the national cause of recovery, other Egyptian notables did the same. These included the heads of the **Wafd party (El-Sayed Belawi),** and of the **National Front (General Ahmed Shafiq).** So did important businessman **(Muhammed Al-Amin and Mansour Amer).** In regard to **Mansour Amer,** he pledged to pay all the costs of construction of the new Cairo University.
- Tourism to Egypt is back; and the new Egypt is gearing up to holding parliamentary elections this summer. The central focus is on inclusiveness and enhancing the representativeness of the previously marginalized groups in Sinai, in Nubia, and in the western desert. Youth, women, and the Copts are expected to win a greater number of parliamentary seats than before.
- Egypt is again rising to see in which ways she and her partners in Saudi Arabia, Kuwait, Jordan, and the Emirates might further contain **ISIS, Hamas**, and a possible third **"Palestinian**

**Intifada."**
The list of signs of an enduring post-revolutionary Egypt goes on and on, including the re-admission of Egypt to the membership of the **African Union.** Above all, Egypt has not been subjected to civil war. Its solidity is, in many ways, similar to the solidity of its iconic Giza pyramids.

**Mr. Friedman:** You may go on with your theoretical fantasies. I sense from your recent commencement speech at the University of **Erbil, Iraq; Kurdistan,** that you are in hot pursuit of peripheral news items. Now with **ISIS** calling itself **IS (the Islamic State),** your little game of words is in danger. That of course unless you try to find a new fictitious resonance between **"IS" and "SI."**

In my view, major issues of stability and historical transitions should be immunized from your addiction to playing with words. More importantly, it behooves you, as a student of the troubled Middle East, not to proceed from that word play to the slippery slope of fictitious, conclusions. ISIS is not a government model, nor is El-Sisi regime doomed to extinction which you seem to predict.

# What Is There in Common Between Charles Darwin and Abdel-Fattah El-Sisi?

Friday, July 11, 2014

My own response is: **"The Theory of Evolution."** During my senior year at Zagazig High School, Sharkia, Egypt, I was, as a science major, one of 20 national contestants in that theory. Studying late at night, aided by the light of a kerosene lamp at our village family home, I plowed through 4 books in English on that theory. It was a very absorbing task, but it taught me a life-long lesson: **evolve or perish.** It is a principle based on **"the survival of the fittest."**

Here is my take on the evolution of **President El-Sisi,** which may also be anchored on what our British professors taught us at that great high school: **"Circumstances Alter Cases."**

**El-Sisi** rightly rode the crest of mass popular anger at the horrible year of Islamist rule in Egypt (June 2012-July 2013). Yes the **Muslim Brotherhood** of the now deposed **President Morsi,** a fellow Sharkawi for whom I voted in 2012, believed in **"One Man, One Vote!!"** But once in power, that principle became, for all intents and purposes: **"One Man, One Vote, One Time."** Their contract with the voters proved to be a sham.

How does the abject failure of Islamist rule in Egypt relate to the evolution of El-Sisi's political though as the 7th president of modern Egypt? (He is #7 after **Nasser, Sadat, Mubarak, Tantawi: (through SCAF); Morsi, Mansour**). Look at what is happening now in Gaza (**Hamas v. Israel**). During the Islamist regime, Hamas revelled in earning **$450 millions** annually by invading Sinai through **1500** tunnels. That was the biggest smuggling operation in modern history. Arms, drugs, terrorists, cars, and house-hold equipment flowed unabashedly. Egypt's army, police and other personnel including large battalions of **Border Guards (Silah Al-Hodoud)** suffered the humiliation of Morsi's orders not to interfere with Hamas illegal operations.

Then suddenly, on July 3, 2013, the hands of these nationalist forces were freed to defend Sinai from Hamasawi attempts to transfer rocketing Israel from Gaza to Sinai. The tsunami of Egypt's defensive measures in Sinai crippled Hamas financially and led to a no-content unity Palestinian government between Abbas and Hamas. And with the heinous crimes of murdering young Israelis and a Palestinian youth, which transformed the conflict from a territorial conflict into an ethnic and religious conflict, Egyptian Sinai stood by, minding its own peace from terrorist aggression. The **Rafah Crossing** remained closed, except for limited purposes of Palestinian pilgrimage to **Mecca.**

With the daily uneven duel between Hamas, through rockets, and Israel through daily bombardment of nearly anything that moves, **El-Sisi** ordered the reopening of the Rafah Crossing to allow injured Palestinians to be properly treated in a specially reserved hospital at **El-Arish.** The evolutionary thinking of El-Sisi and his team made humanitarianism towards besieged Gazans trump their anger at Hamasawi murderous intervention in Egypt's internal affairs. That intervention was aided by Qatar and other outside mischief makers.

As to **ISIS,** the new phantom so-called Islamic Caliphate based in **Mousul, Iraq,** and **Al-Rakkah, Syria,** there could be no more articulated hostility toward that fictitious entity than that of Egypt's secularist community. **Al-Azhar** has declared in August, 2011, that Islam does not admit of a State based solely on religion; the **Coptic Church** watches in horror as Christians in Iraqi and Syrian ISIS-controlled territories are being murdered or chased out of their ancestral lands; and the Gulf States, new and valuable allies of the new Egypt, feel the jitters of an approaching **Sunni-Shii** war of devastation.

While Iraqi Prime Minister **Al-Maliki** is fighting for his political life, and for the territorial integrity of Iraq, **El-Sisi** while condemning the dangers of militant Islam, welcomed Al-Maliki's call of July 8 for broadening the web of relationships between **Cairo and Baghdad.** Attacking **ISIS** and nodding respectfully toward Iraq as a unitary State are clear manifestations of El-Sisi's approach toward this burning issue. In summary, it is a bold attempt to carve out an atmosphere of moderation from the howling winds of an Arab region which is being territorially redrawn.

From all indicators, **El-Sisi** had evolved beyond a total focus on Egypt, to a focus on Egypt as a serious player in the Arab homeland. For **Al-Maliki's** call to **El-Sisi** for **"relationships of complimentarity"** between the land of the Nile and the land of the Two Rivers, was not born out of thin air. Prior to that, **El-Sisi** had declared on July 6 at a meeting with Egyptian editors-in-chief that **"a plebiscite for the independence of Iraqi Kurdistan would be a catastrophe."** No such political backing for the territorial integrity of Arab States -all Arab States - has been voiced with the exception of a reference made to it by Saudi Arabia.

In between the dates of July 6 and July 8, there was the **10th of the holy Muslim month of Ramadan (July 7)**. Since the 1973 war between Egypt and Israel (Egypt calls it the 10th of Ramadan War; Israel calls it the Yom Kippur War), that day is observed in Egypt as a national day (**Day of the Crossing** -crossing the Suez Canal to liberate Sinai).

In his speech to the nation, El-Sisi called for national support of the huge effort to rebuild the economy. An essential aspect of that effort is the doing away with the subsidies on petrol, gas, electricity, and other items of national consumption. This is a very hot potato in Egyptian politics. The poor and the middle classes depend on these subsidies to make ends meet. It caused **"the bread riots"** in February 1977 in Egypt under Sadat. Yet El-Sisi was fearless in declaring that those unpopular measures must stand.

Various heads of Egyptian political parties praised that move which reflected a basic principle: **Leaders must lead.** The head of the **Congress Party (Al-Motamar), Omar Semedah,** said: **"El-Sisi is the first president who tells the public that it should shoulder its economic recovery responsibilities."** A leader of the **Wafd Party, Issam Sheeha,** welcomed El-Sisi redirection of nationalist fever to national acceptance of shouldering the common burden. Even **Al-Noor Party,** the political arm of the **Salafi movement,** stated through its spokesman **Sharif Taha: "We applaud his candor, his transparency."** As to the **Front of National Salvation (Al-Inqaz Al-Watani),** its leader, **Amre Ali,** was by far the most effusive: **"El-Sisi has delivered a declaration which, by the standards of Egyptian presidential statements, is very rare."**

Another evolutionary trend was manifest in El-Sisi's blunt criticism of the incarceration and the sentencing of the three **Al Jazeera** reporters. He had previously declared that he would not interfere in judicial rulings. Now he declares: **"The sentences had negative consequences,"** and that he preferred **"that the journalists be deported rather than put on trial."** I see in this an El-Sisi's edging towards a pardon.

How about the Nile water question? It has stirred deep anxiety on the part of **Egypt (and the Sudan)** whose share of the Nile waters through the **Blue Nile** has been fixed by a **1929 treaty.** That was at a time prior to the emergence of Ethiopia (the Blue Nile descends from **Lake Tana,** Ethiopian territory), of the Sudan, and of Egypt from under Italian and British colonialism. While Ethiopia proceeds at present with the construction of the **Grand Renaissance Dam** at the upper reaches of the Blue Nile, both **Cairo and Khardoum** have been fretting over the possible reduction of their pre-independence share of that precious water.

Under Morsi, an intemperate call went out from a meeting over which he had presided. It was a call for the use of force against Ethiopia. The whole world heard it, because the microphones at that unfortunate war-like conclave were left open. **Addis Ababa** countered with the legitimate argument of self-defence, and **Egypt,** even if the Islamists had gone ahead with their stupid threats, had never won in mountain warfare. No win in **1830** in the war in Greece for the Ottoman Sultan during the reign of **Muhammad Ali;** no win in **Yemen** in 1962-1967 during the go-go years of **Nasser.** And the Islamists forgot or ignored the possibility for employing diplomacy through the **Coptic Church,** a twin historic institution of the **Ethiopian Church.**

Then the Islamist President Morsi was pushed aside, and General El-Sisi, in a land slide, won the presidency in June 2014. While Morsi, the civilian, saw the water issue through the foggy prism of war, General (new President) El-Sisi saw it through the prism of diplomacy. With Egypt's return to the fold of the **African Union** at the June African Summit at **Malabo,** the capital of **Equatorial Guinea,** El-Sisi saw the golden chance of repairing the frayed feelings of Ethiopia, a co-founder with Egypt of the

**Organization of African Unity.**

Now, following an amicable meeting between **El-Sisi** and Ethiopia's Prime Minister, **Hailemarian Desalegn,** an agreement was announced by Egypt's Foreign Minister, **Sameh Shoukry,** and his Ethiopian counterpart **Tedros Adhanom.** Its main points included cooperation between the two sister States, and the establishment of regional projects for developing financial resources to meet the growing demand for water. **Neat!! A welcome evolution from the use of vinegar to the use of honey!!**

Indeed, **Darwin** said it best: **"Survival is for the fittest."** Now even the map of Egypt is changing through redrawing provincial boundaries. From 27 Egyptian provinces, the boundaries, as recently declared by **Adel Labeeb,** Minister for Local Development, may delineate an increase to up to **33 provinces.** The new Governors shall be evaluated on the basis of direct interaction with the Egyptian citizen. This is the essence of evolving the meaning of **"local rule."**

These steps towards rejuvenation did not fail to impact the traditional sources of the tourism industry. Both, **Germany and Italy,** main sources of thousands of tourists to Egypt, are moving towards full nullification of their advisories to their nationals to avoid visiting Egypt. **This is huge!!**

Tourism accounts for 20% of Egypt's foreign currency earnings. This explains the genuine alarm of its **Ministry of Tourism.** In 2013, income from tourism dwindled by 40% as compared to 2012 **(from $10 billion to $5.9 billion).** Italy alone had sent to Egypt in 2004 one million tourists.

**So why shouldn't the Sphinx, hearing about the resumption of the flood of visitors gawking at his feet (I mean paws) be smiling in anticipation? Is it possible that lime stone, of which the Sphinx is made, be also subject to the forces of evolution? The Sphinx has never revealed its inner secrets!!**

# 3 AUGUST 2014

## In the Israel/Hamas War of 2014, Facts Were Smothered By Adding Fiction to the Fray!!

Friday, August 1, 2014

- **Hamas** denies Israel's right to exist. But regardless of the circumstances of its birth, Israel does exist. It is a member of the UN; it has peace treaties with both Egypt and Jordan; it is a party to the Oslo Agreements of 1993 in spite of their rejection by Mr. Netanyahu; and it is in negotiations, now stalled, with the Palestinian Authority which is legally the representative of the Palestinian people.
- **Israel**, as per Mr. Netanyahu, demands of Hamas a **quid pro quo.** It calls for **"quiet for quiet." Unworkable.** Since 2007, Israel has besieged Gaza with a ring of steel. You cannot hold a person's head in a choke hold, cutting off his breathing, then demand of him to stop struggling. Israel claims that the siege is needed for its own security. Israel is entitled to its security within its own borders which include neither Gaza nor the West Bank. History has shown that Israeli security lies solely, not within the framework of its armed might (the 5th biggest army in the world), but in the framework of peace treaties. The Palestinians have been waiting

for one since 1993. Postponing such contractual arrangement is a postponement of security.

- Since 2006, **Hamas** has been in rebellion against the Palestinian Authority. But that authority, though enfeebled by corruption and aimlessness, has been recognized by the UN as an observer State. Hamas has taken over Gaza by brutal force. Hamas has opportuned the wave of Palestinian disgust at the corruption of the PLO. But Hamas is neither a Palestinian government in exile, nor is it a representative of all Gazans, let alone all Palestinians. And, as it calls itself the **Islamic Resistance Movement (Harakat Al-Muqawmah Al-Islamiah),** where does this leave the Palestinian Christians who, together with the Syrian and Lebanese Christians, were the founding fathers of Arab nationalism?!

- **Israel** threatens the Gazans with a return to an Israeli military occupation. It claims that Sharon's evacuation of that territory has resulted in handing the territory over to Hamas. But reoccupation of Gaza by Israeli troops is a sure recipe for continuous bloodshed on both sides. As compared to the West Bank, Gaza is guerrilla warfare territory **par excellence.** Its demographic density is its guerrilla **"weapon of mass destruction."** Like in the case of Israeli withdrawal from South Lebanon, because of the non-defeat of Hezbollah, Sharon, in a wise attempt to save Israeli lives, ordered withdrawal from Gaza in 2005. It was a tactic of Israeli national expediency; not a gesture of Israeli abandonment of its practices of creeping annexation of Palestinian territories.

- **Hamas,** in the course of this **Ramadan War II** (the first was between Egypt and Israel in 1973), has rejected the Egyptian cease-fire initiative. Reason: Hamas was not consulted!! How cynical!! If Hamas is truly concerned with the rising cost in Palestinian blood (more than 1400 Palestinians have thus far perished), does it really matter that Cairo did not place a long distance telephone call to Hamas? That rejection was a transparent search by Hamas for re-recognition by Cairo.

- For reasons of Egyptian security and secularity, Cairo has declared the Muslim Brotherhood in December 2013 a terrorist organization. Hamas, as an offshoot of the Brotherhood, thought it expedient to manifest solidarity with its parent organization. Thus it illogically engaged in terrorist attacks on Egyptian army and police personnel, as well as tourists in Sinai. **A fatal mistake!!** Consequently, post-Brotherhood Egypt is now waging daily defensive actions against Hamas and its poisonous franchises. It was incumbent upon Egypt, for purely national reasons, to label Hamas also a terror organization. From the destruction of Hamas tunnels leading from Gaza into Sinai, to near total closure of the Rafah Crossing, Egypt's actions have already cost Hamas half a billion dollars in annual ill-gotten revenues.

- **Israel,** is reinterpreting those Egyptian defensive actions against Hamas, as **"an Israeli/Egyptian siege"** of Gaza. **No. Egypt is not an Israeli ally in besieging Gaza.** Under the UN Anti-Genocide Convention, a siege is a secondary form of genocide. Egypt is closing its Sinai borders to stanch the flow of murderous operatives into its territory. Both Hamas and Israel, each for its own reasons, pretend that Egyptian sovereign acts within its borders are complementary to the hideous Israeli siege of Gaza. Unlike Israel, Egypt is not blocking Gaza seaports and airports. Nor is Egypt, for example, requiring the registration by Israel of every baby born in Gaza.

- **Hamas,** in its rejection of the Egyptian cease-fire proposals, demanded that those proposals should also include the re-opening of the Rafah Crossing between Gaza and Egypt at all times. **Hello!! Can you read?** Egypt has already declared you **"an enemy"** and **"a terrorist organization."** And when you are gasping for air, because of the war with Israel, you are in no position to dictate terms to Cairo. The violation of Egyptian borders in Sinai by Hamas during the Morsi defunct regime was one of several reasons why the June 30 Egyptian Revolution threw out that pro-Hamas Islamist regime. **Through the Revolutions of January 25, 2011, and June 30, 2013, Egypt has turned secular, nationalistic, internally-bound, and abandoning the unworkable adventures of Arabism of the Nasser to Mubarak period.**

- Egypt has turned away from the hocus-pocus of pan-Arabism and pan-Islamism. The only **"pan"** in the Egypt of today is **pan-Egyptianism** which creates jobs and bestow dignity on the Copts, the Sinai Bedouins, the Nubians, the Shii minority, and the dwellers of the western desert along the Libyan explosive borders. In summary, Egypt has turned inward, deeming intervention in its internal affairs from any quarters as a hostile infraction. The **Rafah Crossing is not a bridge.** It is a sovereign marker which may be opened by a sovereign Egyptian decision. Egypt, because of the human catastrophe in Gaza, has decided on two types of openings: entry into Egypt by wounded Palestinians for treatment, and allowing a Hamas representative to be present in Cairo as a member of Abbas delegation for talks on the cease fire. So please stop spinning!!

- **Israel** in an act of high-handedness, rejected dealing with the unity government declared by Abbas and Hamas in April 2014. Its pretext was that no negotiations could be conducted with a government which includes a **"terrorist component"** meaning Hamas. **This is a legal, political, and diplomatic idiocy.** Though a sovereign State, Israel has no legal capacity to dictate to the Palestinians who should or should not be in their government. **The Netanyahu coalition includes crazies who demand annexation of all Palestinian territories.** Israel's rejection of dealing with the Palestinian unity government is, in effect, a continuation of the Israeli fiction that Israel has no credible negotiating partner.

- Had Netanyahu gotten off his high horse, he might have neutralized the Hamas idiocy of denying Israel's existence. This Israeli rejectionist front deserves what the great Israeli statesman and Arabist scholar, Abba Eban, had once said about the Palestinians. Turning his adage around, he might have said: **"The Israelis never lose an opportunity to lose an opportunity."** In effect, Israel's refusal to deal with the Palestinian national unity government constitutes another form of siege.

- **Hamas,** as a movement is hopelessly fractured. In spite of the blatant obfuscation of its political boss, **Khaled Mishaal,** in his recent interview with **Charlie Rose of CBS and Channel 13 (New York),** it is the military wing, not the political wing, which is now calling the murderous shots. Another Mishaal grand dissimulation during that interview was his response to Rose's question: **"Why are you residing in Qatar, and not in Gaza?"** With the emphasis of a well-practised truth-avoider, Mishaal in effect said through an interpreter: **"The Palestinians are everywhere in the diaspora."** Then later said: **"I cannot be admitted to Gaza."** Of course, Khalid, let your people die in Gaza, while you enjoy a privileged life made sweet by petro-wealth!! Leading from behind is much safer!!

- Neither **Qatar (the mouse that keeps on roaring),** nor **Turkey** (with a Prime Minister who fancies himself the new Caliph) can compensate Hamas for its well-deserved loss of Egypt. Ordogan's insults directed regularly at Israel, and Qatar's gold, channeled habitually to both Hamas and the remnants of the Muslim Brotherhood, cannot replicate Egypt's strategic position bordering Gaza. And neither Ordogan nor Hamas can bring back to Egypt the ousted Islamist governance. Regardless of how often Ordogan raises the four fingers of **"the Rabaa salute,"** Morsi's chances of resuming his Islamist rule in Egypt are as great as those of a snowball in the boiling hot desert.

24

- As for Israel, none of its present practices in Palestinian territories outside of the green line, unless modified through successful negotiations with the Palestinian Authority, is bound to prevail. **Not** its 47 years of military occupation. **Not** its military superiority. **Not** its inhumane siege of Gaza. **Not** its creeping annexation through construction of settlements on lands acquired by force in 1967. **Not** its strategic relations with America. **Not** its coercive negotiations. **Not** its pretense that its forces could legally stay on Palestinian territories following the attainment of a two-State solution. **Not** its prowess in the global field of public relations. **Not** in its contribution to the transformation of a territorial conflict into a religious-ethnic conflict. Not even with Mr. Netanyahu's demand for **"quiet for quiet,"** in effect an imperial call for **"unconditional surrender."**

- **None** of these colonial practices, beliefs and utterances could survive as insuring, in the long run, Israel's security. If no two-State solution can emerge through negotiations, with a fully sovereign State of Palestine, then both the Israelis and the Palestinians are destined to be victims of wars without end.

- Too bad that visionary leaders, like **Sadat and Begin,** are no more. They dared to take a leap of faith by concluding a historic peace treaty in 1979. When Sadat was assassinated by the Islamists in 1981 for that transformative act, Begin marched in his funeral. But the PLO, under Arafat, marched in the opposite direction by intoning: **"May God Bless the Hand that Pulled the Trigger!!"** Had the PLO been blessed by enlightened leadership, responding positively to Sadat's call to the Palestians to join him in reconciliation with Israel in 1978-1979, the Palestinian flag would by now be flying high over the State of Palestine.

- **The Palestinian tragedy** could be traced to the perennial lack of a unifying iconic leadership. Throughout the history of the British mandate over Palestine (1920 to 1948), the **Yishov** (the Jewish community) in Palestine was building for itself state institutions. At the same time, the tribalised Palestinian Arabs led in multiple directions by feudal landed clans like the **Nashashibis and the Husseinis** were busily feuding against one another for pre-eminence as **"southern Syrians,"** even during some furtive armed uprisings against the British and Jewish immigration. The Palestinians have never had either a Mandela for peace, nor a Ho Chi Minh for resistance.

- Another example of the march against history in the unending search for a two-State solution is Netanyahu's present calls for **"a Marshal Plan for Gaza!" Mr. Prime Minister, save your**

**breath!!** When I wrote my Ph.D. thesis at New York University in the 1960s on decolonization, I realized that the colonized, such as the Gazans today under Israeli siege, would never exchange their freedom for butter. **They are not seeking your bread. They are seeing their very being.**

- Would the warlords of Hamas and Israel of today ever come together? In this I have no doubt. **Their portraits shall forever hang side by side in history's Great Hall of Infamy.** Admission Free!! There is no exit through adding fiction the the fray!!

- **This is habitually the fate of crazy deadenders, ideological maximalists, and deranged theocratic psychopaths. Their wounds are self-inflicted. But the wounds which they inflict upon others remain as gaping holes igniting the next genocidal round.**

# The Distance Between ISIS and Islam: Is Greater Than the Distance Between Mosul and the Moon!!

Monday, August 11, 2014

They call themselves a Caliphate -a successor regime of whom? Of the Prophet Muhammad? He defined Islam as **"the system where people are not harmed by its word or its hand (action)."** Of the four successors of **Muhammad (Abu-Bakr; Omar; Othman, and Ali)?** They advocated learning from Byzantium, Persia, and Egypt. Muhammad called for searching for knowledge **"even in China."** Of the Ottoman Empire? But that Empire was built on **"the Millet"** system where all religions were allowed to thrive.

Then it must be a Caliphate of their lunacy, of their insatiable hunger for brute power, of their worship of an age of darkness led by a crazy maniac all dressed in black calling himself **"Caliph Abu-Bakr Al-Baghdadi."** Even Al-Qaeda, of Bin Laden and Al-Zawahri, the criminal perpetrators of 9/11 among other calamities, have cut ISIS loose.

Their faith is in the sword; their mode is blitzkrieg; their joy is in decapitation of their opponents; their **"Islam"** is a black flag and a stolen Humvee; their advocacy is death to the Christians, the Yazidis, the Shia, the Jews, the Alawites, the unveiled women, the secular governance, and those who do not pay them their ransoms and their **"estimated taxes."** Works of art are their enemy; the great mosaics of Church windows and Islamic mosque domes are a threat which is brought down by dynamite; music and dance and cafe social gatherings are sinful; the West and the East should all perish. They are the new pretenders, the masters of the universe, the holy-inspired throngs with shoulder-carried grenade propellers and Kalashnikov rifles. National borders, indicative of sovereignty, are to be erased. Sovereignty resides in Caliph Al-Baghdadi -a street thug from Anbar!!

How do we measure the distance between ISIS and Islam, a distance co-equal to that between their temporary **"Mosul"** and the Moon?

The only verifiable yardstick is the **Quran** and the **Sunna (the words and conduct of Muhammad).** For these two sources are the primary sources of **Sharia (Islamic Law).** And they have so much tarnished Sharia to the point that several States within the American Union have adopted legislation banning its citation as a source of law in their courts!!

On this alone, ISIS has scored a crucial victory for their lunatic interpretations and actions. They have converted us to their own interpretation of Islam, thus causing us to ingest their poisonous pills. **A historic ISIS contribution to Islamophobia!!**

Their lunatic interpretation of the **Quran** and the **Hadith** (the traditions of Muhammad), combined with their savagery in the field reflected Islam in their ugly mirror. Relying on that false image, and suffering from anxiety about national security, the non-Muslim would become hostage to their propaganda. That ominous trend toward Islamophobia was also propelled by mistaken writings in the west about Islam. In his several books about Islam, Professor Bernard Lewis of Princeton University falsely asserts that there is a clash between Islam and modernity. Nonsense!!

The first word in the Quran is **"IQRAA" (Read)** meaning **"Learn."** Thus early Muslims avidly sought knowledge from Persia, Byzantium including Greece, and Egypt. In their wars, the ransom for a non-Muslim Prisoner of War was a book. That was the golden age of Islam which criminal gangs like ISIS wish to skip over, rewriting the thought and action parameters of **"fundamentalist Islam."** Fundamentalist Islam and reactionary Islamic are very opposite concepts: the former is light and tolerance, the latter is darkness and banishment of **"The other!!"**

The primary Islamic method of learning was developed by **Al-Azhar** which was established by the Shiis in Cairo in 975 AD as a citadel of Islamic learning. That was the seminar method whereby the student selects the instructor -a method which later travelled from Cairo to Andalusia (Spain) to Germany, to the Sorbonne in Paris, then to Oxford and Cambridge in the U.K. **Islam and modernity go hand in hand, Professor Lewis,** except in periods of decline such as the present one which we are sure to be transient.

So instead of what they say in televised sports, **"let us go to the tape,"** we say **"let us go to the Quran and to Muhammad's tradition, the primary sources of Islamic Jurisprudence."**

ISIS (I don't care whether they call it ISIS or IS -both are deceptive appellations) declares that only Sunni Muslims are entitled to existence. Nobody else as they are the only **"believers."** Total idiocy!! The primary principle of Islam is **Tawheed** (the oneness of God) which means direct relationship between the individual and his/her Creator. There is no middleman.

This concept covers: the elimination of someone declaring the other **"an apostate;"** the equality between every faith and other faiths; and equality before the law. In fact, this doctrine accepts **"non-faith,"** as the final judgement is left to God. The Quran, which in Islamic dogma, is the word of God as revealed to Muhammad, says: **"Say, the truth is from your Lord. Let him who will, believe; and Let him who will, reject!!"** (Chapter 18, verse 29)

On diversity and the need to welcome **"the other,"** the Quran says: **"Then will God says:" O Jesus the son of Mary! Recount My favor to thee and thy mother. Behold! I strengthened thee with the holy spirit, so that thou didst speak to the people in childhood and in maturity. Behold! I taught thee the Book and wisdom, the Law (the Torah) and the Gospel! and thou healest those born blind, and the lepers by My Leave. And behold!! Thou bringest forth the dead by My leave."** (Chapter 5, verse 110).

ISIS hypocrisy is challenged forcefully by these Quranic admissions and instructions. And hypocrisy, in Islamic tradition, is a non-forgivable way of life. In fact, the Quran devotes an entire chapter of a total of 114 chapters to hypocrisy which ISIS has mastered. The Quran says: **"When the hypocrites come to thee, they say, "we bear witness that thou art** indeed His Apostle of God? Yea, God knoweth that thou art indeed its Apostle, and God beareth witness that the hypocrites are indeed liars." (Chapter 63; verse 1). **Have you heard that Caliph Abu-Bakr Al-Baghdadi?**

But obviously the great pretender **"Al-Baghdadi, who is busy killing anybody he could catch, if he is not a ransom-paying Sunni, has no time for such Quranic details!!"** Yet his delegitimation, as a pair of hands dripping with blood, lies in this Quranic statement: **"On that account: We ordained for the children of Israel that if any one slew a person -unless it be for murder or for spreading mischief in the land - it would be as if he slew the whole people; and if any one saved a life, it would be as if he saved the life of the whole people."** (Chapter 5; verse 32) On that basis, the air strikes and humanitarian air drops in Kurdistan by the U.S., the U.K. and France, which began as of last Thursday to save the Yazidis, Christians and Kurds, are, under Islamic laws, to be regarded as fully sanctioned and justified.

In all of these arguments, the Quran is not the only yardstick. It is bolstered by the concept of **"Wisdom" (Al-Hikmah),** which is equally emphasized under Islamic Law by both the Quran and the traditions of Muhammad. It is the pillar of **Ijtihad** (the application of reason to the revealed text of the Quran). Unfortunately, the non-Muslim world has focused on jihad, not on ijtihad. Even that focus was largely mis-directed. **In Islamic Law, there is no aggressive war; only defensive war** for the dual purposes of territorial protection and self-defense, both within national frontiers. Thus killing of the innocent, as in Mosul or Rakka or in Kurdistan, is totally abhorred by Islam.

Returning to Al-Hikmah (wisdom), we find the Quran saying: **"For God hath sent down to thee the Book and Wisdom and taught thee what thou knewest not before, and great is the grace of God unto thee"** (Chapter 4, Verse 113). Herein lies the legal bases of the evolution of Sharia to fit changing circumstances. Thus when the scholars of Islam say that Sharia is for **"all times,"** they mean that it evolves with time.

**Examples follows:**
**On women,** Islamic Law equates between men and women in their respective legal standings. Islam does not preclude women from the work place. During the time of Muhammad and of his four successors, women sat at governance meetings, participated in discussions, and even, at times, contradicted Muhammad himself. **On severance of limbs:** The practice in Islam, as decreed by the Caliph Omar, in his instructions to the judges, is

that the judge should be defendant-oriented. He himself, upon an admission by a malfeasant that he had committed theft, ordered that person to go away, saying **"Your guilt was perpetrated by society which denied you adequate means of livelihood. On the hijab, the Quran only mentioned "modesty in dress." On adultery,** Islamic Law made it impossible to prove. For it provided for four persons to perceive penetration (an impossibility). **On Quranic texts,** legislated laws are a necessary supplement and modifiers (such as in the laws of inheritance, and in criminal law, and co-education).

As to religious fanaticism, the hallmark of ISIS, the Quran could not be clearer. It says: **"O people of the Book! Commit no excesses in your religion; nor say of God aught but the truth."** (Chapter 4, verse 171). ISIS cruelty is abhorrent to Islamic Law as based on Islamic legal outlook and practice. The Quran advises Muhammad to be kind and tolerant. It says: **"It is part of the Mercy of God that dost deal gently with them. Wert thou severe or harsh, they would have broken away from about thee."** (Chapter 3; Verse: 159).

Now behold ISIS, as it decapitates its hapless victims, shrieks **"Allahu Akbar!!"** That invocation which they have turned on its head means: **"We humans are all equal before God regardless of our beliefs."** Yet they call their fallen **"a Shaheed"** (martyr). But the martyr is the victim not the would-be executioner. The same process of upending Islamic definitions and values manifests itself through their recruitment of foreign fighters. Islamic Law calls on immigrants to abide by the laws of their newly-adopted countries, as they practice their inherited faith.

When ISIS took over control of the Mosul Dam, the main water regulator and feeder for Iraq downstream, they have engaged in another form of genocide -the tactic of siege through the threat of either flooding or manipulation of water resources. It was in Iraq, 1400 years ago, when **Imam Ali,** the fourth Caliph and cousin and son-in-law of the Prophet Muhammad, who upon prevailing over his war adversaries, the ummayads, directed his victorious troops not to withhold access to water for these rebels. Before their defeat, his adversaries have committed the opposite against that great founder of the Shiism.

May the U.S. air strikes vanquish the new barbarians!! ISIS has no place either in Islam or on any geographical map. Their war crimes may, unfortunately, go on for a while. But their end cannot be in doubt. Neither their war materiel, nor that ill-gotten wealth, nor their horrific videos by which they are seeking to propagate fear, shall ever, in the long run, insure their existence.

**Their prediction of one day hoisting their black flag over the White House is proof of their unprecedented hallucination. A more assured bet is on a white flag of surrender flying over their black abodes. Neither God nor humanity are on their side. Compared to other similar jihadi organizations, ISIS is more distant from being Muslims, let alone human.**

The translation of the Quranic quotations cited above are from **Abdullah Yusuf Ali, The Quran: Text, Translation and Commentary (U.S. edition, 2008). I teach "Islamic Law and Global Security" at Fordham University School of Law, New York City.**

# When Human Rights Watch Turns Its Advocacy Into a Comedy

Friday, August 15, 2014

While riding a Manhattan bus, a headline of a report by **Kareem Fahim** in **The New York Times** of August 12 quickly caught my eyes. It read **"Systematic Killings in Egypt are Tied to Leader, Group says."** Emanating from Cairo, it meant by **"Leader" President El-Sisi;** the **"Group"** was **Human Rights Watch.**

I am not usually a speed-reader, but quickly became one, till I stopped at a paragraph before suppressing my laughter. The paragraph reads: **"The report calls for an investigation of Mr. Sisi who was commander of the armed forces at the time, and several other sitting government officials, including Egypt's interior minister."**

So Human Rights Watch, a non-governmental organization based in New York City, has, by an act of God, made itself an international criminal court!! But there is one ICC which is based in the Hague, which came into being by the Rome Charter of 1998, with Egypt acceding to it, and the U.S. rejecting it, even though it had negotiated it.

To my knowledge, the ICC has no subdivisions, no chambers, no branches anywhere! Nor can the ICC be succeeded by an NGO which, from that report in **The New York Times** is sitting, without any legal standing, in judgement of a sovereign State **-Egypt.** The funny thing is that, as reported, Human Rights Watch **"had conducted a yearlong investigation into violence that followed the military's ouster of former President Mohamed Morsi."** A HA!! So we are back celebrating on August 14, 2014, the first anniversary of the events leading to Egypt's security forces, backed up by the army, breaking up the **Muslim Brotherhood's** double sieges at **Rabaa** and **Al-Nahda** by force.

Now that Human Rights Watch has completed its one-year long investigation into those momentous events, it now wishes to label **El-Sisi** and the **Minister of Interior** and other senior officials as defendants **"accused"** of **"wide-spread and systematic killings of protesters...more than 800 people, and possibility more than 1,000!!**

A very tall order by an NGO from whom I have seen no similar reports calling for investigations into **Guantanamo, Abu-Ghraib, Helman, Gaza, Yemen,** or... These are large geographical areas where dragnets caught thousands of citizens in their webs to throw them away into a forever-legal limbo combined with degrading torture. That is where an American NGO should go, and claim jurisdiction over the likes of **Cheney, Rumsfeld,** and company who still claim that **water boarding is not torture!!**

OK!! Let us stay with Human Rights Watch's uninvited focus on post-Arab Spring Egypt which has fought off the Islamists attempts to turn it into an Islamic Emirate.

The Muslim Brotherhood was given a historic chance to rule Egypt under a presidency of their own. Morsi became President in June 2012, promising inclusiveness, security and development. Within only 5 months, he proved to be not the president of all Egyptians. Copts, Shias, and secularists were excluded. During a period of one year, he distinguished himself by **"I am above the law"** through his **"Constitutional Declaration"** of November 2012!

Let us ignore for a few moments the report of those false pretenders to universal jurisdiction, the Human Rights Watch. Let us focus on the **"achievements"** of the Morsi **"one man, one vote, one time"** during his incumbency -an incumbency which was terminated by **35 million Egyptians** calling on June 30, 2013, not for his head, but for his seat. The armed forces, under El-Sisi, were only the auxiliaries of that Second Revolution, not its igniters.

Morsi, in a booklet published in Arabic by the Muslim Brotherhood in April 2013, called his program for Egypt **"The Islamic Project."** In its introduction his adversaries, the secularists, were attacked as **"aiming at causing the public to reject the Islamic/Brotherhood experiment in order to perpetuate the environment of corruption which enabled them to accumulate ill gotten gains."** (p.7) That 24-page booklet went on to cite the tactics of the anti-Morsi opposition. It listed 13 such tactics, including **"the manipulation of the judiciary (tactic #5), "the fomenting of sectarian and ethnic violence" (tactic #6),** and the propagation of **"civil disobedience (tactic #13) -all of which on p. 8.**

Then the Morsi manifesto goes on to respond to the question: **"Is President Morsi a weak president or a strong president?"** It answers as follows: **He removed Field Marshall Tantawi: and General Anan; he cashiered the chief of National Intelligence; he dismissed the Attorney General, Abdel-Meguid Mahmoud; and he issued "the Constitutional Declaration"** (of November 2012) concentrating all powers in Morsi's hands). On that achievement, the document cites Morsi as a genius because **"although he rescinded that Declaration, he, in practice, preserved it effects."** (p. 9)

The manifesto of April 2013 ridicules national secular opponents by name; denigrates Egyptian economic leaders; calls Israel **"the Zionist Entity, and ridicules national consensus as destabilizing** (pp.10-11)

The Morsi manifesto confronted Egypt with a clear and present danger: from civil war to splitting the country between North and South. That is not to mention their transparent attempt to ween away the public from its army at a time when the Brotherhood had its militias and **Baltagias** (thugs) as the enforcers of Islamist rule. A mere reading of the Islamist constitution of 2012 provides a non-controverted proof: The secularists, including the Christian minority, were pressured to abandon their seats on the Constituent Assembly; and articles agreed for inclusion in the final text were either deleted or re-written Islamicly. The plebiscite on that defective Constitution attracted only 22% of 53 million eligible voters, and its faked approval was less than 50%.

And when the call to prayer sounded in the parliamentary chamber, for the first time in any Egyptian Parliament since 1936, it was in effect a call to arms between the secularists and the Islamists. The former had their eyes on Egypt whose monuments were threatened by destruction a la **Bamian Buddhist Temples** by the Taliban in Afghanistan. The latter had their eyes on pan-Islamism, where Egypt historically does no belong.

33

When the Second Revolution of June 30, 2013, erupted, the lines of battle had already been drawn leading within 3 days to the ouster of a hated Islamic regime. That regime would have found common cause with **ISIS** on the **Tigris and Euphrates Rivers in Iraq and Syria.** The Nile is immune from that sectarian lunacy.

With Morsi's ouster by the will of the masses **(the Islamist Constitution contained no provision for presidential recall),** the Islamists struck back. In Sinai, a war by proxy with Hamas, an offshoot of the Brotherhood; in Cairo, guerrilla urban warfare at Rabaa, east of Cairo, and Nahda, west of Cairo. Two small emirates arose in the capital of Egypt whose 93 million inhabitants constitute 30% of all Arabs from the Atlantic to the Gulf.

Time now to review the urban Islamist rebellion from July 3 to August 14, 2013, the period of the so-called **"investigations"** by Human Rights Watch -the new self-appointed Trustee over sovereign Egypt.

**"The Watch"** claims that Egypt's security forces struck on August 14 with a scant warning to the Rabaa demonstrators. **A blatant lie.** The government of Interim President, Counsellor Adly Mansour, pleaded with the occupiers who paralysed life in two major sections of Cairo, for 6 weeks, to leave peacefully. In New York City, the **"Occupy Wall Street"** movement was given 15 minutes by the New York Police Department before they were dispersed by well-justified force.

**"The Watch"** claims that for 12 hours elapsed before the Egyptian security forces allowed the demonstrators a safe exit. **Wrong again.** The guerrilla warfarers were permitted two safe exits publicly and repeatedly announced by the authorities. The central purpose of the authorities was to effect a peaceful end to a trench warfare by the Brotherhood.

**"The Watch"** claims that the demonstrations were **"largely peaceful."** **Wrong.** In the two emirates of Rabaa and Nahda, weapons were stored; hostages were taken; firearms were used; the first casualty, a police officer, was felled by bullets shot from within the rebellious crowd; street pavements afforded the well-rehearsed fighters plenty of stone-power to lob at the forces of law and order; the so-called **"martyrdom"** was celebrated; **"Down with Egypt"** became a battle cry; calls on the members of the police forces and the army to defect were broadcast; and foreign intervention and funding were invited.

**"The Watch"** claims that the Rabaa stand, the field hospital, and the mosque were torched, **"probably by the security forces."** Probably?! A case of conjecture whose advocate I would not admit to my lectures on the law of evidence. **If you have no proof, zip your mouth!!**

**"The Watch"** again shows how soft its head is on the law of evidence. It had to admit that **"few of the demonstrators were armed;"** but its selected evidence asserts that **"the police killed hundreds of unarmed demonstrators."** It also had to admit that the demonstrators lobbed Molotov cocktails at the police. Then it states that it was able to document these episodes in **"a few cases." How few?** And are you professionally capable to reach these vague conclusions on the basis of **"hearsay evidence"** gathered over one year of the occurrence, and collected from witnessed already biased for being a party to that conflict? **Get Real!!**

Egypt has lost nearly 500 army and police personnel, even before declaring your beloved Muslim Brotherhood and its franchise, Hamas, terrorist organizations. Its public is still under a terrorism alert in the subways and above ground. Its forces are still confronting the Islamic marauders in Sinai and on the Libyan borders. Yet at the same time, Egyptian engineers are now rebuilding the Coptic churches destroyed by the Islamists during their reign of terror in upper Egypt. They are also refurbishing neglected Jewish temples. Its diplomats are in an overdrive to rescue the Palestinians in Gaza from further death and destruction through the Egyptian cease fire initiative which is being prolonged whenever it comes to its end.

And now **Human Rights Watch** is calling for an investigation of the country's leadership including the Interior Minister who had nearly lost his life to a drive-by terrorist bomber. You must be nuts!!

When the State is fighting for its life, security takes priority front and center. The hundreds who were unfortunately killed at Rabaa and Nahda were put on harm's way by the Brotherhood whose baby organization. Egypt is a part of the presently-boiling Middle East in regard to which President Obama, in a recent interview on August 8 with Thomas Friedman said: **"Our (meaning the U.S.) politics are dysfunctional, and we should heed the terrible divisions in the Middle East as a warning to us: societies don't work if political factions take maximalist positions."**

Well said, Mr. President!! Maximalists, like the Brotherhood, Hamas, Jihad, and ISIS, never win. This is because they demand of their opposing party only one small thing: **non-existence!!**

So Mr. Kenneth Roth, Executive Director of Human Rights Watch, and Ms. Sara Leah Whitson, Director of its Middle East Division: You were not deported from Egypt when stopped at the Cairo airport on Sunday, August 10. You cannot be deported if you were not admitted into the country.

And how arrogant can you get to proceed to Cairo after being denied a visa in order to perform another stunt for publicity as you presented yourselves to the airport authorities as **"tourists."** You were no tourists. You were **"agent provocateurs"** who wished to unfurl your report calling for investigating El-Sisi and others on the basis of an evidence-free report intended to harm, without credible cause, Egypt's standing worldwide.

To repair the damage to your reputation, and in the absence of the status of a super power, I strongly urge you to stay home to take care of the multitude of human rights issues on which you would be luckier in collecting credible evidence.

Unless you claim immunity from reason, it is **"The Watch,"** not Egypt, that has a lot to account for. Egypt, through its venerated judiciary which was pummelled during the Brotherhood's rule, is capable of handling the events of August 2013. It has, without your prodding, appointed my friend, **Counsellor Fouad Abdel-Monim Riyadh,** formerly of the ex-Yugoslavia Tribunal, to head a national commission of inquiry into those events. **So butt out!! Egypt is not a banana republic.**

Your claim to world-wide concern everywhere for human rights rings hollow. Your **"Watch Tower"** must have been on vacation during the Bush Jr. administration. Where were you when **John Yoo** as counsel for the Department of Justice advised that the **Geneva Protocols of 1949 providing for the protection of civilians during times of war** are obsolete. Acting on this advice, the U.S. detained and tortured hundreds of civilians from various Muslim countries. The highly-placed perpetrators are still at large in the U.S., yet fearing detention if they ventured abroad.

Mr. Ken Roth, also known to me as **"Mr. Watchman"**: I wish I were the attorney for **"plaintiff Egypt"** in a case against you and your funders in Cairo, a proper venue where the events took place. The cause of action would have been **incitement to violence.** The evidence would have been the limited riots of your **"Muslim Brothers"** in Egypt this August 14. Your attorney would have advised non-appearance at that trial. But in abstentia, I most probably would have secured a favorable verdict. And under **the theory of universal jurisdiction,** you would have been a target of detention in any of the members of the League of the Arab States (22 minus **Syria** -suspended membership, and **Qatar** -no diplomatic relationship with Egypt for its support of **"Brotherhood"** terrorism in Egypt). No statute of limitations.

But wait, here is a tip from this blogger: **There is an exit!!** Declare your actions as immunized as **"Acts of State,"** under the official seal of **"The People's Republic of Human Rights Watch."** Then the whole world would have joined me in a prolonged and hearty laugh!!

# Honoring Isis, the Egyptian Goddess of Mercy 5000 Years Ago; Dishonoring ISIS of Today as Murderers Without Borders

Friday, August 22, 2014

In Islamic jurisprudence, Jim Foley of New Hampshire is a martyr (a Shaheed). **In memoriam, James Foley;** decapitated by ISIS on August 19.

ISIS's very name is a cause for acute revulsion. The reasons are myriad. Foremost among these is their vocation. They are **"Murderers Without Borders."** **Jim Foley** was a photo journalist without borders. Add to that, ISIS's fanciful assumption of being the resurrected **"Caliphate."** A painful joke!! Under a street thug from Anbar, Iraq, called **"Abu-Bakr Al-Baghdadi."**

On top of that, comes the abuse of the term **"ISIS."** It should not be confused with the heroine of ancient Egypt, **Queen Isis**, the goddess of mercy, and compassion, the loving wife of **Osiris,** and the celebrated mother of **Horus** who appears in relief as a falcon.

**Osiris/Isis/Horus** is the ancient trinity of which the great Egyptologist, **Professor James Breasted** of Chicago University said in his 5-volume work on ancient Egypt that it presaged the trinity in Christianity.

It was in the 1950's when, as a junior researcher at the UN, I was asked to help find if genocide was ever practiced in ancient Egypt. At the New York Public Library, I read Breasted's five volumes in search for clues. I found none, with the exception of two episodes of **"secondary genocide:"** a siege, and the destruction of wheat fields. No mass killings of other humans, non-involved civilians. That was five-thousand years ago, with no national, let alone international conventions, on genocide. **Only the rules of common sense for common humanity.**

So from Isis the Queen, to ISIS, **the head cutters;** from giving life, to decapitation; from the creation of great monuments, to the destruction of temples, churches and mosques; from the belief in great science and engineering on the banks of the Nile, the Tigris and the Euphrates, to the stockpiling of material intended for destruction in the name of God. An amazing decline in values, an uptick in the elevation of fiction to the level of belief such as jihad in the ISIS fashion. **History does not repeat itself; its gears are pushed in reverse.**

The decapitation of Foley is a clear signal for a close look at our interpretation of **faith and force. They don't mix.** ISIS mixes them because it serves the purposes of using the garb of Islam to hide their tools for decapitation of civilization. They use the rage against the West on the Arab and Muslim streets as leverage; the lack of cohesiveness among the 1.6 billion Muslims as an incubator for breeding brainless future jihadis, **ready to proclaim an Islamic People's Republic of Terror.**

It is amazing how such vicious Muslim renegades can be thought of as possible negotiating partners! There are no values, no commitment to law either domestic or international; no feeling for the right of others to their beliefs; and no regard to their own book, **the Quran,** that murder is a capital sin!!

Holding Foley's severed head with one hand, and the black flag of ISIS with the other, is a gruesome macabre. On that black flag is the Islamic inscription of **"Muhammad, God's Messenger."** Neither Muhammad nor God have anything to do with these animals who are masquerading as humans. In fact the common blessing in Islam is **"In the Name of Allah, Most Gracious, Most Merciful."** Where is the ISIS belief in God's graciousness and in God's mercy?

By their deeds, they mock Islam, let alone other creeds. In non-recognition of their flag, the Quran says: **"And now they reject the truth when it reaches them: but soon shall they learn the reality of what they used to mock at"** (Chapter 6, verse 5). The future cannot be on the side of darkness. ISIS began with 3000 fighters; says it now has 20,000. But as they lost at the Mosul Dam, so they shall lose what they had gained by stealth, jihadi false propaganda, ransoms, and commandeered resources. May their loss at the Mosul Dam, thanks to U.S. air strikes and indigenous military footprint on the ground, be the beginning of the end of their farce.

But to defeat them, we first have to go into the ISIS brain. I needed to find a manifesto, an interpretation of their outlook on jihad. I needed to read their words to assess their idiocy. Coming back empty, I looked into the declaration of their cohorts -**"Ansar Beit Al-Maqdis,"** the Gaza-based lunatics. Here is a summary of a video released in late August urging Egypt's army and police to defect. Just read and wonder about the **voodoo rationale of these transnational non-State actors.**

Using the modus operandi of ISIS, that terrorist group whose name translates into **"The Friends of Jerusalem,"** show how they kill members of Egyptian forces in Sinai. Their leader, **Ibrahim Al-Rubaish,** taunts his targets by saying: **"You have sold your faith for a loaf of bread."** Then he adds: **"You have worshipped El-Sisi instead of God. Do not blame us for killing you only because you pray and fast. You do not cry for the death of the noble Mujahedeen as you murder them."**

**"The Friends of Jerusalem,"** whose terrorism in Sinai has forced Egypt to declare them and their allies, Hamas, a terrorist organization goes on in its video to say: **"El-Sisi is standing by his friendship with America. He would have no chance of survival without your weapons guarding him and obeying his orders. By doing that, you have disobeyed your Creator and sided with El-Sisi."** Then Al-Rubaish adds: **"I have searched the Quran and the Sunna (Muhammad's prenouncements and conduct) and found no justification for you, soldiers and policemen, to put your duties above God's orders. Your livelihood is in the hands of God, not in the uniform that you are wearing."**

This is only a small segment of their heinous propaganda, which proclaims them as the interpreters of Islam. **Disobeying them is made to sound as rejecting God!!** It is a savage psychological warfare aimed at untutored masses and intended for mass panic. From **"The Friends of Jerusalem,"** to Hamas, to the Brotherhood which gave birth to Hamas, to ISIS -it is one single tapestry but with different colors, woven in hell. That tapestry hangs together; its elimination needs regional hands and international shock and awe actors. A piecemeal approach is likely to needlessly prolong the agony.

Against this incredible array of facts against ISIS and similar organizations, it is unbelievable to find American media calling on Egypt to make peace with the Muslim Brotherhood.

On **CNN** last Sunday, August 17, **Fareed Zakaria** once more is stuck on his old script. He proclaims that **"the Arab Spring in Egypt has failed to advance the cause of democracy in view of its crackdown on the Muslim Brotherhood."** Do the CNN pundits think that bringing Morsi back is possible? Is disfranchising the huge majority which voted for **"El-Sisi Raiisi (my President)"** a workable answer? When Egypt is fighting today for its secular identity, are those talking heads advocating a halt, so that their definition of democracy would prevail? Have they heard of **"The Islamic project,"** called for by Morsi when he was in power, which was a scheme excluding everyone else except for Morsi's real base **-the Muslim Brotherhood?** Shouldn't the rise of ISIS change Zakaria's outlook in view of this game -changing menace?

This week, the Sinai authorities discovered five headless bodies in various parts of that desert province. The trademark of ISIS is already discernible in Egypt!!

The big question is: In an existential struggle, such as that of Egypt's secularists vs. the Brotherhood and its affiliates, which should come first, classical democracy or classical security?

During America's civil war, President Lincoln suspended **habeas corpus,** together with other provisions of the American Bill of Rights. The American Union was fighting for its existence.

So is with Egypt of today: The survival of the State's identity within its historic character comes before Mr. Zakaria's definition of what should constitute ultimate freedom. He is blissfully immune from the politics of Tahrir, and from the aspirations for a better life for 93 million Egyptians. **Zakaria's silence would truly be made of gold for the land of the Nile.**

The truth does not exist within the CNN studios. **It only shows its face on the Egyptian street so that a repeat of the James Foley's decapitation would never be attempted in Tahrir Square. Queen Isis stood for the victory of good over evil. ISIS stands for evil pure and simple. May the soul of Jim Foley rest in peace!! And may the Murderers without Borders receive their punishment from above and from below!!**

# In Libya's Civil War: How to Judge a Declaration as Confused and/or Idiotic?

Friday, August 29, 2014

Qaddafi is gone forever from Libya, Egypt's neighbor to the West. But the ghosts of destruction through civil war between the Islamists and the Secularists keep on multiplying. Libya has become a dangerous place for its people and the region, and the world lying to the north, across the Mediterranean. Militias fighting militias; Qaddafi's nuclear arsenal is gone, but the huge amounts of conventional weapons remain; deadly weapons keep on crossing the Egyptian borders to the east, the Tunisian borders to the west, and to Al-Qaeda in the Maghreb (AQIM) and beyond to the south, through Chad and Niger. **A real security mess!!**

But Egypt, though with a million-man army, both in active service and reserves, feels the jitters. The Sisi government, with pledges to **93 million Egyptians (a full 25% of all Arabs)** of security and stability, cannot close its eyes to its long borders with a **militias-run Libya.** The Islamists of Libya are an integral part of the flying Islamist carpet of the Muslim Brotherhood, now banned in Egypt, but keeps on floating from Hamas, east of Suez, to Tripoli, Libya. A vaunted pan-Islamism, which now calls itself a caliphate in Iraq and Syria **(ISIS),** and a caliphate in northern Nigeria **(Boko Haram: "Western education is a sin")** in western Africa.

This gathering Islamist storm is already rattling the windows of power in security-conscious Cairo. Storm windows need to be quickly installed, as Cairo uses its soft power to contain blood-shed in Gaza, and uses its iron fist to annihilate the terrorist **"Friends of Jerusalem,"** a Hamas franchise.

The El-Sisi's one-two punch cannot be of lasting effect without at least some gesticulation in the direction of presently law-less Libya. This is the heart of the lesson of US air strikes against ISIS in Iraq, US air surveillance together with special forces operations in Syria **(the Iraq-Syria borders are gone),** and the pilotless drones over Yemen to contain the Al-Qaeda in the Arabian peninsular **(AQAP)** of Al-Awlaki fame (or lack thereof).

Though seemingly regional, this is a global struggle for the defeat of those who claim that **God (Allah)** has permitted them to claim the entire world, beginning with the Arab/Muslim regions) for Sunni Islam. The Islamists have anointed themselves as jihadis (soldiers of God), even though the

41

word of God is vastly at odds with those moronic jihadists. These terrorists, now waging a World War III against civilization, tell the befuddled youth from the U.S., Europe, Asia and Africa: **"Come join us and be rewarded by paradise in the hereafter."** But the **Quran** confronts their thesis of **"cooperation for murder,"** by these words: **"You help one another in righteousness and piety, but do not help one another in sin and rancor."** (Chapter V, Verse 2).

This confrontation between the secularists (who won in Egypt) and the Islamists (who seem to be winning in Libya, Iraq and Syria) is **existential.** It is a zero-sum game, and after the dust of battle settles, only one of the two global factions shall remain standing. And it shall not be the Islamists, what with their fragmentation, territorial non-contiguity, savagery, and alienation of the vast Muslim masses in 57 States!!

However, on the side of the Islamists, stands idiotic western media, vacillating western leadership, hood-winked non-governmental organizations, and an America which is still looking at the jihadis as reformable, potentially democratic and a counterpoise in the Arab Spring to what the U.S. perceives as a lurch towards military governance. And when America gets really stunned by the Islamists barbarism, such as in the case of the beheading of the American photojournalist **James Foley,** America gets dressed up as a cop holding a search warrant, knocking on the door of the jihadis, entering their lair (where animals lie down) and solemnly declare: **"You have the right to be silent!!"**

**Come on, America:** this is war which is more ferocious than that in Iraq where, in 2003, you suspended the iconic Geneva Conventions of 1949. It is amazing that you enjoy nearly silently, Egyptian initiatives for peace for the Gazans and the Israelis, yet condemn Cairo for what you miscontstrue as Egyptian intervention in Libya. **What a mockery!!** Washington hits ISIS from the air under the justifiable claim of ISIS being an existential threat to the homeland 10,000 miles to the west. But looks upon a presumed Egyptian act of self defense a **dangerous intervention by Cairo in the Libyan affair.**

This is not only double standard. It is beyond being confused. It is a sheer self-defeating fantasy:
- The Islamist intervention in Egyptian domestic affairs is on, since the popular unseating of the Islamist reign of terror in Egypt under Morsi from June 2012 to July 2013;
- American media and non-governmental organizations, **including Haman Rights Watch,** still obtusely describe the elected

presidency of El-Sisi as a coup;

- Simultaneously, the spokeswoman of the U.S. State Department, **Mary Harf,** in effect declares on August 19, 2014 that President El-Sisi was leading the process for democratization in Egypt, but this would take a long time. **Thanks, Ms. Harf, your assessment of democratization in Egypt has not been invited,** unless you wish to eat your words about Egypt a couple of weeks earlier. At that time you charged Cairo of using U.S. aid to **suppress peaceful demonstrations.** In a riposte, the Cairo Foreign Ministry did not mince its words. It said that your statements reflect **total incompetence and ignorance** of the facts on the ground in Egypt;

- Compounding these contradictions, are the declarations of **"The Friends of Jerusalem"** (Ansar Beit Al-Maqdis) that it shall keep on liquidating Egyptian security forces in Sinai because they were the enemies of God through their fealty to El-Sisi -an enemy of God (as per Ansar);

- Now come the American charge that Cairo has placed its airports at the disposal of the air force of United Arab Emirates to attack the Islamists in and around Tripoli.

Aside from being a non-substantiated charge, let us suppose that it is true: how would it differ in its ultimate effect from U.S. similar and more direct actions elsewhere in Arab lands? And who gave the U.S. the right to complain that it was **not consulted in advance of such actions**? Does the U.S. consult Egypt before it undertakes its justifiable actions against ISIS and similar terrorist organizations? Is Washington, in its justifiable desire to defeat ISIS, consulting with Cairo on American rumored contracts with **Al-Assad and Iran** under the theory of **"the enemy of my enemy is my friend?"** Not so!!

- Then as **"icing on the cake,"** enters **The New York Times** of August 26, with the provocative headline on its cover page: **"Arab Nations Strike in Libya, Surprising U.S."** The paper's demagogic reporter **David Kirkpatrick,** supported by his usual coterie ensconced at the **Carnegie Endowment for International Peace** (What kind of international peace do they advocate?) pipes in: In an interview with the **New York Public Radio** on August 26, that correspondent, in a self-convincing voice, says: **"Egyptians lied to the U.S. This is a cold war between political Islam versus stability. The military government in Egypt never forgets U.S. backing of Morsi when he came to power."** Thanks, David!! Apparently you see Cairo always from a faulty lens of an Egypt descending into dictatorship!!

- Now how does Mr. Kirkpatrick reach these conclusions? And

more to the point, how does **"one senior American official"** perform an acrobatic outstretch in describing the presumed actions by the **Emirates and Egypt** in the following confused and/or idiotic words: **"We don't see this as a constructive at all."** Well, the Carnegie people went even beyond these interventionary hallucinatory statements. A **Michele Dunne,** a senior associate at the Carnegie, raves from the bottom of a well of fiction when she solemnly declares: Such actions have **"proved to be a gigantic impediment to international efforts to resolve any of these crises."** Michele: time for you to take a break from your overworked brain at Starbucks;

- In what seem to be an anticipation by Cairo of these official and non-official American blitz against Cairo's self-defensive measures, President El-Sisi had a completely different version. Addressing one of his periodic meetings with Egyptian media, he referred to the allegations by the Muslim Brotherhood in regard to Egyptian armed forces involvement in attacks on the Islamist militias in Libya. The Egyptian President declared that there was no involvement by Egypt **"outside of its borders."**

- El-Sisi was on point in addressing the issue from an Egyptian sovereignty perspective. All other foreign declarations were fumings with no tangle effect on the existential battle between the Islamists and the secularists in Arab lands. It is a combat between those who declare their adversaries **"apostates (Takfiris),"** a fancy term by the Islamists, and those who declare that **"Allahu Akbar" (God is Great) (Tawhidis),** a term that says faith is a matter of choice and conscience. The **sword has no place.**

**It is high time for America to stop acting confused. The Hamlet persona of "To Be or Not To Be" is not befitting a great power!! The struggle against terrorism, especially when it raises deceptively the banner of faith (Islam), is globally indivisible. You are either on the side of humanity and international humanitarian law, or on the side of darkness, amply represented by the flag of ISIS -a flag which amply deserved a recent act of maximum disdain performed in Sweden by two young Egyptian women!!**

# 4 SEPTEMBER 2014

## In Civil Wars, Seeking a UN Solution Is Like Seeking Dental Help From a Toothless Dentist

Friday, September 5, 2014

The U.N. General Assembly starts its 69th session in New York City later this month. Let us peek under the blue canopy to separate the wheat from the shaff. **Mostly shaff.**

The die was cast in San Francisco in June 1945. The course, character, function, role and mission of the U.N. **were all irrevocably decided forever.** The U.N. Charter gave birth to a World War II organization which was basically a clone of the **League of Nations,** except in few cosmetics. An inter-State system which falsely described its existence in a contradictory fashion for public consumption -a feel good heading!! The Charter begins with the words **"We the people,"** but the **"Nations"** were only united in one respect: **to prevent any surrender of substantive sovereignty.**

The U.N. bestowed equality of sovereignty on its now **193 States. Great!!**

But in effect it saddled itself by two systems: equality in the General Assembly (the Parliament of Man/Woman); and a Security Council where the five **"great powers"** were respectively armed by an extinguisher of that equality -**a veto power.** In effect, we have under the charter a **house of commons** (the General Assembly) and a **house of 5 lords** (the powers possessing a veto), plus 10 non-permanent States as extras. This is the first split personality in the U.N.

If I say the **"first split,"** I must produce **"a second"** without inventing it. The second split is **Article 2, para. 7** which, in part, states: **"Nothing contained in the present charter shall authorize the United Nations to intervene in matters which are essentially within domestic jurisdiction of any State..."** So the State, at the U.N., is not only **"sovereign;"** it is also omnipotent because it can put a **"domestic jurisdiction"** label on any matter it could assert and defend as an internal matter.

In consequence, the hallowed **"right of peoples to self-determination"** is established only with regard to the inhabitants of an established State. It does not exist in regard to groups seeking to secede from States, or to the right to reunification in divided States. It is even more remote as to the **exercise of minorities** of their right to preserve their own separate identities, except what the State would authorize. As a matter of fact, there is no consensus on defining the word **"people."**

This uncertainty seeps also under the foundation of **"the right of peoples to self-determination."** Why?! Because it conflicts with the better established principle of sovereignty. This in part explains why States value their U.N. membership: **it freezes the lines of their national boundaries at the time of joining** the U.N. club.

**But wait a minute!!** The U.N. Security Council, in spite of the existence of the veto, has been able to play some role in deterring aggression. **Yes, but** only when the U.S., the U.K., France, China and Russia are together in accord, or when one or more of them decide to abstain or be absent.

This explains why **Al-Assad** has so far survived the hurricane of the Syrian civil war (the **Russian veto either cast or threatened**), and why Israeli Prime Minister Netanyahu could flout international law as he grabs more Palestinian land (the **U.S. veto is the real iron dome for the State of Israel**). Building settlement on occupied lands is anathema to the Geneva Conventions of 1949, and is totally not covered by the right of Israel to defend itself.

Of course, the Security Council can impose sanctions, either military or economic. But what the popular eye misses in this comforting scenario is that the Council does not possess what the charter had anticipated. It says, in **Article 42** that the Council may use **"armed force"** by **"air, sea or land forces."** However, due to the cold war which followed on the heels of the victories of World War II, **it is the State that can produce** and can volunteer such armed forces. The Council has none of its own. In fact, the term **"peace keeping"** does not exist in the U.N. Charter. The term is the product of a transitory chance: **The Suez War of 1956** which brought the U.S. and U.S.S.R together on the same page during the **Eisenhower** and the **Khrushchev** administration -a rare moment of common purpose.

In consequence, these national military contingents, which may be volunteered only by the will of the State, and also withdrawn by the will of the same State, have no ascertainable command and control at the U.N. Headquarters. The **U.N. Secretary General** is not a commander-in-chief; he or she is only the bursar who funds these operations as per decisions of the Security Council and the General Assembly.

When we teach the laws of the U.N. Charter, we, as professors of law, tend to make a great deal of the presumed importance of the difference in powers between the Secretary-General of the League of Nations, and his successor at the U.N.

We point to **Article 99** of the Charter which enables Mr. Ban Ki-Moon, for example, to **"bring to the attention of the Security Council any matter which in his opinion may threaten the maintenance of international peace and security."** The League's Secretary-General did not enjoy that capacity. He was primarily a mere clerk. But what can Mr. Ban do with this power in a Security Council whose decisions have to traverse the obstacle course of the non-exercise of the veto? At most, a resolution which reflects the diminished will of a toothless U.N.

In practice, the power granted to the Secretary-General under Article 99 has largely manifested itself in two procedures: formation of **"Friends of the Secretary-General"** from 4 to 5 Security Council Members. The other are statements by the Secretary-General of either support or condemnation of a global event -mere soap bubbles in the wind!! Ceremonizing!!

Some would say: But the General Assembly could also adopt resolutions on war and peace!! True. But those resolutions are only a wish list, **mere recommendations,** implementable only by the will of the **sovereign**

**leviathan** called, the Member State.

So far, I have painted a bleak picture. **I am right and wrong at the same time.** I am right when I state that the U.N., as an inter-state system, is unsuitable for effective action in civil wars. Civil wars are domestic jurisdiction catastrophes, such as in Syria, Libya, Yemen, Iraq, the Ukraine, Afghanistan, and Somalia. . In such situations, any U.N. resolution is only carried out by the State.

Now let us look at where I am wrong in **not delving in the exceptions.** The most important exceptions are: When human rights are so vastly violated to the point of shocking the conscience of mankind. This is when States may intervene under the newly-minted doctrine of **"international human intervention."**

Also when the Security Council and/or the Assembly might call on **regional organizations,** such as the European Union or the African Union or the League of Arab States to act on behalf of the U.N. under **Chapter 8.** Also when the U.N. call goes out to capable individual members hidden within the vague term of **"the international community"** to come to the rescue. Also when a U.N. resolution emboldens **domestic opposition** to rise up and throw off the yoke of the local dictator. Also when a group of States get together, in their exercise of converging self-interest, to take collective action. In all these situations, you see in the U.N. only a flag, but no direct executive action.

We also have on the bright side of the U.N. value, the vast developmental and humanitarian assistance carried out by what is called **"the Family of the U.N. Organization"** -30 specialized agencies (e.g. World health, civil aviation, refugees, food).

This is not to mention the **2000 non-governmental organizations** which truly represent **"We the People"** in the U.N. Charter. But their input, even when invited, is hardly translated into direct U.N. action. In any case, such NGO input is safely channeled, not through the Security Council, but through the Economic and Social Council (ECOSOC). ECOSOC is hardly mentioned in media headlines. This is although it carries out the greatest bulk of global action relative to enhancing the quality of life for billions of human beings in the so-called **"developing countries."**

In spite of all of these bright spots in the global performance of the U.N., I am looking through the window of **civil wars and ISIS animal kingdoms!!** What I could see are pillars of dark smoke, with the fire department, called the U.N., with no engines to rush to these fires.

Could we repair these engines? How?! The Charter cannot be amended - except, except, except, by a new beginning to be called: **"The World Under United Peoples!!"** **Sweet dreams!! Wake up, Pal!! You are now in the world of the non-State actor. Also known as "The Twilight Zone!!"**

# Hey, ISIS!! You Are Neither Islamic Nor a Caliphate!! But You Are a State -Only For the Insane!!

Friday, September 12, 2014

Now here is something which we attorneys live by: **"Show me the evidence."** The second Caliph, **Omar,** in his instructions to the judges in the middle of the seventh century, laid it down. He said: **"The burden of proof is on the plaintiff."** In this posting, I consider myself a **"plaintiff."** So here is my proof.

You, ISIS, call yourselves **"Islamic."** But **Islamic Law (Sharia),** which I teach, denies you that status. None of your **"jihadi"** forays accords with **Sharia.** The list of my evidentiary items is long. But I shall abridge it to avoid cumulative evidence:

**(1)** You declared that your **raison d'etre** is for the propagation of Islam.
- But **Islamic Law** does not extend jihad to the propagation of Islam.

**(2)** You claim that your mission is to rescue the West and other part of the non-Muslim world from ignorance **(Jahiliah)** of the present time.
- But in Islamic Law there is no proselytization. Islam, through the principle of **Tawheed (God is one),** has equated between all faiths. It left the final reckoning not to you, but to **the Creator.** There is no middle man who decides who is faithful to God and who is not. The **Quran** state: **"If anyone invokes, beside Allah (God), any other god...his reckoning will be only with his Lord."** (Chapter 23 **"The Believers;"** verse 117).

**(3)** You hug your sword, or your knife, or your artillery, as a means of coercing others, Muslims and non-Muslims, into seeing life and the world

49

through an ISIS distorted prism. Thus, you assume that Islam has tasked you with being **"an army of God."**

- But Islam abhors any use of force except for self-defense. Same with international law. The Quran states: **"Invite to the way of your Lord with wisdom and beautiful breaching; and argue with them in ways that are best and most gracious."** (Chapter 16; verse 125). Your most gracious way is **head-cutting!!**

**(4)** You claim that your jihad is akin to what **Muhammad** and his companions waged at the inception of Islam.

- But prior to Muhammad's flight from Mecca to Medina, Muhammad and his Companions confronted their tormentors with the **jihad of wisdom, the friendly advice, patience, endurance and immigration.**
- The first Muslim immigration was to a **Christian country, Ethiopia** which welcomed them with open arms. It was later followed by the immigration **(hijrah)** of Muhammad from **Mecca to Medina. This is where the true Islamic State was founded.**

**(5)** You confuse between the concept of **"jihad"** and the concept of combat **"qital."**

- In Islam, jihad is an internal striving for self-improvement. It **becomes external only for self-defense.** Islam regards the defensive war as the only just war. Muslims do not aggress; they only defend against external aggression.

**(6)** Your jihad is mayhem through an endless war which eliminates borders **-a borderless State.**

- But this is neither **jihad,** which is a legal concept, specifically circumscribed, and judicially sanctioned. Nor is it **Qital (combat)** which is limited in scope as it arises from the exigencies of the State **-the sovereign right to exist.** This leaves you only with a threatening black flag which declares: **"God, and Muhammad, his Prophet."** You abide by neither.

**(7)** You deny all others **(Shias; Christians; Jews...etc.)** the right to exist. To you, the only humans who are entitled to live are the Sunnis. Even those must be extremist Sunnis.

- But the **Quran** establishes an inclusive community of believers across the entire spectrum of humankind. It speaks of **"the people of the Book."** It glorifies **Jesus** as **"the word of God,"** born through immaculate conception. The Quran, which your practices have shredded, describes Moses as **"God's Interlocutor" (Kaleemullah).** It treats all others as equal through the call **"Allahu Akbar"** -meaning **we are all equal before God.**

**(8)** You have enslaved women through captivity, lust, and dehumanization through an austere forms of dress and conduct.

- Contrary to sterotypes, Islam, through **the Quran and the Sunna,** has equated between male and female. The Quran's verses in that regard are misread as to mean inequality in terms of inheritance, giving witness, and the like. These have been amended or supplemented by legislated law **(man-made; not God-made).** Thus today we have female judges even in **Aden (Yemen), women pilots in Egypt, Presidents of States, and paratroopers in Jordan.**

**(9)** For purposes of recruitment, you prey world-wide on the young who are disaffected, aimless, misunderstanding of Islam, or simply seeking either an identity or a job. Now, out of your 30,000 troops, you have 8000 from east, west, north and south. These are being raised by you as killers -all in the name of God.

- Islam establishes the principle of cooperation for good work. (the Quranic verse is **"cooperate in doing what is good."** Islam abhors deceptive propaganda, epitomized by your savage videos, which advocates **chaos (Fitna). Chaos is a formless void of confusion.** In its allocation of degrees of danger to society, the Quran regards **"Chaos" (fitna)** as more destructive of society's fabric than murder. Reason: **murder affects one; fitna affects all.**

**(10)** Your distorted advocacy of a concept of jihad without borders instills hostility amongst States. Your so-called **"islamic program, a projection of a Caliphate,"** aims at leading to raising the ISIS flag over all capitals. This idiocy has generated a world-wide wave of **islamophobia.**

- Yet all the members of the **Organization of Islamic Cooperation (OIC)** -all 57 Member States are parties to a world-wide contract, called the **U.N. Charter.** The Charter is a treaty. The treaty is a contact. **"O ye who believe! Fulfil all obligations"** (The **Quran;** Chapter 5, verse I). Emphasis on **"friendly relations"** between States, which you are bent on disturbing, is of such importance, that it is a part of written in the preamble of the U.N. Charter.

**(11)** You pick and choose from among the nearly **6400 verses of the Quran.** Thus you do what you are enjoined not to do by the primary source of Islamic Law.

- The Quran abhors saying by the mouth what one does not do, either by deed or at least by intention. Thus it says: **"Why do you say what you do not do?!!"**
- You lack the knowledge of **Tafseer** (interpretation of the intended words or speech). You lack the qualification for issuing **Fatwas (a non-enforceable religions advice anchored in deep knowledge of Islam).** You lack the support of **Ijmaa** (unanimity among Muslim scholars at a given time -a form of **ijtihad).** This is the

application of the mind to the written verse.

- You lack basic knowledge of Islamic history. Muslim ministries of defense in various countries from Istanbul to Cairo to Khartoum were called **"The Jihadiya Ministry."** That was a proper usage of the term **"jihad"** -self-defense, proceeded by self-policing.

- **In this context, you ISIS, are nowhere to be found, except as marauders, head-cutters, ransom-extortionists, natural resources snatchers, Islamophobia generators!!**

- **I am not finished yet, ISIS. This is only Part I. Part II shall be in a future blog. -IS (Insane State): Stay tuned. But keep your black masks on -another method of separating you from the rest of the human race!!**

# Defeating ISIS Through This Coalition? Are You Serious?!

Sunday, September 21, 2014

That would be a miracle!! This coalition which is being cobbled together by the U.S. for that worthy cause is **"a collection"** of States. As is customary during church services, a basket is passed around to collect from the faithful financial donations for the poor. Some of the congregants drop money in the basket; others pass it down the pew while kneeling at worship.

Let us see what the Obama administration has garnered in its basket for the purpose of **"degrading and defeating"** ISIS -which **British Prime Minister Cameron** has aptly called **"pure evil."** From **Saudi Arabia**, we got funding and training of carefully selected Syrian opposition elements. Please underline the words **"carefully selected,"** because nobody knows for certain the good guys from the bad guys. ISIS itself, though born in Iraq (2003-2010) matured in the Syrian civil war as of 2011.

OK!! Back to the **Obama/Kerry/Hagel/**basket of collected donations to defeat ISIS. Oh yes, here is the **Jordanian** donation: intelligence!! Good!! No troops? No!! Now here is the **United Arab Emirates** -ready for bombing ISIS from the air!! **Hmm!!** But who will coordinate these aerial missions? And don't we already have the U.S. doing this in Iraq, and now extending these assaults to Syria?

How about the **Turkish** donation? None!! Turkey has a long porous
border with Syria, and has just been worried sick by ISIS holding captive
around 50 Turkish consular officials trapped in Mosul. Remember that
Mosul was an integral part of the Ottan Empire until its defeat in World
War I. This resulted in Mosul's detachment from the Turks, making it a
part of a new Iraq. The Emperial British plan for the re-conquered Middle
East included ruling the newly minted Iraq, not from Baghdad, but from
New Delhi, India.

Turkey is now jubilant, as it should be, for its success in getting its citizens
released from the murderous ISIS grip. How? They negotiated, and ISIS
released. From ISIS perspective, these were Muslims whose country
refused to join the coalition, except for a promise (seemingly illusory) to
tighten border controls over ISIS sympathizers crossing from Turkey into
Syria, and thence, into Iraq. But wait a minute!! **Negotiating with
terrorists? Yep!!**

The rules for freeing hostages are non-written; and this was the largest
consular detainee contingent since 1979 when the Iranians held 59 U.S.
consular officials for 444 days. The U.S., under **Carter,** tried force but
failed (remember the special forces helicopters rescue operation which was
obliterated by a desert storm). **Reagan** came along, bargained through
Colonel North an Iran-Contra arms deal, and the U.S. hostages were flown
home.

Where the U.N. Convention on **"Protected Persons"** (meaning those
covered by diplomatic or consular immunities) of the 1960's failed, dealing
through **quid pro quo** with the devil succeeded. There is a need for new
international rules to regulate the unregulated: **the age of the non-State
actor!!** Don't you wish that poor **Jim Foley, Sotloff** (of the U.S.) or
**Haines** (of the U.K.) had been given, through some flexibility, the chance
to survive the butcher's knife?! As they met that horrible end of life, they
took also with them what they might have been useful as intelligence about
ISIS.

**Back to the collection basket!!** How about **Egypt's** contribution to the
coalition? Notice that all the nonsense about Egypt under El-Sisi becoming
a military dictatorship -a fabrication by U.S. decision-makers, pundits, and
neo-conservatives -has suddenly vanished. Of course Cairo is still smarting
from such interventionary attacks, including the withholding of $250
million in aid mandated by the Egypt/Israel Peace Treaty of 1979. There
are now some friendly U.S. noises about releasing those blocked funds as
well as sanctioned military hardware.

Yet even with these palliative inducements, Egypt is emerging as a non-beast of burden, Mubarak era styles, for automatic support of continuously fluctuating American policies. Some of the U.S. friendly approaches to the now banned **Muslim Brotherhood** have left a bad taste in Egypt's mouth. Through the rise of ISIS, they have also been proven to be foolish. You don't force on historically-secular Egypt a stupid Brotherhoodization agenda for the sake of conforming to American expectations of an Egyptian opposition at all costs.

Aside from these considerations about Egypt and the anti-ISIS coalition, Cairo has its own absorbing campaign inside Sinai. It is a relentless struggle against other terror franchises, like **"The Friends of Jerusalem" (Ansar Beit Al-Maqdis).** Thus Egypt is a front in the anti-ISIS campaign, a front covering the sands at Sinai, not the sands of Anbar, Iraq.

However, Egypt has in its arsenal against terrorism what others cannot match. It is a veritable arsenal that goes by the name of **"Al-Azhar,"** the citadel of proper Islamic learning, both Sunni and Shii, since **975 AD.**

**Al-Azhar** is a unique combination of mosque, university, market-place of ideas, pan-Islamic, and the first **"Tahrir Square"** in Egypt, rallying national forces against Napoleon in Egypt (1798-1803), and the British (1882-1954). **Al-Azhar** even survived the amateurish attempts during the Islamic reign of the Muslim Brotherhood (2012-2013) to co-opt it.

But under the secular **Constitution of 2014, the remarkable achievement of the Revolution of June 30,** 2013, Al-Azhar's independence was restored; the election of its Rector (the Grand Imam) reverted, not the State, but to its Council of Scholars; its amity with the Coptic church was assured.

Above all, **Al-Azhar's Document of August 2011** put truly Islamic fingers in the eyes of jihadi Islam as it declared that **"no recognition could be accorded to any State which is solely based on religion."** The Muslims are a community **(UMMAH),** not a State **(Dawlah). Sharia** is supplemented by legislation. With this type of booming and authentic voice from Egypt, makes the country akin to a **Coalition's Department for Public Information."** The delegitimation of ISIS is the only credible contribution against that crazy caliphah **Al-Baghdadi** -a mere street thug from Al-Anbar, Iraq.

Other contributors to the coalition (the number stands now at 40 States) have their roles: Bombing by **France;** training by the **British and Australians; Qatar** by arms and funding anti-Assad forces ... etc.

International organizations, like the U.N., have become more factories of statements of denunciation or support **-soap bubbles in the wind!!**

In that mix, everyone is wondering about the real weapon that has a chance of an immediate effect on containing ISIS: **the foot soldier.** None from the U.S., except for non-combat advisers whose task is **"tactical."** President Obama, reflecting national aversion to wars, has ruled it out. In fact, American history has ruled this out too. Since World War II, the mighty U.S. was involved in 5 wars: **Korea; Vietnam; Iraq I (1991); Afghanistan; and Iraq II** under Bush Junior.

With the exception of Korea, all the other wars were lost. Why? This **is the age of asymmetric war,** where the individual with an **RPG (Rocket Propelled Grenade)** is an awesome combatant with neither a uniform, nor a copy of the **Geneva Conventions of 1949** on the protection of civilians at times of war.

The coalition strategy calls for the training and equipping of **Iraqi shii** troops, **Iraqi sunni** tribes, **kurdish troops,** and **trustworthy anti-Assad forces inside Syria.** The U.S. Congress has, at long last, approved US arming and training **"safe"** anti-Assad fighters. Even **Iran,** an Assad supporter, is now tolerated by the U.S. to jump in the fray through Iraq, to combat ISIS. Indeed, wars makes for strange bedfellows!! The **enemy of my enemy is a kind of friend.**

The one billion riyal question is: **Can This Coalition Win This Just War Against ISIS?** We should all wonder. General **Martin Dempsey,** Chairman of the Joint Chiefs of Staff described this phase as **"extraordinarily complex."** And when it comes to clearing out Iraqi and Syrian cities in the Iraqi north and west, and in the Syrian east, Pentagon officials say: **"There is no one in this building who does not know that clearing out the cities will be much harder."**

On the eve of the **Normandy** invasion against **Hitler** in June 1944, **Churchill** is quoted as having wondered: **"But will the troops fight?"** The same question should be asked of the Iraqi amalgam of foot soldiers, but in a different way: **"Will the Shii troops turn their guns against the Sunni contingents, and vice-verse, after their U.S. training?"** And: **"Will the fractious Free Syrian Army, with its various ideological shades, go into combat against BOTH Assad and ISIS with the same** goal in sight?" And **"Where will Russia and Iran and Hezbollah be if the noose is tightened against Assad, their Damascus Killer-in-Chief, causing another regime change in the Arab world?"**

U.S. media have pointed out that **"the more the President and his aides have talked, the more confusion they have sown."** The Pentagon has not yet given this U.S. mission a formal name.

**Said a commentator whom I respect in his column in the New York Times, a few days ago: "For now, we seem to be settling out on an uncertain mission with unclear objectives on an unknown timetable using ambiguous methods with unreliable allies."**

The icing was on the cake as Assad expressed his desire to join the anti-ISIS coalition. An Arab adage sums it all up: **"Everyone is singing his own love song for his beloved Lailah!!**

# 5 OCTOBER 2014

## SATANIC ISIS Led to a World-Wide Discovery: It and Islam Have Never Met

Friday, October 10, 2014

### Don't call it IS (Islamic State). Call it SI (Satanic ISIS)

This is a veritable case of misrepresentation. **Whatever ISIS is, Islam is not.** Unfortunately for the 1.6 billion Muslims, the term **"Islam"** cannot be patented.

Sometimes, crooked businesses, in furtherance of their under-handed schemes, steal trademarks. On an assignment in the year 2000 from the World Bank in Yemen, I was informed by the Aden judges of an amusing case. NABISCO is a well-known name brand for biscuit production. A Yemeni company jumped in with a biscuit product which it called YAMISCO. Their ruse was short-lived. NABISCO sued YAMISCO in Aden. The court verdict was for NABISCO. Its trademark which is internationally recognized, could not be stolen.

Such protection is unavailable for Islam as a term. So ISIS and other murderous organizations which call themselves Islamic could use that great term/name for their sinister reasons. From recruitment to funding; from legitimation to globalization; from salesmanship on behalf of dark causes to intimidation of millions who mistake **"the Islamic State"** for a real State.

But gradually, ISIS, unintentionally has led the world to a discovery **-Islam and ISIS have never met.** For the following reasons, the claimed encounter is revealed as **"the lie of century"**:

- **"Holy War,"** as a term, does not exist in Islam. Jihad, meaning struggle, does not mean **"holy war."** Thus raising a black flag with an inscription of **"God and Muhammad"** for the purpose of war is very alien to Islam. It is anti-Islamic. Even the term **"just war,"** does not exist in Islamic jurisprudence. But **"self-defense,"** as a basic human right, does exist, as in every legal system and culture, including Islam.
- Islam defines killing as a crime against humanity, unless done by a sovereign empowerment; meaning by State action for self-defense. There is no recognition in Islamic law of free-lance killing.
- For this, the Quran, the overriding source of Sharia, gives a specific definition. It says: **"We ordained for the children of Israel that any one who slew a person -unless it be for murder or for spreading mischief in the land -it would be as if he slew the whole people; and if any one saved a life, it would be as if he saved the life of the whole people." (Chapter V, verse 32)**
- Over the past six weeks, four westerners were butchered by ISIS. These martyrs were American journalists **James Foley** and **Steve Sotloff,** and British aid workers **David Haines** and **Alan Henning.** This depravity attests to a central fact: Creating martyrs through a butcher's knife shall be the global force which is destined to annihilate Satanic ISIS.

Humanity can clearly see its face in these two journalists, reporting on the evolution of the Arab Spring into a tragedy in Syria and Iraq. That human face can also be discerned in **Haines** and **Henning** providing aid and comfort through Christian hands to Muslim and non-Muslim victims of these tragic upheavals.

The words of the executioner addressed to the U.S. President reflect ISIS total detachment form the human race. He claims that Obama has started aerial bombardment of Syria, and adds with the callousness of a coward: **"So it is only right that we continue to strike the neck of your people."** These victims were not only Obama's people. They were the people of every decent human being every where.

Obviously, the desert murderers who call themselves **"Islamic"** have no values to share, no principles to uphold, no cause and effect to demonstrate, no faith to defend. Nor do they have feelings for the appeals by the families of their victims or the exhortations by the world-wide Muslim leadership, and **even by Al-Qaeda,** to sheath that knife and let these brave men go.

How can ISIS be not anti-Islamic when it fights for a non-existing cause, except that of power enveloped in darkness? It has never met the Quranic injunction against crimes against humanity. For the Quran states: **"Fight in the cause of God those who fight you, but do not transgress limits, for God loveth not transgressors." (Chapter 2, Verse 190).**

**Satanic ISIS** may, for a while, control 25% of Iraq and large Syrian territory. But eventually, there shall be just reckoning whose day shall dawn over that desert where the sands is soaked with the blood of the innocent.

Calling **ISIS, Al-Qaeda, Al-Nusra,** or **The Friends of Jerusalem** jihadi organizations reflects ignorance of what jihad in Islam means. Those entities wrap themselves in these terms seeking legitimation, recruits and funding. To them the term **"jihad"** is the other side of their false coin of **"Islamic."**

Since **"jihad"** does not mean **"combat,"** but means **"struggle,"** let us seek the meaning of **"struggle"** from the words of the **Prophet Muhammad** himself. Praising non-violence, he said: **"The best struggle (jihad) is to speak the truth before a tyrannical ruler."** Speaking truth to power!! He also admonished: **"The best struggle is to struggle against your soul and your passions in the way of God Most High."**

These are the immutable values of Islam. ISIS depravity has no limits. And in the name of what? Islam? Satanic ISIS and Islam have never met.

**Oh!! One more thing, Satanic ISIS: Don't look upward to heaven!! The skies above have nothing for you except -except rain of bombs. You started that war, against humanity. Now humanity shall know when to end the conflagration which your jihad for Satan has triggered!!**

# Descending Into the Arab Cellar For Bottles Labelled "Hate the West"

Friday, October 24, 2014

It is invoked at every corner. It is the substance of nearly every conversation. It is a negative wish that binds positively. But why? Let us go to the roots, both factual and perceptional.

In 1916, the Arabs joined Britain and France in their campaign against the Ottomans. The prize was to be a State, independent from the Turks. Liberty was a priority trumping the ailing Caliphate. Lawrence of Arabia was an embedded witness, spy and advisor. Sherif Hussein and his sons, Faisal and Abdullah, could taste the sweetness of an Arab power stretching from the Mediterranean to the Euphrates, and from South Anatolia in the north to nearly the Arabian Sea to the South. A great expanse, strategic, where Arabic was spoken.

But London and Paris had up their sleeves a different expanse. France, in secret and deceitful agreement with Britain, would chop up that Arab territorial dream. France would take Syria and Lebanon. The rest, with the exception of arid and pre-oil Arabian peninsula, minus the Gulf, would be the share of the British lion. In North Africa, Egypt was, as of the defeat of the Turks at Suez in 1917/1918, to become a British protectorate; the Sudan would have two flags, the Union Jack and the Egyptian flag that fluttered but was not sovereign. The great Arab/Berber west from the Egyptian borders to the Atlantic would be ruled from Rome, and Paris.

Gone with the western winds all dreams of Arab independence. Western treachery? To a reasonable person, **"yes;"** To western capitals, **"well, reasons of state;"** to future Arab generations, only the daily prayer **"Death to the West."**

In Egypt, rebellion against British occupation, was a nationalist reaction. In 1919, the great Saad Zaghloul, raised the banner of the Wafd (The Delegation -inspired by the Indian and Irish struggles against London). It was a banner of modernity, secularism, articulation, mass support behind an enduring national symbol bearing both the crescent and the cross. Seeking to make a plea before the Paris Peace Conference, the Egyptian Delegation was quickly shown the exit. Colonialism became the order of the day, and **"the white man's burden"** became an accepted norm.

At the League of Nations, the enfeebled organization sanctified Lord Balfour's 1917 declaration of a homeland in Palestine for the Jews. He was Britain's Foreign Secretary bequeathing non-British lands. Palestine would accommodate a homeland for the Jews, with the rights of other communities unaffected, the word **"Arab"** slipped from the typewriter at the British Foreign Office -sorry, an intentional typo.

Oh, but don't worry, look all of you Arabs what we have for you -a lollipop -the British Mandate over Palestine west of the Jordan. You see, Arabs, the Mandate is intended to help people like you to learn how to govern. When you, Arabs, graduate, we shall certify that you may now govern yourselves - a governance which we, Brits, shall mentor.

In Palestine, both Jews and Arabs rose against each other and against the Union Jack. The Jewish population proceeded to build a State; the Palestinian Arabs, accustomed to feuding tribally internally, looked to other Arabs to adopt their cause. Relying on several **"intifadas,"** and on their being the majority in the land, state building was perceived by the Palestinians as an enterprise which might automatically happen. When the UN was born, its Charter provided for some hope: the mandates would become trusteeships.

But Southwest Africa (new Namibia) under South Africa's mandate, and Palestine, under British mandate, were the exceptions. No trusteeship; continuation of the mandate!! In 1947, the US, under President Truman was for a UN trusteeship over Palestine. Then, it switched its affections, voting for partition. Ben Gurion, accepting partition, declared **"the State of Israel"** on May 15, 1948, the date of the mandate's death. The Arabs, leaderless, refused partition, and no State of Palestine was declared. The Arabs wrongly felt that you don't declare the establishment of what you already have -Palestine. Subsequently, their armies, untested in battle like the Haganah of Israel, failed on the battlefield. Another Arab deep wound. And it is still throbbing.

Defeat, on top of defeat, on top of yet another defeat. But these setbacks were, to the Arabs, bad wind, seemingly blowing only from the bad west. Thus they immersed themselves on three non-winnable fronts: building up armies without building industrial societies; sanctioning dictatorship as a way of creating a unifying national consensus; and interpreting Islam in a way which made western ways nearly an apostasy. Three losses wrapped in one: loss of material advancement; loss of individual liberty; and loss of the Islamic tradition which is governed by the **Quran** whose first word is

IQRA (Read-meaning: acquire knowledge).

Within that hopeless mix on the part of the Arabs, a new Western bad wind began to blow: Orientalists rewriting Arab history and Islam in the image of its authors. These advocates painted the Arabs as a pitiful bunch. A prime example was Bernard Lewis's two books: **The Crisis of Islam** and **What Went Wrong: The Clash Between Islam and Modernity.** A total misreading of the faith of 1.6 billion Muslims. Yet Professor Lewis of Princeton was considered in the U.S. the guru of Islam. His misleading books were freely given to the US armies heading for the subjugation of Iraq in order to help the troops deal with the Iraqis!! A double calamity: invading an Arab country, while misrepresenting its faith -both reminders of earlier acts of western aggression.. While the American War chieftains, Vice President Cheney, and Secretary of Defense, Rumsfeld, cheered, the Arabs seethed. And a wave of sectarianism became a permanent weather-changer!!

Yet the Arabs, in defending Islam, their last ideological refuge for their bruised dignity, went about it in the most ill-advised way. Not fully understanding it, they interpreted Islamic law as if it was incapable of evolution since the time of the Prophet Muhamaad, 1436 years ago. The primary casualty was their minorities, especially the Christian and the Shiis. That slippery slope led to the engineering of an alien concept of **jihad.** Jihadism is basically un-Islamic, and was totally contrary to the concept of **ijtihad** which is luminously Islamic. To them, jihad was death to **"the other,"** yet ijtihad (application of reason to the revealed text) was acceptance of the other. Even the great institution of **Al-Azhar,** established in Cairo by Shiis since 975 AD as a beacon of an Islam which is moderate, inclusive, minority-oriented, and progressive. Yet Al-Azhar could not effectively overcome the tsunami of that colossal ignorance.

The west watched, and became convinced that its outlook on the Arabs was well-founded. It perceived Islam was warlike, and that democracy and the Arabs are mutually opposed to one another. Western media propagated that mythology; Arab media, unable to respond in ways understandable to the western mind, underpinned **"Death to the West."**

As the Arab Street, oppressed by its domestic dictators and buffeted by the hated West, was burning Western flags, especially the American flag. Suddenly the Arab street had a new adversary. It had previously thought the Soviet Union was a friend. But in the late 1960s, the Soviets struck with thousands of red troops pouring into Afghanistan. That was the first Soviet grab of Muslim lands since Russian absorption of the great Islamic **"Stans"** to the north of Shii Iran.

Equally suddenly, the west saw in jihad a weapon of manipulation -a ready-made tool for Soviet containment. The West, especially the U.S., discovered **Osama Bin Laden** spearheading guerrilla warfare against the U.S.S.R. An opportunity to be exploited in the context of the Cold War. Al-Qaeda benefited from military training by the US and Pakistan, and stinger missiles became readily available. Fired at Soviet aircraft from the shoulders of the Mujahedeen, these missiles became the weapon of choice.

The Soviet fled the onslaught; America and the rest of the West cheered prematurely; but the jihadists now saw their window of opportunity to even the old score with the hated West. The Mujahedeen marriage of convenience with the West was over. A new pan-Arab/pan Islamic Foreign Legion began to look for recruits and targets.

With fury, Al-Qaeda struck on 9/11. A total tragedy for the families of 3000 innocent civilian victims, including hundreds of Muslims, and for Islam itself. Now Islam was broadly perceived by the West as a faith of death through terrorism. Consequently, every beard became suspect; every hijab became a threat; every traveller to the West under the name of **"Muhammad"** or **"Ahmed."** was subjected to enhanced scrutiny. On my return from co-defending in Iraq an Iraqi wrongly detained by the marines, my U.S. passport was subjected to that over-scrutiny by Customs at JFK. The police inspector asked: **"Don't you know that an Egyptian-born person like yourself travelling frequently to Iraq, raises a warning flag?"** As an attorney whose profession exalts forked-tongue answers, I responded: **"The only flag I am raising now is the U.S. flag!!"** Smilingly, he shook my hand, while returning to me my passport. On the next arrival at JFK, the same Customs officer greeted me warmly: **"How is Baghdad this time, counsellor?"** I responded, describing Baghdad of 2007 with an unprintable epithet as it was mired in sectarian strife.

Now with the Arab Spring, calamities began falling on Arab heads like Autumn leaves: the Gaza recent massacres; the Syrian civil war; the Sudan's fragmentation; the Libyan rule by militias; the rise of the Islamic State of Iraq and Syria (ISIS); the Yemeni territorial conquests by Al-Qaeda; the conversion of the great city of Mosul to be the new presumptive capital of a lunatic by the name of Caliph Al-Baghadi; the renewed sectarian battles spilling over from Syria into Lebanon. With no end in sight, who can blame the West for fearing the Arabs, and who can blame the Arabs from daily intoning **"Death to the West!!"**

Keep in mind that historic frustrations have been seeding the fertile field of "Loving to Hate!!"  A type of psychosis bequeathed by accumulated injustices which cannot be easily overcome.  It is also hereditary!!

# 6 NOVEMBER 2014

## In Favoring Morsi Over Sisi, America Looks Like a Sleep-Walking Uncoordinated Hulk!!

Friday, November 7, 2014

The American media are on a mission. A crazy mission. Day in, day out, the shrill voices rise in unison. A prolonged lamentation of the removal of Morsi from power in Egypt. And a prolonged unreasoned condemnation of the seating of El-Sisi as Egypt's president.

Like a sleep-walking uncoordinated hulk, pundits, politicians, op ed pages, panels and interviews with a pre-selected corps of commentators, the bottom line is one and the same. **"ISIS is a menace!!"** OK. Correct. Good. Bravo. Simultaneously, the talking machine laments: **"El-Sisi has come to power through a military coup."** **How ridiculous!!**

When America started on this dangerous obfuscation, people like me, with one foot by the shores of the East River in New York, and the other foot by the banks of the Nile, said: **"A misunderstanding ."** Now with the passing of time, and the singularity of this hopeless American myth, I say: **"Even ignorance has a shelf life. ENOUGH!!"**

What does America want? Mind you that Egypt and the U.S. need one another. For a historic purpose: **Defeat terrorism which is**

**masquerading as Islamic!!** Yet from Fareed Zakaria, to Thomas Friedman; from David Kirkpatrick of the **New York Times** in Cairo to the Carter Center; from the so-called think-tanks in Washington, D.C., to some faculty voices at the American University in Cairo: the bad wind of trying to delegitimate El-Sisi, together with the secular Constitution of 2014, keeps on blowing.

**Well, let it blow; let it blow.** It shall not lift the sphinx from its desert moorings one single inch. For Egypt is not just an Egypt of El-Sisi, who won his post of President in an openly-contested elections in June 2014. Of course the crows of **Egyptophobia,** attempting to impugn that process, tried to find loopholes. So they found a tiny one: **the turnout was low.** Really?! At 45% turnout in a population with 40% illiteracy, in the midst of trying to rescue Sinai from the **Hamas/Friends of Jerusalem** terrorist barbarians, that percentage is higher than that of the U.S. in these midterm elections.

Nonetheless, the shrill voices of doom, emanating from the U.S., which still demands from its first black President to produce his birth certificate, never stop. Here are samples of their **"Road Runner"** imbecility attacks:

## Imbecility/Mental Weakness #1
- Morsi is the first freely-elected President in Egyptian history!!
- Well: What did Morsi do with his win? Broke his social contract with secular Egypt: Attacks on the Copts; torture of the Shiis; veiling the monuments as pagan relics; changing the curricula to cleanse secularism from children's books;
- Furthermore, humiliating the forces of law and order of the Ministry of Interior; calling for prayer in the midst of a Parliamentary session; downgrading the independence of **Al-Azhar** as the highest locus for **Fatwas,** and the loftiest oracle of moderate Islam; and inveighing against the Judiciary to the point that the head of the Judiciary Club, **Judge Al-Zind,** threatened to sue at the **International Criminal Court** (though he has no standing at the ICC);
- Morsi's elections and assumption of the presidency for one year (June 2012 - July 2013) **cannot be regarded as a free ride to power.** Legally speaking, that victory and its consequences are akin to somebody purchasing a token to ride the subway. That purchase of subway fare is no excuse for harassing the passengers. **Felonious assault is a negation of the right to ride mass transit.**
- Morsi's most despicable assault was his **November 2012**

66

**declaration** (so-called Constitutional declaration) to the effect that **he was above the law.**

- Have the American supporters of the Muslim Brotherhood noted that? **No!!** Had Ayatollah Morsi not been forced to recant his ridiculous claim to totalitarian power, Egypt of 93 millions would have been engulfed in a **bloody civil war.**

## Imbecility/Mental Weakness #2

- The American nay-sayers claim, that the Egyptian Revolution of June 30, 2013 constituted, together with the removal of the Morsi/Brotherhood regime from power, a **"brutal military coup."**
- We learnt in civics course 101 that sovereignty resides in the people; that that sovereign has the right, indeed the obligation, to remove a tyrant from power, if they can; **35 million Egyptians raised that historic call** for the removal of Morsi; the national army of Egypt protected that revolution, as they had duly protected the incoming wave of the Muslim Brotherhood as of **January 28, 2011,** 3 days after the start of the January 25 revolt of the masses;
- After the ouster of Morsi by means of **recall by the masses,** in the absence of a presidential removal clause in the defunct Islamic Constitution of 2012, the **interim President of Egypt, the venerable Judge Adel Mansour** (of the Egyptian Supreme Constitutional Court) paved, as a Care-Taker, the road for new presidential elections. That exercise of sovereignty brought General El-Sisi **from the military barracks** of the Defense Ministry **to the Ittihadyiah Presidential Palace.**

## Imbecility/Mental Weakness #3

- The pundits and others of the U.S. non-coordinated hulk viciously claim that the fact that President El-Sisi was a military man, thus Egypt is now ruled by a military regime!!
- Really?! Does that mean that the great administration of say, **President Eisenhower (formerly General Eisenhower)** who scored electoral victory in 1952, with Nixon as his running mate, was a military regime?
- Have the American supporters of the Muslim Brotherhood absent-mindedly forgotten that it took the Egyptian Government of Adly Mansour (interim President) and Dr. Mehleb (Prime Minister) 3 full days (from June 30 to July 3, 2013) to dialogue with the Islamist opposition to no avail? Even the Muslim Brotherhood, a monolithic organization which is not given to admission of self-inflicted wounds is now saying **"We were wrong!!"**
- The ultimatum by the military of 72-hours for compliance by Morsi, **who was not even the first choice for presidential**

candidacy by his own Brothers (El-Shater was) was a warning signal. It was also a rescue call. It saved Egypt from impending disaster in which **Qatar and foreign funds and agents** were active as **"agents provocateurs."** A popular voice for the removal of a dictator, needs, for its enforcement, the backing of a national army. That national army timely acted. And the Egyptian public which sings even through its critical moments chanted: **"May God Bless the Hands of Our Army!!"** (Teslam El-Ayadi. Ayadi Qaish Bilady). The Copts sang even lounder!!

### Imbecility/Mental Weakness #4

- The security forces committed a war crime by killing **"more than a thousand peaceful demonstrators at Rabaa and El-Nahdha squares in Cairo!!"**
- **Well; isn't that fanciful?!** For six weeks from July 3 to August 14, the government called on the hordes to end **their emirates** which they declared in the heart of Cairo of 10 million inhabitants. The governments pleaded to **"please, go home and avoid bloodshed!!"**
- **Response:** more defiance; more smuggling of arms; killing by throwing someone from the roof of a building at Rabaa; calls by the armed demonstrators for outside intervention; non-sensical support from the new **Ottoman Caliph, Mr. Ordogan** from his multi-million dollars palace in Ankara; felonious attacks against the besieging security forces which kept exits open for those wanting to end that open rebellion.
- Finally, the Rabaa and Al-Mahdha sieges had to be broken by force. **Yes, people died:** demonstrators and security forces. A tragedy; self-inflicted wounds by the murderous gangs of the Brotherhood.

### The sad list of imbecilities goes on and on and on:

- **Suppression of free expression!** Response: Shouting **"fire"** in a crowded theater, causing a stampede and death is not a **"freedom of expression."** In national emergencies, communal rights temporarily trump individual rights.
- **Abortion of democracy!!** Response: **What is your definition** of **"democracy?"** In the global dictionary, there is no consensual definition of three terms: **democracy, terrorism, and aggression.** If Egypt needs time to put its house in order, who are these alien voices to judge an incomplete process?!
- **Terrorism in Sinai is the result of suppressing the Islamists!** How laughable is the claim that action on security is the cause of terrorism!! Show me on the world map a major region which is free today from some acts of terrorism!! This includes the U.S.,

Canada, Great Britain, France, Russia, China, Australia, India. Muslims ignorant of their own faith commit these horrendous acts. Motivations: imagined injustice and a cultish belief in rewarding their crimes by palaces in paradise.

- The **Egyptian Law on Public Demonstrators is brutal!!** Well!! I have examined the U.S. laws on the same issue, and found that by comparison, the Egyptian law is less stringent.

**Now:** Let us hear **the voice of El-Sisi** at the U.N. General Assembly on September 24, 2014 put the ravings of the Uncoordinated Hulk to rest. In response to the global demand to stand united in the face of terror through religion, this President who came to power only in June 2014 declared:

*Terrorism is a plague that does not differentiate between developing and developed societies as it spreads. Terrorists come from different societies. They are not bound together by any true religious faith. That is why it is imperative that we all intensify our cooperation and coordination efforts, pursuant to the principles of the Charter of the United Nations and in fulfilment of its objectives, to end the support provided to those terrorist organizations that enables them to continue perpetrating crimes.*

America's siding with the Brotherhood shall not bring Islamic rule back. U.S. pundits, media and NGOs, through their interference in the internal affairs of Egypt, are summarily rejected. America's **"exceptionalism"** should stay at home; **it is not for export, especially to the New Egypt.** The New Egypt shall move, at its own pace towards democratization and freedom from terror and want without uninvited helping hands.

# With David Kirkpatrick in Cairo, The New York Times Becomes An Oracle for Fear-Mongering of Cultish ISIS!! How Brain-Dead!!

Friday, November 21, 2014

Of course, reporter David Kirkpatrick is no Franklin Roosevelt. Kirkpatrick, through slanted reporting on Egypt , is a fear-monger. President Roosevelt is hailed as calming the nation following the Pearl

Harbor attack in December 1941. David's article of November 11, 2014 headlines **"Milestone for Islamic State"** as it **"widens reach."** Insane!! Roosevelt calmed the nerves of the U.S. when he uttered: **"The Only Fear Is Fear Itself."** Kirkpatrick is providing evidence of his becoming an Egyptophobe. Roosevelt was providing evidence on the new dawn of **"The American Century."**

Kirpatrick's analysis, if one glorifies it by calling it **"analysis,"** is a see-through to a bunch of non-factual depictions. His point of reference was that: **"On Monday, Egypt's most dangerous military group, Ansar Beit Al-Maqdis, pledged obedience to the organization that calls itself the "Islamic State."** So what: a group of marauders declaring fealty to another group of maniacal marauders.

No!! To Egyptophobe Kirkpatrick, that recognition by a bunch of criminals of a bigger bunch of criminals is very **"significant."** It is a as if the U.N. Security Council recommended to the General Assembly the admission to UN membership of a new State - **"The Islamic State."** But, El-Ayouty, you do not get it: That recognition of subservience to ISIS is a historic change of regional power balance. **How, Mr. Kirkpatrick?!**

It is the first significant international affiliate in the bet that **the link will provide new money, weapons and recruits to battle the government in Cairo!!** Oh my God, Mr. Kirkpatrick: where were you when El-Sisi administration declared in December 2013 the Muslim Brotherhood and all of the branches of that poisonous tree, **including Ansar Beit Al-Maqdis,** to be a monolithic structure?! Under a rock?!

The declaration by **Ansar Beit Al-Maqdis,** the criminal gangs infiltrating Sinai from Gaza and from sleeper cells in Sinai, of their fealty to ISIS is no new development. They and other such anarchic outfits seek one another. With their umbrella, the Muslim Brotherhood, folding, they grope for publicity through Egyptophobe media **to project an aura of an imperialist reach.** Your expose of that declaration by the **Ansar/ISIS** axis, whether out of your agenda or out of your ignorance, acts as a **fear weapon.** It is a blunt weapon, as far as the New Egypt, and its Arab and non-Arab allies are concerned.

So please save your breath and your fanciful projections of an Egyptian rout before the cultish hordes. Did I say **"rout"**? Yes I did. Here are your words, David, in the New York Times -your unholy pulpit dated, November 11, 2014. They, meaning, Ansar, have **"recruited experienced fighters; staged increasingly sophisticated raids from the western** desert to the Sinai peninsula; beheaded informants."

Then you go on with your **hopeless efforts at psychological warfare.**
You, sir, have no shred of evidence!! Your Bla Bla Bla is no evidence!!
You describe that declaration of affiliation of Ansar Beit Al-Maqdis with
ISIS in words of gloom and doom affecting Egypt's attempts to rise up
economically. Again to your words, Mr. Kirkpatrick: **"The pledge alone
could undermine the government's efforts to win the trust of western
tourists, a vital source of hard currency."** Reaching for a crescendo, you
emphatically provide a conclusion which only idiots can subscribe to.
**"The endorsement is a major victory for the Islamic State in its
rivalry with Al-Qaeda... and could now help recruit fighters and
affiliates far beyond Egypt."**

As I gradually absorb the contours of your tortured claims, I cannot avoid
wondering to myself: **"On whose side is David Kirkpatrick and his
newspaper on?"** Have the Muslim Brotherhood achieved a brain-washing
coup to the point of no return? **I don' think so.** Why? Because the
tradition of **"a security State"** is so ingrained in Egypt of 5000 years. This
is to the point of safely predicting an eventual defeat of jihadism.

This is the nature of things in old civilizations: **Could be down for a
while, but never out.**

Just look at the **recently-promulgated Egyptian law on deportation.**
One day following Kirkpatrick's predictions of an Egyptian collapse in the
face of an Ansar declared affiliation with ISIS, which is now reeling from
the slow but sure loss of territory, President El-Sisi issued a new law. It
allows him, in the present absence of **a House of Representatives,** to
**"deport non-Egyptians convicted of crimes to their home countries."**
**Weakening States do not do that.**

In the meantime, **Abu-Bakr Al-Baghadi, the pretending Calipha,** is
playing house. His house is a State -the Islamic State, a fictitious cult. His
**"State of the Union"** recent speech, said it all. All bluster, all swagger, all
threats. In his 17-minute of November 14, 2014, he belittled not only
Obama. He belittled all foreign leaders, **especially those of Arab and
Muslim States.**

These repairs came from none other David Kirkpatrick from Bagdad. This
is the capital of Iraq where one third of its landmass raised, not the Iraqi
flag, but the ISIS black flag. Al-Baghdadi, the **street thug from Al-Anbar,**
thunders as follows: Calling on **"the Mujahedeen among the disciples to**

erupt volcanoes of jihad everywhere."

If that is not enough, Al-Baghdadi of what is expected to be the shortest lived Caliphate ever, adds other layers of bluster. He exhorts all Muslims **(the 1.6 billions of them)** to: **"rise up against the agents of the Jews and crusaders, their slaves, tails and dogs."**

Would Egyptophobes, like Kirkpatrick or Human Rights Watch, take positive note of the recent Egyptian law releasing representatives of errant organizations like Al-Jazeera from incarceration? I cannot bet on it. Because **their specialty is poisoning the well of facts** in a brain-dead support of the propaganda line of the Muslim Brotherhood.

The well has been sufficiently poisoned by the likes of David Kirkpatrick and his mouth-piece, **The New York Times.** The poison here is in the form of myth-information and misinformation. It has even seeped into the thinking of well-recognized law organizations such as the **New York City Bar, the oldest Bar in the U.S.**

A recent event was held on November 13 by the Middle East and North Africa Committee. It featured the **Consul-General of Egypt, Ambassador Ahmed Farouk.** He addressed that forum at a standing-room only affair. That was in the presence of a galaxy of senior diplomats including the Consul-General of Saudi Arabia, **Khalid Al-Sharif,** the UN Under-Secretary-General for African affairs, **Ambassador Maged Abdel-Aziz,** and the permanent observer of the League of Arab States, **Ambassador Fathallah.** His speech was luminous, especially with regard to a controversy maliciously generated by elements of the Muslim Brotherhood. Namely: Is the present government of El-Sisi the outcome of a **"revolution"** or a **"coup."**

In his speech, Ambassador Farouk did his best to lay this controversy to rest: **A Revolution.** Yet during the Question and Answer period, one of the attendees, an attorney, screamed his head off about **"total absence of respect for human rights in Egypt."** The questioner was obviously unpersuaded by the plain logic set forth by the speaker. And being a veteran diplomat, Ambassador Farouk, referred the questioner to the speech.

Being not beholden to the restrains of diplomacy, I jumped to my feet. Among other points, I asked that opponent: What do you read when you say, with undeserved haughtiness, that the demonstrators at Rabaa and Al-Nahda were peaceful? **Moreover why do you hold the Egyptian process**

leading to democratization at a a standard which you do not apply to
the U.S. -such as in regard to Guantanamo torture, the declaration
that the Geneva Conventions were obsolete, and the rendition
policies of the Bush Jr. administration?

He looked ashen, and ready to jump ship. **Good!!** But the point is that the
likes of Mr. Kirkpatrick are having their way with the facts of the situation
on the ground in Egypt. Ambassador Farouk said it best: **"Call it what
you want: A Coup!! A Revolution!! It is up to you. I provided the
facts. You provide your own conclusion.**

**Here is my own conclusion:** The Muslim Brotherhood is active and is
heard in America. They have the funds, the penetration, the voice, and the
professionalism of lying to their audiences. In this, they are well practiced.
**For over 86 years!!**

America, in sum, is taken for a ride by **the mother of all jihadism -the
Brotherhood!!** The government of the New Egypt should bear in mind
that fighting terrorism in its deserts should not be by armed might alone. **It
should also be by articulated voices which know how to respond to
an American environment which is being manipulated by the scum
cells of the Brotherhood in the hope of bringing back to Cairo the
nightmare of the Islamic one-year rule!!**

# Who Are The Village Idiots In The U.S. Who Support ISIS?: The American Islamophobes and the American Jihadis!!

Wednesday, November 26, 2014

The American Islamophobe is probably the most dangerous!! He or she
is akin to a sleeper cell and a fifth column combined. People like **Sam
Harris** and **Bill Maher!!** Sam, with his two stupid books calling Islam all
kinds of nasty names. Bill, with his antics, and his tongue on talk shows
quoting from the **Somali Ayaan** her negative tribal experiences in Somalia.
What both of these **"village idiots"** say in the safety of their mock salons
in the U.S. endangers the safety of this great country.

They hurt the homeland, advance the cause of religious apartheid, and assist
ISIS in its idiotic claim that all of Islam is under attack by the U.S. None of

these idiots, including their propagates on the extreme right of US politics, such as **Michelle Bachman** and **Sara Palin,** know anything credible about Islam or the 1.6 billion Muslims. They swallow as objective truth what the jihadists say about Islam and do to non-Muslims. Then proceed to make the most atrocious and negative conclusions about that great faith.

It all seems to stem from the likes of **Bernard Lewis** of Princeton. In his books, especially **"What Went Wrong With Islam?,"** he imagines that the Muslim of today **(a)** wants to establish a Caliphate; **(b)** his (the Muslim's) faith suffered from no reformation movement; and **(c)** Islam and modernity are antagonistic. That celebrated guru of Islam is no guru at all!! The Caliphate is as dead as King Tut; Islamic jurisprudence (Sharia) is continuously evolving through ijtihad and legislation; the Christian Reformation and Counter-Reformation of the 16th and 17th centuries were rebellions against papalist regimes which glorified symbols over substance.

As to Islam being antagonistic to modernity, this is an Islamophobic trait that has no relationship to Islam itself. It has to do with the demagoguery of terrorists like **Boko Haram** which regards Western education as un-islamic. So **Lewis, Harris, Maher, Ayaan, Bachman, Palin and Fox News** are in the camp that judges Islam from their dark corner of ignorance. They are playing on the post 9/11 fears, and on their desire to manifest loyalty to America.

They in fact drink from the well which has been contaminated by jihadi propaganda against the West, and by jihadi abhorrence of any rapprochement between the 1.6 billion Muslims and the rest of humanity.

**Here is what they do not comprehend** about **Sharia (Islamic Law)** of which I am professor at Fordham University School of Law, New York City:
- Islam is the submission to the will of the Creator. **"In God (Allah in Arabic) We Trust,"**
- Unless you are a jihadi butcher, **"Allahu Akbar"** means: **We are all equal before God,** regardless of whichever faith we hold. **Equality before the law;**
- The principle of **Tawheed (There is no God but God)** is a principle that ties every faith to all faiths. For the oneness of God is a commitment to non-discrimination -**the acceptance of the other (diversity);**
- In that principle there is no middle man between man/woman and their Creator. There is a hotline between earth and the heavens, with no server or intercessor;

- **"Infidel"** is not what **Somali Ayaan** stupidly describes as non-Muslim. **"Infidel,"** in Islamic jurisprudence, means someone with no values;
- The **Prophet Muhammad,** a messenger of revelation, was born a natural birth. And died a natural death. Christ, in the Quran, is **"the word of God."** born of **"immaculate conception,"** and **"will come again,"**
- A tyrant should be removed from power, if the means exist for avoiding a total breakdown of law and order **(Fitna - Mayhem)**;
- Maslahah (public good) trumps the religious text. In fact there is an entire jurisprudence entitled **"The Non-Textual jurisprudence,"** on **which I shall refocus my course for the Fall of 2015;**
- Jihad is not the equivalent of combat. The jihadis criminally mix between the two. Jihad is both inner **(self-improvement),** and outer **-self-defense** (The UN Charter, Article 51);
- The law of war in Islam is fully compatible with the **Geneva Conventions of 1949.** In all respects. Including the protection of civilians in times of war.
- Under Sharia, there is no **"Holy War"** -as the Islamophobes claim. **Holy War is a western expression** from the time of the Crusaders of the 10th, 11th, and 12th centuries. It has never been an Islamic jurisprudential term.
- Torture is fully repugnant to Islam. For Islam, like every other faith, values the sovereignty of the individual. US warlords like **Dick Cheney, Donald Rumsfeld, Condelesa Rice, Wolfowitz, Feith and John Yoo** believe that torture is a state exigency. That waterboarding is OK. That Guantanamo is a Maginot Line of defense for America. That holding Muslims for a dozen years without being either charged or released is OK -the new order (in effect, the new disorder),
- **Ijtihad (the application of the mind to the text)** is the means by which Islamic law evolves. Both through unanimity **(ijmah)**; analogy **(Qiyas)**; or public policy for public good **(Maslahah),**
- Regardless of counter-practices within the variegated spectrum of 1.6 billion Muslims, **Islamic Law guarantees gender equality.** Where the text connotes differences, legislation has remedied that disparity. A woman has the unilateral right to divorce her husband, and her wealth cannot be commingled with that of her spouse by his own wish,
- The judge in Islamic Law is defendant oriented. And the **fatwa (religious pronouncement with no enforceability)** is the preserve of licensed Muftis; thus the likes of Bin Laden or the

crazed so-called ISIS Caliph, Al-Baghdadi, are rogue muftis. **You might as well take their fatwas to the toilet;**

- As to the use of force, there is no self-help in Islamic Law. The State under that law has the **monopoly of the use of force, not the crazy jihadis, and**
- **Blasphemy** laws in Pakistan are nothing **but a heap of crap!!**

This is only a fraction of Islamic Law. **Isn't it ridiculous:**

- For several states in this United States to pass laws preventing citing Sharia in state courts as a source of law?
- For the U.S. policy-makers to slap sanctions on Egypt for removing an Islamic tyrannical rule of the Muslims Brotherhood by public recall of Brotherhood? Morsi had threatened the Copts, the Shiis, women, other broad sectors of Egyptian society and secularism!!;
- For the great majority of Americans to **regard the Saudis -all Saudis -as potential terrorists,** while the U.S. is assiduously seeking cooperation from Riyadh as a member of the **anti-ISIS coalition?** Was **David Koresh** of Waco, Texas, a representative of all Texas, **"The Lone Star Republic?"**
- For the overwhelming majority of the members of both houses of the US Congress to **regard the Israeli/Palestinian unresolved conflict** as having no impact on the growth of jihadism?

None of the above writing has the central intention of defending Islam as a faith. No faith needs a defense, because faith is non-negotiable!!

It is an illustration of how attacking any faith can only backfire. **Pogroms and the holocaust** have not succeeded in vanquishing judaism; Jihadism shall not vanquish Islam; Western colonialism did try to be a vehicle for Christianization. It largely failed. ISIS is only a passing disturbing phenomenon.

The clearest fact is what you can prove to be supported by demonstrable experience. **The fact is that both American Islamophobes and American jihadis cohabit the same tent.** Over that tent, the black flag of ISIS flutters.

**To the village idiots, I say:** You have no future. Hate and cruelty paralyze the human brain. That brain no longer does its work -thinking. It is in a coma!! And when that coma is over, the village idiots shall discover that: **the suicide bombers commit anti-Islamic acts of destruction; that they have taken an express train, not to heaven but to hell; that there are no 70 virgins awaiting them, as it is only a parable, which may in reality exist only in Playboy, porn literature and in the so-**

called "jihad by fornication." In summary, neither Islam nor Sharia has anything to do with the criminality that goes nowaday by the name of ISIS, Jihadism, or the Friends of Jerusalem.

# 7 DECEMBER 2014

## Through Default, ISIS LIVES And Shall Die!! Here is Why?!

Saturday, December 6, 2014

We are back to an analysis of ISIS -the vaunted phantom which crystallizes jihadism. Born through fissures in governance in Iraq, and absence of governance in Syria. This is the cleanest slate any barbaric movement would hope for.

In Iraq, the fissures were already there under **Maliki,** the former Prime Minister of an Iraq orphaned by lack of truly national leaders. Maliki, a Shiite boss who commands allegiance centered on Tehran, saw a mirage of an Iraq dominated only by Shiis. Not by an amalgam of all Iraqi sects. Neither the Sunnis of the great North, nor the Kurds of Iraqi Kurdistan saw in Maliki the visage of national unity. For he was a divider, not a uniter. His ethos was **"divide and misrule."**

Pandering to his handlers in Tehran, he refused to sign a security agreement with the U.S. That was before the American military turned tail, and completely departed from the **"Land of the Two Rivers."** In the wake of that withdrawal, was a Sunni dormant volcano ready to erupt in the face of the **Sectarian-in-Chief Maliki. Bremer,** the genius of a misguided American invasion of Iraq in 2003, had disbanded the huge Iraqi army. An insane blunder for which America dearly paid.

That formidable Iraqi military machine had been officered for years by highly-trained Sunni general officers. Now, without jobs in Anbar, Mosul and Faluja, highly trained but unemployed, imbued with Iraqi nationalism, but excommunicated by the Baghdad Shii-powered structure, they readily welcomed ISIS. **An act of Qassass, revenge, against Maliki.**

Acting on the basis of **"the enemy of my enemy is my friend"** (sectarian Maliki v. Sunni north), this cadre of battle-tested military were a boon to **Al-Baghadi** of ISIS. It was an alliance to which the tribal leadership of the north and west were eager to seek out and pay homage to. The tribal leadership of Tikrit, and other Saddam geographic centers of power, had been humiliated by both the American invaders, and by their shii-based Iraqi successors.

They saw in ISIS an entity through which they could hit back at their tormentors. And hit they did. By the huge American-made arsenal, nearly trillion-dollar worth of the best offensive equipment money can buy. ISIS knew the Sunni desire for revenge: They have been in bed with them in Iraq, even before ISIS was an ISIS fighting in Syria to topple Assad.

The field was clear. In both Iraq (north and west), and in Syria (north and east), you could see no border markings. I was there as a defense attorney. It was, and continues to be the biggest no man's land in the world. **TERRA NULIUS!!**

Having been declared by **Al-Qaeda** as too brute, and by **Al-Nusra** as too independent, and by the world as an outlaw, ISIS reality showed its ugly face. Through a different modus operandi moving massively eastward astride both Syrian and Iraqi territory; cease the no man's land and hold it; inherit the Sunni desire for revenge against the shiis; **re-employ Saddam's battle-hardened colonels and generals.**

More importantly, declare a caliphate -the Muslim equivalent of an imperial system!! It evokes memories of a robust governance which could put an end to Islamophobia and the humiliation of Muslims in Afghanistan, Iraq, Pakistan, and Palestine of the mandates. No more Guantanamos; no more Abu Ghraibs; no more Pagrams; no more collaboration of peace between Arab capitals and the West, including Israel. Payback time through a caliphate, headed by **Abu-Bakr Al-Baghdadi**. Hail to the Caliphate, and come you all disgruntled young from the West and East, and cleanse the Middle East from all vestiges of westernism, including even Christian

Arabs!!

In a matter of days, the newly trumpeted caliphate had two capitals: **Raqqa in Syria, Mosul in Iraq.** Oil fields, and huge water dams were targeted; **the shias had no real army in Iraq,** only disjointed militias; the collapse of the Iraqi army of the north proved the falsehood of the modern State; **over the necks of western hostages, knives were a tool of terror;** over the modern tanks abandoned by leaderless Iraqi recruits, black banners fluttered with the familiar inscriptions of **"Allah, and Muhammad, His Messenger."** Neither Allah nor Muhammad have anything to do with that barbarism.

Various jihadi factions declared their fealty to the new phantom caliphate, including the **Friends of Jerusalem, a Hamas offshoot,** which went as far as declaring Sinai of Egypt an emirate of the new caliphate. A pie in the sky.

The hit and run acts of the Muslim Brotherhood, now declared a terrorist organization in the largest Arab State demographically (Egypt), were celebrated. ISIS called it, through social media, the beginning of the collapse of El-Sisi government, and of the restoration of the faschist Islamic rule of 2012-2013 in the heart of Arab lands.

And when the anti-ISIS international coalition of 60 countries was declared and began raining bombs on ISIS command and central centers, ISIS called the campaign against terrorism a campaign against Islam itself. Through confrontations at holy sites in the West Bank and Jerusalem, between Palestinians and Israelis, **the Palestinian-Israeli conflict was changing labels: from a territorial conflict into a bloody religious conflict.** A huge assist to the propaganda machine of ISIS.

But can all of this chaos translate into an ISIS durability and longevity? **Absolutely not.** Through all sorts of default, ISIS lives. And through the same defaults it shall gradually die. Here is why:
- The international anti-ISIS coalition is fast learning. Air campaigns shall gradually be supplemented by foot soldiers from the localities affected;
- The Sunni-Shii divide, exasperated by jihadi propaganda and Western Islamophobia, shall eventually shrink. This is being done by age-old solid institutions, such as Al-Azhar of Egypt. And by the centralization of **sources of fatwas** in various Muslim countries;
- Weak institutional responses to ISIS and other jihadi organizations

have been the hallmark of inter-State systems, such as the UN, the League of Arab States, and the Organization of Islamic Cooperation.

- These organizations are now being sidelined by more robust non-governmental organizations which are less bureaucratic and more adept in confronting false jihadi propaganda. They are more suitable to deal with the actions of non-State actors as regards recruitment, funding and mission-statements.

- **Anti-jihadi forces are quickly learning from their jihadi adversaries.** Military training is accelerated; modern technology is being employed; nationalism is overwhelming their daydreams of a caliphate; **Islamic law (Sharia) is being learnt;** protection of minority rights is being rediscovered; parliamentary systems are being refashioned to suit the environments of Egypt, Tunisia, and Bahrain; women empowerment is becoming a national objective in several Muslim countries including Saudi Arabia.

- **Assad may stay on, but eventually presiding over a partitioned Syria;** the Islamic militancy by which Turkey and Qatar are approaching their neighbors is not gaining traction especially in the New Egypt; and Iran is struggling to find a middle ground between its sovereign right to nuclear energy and western fears of proliferation of nuclear arms.

It is indeed tragic that some Western analysts seem to have become spell-bound by the din of jihadi self-aggrandizing publicity. A recent example could be here cited by **"An Analysis"** posted online by, **George Friedman** of **Geopolitical Weekly,** dated November 25, 2104. Its title is **"The Islamic State Reshapes the Middle East."** A tantalizing title for an article which dealt mainly with various readjustments in external policies by Middle Eastern Arab States. The author was off the mark where he described ISIS as **"a new territorial power in Syria and Iraq." Sound analysis?! No!! Alarmism: Yes!!** Slowly but surely, anti-jihadi forces are rising, organizing and coalescing.

The dream of Al-Baghdadi of flying his ISIS black flag over the White House in Washington or over Al-Ittihadyia Palace in Cairo, or over Mecca and Medina, shall in the long term prove to be less credible than the flying carpet of Ali Baba and the Forty-Thieves!!

# For How Long Can the Arabs Continue To Blame "The Others" For THEIR

# Retardation?

## Saturday, December 6, 2014

Time for the Arabs to get up from their easy chairs, look in the mirror and say: **"We too are to blame!!"** Self-criticism is a virtue, a sign of maturity, and the point at which the Arab World would begin to own its future.

Yes, we know!! The **Sykes-Picot** secret agreement between Britain and France during World War I was a huge betrayal to Arab nationhood and independence. Colonization of Syria and Lebanon by France; Iraq and Palestine and Jordan by Great Britain; Balfour Declaration for the creation of a national home for the Jews in a part of Palestine; and a free hand in the Gulf for the Union Jack.

Prior to these national calamities, visited upon the Arab homeland nearly a hundred years ago, was the continuation of British occupation of Egypt and the Sudan; Italian hegemony over Libya, and French protectorates over most of the Maghreb, west of Tripoli.

During those dark ages, the Arabs were humiliated; their national leaders were exiled, killed, or imprisoned; their language, the language of the Quran, was given secondary importance in the curriculum. Arab culture was denigrated; national uprisings were put down ferociously as if they were crimes against humanity. **From ages of glory, to ages of western imperialism and in your face ascendancy!!**

But that was more than a hundred years ago. Yes the Wilsonian **"right to self-determination"** remained mere ink on worthless paper. But by the end of World War II, an earlier Arab Spring of national liberation changed nearly everything. By 1962, with Algeria's independence, which I witnessed as UN spokesman, the Arabs, with the exception of the Palestinians, became masters of their own houses, **or shall we say palaces.**

However, who replaced the western colonialists? **Arab dictators!! Inter-Arab Cold War!!** Swinging from alliances with either the West or the East!! Or being non-aligned!! **Politics became the sport of an indecisive elite.** But the street and the mosque were left to religion largely defined as mere rituals not as renewal of values especially **"the acceptance of the other."**

Armies marched proudly, but on parade grounds, except when enforcing the will of the dictator. Education became largely costless but also worthless. The press became mere gossip sheets, or poor translations of how the developed world perceived us. **Gender inequality found its support in the misunderstanding of Sharia (Islamic Law).** Oil made the Gulf rich in liquidity, but did not create truly industrial societies. Federations were fabricated from the top, and quickly dissolved through either inter-dictator piques or through putsches.

The Baath party was born, so was the Muslim Brotherhood. **The one became secular fascism, the other became religious fascism.** Nascent democracies became a tool to paper over one-party rule. College degrees could not qualify the holder for jobs.

The League of Arab States (LAS) was trumpeted, but remained a mere talk show. Membership in the UN Security Council, though it continued to be **"The Great Hall of Deadlocks,"** became a phony badge of national prestige!!

Qaddafi called Libya **"The Great Popular Socialist Jamahiryah;"** Saddam thought Kuwait was his to take by force, and Arafat rushed to hug him as an Arab gesture of solidarity. How Machiavellian!! The Sudan fragmented. Israeli settlerism in territories allotted to an Arab State remained largely immune from condemnation as flouting international law.

With the 40's, the 50's, the 60's and the 70's gone, came over the Arab world, **the dark cloud of militant Islamism.** The great content of Islam was replaced by the disturbing context of **"Islam Is the Answer."** Images without substance.

**Al-Qaradawi assumed in Qatar the mantles of the great Gamal El-Deen Al-Afghani, Muhammad Abdo and Rasheed Ridha.** His fatwas were sought as if emanating from a great oracle or from the great Al-Azhar in Cairo. The Khomeini Revolution of 1979 attempted exportation. But deservedly failed, except -except for making the veil and the long beard Islamic requirements.

**That was the first wave. The second wave (waves always overlap)** was jihadism born of Al-Qaeda's rise in consequence of the defeat of the Soviets in Afghanistan. And from pin-pricks to the catastrophic **9/11.** Don't laugh, but some Arabs blames it on the CIA. And from here Islamophobia reared its head, especially in America and Europe. **A boon for jihadism which grew out of ignorance of Islam by the West.** It also grew out of the Muslims ignorance of the continuous evolution of Islamic Law in the direction of **"The Maslaha Jurisprudence."** (The Laws of Communal Interest).

**The third wave was the Arab Spring.** A rumbling earthquake. It began, but seemingly without and end. Its ugliest form is the Syrian civil war. A family of dictatorship, the Assads, which would rather pulverize Syria as a structure, and annihilate its population, than relinquish its ill-gotten throne. **Yet its most promising form is Egypt and Tunisia.** This is where the battle between secularism and Islamism has been decided by popular vote in favor of secularism and inclusiveness."

Throughout all the above, one could see that the Arabs, since the early 1960s, have chosen their twisted paths toward tomorrow. **"The Others"** had virtually no hand in fashioning it.

- **"The Others"** did not cause developmental retardation;
- They did not bring one dictator after the other to the seat of power;
- They did not wreck the educational system;
- They did not enhance corruption in public life; for corruption is invariably locally manufactured;
- They did not dictate to the judiciary;
- They did not write the rubbish which is daily published under the name of **"thoughtful analysis;"**
- They did not degrade TV shows to their present level of superficial pastime;
- They did not cause the young and the restless to want to die crossing the Mediterranean in search of a future; and
- **They did not even anticipate the Arab Spring with its popular calls for Dignity, Development, and Democracy.**

It was the Arabs who, by and large, have mismanaged their affairs:

- They have looked upon their oil wealth as a non-ending bonanza;
- They have lagged in the creation of their own defense industry;
- They have condemned terrorism but stopped short of creating powerful indigenous anti-jihadi structures;
- **Their Sunnis have looked upon their Shiis as non-Muslims;**
- Their only Shii State, Iraq, has bungled its relationship with its Sunni population to the point of the latter opting for joining Satanic ISIS as a means of revenge;
- Libya has become a State of militias; Sudan continues to fragment beyond the loss of the South; Yemen is in the grip of a combination of tribalism and Houthis revival; the great Sahara in both Libya and Algeria have become a prime source of jihadi

military hardware; Qatar is closer in foreign policy to Turkey than it is to Saudi Arabia, the largest stakeholder in the Gulf Cooperation Council; Dubai has become more of a western implantation than an Arab enclave; and the Palestinians are still in search of national unity under a dysfunctional leadership which is expert in corruption; and Islamic Law is still unlearnt by the majority of Muslims.

*For how long can the Arabs continue to blame "the others" for their retardation? For as long as they do not see their reality in the mirror and decide to become "the new India": hundreds of languages and ethnicities; a democracy deemed to be the largest in the non-Western world; a tradition imbued with technology; and leaders who are proud to see their vehicles in outer space.*

India even had a Muslim president, a Sikh Prime Minister, and a Catholic woman born in Italy as head of the former governing party, the Congress Party which the Wafd party in Egypt tried to emulate!!

**Let the Arabs compare between India and Pakistan: sky above, and turmoil below. This is the magic of forgetting the colonial past and espousing diversity. When are the Arabs going to learn that: "Salvation comes from within?!"**

# How and Why Has Egyptophobe Michelle Dunne Gotten the Reputation of the Carnegie Endowment Undonne?

Wednesday, December 24, 2014

This is the first of two Christmas letters to **Michelle Dunne.** Its title is **"The Contrived Drama a the Cairo Airport."** She, the queen of that drama, is reputed to be a diplomat and a scholar in the pay of the Carnegie Endowment for International Peace. I am the founder of **"ELIFAS - El-Ayouty Institute for Arab Spring Studies"** and in the pay of myself.

Before I present the non-controverted facts, Dunne and El-Ayouty share in two values: Love for the U.S. as citizens; interest in Egypt with Dunne as the ideological attacker, and I, a **"one man platoon,"** as a defender of my other and older nationality -an Egyptian who came to America as a

Fulbright 62 years ago.

I served America well through teaching since 1954. She serves America not so well through attempting, not to bring Egypt and America closer, but to drive them apart, by casting unmitigated doubts on the Egyptian Revolution as a failure. Dunne's motivation for her Egyptophobia is unclear to me. The only clarity is that a scholar and a diplomat are soldiers for peace. From the facts below, she comes across as a stalwart for hate.

Ms. Dunne was invited to speak at the 15th Anniversary of the **Egyptian Council for Foreign Affairs (ECFA)** in Cairo in mid-December. ECFA, which I represented at the UN from 2002 till recently this year, is a prestigious NGO. It brings together the best Egyptian minds in diplomacy, academia, business, politics and the arts under one umbrella. I was in Cairo at the celebration time. But could not attend because of a nasty bout of cold. However, I came to know about the **Michelle Dunne** saga from ECFA's top echelons, and from the media which carried mostly Dunne's view of what she was subjected to upon arriving at the Cairo Airport.

From my investigations, the following picture emerged:
- Opposition within ECFA to inviting Dunne was based on her persistent attacks on the legitimacy of **El-Sisi's** assumption of powers as President. Casting doubts by Dunne in that direction is baseless. Thirty-five million Egyptians congregated on **June 30, 2013** in every square clamoring for **Morsi's** ouster. His Islamic iron fist and the Brotherhoodization of Egypt were about to plunge Egypt of 100 million population, both Muslims and Copts, in a Libyan/Yemeni style civil war. It was a popular recall of a hated Islamist regime, an appeal for the rescue by the national cohesive Egyptian army, not unlike 1958's uprising in France which brought **DeGaulle** to power.

States in transition are traditionally sensitive to outside intervention, even if that intervention is by the so-called **"Global Think Tank"** -the motto of Dunne's paymaster, the Carnegie Endowment. Yet the ECFA leadership won the day over those who opposed Dunne's participation. The leadership said, **"Let her come so that we might reason with her."** If I had a say in the matter, I would have joined the opposition. Ideologues like Michelle Dunne are beyond reasoning. Like Amtrak, they run on iron rails, not a Greyhound bus navigating the bumps and taking alternative back roads.

Dunne was advised by ECFA to pay for her air travel and secure her visa. ECFA was to house her, together with other invitees from abroad, at the

Conrad Hilton, a 5-star, by the great Nile River in Cairo. Dunne submitted her passport to the Egyptian Counsular section of the Embassy in D.C. for the purpose of a visa. But quickly withdrew it before any official response was made. **Why?** I don't know. But she did, and opted to travel to the country which she, from her writings, considers a dictatorship, only **because she says so.**

Arriving in Cairo late at night, Dunne presented herself to Passport Control at the Cairo International Airport (Terminal 3). Her request was for **"a tourist visa,"** while the purpose of her travel was **"business."** By checking her name on their **"No Admission"** list, Michelle Dunne's name was emblazoned, and her admission was denied.

   **Was that a contrived move by Dunne to prove to the world that Egypt was in the grip of a dictatorship, and that she was justified in her Egyptophobia?** I truly don't know. But as an international defense attorney, I would be foolish to discard it, though I am not generally a believer in conspiracies.

So here I must say in this **First of Two Christmas Letters** to Michelle Dunne: Had you left your passport at the D.C. Egyptian Consulate, you would have been warned that you were not welcome to enter Egypt. That unvisa'ed trip and the obfuscation in your application at the Cairo Airport for a **"tourist visa"** cascaded into what followed.

Undoubtedly, it fed you with the Egyptophobe nourishment which you, from your writings and other utterances seem to crave. Addiction to hate is a real malaise, though you pretend to work for **"international peace."**

Midnight of Dec. 14/Dec. 15 at the Cairo International Airport is not an opportune time for negotiation with the security services of Egypt. This is a country at war with terrorism and other myriad opponents, and lifting of **"the non-admission"** status is a lengthy process.

You called the U.S. Embassy in Cairo -no help. You called another soul mate of yours -another Egyptophobe, **David Kirkpatrick,** reporter of the **New York Times** in Cairo -no help, except for a commitment to persevere in **calling the elected El-Sisi administration a coup.** I am certain that you called others as well, especially in the U.S., at around 5:00 pm Eastern Standard Time.

Lots of empathy for you, Michelle, from those helpless quarters. But still **"no admission."** Mind you, as a presumed scholar and a diplomat, you should know that legally **"no admission" is not detention.** But for enhancing the dramatic effect of what you, by your unreasonable actions, had brought upon yourself, you allowed yourself to call it **"detention."** Even a cup of tea in a private salon offered to you by the Airport Security Officers out of sheer Egyptian kindness to your unresolved dilemma, was described as **"isolation, intimidation."** How ridiculous!!

Then your veil of victimhood fell off. **Ambassador Shalaby,** the able, gentle and scholarly Executive Director of ECFA, having been informed while in bed at or about 1:00 AM of your dilemma, called top officials to allow you to enter even for one day. He regretted that he was unsuccessful, and that ECFA had not known about your being on a **"no admission"** list.

Calling you through a teleconference while you sat waiting for a plane to fly you out of Egypt, **your haughty response was truly imperial.** You told him in effect that **"I came in the hope of changing my mind about Egypt. Now I am confirmed in my views about Egypt!!"**

**A threat,** combined with arrogance and ingrained malicious intention about Egypt -one third of the Arab population!! So please go ahead with your theatrical threats. You and the entire **"think tank"** of the Carnegie shall not move the New Egypt one inch from the march to its own drummers - its secular society. **Rivers of your ink shall not change the color of the Nile water,** because, in your fantasy, you ignore the **following realities:**
- A visa is a recognition of the validity of a passport, issued by the proper officials of the country which the bearer wishes to enter;
- A visa is a product of a State sovereignty whose denial is known in international law as **"a protective principle"** with respect to certain conduct outside of its territory by persons, **like you Michelle Dunne,** not of its nationals;
- According to international law, the U.S. cannot interfere with the laws of another sovereign regarding conduct occurring within that other sovereign's territory; and
- **The New Egypt, unlike the pre-El-Sisi era, is not going to be supinely the tool of other powers.**

As an example, the U.S. has denied the entry of **Professor Tariq Ramadan** to the U.S. 3 years ago, following his application to the U.S. Embassy in London for an American visa. That world renowned professor of Islamic Studies at the Faculty of Theology at Oxford, was responding to an invitation to speak at Stanford University. Though a nephew of **Hassan El-Banna,** the founder of the Muslim Brotherhood, and based in Geneva, he has never engaged in anti-US or anti-Western activities to warrant that senseless denial. **Le Monde Diplomatique** has said about him:

**"Ramadan has started to pave out the road to reform and changes in the understanding of Islam in Muslim communities in the West."** I have assigned his book entitled **"Islam and the Arab Awakening"** to my graduate seminar at **Fordham University School of Law, New York City** where I teach a course entitled **"Islamic Law and Global Security."**

Everyone took that visa denial in stride. **But not the omnipotent Michelle Dunne of the Carnegie Endowment for International Peace!** She is **UBER ALLES!!**

- **David Kirkpatrick,** Dunne's cohort in Egyptophobia, wrote two pieces on the Dunne's seemingly pre-fabricated victimhood. The title of the first article in **The New York Times** was **"Egypt Denies Entry to American Scholar Critical of Its Government."** In it he refers to recent Dunne's writings by saying: **"Ms. Dunne has pointedly criticized Egypt's attempts to carry out what she called 'draconian' restrictions on nongovernmental organizations as well as its "harassment and intimidation of activists."**

- **Thanks, David!!** You are a Prince in the mold of Prince Vlad!! I hope that you have enjoyed reading about your lack of ethics in reporting in **Media Ethics,** by **Rhonda Roland Sheaver,** dated **Dec. 18. Media Ethics** investigations revealed, among many other lapses of ethics, that you lied about the **Grand Mufti** of Egypt, **Shawki Allam.** You, **a lying weasel,** featured him as **"defending forced evacuation of families from Sinai."** Mr. Kirkpatrick: you did not even contact Dr. Allam. You seem to ignore the fact that in Sinai, **Egypt is at war with terrorism.**

- Its action in Sinai does not even come close to **Roosevelt's brutal herding** of US citizens of Japanese descent in 1941 in horrible concentration camps after **Pearl Harbor.**

- **Media Ethics** proved by statistics that 12 of your stories relied in **38 anonymous sources;** that nearly half named no sources interviewed by the **Times;** and that your lopsided stories quoted **15 critics of Egypt's government and a single Sisi supporter.** 40 of your stories, Kirkpatrick, quote the Egyptian Initiative for Personal Rights, of Cairo, a well funded attacker of Egypt's actions against Islamist marauders in Sinai and elsewhere.

- **Shame on you and on other Egyptophobes like Dunne** for calling Egypt's Grand Mufti **"a lackey for the Egyptian government."** And that the Mufti's ruling was **"the latest attempt by the government of President Abdel-Fattah El-Sisi to invoke interpretations of Islam for its own legitimacy."**

- Confirmed ignoramuses like you and Michelle reflect a disgusting mix of Egyptophobia, Arabophobia and Islamophobia. All wrapped into one. An Egyptian version of Islam, exists only in your deranged approach to public reporting.

**Returning to Dunne:** The Carnegie entire board published an editorial in **The New York Times** of Dec. 15 entitled: **"Egypt's Latest Outrage."** In it, that Board for international peace called American approval of $1.3 billion in military aid to Egypt **contradictory. Why?** Because that aid, which is treaty-based, and in line with Egypt's performing in the global war on terror, was claimed by Carnegie as supporting the continuation by El-Sisi Government of repressing **"Egyptian citizens"** and of **"harassing foreigners like Ms. Dunne."** No wonder that Cairo is pivoting to the East!!

Yet the Carnegie endowment of Michelle Dunne falsely claims that it continues to be **"dedicated to advancing cooperation between nations and promoting active international engagement by the United States" YA SALAM!!** Equivalent in Arabic to **"Oh My God!!"** Give it up Carnegie: **your fig leaf has fallen and the visuals are far from appealing.**

Through Dunne and others like her, the Carnegie does not deserve the title of **"The Global Think Tank."** In reality, and with reference to Dunne, you have become, at least in respect to the New Egypt **"THE GLOBAL STINK TANK."**

Await Christmas Letter No. Two to Dunne on **"Analysis of Dunne's So-Called Scholarly Writings."**

# Christmas Letter No. Two: How and Why Has Egyptophobe Michelle Dunne Gotten the Reputation of the Carnegie Endowment Undonne?

Wednesday, December 24, 2014

This is the second and final Christmas Letter addressed to **Michelle Dunne** from **ELIFAS (El-Ayouty Institute For Arab Spring Studies).** ELIFAS is a truly biased and self-funded organization in New York City. We are biased in favor of justice globally speaking, especially towards

Egypt, the Arab homeland and Islam as a force of moderation. These three entities have been the favorite targets of three American inter-related phobias. These phobias are the result of the U.S. taking a sharp turn to the right as of **9/11,** of America losing every war since World War II, and of the rise of China and India.

Devoting this Christmas Letter No. Two to an **"analysis of Dunne's so-called scholarly writings"** requires an ideological preface. Here it is:

- The growth of international law has been largely the consequence of the growth of human rights since the Nuremberg and the Tokyo military trials of **1945** and **1946;**
- In the train of that growth, came the **Universal Declaration of Human Rights of 1948.** On its heels came the **Geneva Conventions of 1949,** and two UN Conventions on Civil and Political Rights; and on Economic and Social Rights in the mid **1960s.** Africa's independence movements of the early **1960s** gave an additional push.
- In consequence, and largely as a reflection of the Holocaust tragedy of the late **1930s** and early **1940s,** two theories of international law were born: the **Human Rights Law** (largely affecting individuals) and the **International Humanitarian Law** (affecting larger groups). Together, these theories gave States some right to intervene in the internal affairs of other States where violations of human rights were perceived.
- These important developments stood largely inactionable due to the rise of the non-State actor, especially with regard to the illegal occupation by Israel of Palestinian territories beyond the line of demarcation of **June 4, 1967.**
- Yet three terms remained lacking of consensual definitions in the legal dictionary: **Democracy; Aggression; and Terrorism.** The absence of translations into Western languages of the languages of the East, such as **Arabic, Farsi, Urdu, and Pashtu** expanded the area of darkness about Eastern/Western understanding. In these domains, the UN and other international regional organizations stood nearly motionless: they were inter-state systems facing almost leaderless mass movements of non-State actors unbound by the conventional legal strictures. The catastrophe of **9/11** was only but one example of State paralysis of action in a globalized context.
- At that juncture, non-governmental organizations dealing with human rights issues generally took the wrong jump. Organizations like **Human Rights Watch, Amnesty International, Human Rights First, the Carter Center, the Carnegie Endowment for International Peace** began to meddle in the internal affairs of

sovereign States. This is while ignoring, perhaps for funding reasons, the infractions of human rights by States in which they are chartered.

- Hence the under-reporting on **Guantanamo,** the destruction of **Habeas Corpus** jurisdiction (every person has the right to his/her day in court to question the legality of their detention); forcible renditions; the torture practices by the CIA; the military commissions replacing regular U.S. Article III Federal Courts; detentions for years without either charges or release; and the downgrading, under Bush II administration of the Geneva Conventions as obsolete.

- Rationale: The so-called **"War on Terror"** needed new tools. Coercive interrogation, guilt by association, and claims of the need for total U.S. security became parts of the U.S. arsenal. That arsenal included killing of U.S. citizens abroad in an extra-judicial manner, and floating hostility toward Islam and Muslims.

Enters the likes of **Michelle Dunne; David Kirkpatrick; Fareed Zakaria; Tom Friedman; Michelle Bachman; Sara Palin; Ted Cruz;** and the rest of the party of war, **the Republicans.** Ironically, they saw victories in the destruction of Iraq, Pakistan, Afghanistan by an unrelenting military machine. The Islamophobic side seems to be left as the preserve of **Fox News** and **Bill Maher.** Books began appearing such as that by **Sam Harris attacking Islam as a bundle of crazy ideas.**

Through such a crowd of ignoramuses, the jihadis, including ISIS, won in two ways: Their criminal interpretation of Islam became an accepted norm; and America's embroilment in wars in Muslim countries, sanctions on countries like Egypt became the best jihadi tool for recruitment and funding.

Against that lengthy, yet general background, we begin to examine **Michelle Dunne's** writings as reflecting her untoward intervention in internal Egyptian sovereign affairs. This has been behind the transparent veil of concern for human rights. The following is an illustration of Dunne's half-baked scholarship and holier than thou attitude.

In a Carnegie article dated **September 22, 2014,** entitled, **"Syria in Crisis - What Egypt Can and Cannot Do Against the Islamic State"** she posits the **following imbecilities:**

- **"Many assume that Cairo will have a significant military rule to play in the fight against the Islamic State."** Then disparagingly, Dunne goes on to say: **"Kerry recently bolstered the impression of Egypt's 'critical role' by including Cairo in**

**his tour of the region, by touting Egyptian Sunni Muslim institutions as key to the ideological fight against extremism, and by stressing the importance of defeating extremism in the Sinai."**

- Dunne is dead wrong about all the above because: **(1)** Cairo's role in the anti-ISIS coalition is bifurcated into **(a)** combatting **Ansar Beit Al-Maqdis** on national territory; **(b)** resonating to Al-Azhar's huge impact for more than 1000 years throughout the Muslim world in attacking the criminal jihadi interpretation of Sharia; **(2)** Dunne gives the impression that she knows what is needed to be done better than the U.S. Secretary of State; **(3)** Dunne looks myopically at Egypt, with its 100 million inhabitants as a marginal factor in the global war on terror; and **(4)** Dunne stupidly and cavalierly discounts the role of fighting jihadi criminal ideology by the precepts of Islamic jurisprudence.

Furthermore, she treats Egypt as if its contributions to the U.S. -led anti-ISIS coalition were to be taken for granted. Egypt, Ms. Dunne, is not a vassal State beholden to Washington, D.C.

Michelle offhandedly posits the following: **"Expedited Suez Canal transits for warships for which the U.S. government pays a handsome premium are routine features of the bilateral relationship."** In the same paragraph, she does not lose the opportunity to tarnish the legality of El-Sisi administration calling it again and again the result of **"Egypt's July 2013 military coup that ousted then president Mohammad Morsi."**

Attacking **Al-Azhar** and the **Mufti of Egypt,** Dunne, with her crooked pen dripping of Egyptophobia, describes these iconic personalities as **"complicit"** in the ouster of the heinous Islamic rule of 2012-2013. Michelle Dunne unthinkingly speculates as follows: **"Egyptians and other Sunni Muslims susceptible to recruitment by the Islamic State are unlikely to pay heed to statements by the grand sheikh of Al-Azhar, Ahmed el-Tayeb or the grand mufti, Shawki Allam; many consider them to be no more than civil servants who put out a government-sanctioned brand of Islam."**

Dunne's total ignorance on that score is plainly manifest in: **(1)** Her non-recognition of the return of Al-Azhar under the secular Constitution of 2014 to its prior status of independence; **(2)** Her non-recognition of the Al-Azhar's seminal document, co-authored with the **Coptic Church** in August 2011. In that document of 11 principles, is included **"the non-recognition of a State based solely on religion;"** **(3)** Her stupidity in the heinous assumption that in Islam there is **"government-sanctioned brand of**

Islam." Michelle, as a presumed scholar, does not seem to know that Sharia everywhere is based on the **Quran, the Sunna, and ijtihad.**

Egyptophobe Dunne ends up her diatribe in that poorly argued article made up of a mix of contradictions, by the following: **"The political repression and human rights abuses associated with this crackdown, which are on a scale not seen in Egypt's modern history are a recipe for breeding recruits to Islamist militancy and ideologies such as that of the Islamic State."**

**Yes, Ms. Dunne: Right, Right, Right: Egypt by ousting a hated Islamist regime, has ensured the emergence of ISIS!!** Not the U.S. disbanding of the Iraqi army; not the U.S. contribution to sectarianism in Iraq through hugging the **Sunni Sahwas** one time, and casting them aside the next time; not by Obama's announcement of red lines in Syria then backing down under the pressures of a dysfunctional U.S. Congress.

**It is all Egypt's fault!!** Your stupid arguments reveal the shallowness of your presumed scholarship, and the surface commitment by a discredited Carnegie Endowment to a **proper engagement with the U.S.** Please remember again that Egypt is not a U.S. colony, but a sovereign State whose roots go back 10,000 years -40 times the age of the establishment of the U.S. which largely still treats Obama as a racial figure fit for demonization.

Now to another example of garbage emanating from the hateful pen of Michelle Dunne. Co-authoring in the **Wall Street Journal** of **Nov. 4, 2014,** an article with **Frederic Wehrey,** she emblazoned it with the title of **"3 Risks of U.S. Cooperation With Arab Allies Against Islamic State."** Dunne knows it all. The rest of us in the Arab and Muslim worlds are non-thinking dummies!!

So just mention the word **"Egypt"** once, and the hate enzymes start oozing out of Dunne's pores!! **As if she is a pre-programmed hate machine.** To her, every act of Arab cooperation with the US is either suspect or futile. The zone of hate now envelopes her in a trance of Arabophobia. Thus in her **"3 Risks"** piece **(only 3 Michelle?)** she asserts that **"while U.S. cooperation with Arab allies against Islamic State and other terrorist groups is essential, it is also problematic."** Real funny: she seems to treat the mirage of the so-called Islamic State as real!!

But Michelle: This is how alliances work. They are not a fusion. They are arrangements among sovereigns. Leave it to Dunne. **She knows better.**

Thus with regard to the Arabs, with whom America is deeply involved, regardless of the likes and dislikes of Michelle Dunne, she arrogantly says: **"As they compete for influence, some are enacting repressive policies that fuel the extremism that they purport to fight..."** Again Arab **security measures, not the espousal by the US authorities and media of the cause of Islamists,** are to blame!! For good measure, she adds: **"And in the rush to build support from Arab partners, the U.S. is largely ignoring these policies."**

Michelle's idea of inter-State relationships is terribly at odds with the way international comity works: cooperation in one area does not translate into submissiveness in other areas. **Otherwise it is colonialism all over again. Just look at the rocky relationship between the UK and the European Union.**

But Dunne's recipe -a recipe for increased US isolation in the Arab Middle East takes in a very confusing element. She manifests her patent confusion about the meaning and content of terms when she proclaims haughtily that: **"By focusing on winning the battle against ISIS, the U.S. will (WILL) lose the war against extremism."** Is there a difference?

Please explain Ms. Dunne. And she does: **"America's counter-terrorism focus with Arab States reduces its leverage, and bandwidth, to advance reforms that would address the root causes of radicalization."** Oh, I got it. Michelle, while shifting her arguments, is advocating that the U.S. should imperially take upon itself the task of intervention in the internal affairs of Arab States. **Are you nuts?!**

This is aside from the plain facts of the tragedy of decline in the U.S. style and manner of democracy: Dollars buy Congressional seats; redrawal of congressional districts to curtail minority participation; and obstacles placed by several States in the path of one person one vote through ID requirements. There is an Arab proverb which says: **"You cannot offer what you don't have."**
More laughable idiocies from the Carnegie's Michelle Dunne.

In **Al-Jazeera,** Dunne on Nov. 4, 2014, states without any credible evidence that: **"The question is whether the scorched earth methods practised by Sisi and his government are helping to build legitimacy among the Egyptian population, including in economically disadvantaged areas such as north Sinai, the Western Desert, and upper Egypt."** El-Sisi does not need to build legitimacy. He won the Presidency against Sabbahi in 2014 through the ballot box.

**No end to her hysteria; no end to her venom!!** But for the record, she and her likes among the Egyptophobes and the Arabophobes **must realize** that:

**(1)** US wars of choice in both Afghanistan and Iraq as of 2002/2003 have spawned criminal ideologies by jihadis who wished the Americans ill in order to get even;

**(2)** Total denial by the US of human rights on the field of battle and in detention camps such as **Pagram** and **Abu Ghraib** and force feeding in **Guantanamo** has super-charged millions of Muslims with hate for the U.S. and its institutions;

**(3)** American reliance on military means in the Middle East and Central Asia, without any meaningful attempt to understand Islam, in both its religious and cultural aspects, have compounded the task of many governments in the area with regard to containment of jihadism;

**(4)** The so-called human rights organizations have tried but failed to jump over the fence of sovereignties under the guise of protecting human rights;

**(5)** The recent Egyptian law on regulation of public demonstrations is much less stringent than its US equivalent; just remember **"Occupy Wall Street;"**

**(6)** It is patently stupid to measure the transition of the Arab Middle East from brute dictatorships which America supported for years with the same measures used in the US.

**(7)** In the U.S., we have a former Vice President, **Dick Cheney,** who is so insane that he still believes that **water boarding is humane!!**

**Michelle: Bark as you must!!** As far as Egypt is concerned, your hate shall topple neither the pyramids, nor the sphinx. Nor shall it bring your beloved Islamists back. For I have just returned from Cairo after watching **El-Sisi** in Hurgada, calling movingly for **"A Strong Egyptian State."** So **Buzz Off.**

**Lady!! You NEED A Psychiatrist Real Fast!!**

# After 6 Months of El-Sisi Presidency - An Egyptian Version of "Yes - We Can!!"

Wednesday, December 31, 2014

It was one of the highlights of my ten-days of stay in Egypt in December.  Guest of Hajj Yousri Nagy and his family.  The inauguration of the Passenger's Terminal of the Hurghada Airport on the Red Sea.  An iconic event celebrating the return of the Egyptian spirit of patriotism and the desire to excel.  After all, the inheritors of the land of the Pharaohs were saying, in response to an El-Sisi impromptu speech, **"Yes - We Can."**

Egypt is, after all, a land of symbolism.  Its edifices convey an uninterrupted recorded history of 7000 years.  From the Pyramids and the Sphinx, to the Hanging Coptic Church where the Holy Family hid from persecution. From the Muhammad Ali Mosque, a symbol of an Egypt moving ahead of a dying Ottoman Empire, to the new Suez Canal where water is expected to flow this February, creating **two Suez Canals -each a one-way global waterway.**

It is a confident Egypt, in search of a new age of progress through science and technology, in search of 13 million tourists a year, in search of pivoting to the East to end vestiges of dependency on the West, and in search of assertive secularism over the non-content Islamism of the Brotherhood which dupes its adherents by the fiction of being a Muslim Brotherhood.

Throughout this 10-day period of stay in Cairo, I was able to discern tangible evidence of the framework of the New Egypt after only six months of El-Sisi presidency.  **No -I am not in anybody's pay!!**

**"Tahya Misr" (Long Live Egypt)** is the new motto which reflects a post-revolutionary focus on Egypt itself.  No more ideological preoccupation with non-Egyptian issues under an inarticulate banner of **"Arab nationalism."**

With the Egyptian economy in a sorrowful state, coupled with terroristic attacks targeting Sinai, Egypt is forging an eastern axis with Saudi Arabia, other Gulf States (all sources of generous capital infusions eclipsing any US aid), plus Jordan.

That axis has a **central global mission: combating ISIS and other barbaric marauders.**  It requires coordination with Cairo, an Arab wing of the Anti-ISIS international coalition.  Hence a twenty-one gun salute greeted El-Sisi this December upon his arrival at the Amman airport.  Units of the proud Jordanian Arab army strutted to the tunes of bagpipes as El-Sisi and King Abdulla II saluted.

In mid December, a two-day conference sponsored by **"Dar Al-Tahrir"** and publicised under El-Sisi name, was organized as **"The Anti-Terrorism Conference."** It was addressed by **Egyptian Prime Minister Ibrahim Mahlab** who declared that **"those who seek to transfer their terror trade to Egypt shall fail. For Egyptian culture, and all shades of Egyptian public opinion, confront terrorism through a culture of religious moderation and of total support of the army and the police as they daily combat that scourge."**

The broad representation at that conference of the Cabinet at the ministerial level was indicative of the variety of official contributions to that globalized the historic task of terrorism containment. The ministers of interior, energy, supply, religious affairs, communication, local development, culture, oil, transitional justice, and the presidential advisor on national security.

The conference targeted five fronts through which anti-terrorism should be tackled. Aside from the military blunt instrument, **there are other tasks:** improvement of public services; continuation of Al-Azhar's efforts to rebut the misguided notions of extremists; bettering the advocacy of religious tolerance through mosques and churches; revamping the educational curricula at all levels; and monitoring groups and associations which advocate exclusion.

More anti-terrorism conferences: This time by joint co-sponsorship by **Al-Azhar** and the **Coptic church.** Headed by the **Grand Imam of Al-Azhar, Dr. El-Tayib,** and **Pope Toadros,** their respected voices were raised to stress that there is absolutely **no conflict between Islam and Christianity.** The conferees denounced the mixing between the barbarism of terrorism and Islam, a faith of moderation and tolerance. While terrorism, the conference noted, **seeks the expulsion of Copts from their homeland,** Islam does not decree jihad except for self-defense and repelling aggression against faith and country. Its exercise is the monopoly of governments, not of free-lancers. In this regard, there is no difference between **ISIS, Al-Qaeda,** the **Friends of Jerusalem,** and the **Muslim Brotherhood.** They are all links in the same satanic chain.

Now the thrust of external Egyptian foreign policy beyond the Arab homeland is in the direction of containment of Turkish Islamism, as exercised imperially by **Ordogan.** This seems to be the knob of Egyptian focus on the Mediterranean, which is marked by espousal of **Athens, Nicosia, Italy and France.** An epitome of diversification when seen through the Egyptian **"NACH OST"** (thrust toward the East). Witness the forthcoming visit by **Putin** to Cairo.

As a tenet of this diversification of the New Egypt's foreign policy is the **sidelining of Ordogan** of Turkey as a delusional master of an uncertain destiny. It is a quiet assault on the **neo-Ottomanism** which sees the Muslim Brotherhood as a loyal opposition. **Only idiots may assess the blood-thirsty Brotherhood as a democratizing force.**

Aside from the big picture, **the new normal,** the New Egypt is forging ahead:

- The Giza Zoo is full of visitors, especially entire families;
- The trains are running; the buses are again crowded;
- Thousands of customers are crowding little shops selling produce, fruits, as well as housewares, **all made in Egypt;**
- Syrians are not herded into refugee camps, but are fully integrated within a welcoming Egyptian society;
- Restaurants are busy serving all types of cuisine;
- Tourists are back, **with some of them taking pictures through their apps** even with President El-Sisi;
- International conferences are being held in Cairo and elsewhere;
- The name of a Copt recently martyred by terror gangs in Sinai Kyrollos is now given to, a primary school in the province of Sharkia where the 29th Pharaonic family held sway in Tal **Basta** -a mere 3 miles from my village -**Kanayat.**

**Conclusion:** El-Sisi summed up the surge of new energy in the New Egypt: **"The era of regimes is gone. The era of 'The Egyptian State' has begun."**

# 8 JANUARY 2015

## How Satanic!! A Massacre in Paris Masquerades As Islamic!!

Monday, January 12, 2015

**How can that be?!** A pair of desperadoes, French citizens of Algerian dissent, with Kalashnikov rifles massacre 12 co-citizens on January 7, claiming vengeance for Islam!! **What Islam are they mouthing? And how can January 7, 2015 be different from 9/11?** Except in the number of martyred fatalities!!

The despicable crime against **"Charlie Hebdo,"** a satirist magazine which I have never seen, caused the bullets to ricochet!! As stones skipping on water in a pond, the **ricochet has hit Islam itself!!** There is no faith on the face of this earth that can cover this naked aggression against humanity.

**Massacres of any type are acts of madness.** They are extra-judicial; collective punishment; crime against humanity!! **Charlie Hebdo is the face of humanity.** The offending brothers are the face of real evil!!

From the Armenian massacre by the Ottoman Turks during World War I; to the Jewish massacre by the Nazis during World War II; to the Shii and Kurdish massacres by Saddam!! Three faiths united by a common bond: death for believing, though faith is non-negotiable!! In each of these cases, a fictitious high ground is claimed by the perpetrators. Clear illustration of the **toxic combination of faith and politics,** producing neither faith nor politics which are defined as **"the art of the possible."**

Again to **"Charlie Hebdo:"** Cartoons are not cartridges. They are cartouches which included **Charles De Gaulle, Jesus Christ, and the Prophet Muhammad.** They did nothing to change a belief, not even by one inch!! The rules of war in Islamic law call for **"proportionality."** A **gun** in the hand of an assassin who is not even a warrior is **not the same as a pencil** in the hand of a cartoonist.

The ignominy has not been brought upon Islam and its Prophet by those murdered journalists. But the Kalashnikov guns have caused anxious questioning about the faith of 1.5 billion Muslims. In true Islamic parlance: **"only God Protects Faith."** Instead, infamy has been again brought upon the term **"Muslim."** Confirming the saying by the late Egyptian philosopher, Abbas Mahmoud El-Akkad. **"No imperialism has hurt Islam more than by the hands of its ignorant adherents."**

That ignorance lies like sleeping or in active cancer cells in the various crevices which **hold nearly hidden truths:**

- In Sharia (Islamic Law) the martyr is not the suicide bomber. It is his victim: an uninvolved civilian;
- In Islamic tradition, an immigrant must respect the laws of his new abode. His new abode cannot be the arena for his practices;
- In real governance, faith and the State cannot be interchangeable. **Faith is a choice;** governance is an organized mechanism for communal life;
- In Sharia, there is no proslytization; no missionary endeavours; no in your face conversion;
- In Islamic Law, there are the **Quran, the Sunna, and ijtihad** (reason where the text is absent or unclear). In ijtihad, there is a special jurisprudence: **"Fiqh Al-Maslaha"** (public interest);
- By definition, **"Sharia is for everywhere and every place."** Here lies a total misunderstanding. **This does not mean imposition.** It means adjustment in application to suit changing circumstances;
- It is legally wrong to have several states in America banning lawyers like me from citing Sharia in their courts as a source of law. **The ban is unconstitutional.** But the blame from that Islamophobia lies at the door of jihadism;
- By tradition, **Muhammed** laughed in his councils at the joviality of drunken Arabs;
- In Islamic Law, an **"infidel"** does not mean a **"non-Muslim;"** it means a person without values;
- In Islamic jurisprudence, no one has the authority to declare others

as **"apostates;"** that judgement belongs only to the Creator; no room for an ISIS or other jihadi scum; **no middleman, no broker,** no commission in terms of a religious credit;

- In Islam, the term **"Holy War" does not exist.** Jihad is an internal self-improvement and self-defense of territory and faith in case of external aggression. The State, not free lancers, has the monopoly on the use of force.

Might I also have been in the cross-hairs of those depraved assassins? Possibly!! Well; my recently republished novel in Arab is entitled **"An Impostor In the Village."** It was originally authored and published in 1948 in Cairo. Its republication in 2014 has an Arab Spring reason. The **novel's message is that the manipulation of faith for sordid ends produces catastrophic results.** Thus by implication, the novel depicts the conduct of the Muslim Brotherhood in the two Egyptian Revolutions: **January 25, 2011, and June 30, 2013.**
In both cases, while the Brotherhood was misunderstood in America as a legitimate opposition, its advocacy and practice of terrorism **forced El-Sisi Administration to declare them a terrorist cabal.** Secularism won over the Islamists because Egypt of 100 million has a secular and Muslim/Coptic DNA without which the country is non-recognizable.

**In its historic document of August 2011, Al-Azhar,** that Cairo citadel of more than 1000 years of moderate Islamic learning, responded to the ongoing confrontation everywhere **between secularism and religionism** (excessive religious zeal). One of its eleven principles, all cosponsored by the Egyptian Coptic Church, declared in effect: **"Islam does not recognize a State based solely on religion." This explains why El-Sisi on January 1, chose Al-Azhar as his pulpit from which to call for "a religious revolution."**

The killers at **Charlie Hebdo** cried **"Allahu Akbar!!"** Their war cry belied the huge distance between them and Sharia. For that term, **"God is Great,"** means only one thing: **We are all equal, in the eyes of God, regardless of our faith or non-faith.** They missed that crevice. And hit the wrong target.

The real Muslims in the Charlie tragedy are the **French police officer, Ahmed, a Muslim.** Executed outside of the scene of the murder en masse, on a Paris pavement as he laid injured, but representing the valor of his professions. His execution recalled to mind a young Indian Muslim girl, **Noor Enayat Khan, a French heroine of World War II.** Dropped behind Nazi lines in occupied France to coordinate Morse Code signals in aid of the Resistance, she, a Sufi, was executed in 1944 in a Nazi concentration camp. **Both Noor and Ahmed are the face of true Islam.** So is the Muslim who helped hide jews inside a non-functioning freezer from massacre by a cohort of the assassins at Hebdo at that Kosher deli at the outskirts of Paris.

In Algeria, in the early 1960s, I saw amity between the FLN and the French army outside Oran. De Gaulle has sanctioned my entry into Algeria as UN **Porte Parole** (spokesman) toward the end of that war for Algerian independence. I was a UN junior officer, an Egyptian who spoke French. De Gaulle hated Nasser, but welcomed French-speaking Egyptians. There, **east of Oujda and in Tlemcen,** I saw Algerian and French combatants become brothers. That was the **age of Houari Boumedienne,** not the age of the bottom of the barrel, the evil brothers Said and Cherif Kouachi.

Pity the conflicting reactions from the Muslim world to the **Charlie Hebdo** massacre. It pains me to translate into English those condemnations into Arabic. Following the Paris massacre, **Sarkosi,** former French President, admonished against **"mixing between that crime and French Muslims"** (5 million of them; 8% of France's population). **Rouhani of Iran** blamed the crime on Islamophobia encouraged by France. **"President Rouhani: Blaming the victim for the commission of the crime is like blaming the woman victim of rape for the violation of her womanhood."**

The guiding light for the assassins at **Charlie Hebdo** is **Abu Bakr Al-Baghdadi** -the false Caliph of ISIS, a thug from Anbar, Iraq. The guiding light for the real Muslims, a vast majority, is Salah El-Din. **"Saladin"** in the midst of war **welcomed St. Francis of Asisi** as a peace-maker between the Muslims forces and their crusading adversary.

**France welcomed Muslims to its territory,** including the parents of those assassins. Citizenship is a bestowed right, not an inherent right. Its violation is an act of treachery. **That violation is not redeemable by self-help: individuals assuming the mantle of avengers.**

**"Muhammed: We have avenged you, Messenger of God"** -yelled one of the two killers of 10 French journalists and two police officers. Guess what -Mr. Blood-on-Your-Hands: **Muhammad and his Ummah (community) would never sanction your massacre masquerading as Islamic.** For it is pure Satanic!!

I am a professor of Islamic jurisprudence at a Jesuit law school in New York City -Fordham University School of Law. My father, a graduate of Al-Azhar in Cairo, introduced me properly to the Prophet Muhammad.

From my specialization I conclude the following: **To Muhammmed, terrorism would have been a denial of Allah -the God of all.**

In the Quran, it is said in the name of Muhammad, addressing his community: **"Say: 'I am only a mortal like you; it is revealed to me that your God is One God' (Chapter 18;verse 110). This is the essence of "Tawheed" (the onness of God). This universalizing principle unites faiths of all types together.** It is like a golden thread that keeps a necklace of pearls together. From the smallest to the biggest adorning the neck of every human being.

The first word in the Quran is **"IQRA"** -whose surface meaning is **"READ;"** but its comprehensive meaning is **"LEARN."** The problem with the villains of January 7 is that they live in a bubble of ignorance.

Their like-minded terrorists in Nigeria, who have just massacred 2000 in one incursion, adopted the name of **"Boko Haram"** (western learning is un-Islamic.) By contrast the **Prophet Muhammad** urged his community to seek education -**"even in China,"** his farthest point from Arabia.

While the Ottoman Empire avoided non-Muslim trainers, thus hastening its collapse, **Egypt under Muhammad Ali (the founder of modern Egypt: 1805 -1849) nearly occupied Constantinople in 1839/1840. Reason: French training in every field,** from the army to archeology, since the days of Napoleon in Egypt as of 1798!!

When Khomeini was chased out of his sanctuary in Iraq by Saddam as urged by the Shah after 1975, his refuge was in France. It could, therefore, be safely said that the Islamic revolution in Iran, a shii majority country, was launched from France, the mother of **"the freedom of speech" (liberte de l'expression).**

Nearly a hundred years before Khomeini's Islamic revolution, France was the birthplace of even a more pervasive Islamic movement. Led by two of the greatest reformers, **Jamal El-Din Al-Afghani and Muhammad Abdu,** who were united in Paris, **it aimed at Islamic modernization.**

Upon his return from Paris to Alexandria, well before his death in 1905, **Sheikh Muhmmad Abdu** was greeted at the pier by a group of reporters. He was asked **"How did you find the West?"** His answer fully reflected the values of France's protection of personal liberties. Akin to what Islam calls for, though ignored in the practice by most countries of the Muslim world. His words eternalized by the ages, especially in this age of chaos were: **"I found Islam there, and the Muslims here!!"** An emphasis on value as compared to superficial belonging.

**Now that we all are "Charlie Hebdo,"** and you, the three assassins, have already reached hell, use your hotline with a sizzling message. Text jihadis everywhere: **"Your end is near. The pen is mightier than the Kalashnikovs!!"** A lasting advice from **"Charlie's Angels"** who are now rushing to get a copy of the million copies of the incredible **"Hebdo!!"**

*Your satanic acts in which 17 innocent victims were martyred made Paris on January 11 the capital of the world. At that one-million person rally, the Muslims marched with signs declaring "Not In My Name!!" NOT IN MY NAME EITHER!!*

# 9 FEBRUARY 2015

## Looking for ISIS Enablers? Find Some of Them Among Egyptian Editors

Friday, February 13, 2015

Ironically, some of Egypt's editorialists are in effect ISIS enablers. **Whether through malice or ignorance, they advocate a Cairo surrender!!** On the top of the great Muhammad Ali's Mosque, they, in effect, are advocating that El-Sisi should hoist an impossibility **-a white flag.** The army which dared cross the Suez Canal in 1973 to destroy the Bar Lev Line and reclaim Sinai from Israeli occupation is not likely to heed Egypt's editorialists.

The attacks in northern Sinai by **Ansar Beit Al-Maqdis** (Friends of Jerusalem) may go on for a while. Their terror warfare, though resulting on January 29 in massacring 30 army personnel and civilians, may go on for a while. But with each passing day, Egypt's huge military establishment learns from experience. Its response to the friends of ISIS and the Muslim Brotherhood is becoming more sophisticated.

The pointed advocacy for surrender to global terror is in fact causing massive retaliation, especially through a widening the territorial buffer. Hamas is bottled up in Gaza, and its calls for a Rafah Crossing bonanza are no more than exhalations of desperation. You cannot hurt Egypt and, at the same time, issue deceiving proclamations of a Gazan-Egyptian brotherhood.

That crossing might one day be a bridge between Egypt and an independent State of Palestine. For now, Hamas is no more than an Islamist rebellion against a putative State of Palestine. Perhaps one day it shall submit to commonality with Egypt in recognition of a State of Israel. You cannot deny, as Hamas Charter does, **"the right of any Jew to an inch of Palestine,"** and call yourself a credible member of the international community. Hamas should learn the basics.

Now to Egypt's editorialists -its adversaries from within.

- A genius by the name of **Dr. Mahmoud Khalil** mocks his country's renewal of the emergency law in northern Sinai for another 3 months. That professor at the Faculty of Public Information of the prestigious Cairo University is stupidly sarcastic without cause. He claims, through his empty suit, that **"the military attacks (by Ansar) proves the inability of the present authorities to deal with the situation in Sinai."**

- In his column **(WATANTAN)** of January 31, in **Al-Watan** newspaper, he sounds nearly gleeful. From his comfort zone in Cairo, he opines more blatant imbecilities. **"Ansar Beit Al-Maqdis which carried the operation at Karm Al-Qawadees (northern Sinai) has augmented its lethal power many folds, while the opposing security forces have a diminishing prowess."**

- **Professor Khalil:** Do yourself and Egypt a favor: **learn the art of evidence!!** Have you counted? Or does your measure rest on the mere ability to remotely explode a car laden with explosives, or sacrifice an ignorant suicide bomber? Have you ever learnt anything from the ample lessons of terror warfare? Apparently none!!

So you go on to call on the Egyptian government to abandon its legitimate warfare, come out from its fox holes with hands raised in the air, an declare, to quote your comic phrase: **"We are a failure!!"** You should abandon your classroom and come out confessing your abject failure to even comprehend, let alone to **"teach,"** a new generation of holders of degrees in public information degrees.

Turning now to **Fahmy Howedy,** an Islamist writer in **Al-Shorooq** of January 31. He, apparently without any previous experience in military intelligence, boldly states: **"What happened in Al-Arish, clearly points to significant failure in the gathering of military intelligence."** Sir!! On what basis have you formed that judgement? On the basis of its mere happening?

Have you ever been in Sinai? **I don't mean the pleasure spots of Sharm El-Sheikh, Taba and Hurgada.** I mean through the dunes and crevices of a vast province where trees have surrendered their existence to parched rocky hideaways. I was there. Several times. So was my son collecting Sinai plants to discover their medicinal values -a report by a then 16-year old, now deposited with Cornell University.

If you, Mr. Howedy, wants to be an expert in desert warfare (which I personally gained as a UN officer in Algeria during its brutal war of independence) **go to the scene.** Get some sands in your boots. Get a few lessons on Bedouin life, on tribal disconnects, on the sacrifices of our desert troops, on psychological warfare. Only then could you come back to us. Proclaiming that **"the measure of competence is the ability to sabotage an operation before its happening."** And you call this editorial wisdom?

Then in the language of a defeatist, Mr. Howedy, the Islamist guru of **Al-Shoraaq,** goes on saying: **"Have the measures taken in Sinai diminished the threat of terrorism or enhanced it? The operations undertaken by Ansar are performed with a high level of professionalism while the counter operations are rudimentary and are attributed by the government to the Muslim Brotherhood."**

**Mr. Howedy:** Is that what your pearls of wisdom are all about? Well, if you call raids by Apache helicopters, and the unremitting pursuit of terrorism in Asian Egypt rudimentary, this forces me to call you a **simpleton!!** The term is defined as **"foolish; gullible; a half-witted person."** The terror operations chain of custody couldn't be clearer -**from the Muslim Brotherhood to Hamas to Ansar Beit Al-Maqdis to ISIS.** If you, Mr. Editorialist, cannot make that linkage, it is not surprising that the Brotherhood cells in Egypt and abroad draw comfort from your editorials. **So does Qatar, Turkey, Al-Jazeera TV, and the sheet called Al-Quds Al-Arabi, especially that of February 2.**

Now to our editorialists as cartoonists. **Helmy Al-Tooni** glorifies in the creation of a cartoon in the newspaper **Al-Tahrir** of February 1. The cartoon by that Nasserite artist depicts Egypt as a bride in her wedding gown; flowers held tightly by her right arm; tears streaming her lovely youthful face; pyramids in the background. An arrow has struck her heart. With blood streaming, she bemoans the Egyptian leadership's presumed failure to protect, Bride Egypt, says: **"Whoever married me must be able to protect me!!"**

In support of this fallacy, another grossly misleading argument is advanced. Another editorialist by the name of **Assem Hanafi** makes a fanciful claim: **"The Muslim Brotherhood is armed with a domestically-manufactured bombs which they are at liberty to explode at any time, and at any place."**

With this deluge of non-thinking editorializing by well-known writers within Egypt is it any wonder that that defeatism has infected foreign correspondents? **David Kirkpatrick** of the **New York Times,** who is predisposed to constant attacks against the elected President of Egypt, El-Sisi, pushes the envelope even further. On January 30, he, together with **Merna Thomas**, proclaims to the world a **habitual epitaph for Egypt's ability to confront terrorism.**

In a lead paragraph, they both assert a misleading fantasy. The Sinai terror operations are made to be unlike what is happening all over the world. Those operations, they preach, are **"prompting fears that the Egyptian government's campaign of home demolitions, curfews and sweeping arrests has failed to choke off a budding insurgency there!!"** Then they quote from their already predisposed habitual sources.

From **Khalil Al-Anani** of the Johns Hopkins School of Advanced International Studies -a so-called expert in extremism, they produce a quotation. **Al-Anani** says: **"The insurgency is getting stronger and stronger, and the government's strategy is a failure."** And from **Tamara Cofman Wittes,** Director of the Center for Middle East Policy at the Brookings Institution, another defeatist is quoted. She opines that: **"It is clear that this extremely coercive approach is not working."**

I wonder what **Ms. Wittes, a former deputy assistant Secretary of State for Near Eastern Affairs** is comparing the defensive/offensive Egyptian measures to. With the existence in the U.S. of 50,000 private security firms? With the uncontrolled gun possession in the U.S. of 300 million had guns, a gun per person in America? With the unremitting U.S. campaigns in Afghanistan, Pakistan, Somalia, Yemen, Iraq and through the U.S. Africa military command?

Where has objective measuring of the advance in global counter-terrorism gone? **Apparently nowhere.** Except for a false focus on Egypt which is fighting on two broad fronts: Terrorism and the economy.

The icing on the cake should now be reserved to **David Hearst.**

In the **World Post** he surpasses all the above-cited doom-sayers. He, as if through a bull-horn, shouts: **"Egypt is more unstable than ever, with full-scale military operations in the Sinai and mass protests around the country that never seem to die down."** Last time I checked, I found unfortunately that the **"mass protests in that never seen to die down,"** are in his own backyard: In **Furgeson, Missouri.** Incredible.

Shouldn't the likes of **Kirkpatrick, Al-Anani, Wittes and Hearst** spend sometime learning that their doomsday chants about the New Egypt are akin to mere sound echo at the Grand Canyon? The ABC of wisdom in today's international strategic studies is to shun combat predictions and to keep the U.S. safe from the unintended consequences of intrusiveness in the internal affairs of other States.

This is especially poignant when it comes to the New Egypt. Post-Islamist Egypt has charted a course toward **"The Strong State." No room for an Islamization by the defunct Muslim Brotherhood.** Give it a rest, folks: Morsi. This is in spite of an unfortunate reception accorded recently by the U.S. State Department to his acolytes, calling themselves the **"Egyptian Revolutionary Council."**

Those in D.C. who accorded that group a false sense of recognition should wake up to the realities of a possible Cairo - D.C. rapprochement. On this point, let us cite the **New York Times.**

Written by **David Brooks,** a conservative with Republican party leanings, he, under the title of **"Being Who We Are,"** says:

**"The Middle East is not a chessboard we have the power to manipulate. It is a generational drama in which we can only play our role. It is a drama over ideas, a contest between forces of jihadism and the forces of pluralism. We can't know how this drama will play out, and we can't direct it. We can only promote pluralism -steadily, consistently, simply."**

**Well said Mr. Brooks.** From the Islamic reign of terror in Egypt, under the Morsi regime, a great lesson has been learnt. The Muslim Brotherhood, a determined adversary of pluralism, was given a historic chance which they miserably squandered. ISIS, their related organization, declared through **The Friends of Beit Al-Maqdis,** Sinai as an ISIS Emirate. How brain dead can you get!!

Once more, we see the devilish features of ISIS and its new franchises clearly in the mirror of assassinating the Jordanian pilot and the two Japanese hostages. These features inspire this invocation addressed to all those who predict failure of the efforts of Egypt in Sinai and other related combat activities against ISIS waged at present by the international coalition.

**Our invocation is:** May those who predict failure in the elimination of Jihadism everywhere have their heads examined, their voices stilled, their ink running dry, and their predictions proving as false as their pitiful understanding of this global war of values!!

*In this information warfare, the primitiveness of Egyptian editors is staggering.*

# Here Comes A False Turkish Don Quixote Ordogan!!

Wednesday, February 18, 2015

He is delusional!! Working hard toward the Turkishization of the Arab Spring, especially in Egypt. I knew that something was missing: **One finger in his right hand as he raised it in a Rabaa salute!!** And why a Rabaa salute by Sultan Ordogan: an approving nod towards the Muslim Brotherhood as it waged a coup in 2012-2013 against secular Egypt.

**Don Quixote saw in Spanish windmills hostile knights to be attacked.** In his mold, Ordogan sees in the Egyptian Revolution of June 30, 2013 a tidal wave drowning his dream of a Caliphate. Ordogan's problem does not lie within what he does within Turkish borders. His constant attacks on the New Egypt reflects his being on the wrong side of history.

Our Turkish Don Quixote is welcome to have his palace of 1000 rooms (estimated cost at $750 million); to have his troops welcome Abbas in Ankara in uniforms of 16 stages of the Ottoman Empire; to declare his support for the Palestinian cause. But Ordogan has no business interfering in the internal affairs of Egypt. Especially as Egypt transitions to what El-Sisi calls **"a strong State."**

Having taught in Cairo modern Egyptian history, including Ottoman rule, I find Ordogan woefully lacking in knowledge of why the Ottomans collapsed. The Empire (and the caliphate with it) did not fall because of its opposition to Jewish settlement in Palestine. This is what Ordogan told Abbas during that recent state visit. **It collapsed because it became hostage to three evils: internal corruption; oppression of the Arabs and of minorities; and succumbing to the fatwas of ignorant ulamas (scholars).** Those ulamas advised the Sultans that training of the armed forces by non-Muslim trainers was un-Islamic. **The same stupid thesis of Nigeria's Boko Haram (western learning is un-Islamic).**

By contrast, Egypt even while under Ottoman suzeranity, welcomed training by non-Muslims. Thus Egypt twice was on the verge of burying the Ottomans under an Egyptian flag. Though the Ottomans occupied Egypt as of 1517, Egypt declared its independence from the Turkish yoke twice. **Once in 1769 under the leadership of Ali Bek Al-Kabeer** whose sway extended from Yemen to Damascus, passing through Jedda, Mecca and Medina.

**The second, opting out of the Empire was in 1840 under Muhammad Ali,** whose son, General Ibrahim was about to occupy Constantinople in 1839. He was forced by England and France to retreat out of fear of a dynamic Egyptian empire replacing **"the sick man of Europe"** - the Ottoman empire. As of 1840, Egypt continued to be nominally within Ottomanism. But Cairo looked upon Constantinople only as a notary public for the selection of the successors of Muhammad Ali.

The Arab rebellion of 1916 against Turkish rule was a water shed in Arab history. **That rebellion was led by the Hashemites, not by Lawrence of Arabia.** By joining the Allies against Turkey during World War I, the Arabs put their aspiration for independence ahead of staying within a nominally Islamic Caliphate.

The Ottomans forced the Arabs to make that historic choice. **For it was the Young Turks who reneged on their treaty of 1912 with the Arabs which called for Ottoman recognition of Arabic as the Arabs national language. After all, Arabic is the language of the Quran.** This Turkish chauvinism went further amok. Great Arab national leaders were hung to death in 1915 in Damascus public squares. That was in addition to the Turkish massacre of Armenians due to unfounded suspicion of collaboration with Russia.

**So, Sultan Ordogan, please treat yourself to a refresher course in the history of the Ottoman Empire. Simply leave the New Egypt alone.** Non-interference in the internal affairs of other States is the best recipe for regional and international peace. **Good fences make good neighbors.**

Believe me!! If you want to parade your honor guard in costumes going back to the 14th century, **Egypt might retort by sending you papyri of ancient military Egyptian uniforms going back 7000 years.** Including chariots and charioteers!! But I doubt that the New Egypt would fall for the trap of Ordogan theatrics.

The Turkish Ministry of Education has decided to introduce the old **"Ottoman"** language to its educational curriculum. Egypt, since the discovery of the hieroglyphic language through the Rosetta Stone unearthed in 1801 by the great French archaeologist Champolion, has kept it alive. Contrary to the purpose of reviving Ottomanism by Ordogan, Egypt values the teaching of hieroglyphic as well as the Coptic language at its universities. In this respect, Egypt's reason is for culture not for hegemony.

While Egypt is working for the strengthening of its new axis with the Gulf, Turkey's Ordogan is working toward compensating for the European Union refusal to admit Turkey to its membership. **Hence the Ankara alliances with cul de sac pan-Islamic movements.** While the New Egypt was welcomed at all levels during El-Sisi's visit to Kuwait, including unambiguous Kuwaiti statements of support for the new Egypt, Turkey was critical of Egypt's calls on Qatar to account for its funding of the Muslim Brotherhood.

In the context of Egypt's emphasis on internal development, Abdel-Wahab Al-Badr, head of the Kuwait Development Fund noted the following: **"The creation in Egypt of an additional Suez Canal to be inaugurated in August 2015 is expected to turn Egypt into a new Singapore. 80% of world transit trade shall go through Suez."**

As the Young Turks cracked the whip against non-Turks in their dying Empire, the oppressed began to exit in droves seeking safe refuge. **To where did they flee? To secular and tolerant Egypt, the permanent rebel against the Ottoman Caliphate.** In Cairo and Alexandria, the Lebanese Christians set the example. They launched modern Egyptian journalism, including **Al-Ahram,** now the official printed medium of the Government. They issued the great periodical of **Al-Resalah.** On Al-Resala's high literature, we were nurtured in high school. They established the modern theatre, cinema and comedy; made Egyptian songs the lingua

114

franca of the entire Arab world. And they propelled Arab nationalism on a distinctive secular course.

Thus the loss of the Ottomans was the gain of the Egyptians. **What remained in Egypt from Ottoman days were mere relics: The fez, the titles of Pasha, Bek and Affandi.** More durable are the jokes in Egyptian cafes about Turkish oppression symbolized by **"the whip," over-taxing the poor, and empty fanfare.**

At Davos (2015), El-Sisi, at that World Economic Forum, spoke poignantly about the New Egypt. He stressed the national focus on making it a haven for foreign investors. **Reason: virgin possibilities, and legally insuring profit repatriation.** While acknowledging terror as a global menace, he assured his world audience of Egypt's capacity to undertake the twin tasks: **Development and combating terrorism.**

While Sultan Ordogan was on a visit to Somalia, a failed State, his nemesis, the Egyptian President had a mission with a real future impact. At Davos, El-Sisi was deftly making an apt distinction. **Between faith as a private right, and interpreting faith to the masses, as a communal responsibility.** Sadly, Sultan Ordogan chooses not to espouse that distinction. His Islamism is under attack internally in Turkey. It is also being challenged externally by his formidable opponent, Gullen. **Gullen is a Turkish Islamic powerhouse residing in Pennsylvania and calling for investigating Ordogan's corrupt practices.**

Shouldn't Ordogan, in his foreign policy, give priority to securing Turkey's eastern border against the free movement of foreign jihadis? By the thousands, those misfits pour via Turkey to join ISIS. By contrast Egypt's eastern border has become a priority security issue. **A buffer zone has been created in Sinai** with the aim of degrading the Friends of Jerusalem and their Hamas cohorts who are declaring Sinai an **"ISIS Emirate."**

Mind you, Ordogan is not the only aberration on the scene of globalized Islam. More graphic events are taking place. From the barbaric, as in the case of ISIS, to the ignorant or malicious, as in the multiple cases of self-declared experts in the Islamic faith. Here follows some examples of the latter breed.

- Thomas Friedman declares recently in his Op. Ed column in the **New York Times** that **"there is no real Islam." Tom: There is,** especially if you become at least versed in Muslim culture and the Arabic language.
- A so-called security expert on TV channel MSNBC (liberal)

appeared on February 17 to make a startling declaration. On the reputable talk show of Chris Matthews, that security expert has an incredible explanation for ISIS beheadings and immolation. He declares that **"it is important to remember that Islam spread by violence and the sword."** No, Mr. Expert!! **Islam does not recognize "offensive war." Only self-defense is permissible, as in every other legal tradition.**

- In regard to the air bombing by Egypt and the Emirates of ISIS in Libya, **CNSNews.com** carries a startling report on February 17. **"The United States does not support Egyptian and Emirati air strikes against Islamist militias in Libya."** Amazing!! On the one hand, how can Egypt and its allies not forcefully respond to the massacre at its western borders of **21 Egyptian Christian citizens?** On the other hand, Washington, D.C. does not dictate Egyptian sovereign decisions, nor has Cairo ever interfered with US drone attacks in Yemen, 15000 miles away from D.C.

- A statement of condolences was issued on February 17 by the Egyptian Consulate-General in New York. It reflected Egypt's reasons for national mourning, and added: **"We emphasize that that heinous act perpetrated at the hands of terrorism in Libya shall not weaken the unity or the stability of our homeland. On the contrary. Such barbarism shall only enhance Egypt's determination to uproot terrorism.**

It is gratifying to note that there are also American voices of sanity reflective of a sympathetic understanding of Islam. Even prior to the assassination of 3 Muslim students in the Carolinas, a well-known cartoonist in Arizona, **Steven Benson** contributed to the on-going debate on Islam **and global security** in a very impacting cartoon. In the **Arizona Republic,** Mr. Benson published two frames: One with ISIS operatives clad in black, with swords raised; the other with anti-Afro-American Ku Klux Klan (KKK) clad in white with burning crosses. The captions reflected the whole debate objectively through comparison. Benson wrote: **"ISIS is to Islam what these guys are to Christianity."**

So please, Don Quixote Ordogan: Feel free to raise your hand in **"the Rabaa salute"** (four fingers) anytime you wish. It reminds us not only of the defunct Muslim Brotherhood. It also reminds us of the Nazi salute. The only difference is that the Nazi salute kept the five fingers of the raised hand together. **In your Rabaa salute, I am puzzled as to where you hid the missing finger.**

**You too, Sultan Ordogan is among the latest and meanest aberrations in the enduring Islamic faith.**

# Whistle Blowing By Great Egyptians on Corruption and Terrorism

Friday, February 27, 2015

From the scene, they are gone. But from our historical memory, they cannot be forgotten. **Makram Obeid on corruption, and Ahmed Fathi Soroor, on terrorism.** In present day culture, it is not common to celebrate thinkers and doers of the past. But the focus on the New Egypt should also take into account the whistle blowers of yesterday.

Yes, they are gone either from life **(Makram Obeid),** or from power **(Ahmed Fathi Soroor). A nation that lives on celebrating only its present, is a nation which is bereft of nurturing its young on the model of those who loyally cared for its causes.**

Let us begin with **Makram Obeid Pasha** on corruption. It is the national malaise which contributed to the eruption of the Arab Spring. That great Coptic whistle blower, having split from **The Wafd Party of Al-Nahas Pasha,** addressed a petition to **King Farouk.**

His petition on behalf of **"Al-Kutlah Al-Wafdiya Al-Mustaqillah"** was not in one or two pages. Under the title of **"The Black Book In the Black Era,"** it was a book of 268 pages. Printed at night to escape the sanctions imposed upon him by the Wafd government of the post-Second World War.

Its super-high level of classic Arabic is music to my ears -a person who looks upon his native tongue as his primary anchor in the concept of Arabism as a culture. Before we get to the substance, let us examine his last paragraph on page 268 as he beseeches King Farouk to make right what Makram Pasha perceived as wrong. Lost in this translation, Makram, a Coptic icon who had learnt the Quran by heart, is the cadence of his summation. He says:

**"Your Majesty: Your throne is the refuge of this good nation. We pray that Allah strengthen your hands so that they may pull us up from this abyss. So that you may unburden it from its daily struggle for life's needs. So that you may right what is wrong. So that you**

may restore rightful entitlements to those who truly possess them. So that the Egyptians may again remember what this government caused them to forget: justice in governance; freedom of expression; integrity in word and deed; the true meaning of national and personal dignity."

As if Makram Obeid Pasha, in 1946, was anticipating the signs raised in Tahrir on January 25, 2011. Those signs read: **"Livelihood; Freedom; Social Justice."** As a student at the Cairo Teachers' Institute, Makram Pasha invited me to his house where I was hypnotized by his love of the motherland.

How did he, by his book, raise the alarm with regard to corruption as infesting the governance of Egypt?

He posited that the heart of corruption is putting personal gain ahead of public gain. As a Minister of Supply and Trade, he strictly applied the laws restricting exports needed for home consumption. **"Charity-Starts at Home."** Subverting this judicious rule, namely, equality before the law, **Prime Minister Nahas Pasha** would intervene, without the knowledge of Makram Pasha, to enable his wife's relatives to secure for them sugar, rice and other provisions for export and the black market.

Makram Pasha summed all up as follows: **"The Prime Minister even tried to stop me from bringing before a military court (Egypt, following World War Two was still under martial law) his relatives.** The Public Prosecutor had charged them with illegally trying to export textiles needed to clothe the marginalized Egyptians.

**His assessment was: "This is a scandal. And it is one of many like it. Nepotism, illegal commitments, the prevalence of making governance a personal game for profit. These, Your Majesty, are all forms of corrupt behavior tending to exploit the Government only for the benefit of the ruling class. It makes ruling a game whose goal is to corrupt the trust between those who govern, and those who are governed."**

What more do you need for the clearest definition of corruption in any age, at any time, and in any country? **God Bless your memory, Makram Pasha Obeid.** You were truly ahead of your time. You resigned, not once, but three times. Because you put Egypt ahead of your position, your personal gain, the illusory glow of being the Deputy Leader of a great national party. Your portrait still adorns the walls of the **Wafd**

**headquarters in Cairo.** The main gate is adorned by the symbol of historical Egypt: **A Crescent Hugging a Cross!!** A great image for all of us. Except for the Muslim Brotherhood, on which several **"Black Books"** shall be written!!

Now we turn to **Dr. Ahmed Fathi Soroor, Speaker of the Egyptian Parliament** for many years under **former President Hosni Mubarak.** This scholar of criminal law produced in 2007 in Cairo one of the most definitive papers produced anywhere in Arabic on the issue of terrorism. His removal from office, his incarceration at Tura as one of the top leaders of the defunct National Party, and the charges levelled against him for alleged corruption are not reasonable justification for not benefiting form his unique legal expertise.

In its search for inclusiveness, the **New Egypt** is called upon to abandon what I call **"The Hatshepsut Syndrome." If you lose power or die, all your achievements should be erased.** This is especially dangerous in countries like Egypt which needs every iota of knowledge in order to keep its caravan of progress moving forward.

At my request in his office as Speaker, Dr. Soroor who was previously Dean of the Cairo University School of Law, where I continue to be adjunct professor, gifted me with a copy of his paper. **Within 150 pages, it is a veritable gem.**

Judicious analysis; multi-faceted research in Arabic, English and French; clarity of thought; superb organization of every aspect of terrorism; and a lawyer's approach to a highly controversial issue. **Let the New Egypt be not afraid from one of its great scholars as it battles terrorism in Sinai, on the Libyan border, and within its interior. When you are sick in bed, calling for the help of a competent physician, you don't query that physician's personal history. You need to be cured.**

Under the title of **"The Rule of Law Confronting Terrorism,"** here are the highlights of Professor Soroor's paper:
- In its Introduction, he confronts head on the spurious attempts to link between terrorism and Islam;
- He highlights one of the central facts about terrorism: **lack of an internationally-acceptable definition of that term;**
- He focuses our attention on other challenges: security challenges affecting public law and order, and concern for having those security challenges overwhelm the need to safeguard human rights and civil liberties;

- On this crucial point he suggests a balance anchored in constitutional law, namely: espousal of the exigencies of necessity, together with the proportionality of response;
- He calls on the State to be a **State of laws** which observes the need for democratization, combined with safeguarding human rights;
- He focuses our attention on the globalization of human rights, fundamental freedoms and democratic values. Astutely, Dr. Soroor puts that mix within one container which he describes as **"the values of the international community;"**
- He links between the legal challenges facing the struggle against terrorism both internally and externally. On the external front of these challenges, he reaches out for the precepts of the international human rights law, as well as of the international criminal law;
- **In dealing with the dilemma of defining terrorism, the author brilliantly separates between three types of terrorism: acts perpetrated by individuals, acts inflicted by groups or organizations, and State terrorism;**
- He separates between terrorism and the struggle of oppressed populations for liberty; condemns disproportionate use of military means, and abhors **"extra-judicial killing;"**
- Soroor reminds us of Egypt's penal code as amended in 1992. That is several years before the promulgation by the **League of Arab States of its Convention on Terrorism (1998), and of the Organization of Islamic Cooperation of a similar Convention (1999).**
- In the context of the above, Professor Soroor reiterates Egypt's attempt to define terrorism. As provided in **Article 86 of Penal Law No. 97 (1992),** it states that terrorism is:

*"Any use of force, violence, threat or intimidation, by a suspect in the pursuit of a criminal scheme, either individually of by a group, with the intention of adversely affecting public order or endangering society's peace and security.*

*This includes causing bodily harm or affecting communal freedoms, or damaging the environment or communications or transportation means, or funds, or buildings of either public or private property, or their occupation or sequestration, or impeding the exercise by public authorities of their duties, or affecting the functioning of places of worship, of educational institutions, or hindering the application of the Constitution or the laws and regulations which are in force."*

- This is the broadest ever definition of **"terrorism,"** in both law and procedure which in effect underpins the comprehensive efforts of the New Egypt in combating jihadism in 2015. That was nearly a quarter of a century since the promulgation of that law in 1992 in Egypt. Professor Soroor aptly calls it **"The National Program on Terrorism."** And this many years before the UN acted on this global issue, by the General Assembly in 1999, by the US after 9/11, and by the UN Security Council in 2004.

The **"Egyptian National Project"** as expounded by Dr. Ahmed Fathi Soroor, former Dean of our Faculty of Law, of Cairo University, also deals with the Geneva Convention of 1949. He provides a broad construction of the theory of **"the Right to Protect." His legal construction should be applied by Cairo in its attacks on terrorism in both Sinai, in the Center, and over the Libyan borders.**

So let us not shy away from bringing back to life the work of our luminaries, regardless of the allegations, trials and tribulations of the two Egyptian Revolutions of January 25, and June 30. Let us abide by the British adage: **"Use whatever instrument you have at hand."**

Better still, let us abide, but in a different context, by the great poem by Ahmed Shawqi who admonished:

**"These are our monuments. Gaze on them after we are gone."**

**Our thought monuments on corruption and terrorism have been selflessly bequeathed to us by Makram Obeid Pasha, and Professor Ahmed Fathi Soroor.**

*Would someone volunteer to convey this blog posting to Professor Ahmed Fathi Soroor?*

**For I know that when I stand before my students at Fordham University School of Law in New York City, lecturing on the terrorism plaguing the New Egypt, I feel his presence as a scholar who was amongst the first whistle blowers of the late 20th century on the dangers approaching Egypt.**

*The lessons which we should learn from that unique Egyptian scholar need to be re-learnt at this critical juncture.*

121

# 10 MARCH 2015

## Want To See A Thriller? Watch Hitchcock Not Al-Jazeera!

Friday, March 13, 2015

This is not about the case of Al-Jazeera journalists litigated in Egypt. I do not have before me the file on that case. This posting has to do with a much larger issue: **Does press freedom know no limits?!** Because this is the basic issue confronting Al-Jazeera as it fabricates its case around the world against the New Egypt.

For eight long and productive years, I learnt an important lesson from one great journalists source -**Forbes Magazine.** From 1976 to 1984, I was retained by Forbes great co-founder, the late **Malcolm Forbes.** He, and his four sons, and the editor, **James Michaels,** were my inspirational source. After choosing me to be the editor of the **Arabic edition of Forbes Magazine,** I posed a question to Malcolm: **"What is the most important department at Forbes?"** With a tilt of his head, twinkle in his eyes, and an assertive wave of his hands, Malcolm Forbes drew me closer as he whispered: **"The Facts-Checking Department."** How profound!!

When I began watching **Al-Jazeera TV network,** I felt truly ambivalent about what I was seeing. Captivated by its global resources as it presented documentaries on Arab history. But repulsed by its news presentations of current Arab issues. As if I was watching the production of a schizophrenic network where the past was revered, but the present was slanted.

The Al-Jazeera's slant decidedly pointed to its own funding Mecca - **The Petro-State of Qatar!!** Not one word was ever uttered evaluating Qatar as a family business. But torrents of news and innuendos and oblique hints disparaging nearly every other Arab regime.

Al-Jazeera called itself **"The Pulpit of the Pulpitless" (in Arabic: "Minbar Mun La Minbara Lahu").** OK!! But as the channel's popularity grew, in the midst of the dearth of similar technological resources for other Arab media, a decided tone of pomposity crept in.

Interviews became marked by long leading introductions; assertive interviewers ended their questions with the arms-twisting phrase of **"isn't it so,"** without more; frequent interruptions of the interviewees; non-ascertainable facts peppered the news programs; and clips selectively vouching for Al-Jazeera's editorial commitments ruled the airwaves.

**Conclusion:** ideology took a front-row seat; facts, as gleaned from facts-checking, took a back seat. As in the sordid practice of personal injury lawyers, chasing after ambulances to get injured clients signed up, **Al-Jazeera** was chasing any opposition group in the Arab homeland as the only source of credible news.

One of their leading interviewees was **Abdel-Bari Attwan,** the past editor of **"Al-Quds Al-Arabi."** He, without shame, eulogized in a full-length page Saddam Hussein the day of the execution of that mass murderer. Called him **"The Leader of the Arab Nation!!"** But **"the best"** of Attwan, a Palestinian who was educated for free at Cairo University, was yet to come: On Al-Jazeera, he described the mastermind of 9/11 as **"Sheikh Osama Bin Laden." (Sheikh means an Islamic scholar).**

On Al-Jazeera's airwaves, Attwan advocated a resumption of war between Egypt and Israel. Both **Al-Jazeera** and **Al-Quds Al-Arabi,** described Hamas invasion of Egypt through the Sinai tunnels as **"legitimater for being the strategic depth of Hamas."**

This is not to mention daily attacks on other Arab Governments from Saudi Arabia, Kuwait, and Jordan to the East, to Morocco to the West. Now fast forward to Al-Jazeera's attitude towards the turbulent scene in the New Egypt from December 2010 to the collapse, under massive popular pressure, of the fascist Islamist regime of **Mohamed Morsi** in July

2013.

Two and a half years of misery in the most populous Arab country where the Islamists for a while highjacked the Revolution of January 25, 2011; attacked the Copts and the Shiis; gloried in the burning of convents and museums; attacked nuns; burned books; manipulated university students; side-lined **Al-Azhar;** issued crazy fatwas; allowed uneducated preachers in mosques to celebrate a retrograde interpretation of Islam; aligned themselves with haters of secular Egypt from Hamas to Qatar to Turkey; and called for drastic revisions of security measures in Sinai. For one fateful year, Egypt was ruled by a Taliban-like cabal with one difference: The Taliban espouse Afghanistan; a Brotherhood Supreme Guide said: **"To Hell with Egypt."**

Throughout that period of internal terror, **Al-Jazeera** raised the Islamist flag as high as Qatar wanted; Qatari petro-dollars illegally poured in; foreign NGO, without any accountability to the Government, treated Egypt as if it was a No-Man's Land; and Al-Jazeera's news reports became so one-sided as to qualify for **"news fabrication."** They focused on how **chaos was the daily event in Egypt.**

It was a constant drumbeat by **Al-Jazeera** creating a world-wide false impression of a failed State. No sovereign State on earth could allow such an organization to go on falsely destroying its fabric from within. States have the sovereign obligation to keep national dangers outside their borders.

A sample of Al-Jazeera playing games with the facts on the territory of the New Egypt is Al-Jazeera's reporting of a non-factual article by **Michelle Dunne.** Dunne is described in that article publicized by Al-Jazeera on Nov. 4, 2014 as **"a senior associate in the Middle East programme at the Carnegie Endowment for International Peace."** In her article, Dunne, whose husband was implicated in a case brought before the Egyptian judiciary against an NGO alleged intervention in internal affairs, had plenty to say through which to **vent her incurable Egyptophobia.**

In her own self-proclaimed expertise, **Dunne** denounces Egypt's measures of counter-terrorism in Sinai as follows: **"There were the remarkable scene of Egyptian bulldozers demolishing houses to create a buffer zone in Rafah following allegations that militants or weapons had entered from Gaza to carry out the attacks. While the tunnels under Rafah have been a persistent and serious problem, the total media blackout in Sinai makes it impossible to know what actually**

**happened and whether the demolitions were truly necessary or rather a hasty exertion of collective punishment against Sinai residents."**

How insane can Dunne of the Carnegie Endowment and Al-Jazeera of Qatar get!! **Ansar Beit Al-Maqdis (Friends of Jerusalem),** and based in Gaza, has proclaimed these terror actions to the whole world. They have targeted both Egyptian security forces and foreign tourists. **They have declared Sinai an emirate of ISIS.** Is Dunne and Al-Jazeera so deranged as to expect from Cairo detailed and open access to military operations and measures of self-defense? On what basis in law or fact does Dunne, through Al-Jazeera, characterize internal and sovereign defensive actions by Egypt in Sinai as **"collective punishment against Sinai residents?!"** Total fabrication which is shamelessly uttered behind the facade of **"press freedom."** Is it any wonder that in mid-December 2014 she was refused entry to Egypt? Is that press freedom, on a sinister invention of news and malicious mythinformation?

To me at least, it is the kind of hate-mongering which makes of both the Carnegie Endowment for International Peace and Al-Jazeera Network pro-conflict propaganda organizations. Their manifest purpose is destabilizing the New Egypt. Permanent war seems to be their lifeblood of existence in this age of chaos. **Why is this my conclusion?**

- **Because** freedom of the press is designed to enlighten, not to obfuscate; to shed light on credible facts as the best means of mass education;
- **Because freedom without limitation is the definition of chaos.** Like the Olympic connected circles, the limits of my freedom is where the outer limits of your freedom begin;
- **Because** the age of **Nazi Goebbels** teaches all of us that a steady barrage of lies about other people, whether for religious or ethnic or imperial reasons, shall lead ultimately to catastrophes like the Holocaust;
- **Because** it violates the UN Charter purposes of developing **"friendly relations among nations based on respect for the principle of equal rights and self-determination of peoples"** (Article I, para. 2);
- **Because** interference in the internal affairs of sovereign States, as through negative and non-substantiated media reports, is prohibited under international law **(UN Charter, Article II, para. 7)** except in apartheid-like situations;
- **Because** defamation of States or people or faith through surface conclusions and blatant fabrication of rumors and events, such as manifested by **Al-Jazeera and Michelle Dunne,** are not only

unethical. They are also means of fomenting mistrust of governance. That is especially so in countries like Egypt which is going through the dual difficult tasks of reconstruction as well as containment of ISIS-like terrorism;

- Because *the "Freedom of Expression" does not apply to someone mischievously yelling in a crowded theater "Fire!" causing death and injury by a terrified stampede.*

A seminal article appeared in the **New York Review of Books of January 2015** by **David Cole,** under the title **"Must Counter terrorism Cancel Democracy."** In it, that legal scholar deals with government powers during national emergencies. He says: **"Properly regulated, surveillance is a legitimate governmental function in peacetime and wartime. Every country does it; no country forbids it."** With regard to El-Sisi Administration, Al-Jazeera and Dunne seem oblivious to this reality.

The claim by Al-Jazeera to a bogus total, unbridled, unregulated, and non-substantiated stream of invented facts about sovereign States is rebuffed by law and ethics. Their claim of credibility has been found to vanish through a permanent ideological pattern of smear campaigns against secular Egypt. Al-Jazeera shamelessly manifested its tilt towards a defunct Islamist regime some of whose leaders are now in refuge in **Qatar which bankrolls Al-Jazeera.**

**The Qatar/Al-Jazeera symbiosis** is the clearest evidence of Al-Jazeera's absence of independence. **To Qatar, it is "His Master's Voice!!"**

The New Egypt is charting its own course, come what may. It has a secular constitution which nullified an earlier totally retrograde Islamic Constitution; a president who was fairly and openly elected by secret ballot in June 2014; a cabinet of technocrats under the steady stewardship of **Prime Minister Mahlab;** an upper House of Parliament in which woman, Copts, the disabled, and other previously marginalized communities and minorities are represented; lower house elections are slated to be held later this year.

**And Egypt has an independent judiciary.** That judiciary, through the Court of Cassation, the highest court in Egypt, and of which Bar I am honored to be a member, is the ultimate judicial voice in the case of the remaining two of Al-Jazeera journalists.

How obscene for the **New York Times** of January 2, 2015, to plainly advocate outside intervention in that judicial matter? Can the **New York**

**Times** call for such intervention in a case before the U.S. Supreme Court? How contradictory to the principle of judicial independence does the author of that article, **Kareem Fahim, a clone of David Kirkpatrick,** call for by-passing that judicial process in sovereign Egypt?!

In this morass of malicious one-sidedness which goes by the misnomer of **"Press Freedom," Al-Jazeera** again steps in. In that **New York Times** article, Al-Jazeera condemned the Egyptian Court decision for judicial review. It arrogantly states: **"Al-Jazeera said that the Egyptian authorities had a choice:**

**"Free these men quickly, or continue to string this out, all the while continuing this injustice and harming the image of their own country in the eyes of the world. They should choose the former."**

Yes, Al Jazeera, you, through your fabricated half-truths, know better than the leadership of the New Egypt about what should and shouldn't be done.

But thanks for making my case!! I have always felt that you were not truly engaged in airing news backed by facts. You, and the likes of **Michelle Dunne,** are engaged in imaginary thrillers.

**But when I want to see a thriller, I can assure you that you are not my first choice. Hitchcock is!!**

# The Shaming of America: Republican Congressmen v. The U.S. Constitution

Monday, March 23, 2015

They can't stand having an Afro-American being the President of the U.S. From Day One, in January 2009, Senator Mitch McConnell declared that the Republicans had one mission: **To insure that Obama is a one term President.** They and their supporters on the Right keep on questioning Obama's citizenship and his love of America.

Recently, former New York City mayor, Rudolph Giuliani, wondered in public whether the President cherished America. At a State of the Union message, a Republican Congressman heckled Obama while delivering that message to a joint session. He shouted, **"Liar."** Unprecedented. Obama, unruffled looked at that offender and responded: **"Thank You."**

During campaigning in opposition to Obama, Senator McCain, Republican from Arizona, was asked a question from his audience. The lady asking the question made in fact a comment attacking Obama. She, on national TV, said: **"He is an Arab."** In a subdued voice, McCain, with microphone now in hand, responded: **"No! He is not an Arab."** As if being an Arab in America was a grave national security breach.

Republicans in Congress, now in the majority in both houses, are **shaming America.** Their attacks on Obama have turned into a violation of the U.S. Constitution, especially in the area of foreign affairs.

That document, crafted by geniuses in checks and balances, promulgated in 1787 **"in order to form a more perfect union"** gave the President primary responsibility for foreign affairs.

He is **"Commander in Chief;"** has power **"by and with the advice and consent of the Senate, to make treaties;" "appoint ambassadors,"** with the Senate's **"advice and consent,"** but with a simple majority of one vote; and make use of international agreements and compacts, at times with congressional participation.

On these bases, it has been asserted in case law that the President acts **"as the sole organ of the Federal Government in the field of international relations." (Justice Sutherland of the U.S. Supreme Court, in the Curtiss-Wright case).**

By comparison to the primacy of the Presidential role in foreign affairs, Congress, under Article I (Section 8) of the Constitution, has been accorded limited powers. Congress can **"provide for the common defense,"** can **"declare war,"** and can **"raise and support armies."**

So primarily, Congress real prerogative lies in **controlling the defense budget.** Its power to declare ware has been used in **about 5 cases,** in the course of more than two centuries. Even in this foreign affairs domain, that power has been overwhelmed by the resort by the President to executive agreements which can speedily and privately commit the U.S. to action in foreign affairs without the need of any congressional involvement. This is the essence of what is legally described **"pure executive agreements."**

Also in regard to military action, the President may act unilaterally in actual hostilities against the U.S. When this happens, the only authority left to

Congress is its exercise of **"the spending power."** But limiting the presidential power at times of hostilities can only be done by Congress through its enactment or non-enactment of military appropriations **every two years.**

*The entire weight of legal constitutional scholarship is that the President has paramount power to represent the U.S. in day-to-day foreign relations.*

Yet in the course of this month of March, Republican Congressmen have shamed the U.S., through shaming President Obama. **John Boener, Speaker of the House,** on his own and in service of his narrow interests invites a foreign leader to address a joint **"meeting"** (not session) of Congress.

**Prime Minister Netanyahu of Israel was thus afforded the unheard of luxury of having Congress become a theatrical prop for his electoral aspirations** to secure a fourth term. The repeated standing ovations on Capitol Hill for him represented a massive Congressional indictment of Obama's efforts, still ongoing, to secure a deal with Iran on its nuclear aspirations.

Not to be outdone by these Republican efforts to undermine Obama's primary authority in foreign affairs, a 37-year old **Senator from Arkansas addresses a letter to the Iranian authorities.** The letter from **Tom Cotton** warned Tehran not to conclude a deal on the nuclear issue. Why? Because that inexperienced Senator, with only 65 days in the Senate, offered a crazy warning: **A deal with Obama could be cancelled by a successor.** In essence, Cotton is telling the Iranians and the world: **"Commitment by our President is worth nothing."**

**Are these lawmakers or are they Clowns?** CLOWNS, in a failing roadside circus. For they have:
- Infringed the Constitutional prerogatives of the U.S. President for whom foreign policy is a primary domain;
- Weakened the hands of the U.S. Secretary of State, **John Kerry.** This is in the midst of international negotiations aiming at reaching a consensual deal with Iran and all the five members of the UN Security Council, plus Germany;
- Confirmed the perception in the Arab and Muslim world that Israel, in regard to the Likud attempt **to have and hold a Greater Israel, from the Mediterranean to the Dead Sea,** at the expense of the creation of a sovereign State of Palestine, has the backing of

U.S. Congress;

- Ignored the fact that Israel is already a nuclear power, yet making, through the Likud in Israel, any nuclear program in the Arab Middle East, an existential threat;
- Made a great institution like U.S. Congress represent members who put their aspirations for keeping their seats ahead of the interests of **"a more perfect union;"**
- Hollowed out the incantations of America addressed to the outside world that when it comes to democracy and human rights, America, as Ronald Reagan put it, was akin to **"a City on a Shining Hill;"** and
- Enhanced the trepidations of America's allies that trusting America, especially in this global war on terrorism, is a risky gamble.

Putting perceptions aside, here are some realities drawn from applicable international law:

- If and when made, the deal with Iran is subject to approval by the UN Security Council. A scholar at Princeton University, **Seyed Hussein Mousavian** wrote on this subject an op ed in **Al Monitor.** He aptly titled it: **"On Iran deal, Republicans cut off their nose to spite their face."** In it he points out that: **"If a deal is reached, the Security Council would pass a resolution enacting its terms, which Congress has no authority over rescinding."**
- In his hallucinating letter, signed by 46 other Republican Senators, **Senator Tom Cotton** reminds Tehran of US sanctions. In another swipe at Obama, he in effect states that even if a deal is reached, the US Senate could still maintain sanctions on Iran.

In opposition to a constitutional scholar called Obama, **Cotton must have had real cotton in his ears** during classes in international law. **Sanctions work only if several other States, especially neighbors and big Powers cooperate.** Our "Tommy," in his incongruous role of a volunteer advisor to the Islamic Republic of Iran, should know that in a deal internationally accepted, unilateral US sanctions would not have their intended effect.

- **War is no longer a U.S. option.** Especially in a fanciful war on Iran. Just look at the administration having a difficult time in Congress just to agree to an authorization for the President to combat ISIS. In reality, **Obama needs no such authorization.** In his recent testimony before Congress, John Kerry cleared Obama's objective. The Administration was calling on Congress only to speak **"with a single powerful voice"** at this critical juncture.

One of the four pillars of national sovereignty is the **State's ability to**

**conduct foreign affairs.** Today's Congress, with Republican majorities, is proving that the U.S. governmental system is plagued by more **"checks"** than **"balances."** Retired **U.S. Major General Paul Eaton** said it to the point: **"The idea of engaging directly with foreign entities on foreign policy is frankly a gross breach of discipline."**

The rise of the extreme right in the US, including the Tea Party and the likes of **Ted Cruz, Sara Palin, Michelle Bachman, and Bill O'Reilly,** represents an endemic desire for endless war. The lessons of the wars in Afghanistan (2002) and Iraq (2003), with their consequences of sectarianism in the Muslim world and the economic great recession in America, seem to have been lost.

It is ironic to have the great party of **Lincoln** turning into the **party of war.** American efforts to **"contain and degrade ISIS,"** even through an international coalition, seem to have spawned an internal American war. **A war against Obama.**

A thoughtful commentator, **Dr. Sayed Amin Shalaby,** the Executive Director of the Egyptian Council for Foreign Affairs, recently quoted Zbigniew Brzezinski. In his book entitled **Strategic Vision: America and the Crisis of Global Power,** Zbig, as per his nickname, as quoted by my friend Ambassador Shalaby, argues that America has to understand that its power abroad will increasingly **depend on its ability to face its internal challenges.**

Well said!! A return by Congress to the U.S. Constitution is one such primordial necessity. The shaming of America is an factor in international destabilization.

A great America President, a Democrat, a hundred years ago, wrote while at Princeton University, a great book. It was a must read for me as a graduate student and a teaching assistant in the 1950s in America. Titled **Congressional Government,** President Woodrow Wilson warned against congressional usurpation of presidential powers.

It was Wilson, a real Cassandra, who as U.S. President, crafted the **League of Nations.** The Republican Senate of his day **prevented America's membership in it.** The League, without the US in it, collapsed in 1939, ushering in the Second World War. In spite of that, a Wilson legacy is still standing: **His advocacy of people's right to self-determination.**

An editorial in the **New York Times** of March 13, addressed this weird

132

coup-like Congressional episodes. It said: **"The Republicans are the leaders in Congress. But their efforts to undermine Mr. Obama in every matter are infecting ALL governance."**

An op ed article in the same issue of the **New York Times** by **Professor Kathleen Duval** headlined **"We Have a President for a Reason."** Denouncing that Republican power grab, it concluded: **"It would be strange for a group of 21st Century senators to take advantage of the negotiations with Iran and return U.S. to an earlier age of cacophony and weakness."**

**Time Magazine** of March 23 includes an article by **Ian Bremmer,** a foreign affairs columnist. In it, he says: **"This move undermines the credibility of future Presidents, Democrats and Republicans."**

Yet the process of the shaming of America keeps on going in various directions: President Obama calls Netanyahu to chide him for declaring retreat from the promise of two-States. But Boehner, Republican Speaker of the House, travels to Israel to stand by Netanyahu's side.

*And on March 23, the craziest of U.S. Senators, Texan Republican Ted Cruz, announces his candidacy for President in 2016. This icon of the Tea Party, in his totally unpromising bid for President, accuses Obama of communism. Shameless!!*

# 11 APRIL 2015

## The New Egypt Notion of a New Arab Nation

Friday, April 3, 2015

One of the great novels in Arabic is **"The Return of the Spirit"** (Awdat El-Roah), by Tawfik Al-Hakim. In this blog posting, I shall borrow his title for a contemporary context. Namely the return to the Arab Nation of its spirit. Enunciated by El-Sisi as Chairman of the recent Arab Summit of late March in Sharm El-Sheikh, Sinai, Egypt.

Closing his inaugural summit speech before all top representatives of 22 States, members of the **League of Arab States,** minus one -Syria, the Egyptian President, three times intoned: **"Long Live the Arab Nation."** An apt reminder that after 4 years of the Arab Spring uprisings, the Arab world was discovering, in Egypt, the broad lines of an **Arab concordat.**

It is therefore a time for outlining the notion now held by the most populous Arab State, Egypt, of the newly resurrected Arab Nation. **Adversity, like need, breeds reinvention.** The Arab adversity has been the destructive side of the Arab Spring. Fear has gripped **"the Arab World."** Now after the Declaration of Sharm El-Sheikh of March 29, 2015, it has been renamed **"The Arab Nation."**

The wave of fear began to thunder from barbaric terrorism. Its gusts were submerging the Arab identity. Arab capitals, namely, Baghdad, Beirut, Damascus and Sanaa, were being renamed by extremist Iranian triumphalists as **"cities within the Persian Empire."** Persian versus Arab has become current lingo.

The issue here was misunderstood by the Western media as sectarianism (Sunni vs. Shii). **Wrong characterization.** It was Farsi vs. Arab. And the Arabs were insulted by it. Said **"Amre Musa,"** former Secretary-General of the League of Arab States: **"I have never felt so insulted in my whole political life."**

As Sanaa was being run over by the Houthis, supported by Iranian funds and arms, the Arab leadership, including the exiled Yemeni President, Abdu Rabbut Mansour Hadi, hurried to the Arab summit at Sharm El-Sheikh. They were in search, not for identity, but for affirmation of what to do about refurbishing their ID.

Saudi Arabia led the purposeful parade; the Gulf States coalesced, including Qatar; El-Sisi and his team, together with the institutional host, the League of Arab States, prepared the ground work; the Saudi air campaign which brought together an Arab Coalition of 9 other States was disrupting the Houthis advance towards Aden; and a revitalized Arab Nation was taking shape, pushing back against what a third of a billion Arabs perceived to be a revival of a massive inter-cultural clash with Tehran. A clash with massive geo-strategic dimensions.

**So what were the policy ingredients of Cairo's notion of a New Arab Nation?** These ingredients are still not receiving a unanimous vote of support from the other 20 Arab capitals. Nonetheless, the broad framework is emerging. Its shape is crystallizing along the following lines:

- Egypt now describes itself as **"The Home of the Arab Family ."** A softer definition and a lesser involvement, and at a much lesser cost than **"The Arab Leader."** The Nasserite ideology has become a museum piece;

- Recognition that the primary challenge facing the New Arab Nation is not ISIS, Khorasan, Al-Qaeda, or Al-Nusra. Egypt, especially now with the release of previously-withheld US offensive armament, is confident of its combative efforts on these transitory fronts.

- The main challenge is posed by outside neighborly powers (Iran; Turkey) whose regimes are looking westward, in the case of Iran, and eastward, in the case of Turkey. **"The cultural war"** is no longer a term which is reserved to **"a religious revolution;"** it has been expanded into a confrontationist term which is backed not only by sermons, but by swords as well;

- **"The New Arab Nation"** is regarded as an amalgam of various faiths, creeds, allegiances and manners of worship. The reference to a **"Muslim Nation"** seems, at present, to denote a Sunni/Shii amalgam where **Al-Azhar, Kufa, Karbala, Najaf, and Qom** shall continue to hold religious sway. Within that concept of Arabism, the attacks on Christians, especially after the Libyan massacre of the Copts, have become attacks on Arabism. For Egypt, at least, there can be no more repetition of the attacks on the **All-Saints Church in Alexandria** on the eve of celebration of the new year of 2011.

- **"The New Arab Nation"** is now sounding the alarm regarding the fragmentation in more than one Arab State into Statelets. Especially in Libya, Syria, Iraq and Yemen. Sectarianism, especially with funding from the outside, is the trojan horse whose objective is to **replace the flag of the State by tribes with flags.** El-Sisi at the 26th Arab Summit, described this process as the **"kidnapping the homeland."** This call for the need of a coordinated inter-Arab push-back was reiterated by a former Egyptian Minister for Foreign Affairs, **Muhammad Al-Orabi.** In a speech in Abu Dhabi (the Emirates), he, on March 31, stated: **"Today's challenges impose on all Arab States the obligation of interdependency in order to escape the dangers of this bottleneck (of simultaneous challenges)."** Minister Al-Orabi had, on March 1 launched an initiative called **"With Our Money We Build Our Army."**

- At the Sharm Arab Summit, the League of Arab States was resurrected. From dormancy to vibrancy, **through the decision to create a unified Arab armed force for quick intervention.** No more total dependency on a Western military handout which at times, especially in the case of the U.S., was held hostage to the whims of internal politics.

- El-Sisi advocated; Saudi Arabia led; the other Gulf States coalesced;

air forces were scrambled for a showdown over who rules Yemen: the Houthis and a deposed ruler (Saleh) or the Hadi government which came to power through consensus.

- The Arab summit resolution on a unified Arab military force, adopted toward the end of March, had no non-Arab finger prints on it. Propelled by real concern for fraud committed on the Arab ID card, it had an old and nearly forgotten foundation: **The Arab Defense Pact of 1950.**

- But that was only a part of the legal context. The Charter of the League of Arab States, set forth in Alexandria in 1945 well before the drafting of the UN Charter, was invoked at Sharm. And the UN Charter was also cited (by implication Chapter VIII, on regional organizations).

- That Arab expeditionary force, to be created in a few weeks before having the Arab Defense Council issue its birth certificate, has become the center piece of the functioning of the New Arab Nation. Its creation, declared both the Arab League Secretary-General, **Dr. Nabil El-Araby,** and Egypt's Foreign Minister **Sameh Shoukri,** was largely due to **"unprecedented challenges."**

- That Arab expeditionary force benefits also from a political road map: membership in it is voluntary; not intended as a threat to a neighbor or another Arab State; defensive in nature.

- However the triple threats of terrorism, fragmentation and external intervention were cited geographically by President El-Sisi in his inaugural address to the Arab Summit. These were: **Yemen, Libya, Syria, Iraq, Lebanon, Somalia, and Israeli illegal practices in the occupied Palestinian territories.**

- Other aspects necessary for the resurrection of a New Arab Nation, were not left out. All the 21 Arab States (with the Syrian seat remaining vacant for now) addressed complementary issues needed for an Arab national renaissance: economic and social development; emphasis on equality before the law; the role of religious institutions in combating terrorism, the elimination of illiteracy by 2024, and the inclusion of women and youth in the efforts of an Arab Nation now under construction.

- In an interview with **"The Voice of Lebanon,"** Amre Moussa, on March 30, commented as follows: **"There are basic strategic considerations behind this regional Arab surge towards coordinated action. Egypt has also a primordial interest in maritime security in the Red Sea and in the national security of Saudi Arabia."**

- In that context El-Sisi's visit to Riyadh in very early March, and the meeting of minds between him and King Salman of Saudi Arabia have laid the ground work for the historic Arab summit held in Sharm.

- The Gulf's financial liquidity, now partly channelled through these new defensive inter-Arab structures, shall make non-Arab financial support to States like Egypt less conditional on meeting the donor's restrictions.

As the British adage goes, **"nothing succeeds like success."** The anti-Houthi coalition now count 10 States: Saudi Arabia, Egypt, Kuwait, Jordan, Bahrain, Qatar, Morocco, the Emirates, anti-Houthi Yemen and the Sudan. Add also Pakistan, a Muslim non-Arab State.

US logistical and intelligence support to that formidable coalition, to which Egypt offered ground troops, cannot be underestimated. Nor can the timely action by President Obama removing the weapons freeze against Egypt on March 31. A thoughtful New York Times reporter, **Peter Baker,** attributed that action to Washington **"seeking to repair relations with a longtime ally (Egypt) at a time of spreading war in the Middle East."**

Despite continued terrorist attacks in Sinai, including the human loss by the security forces on April 3, there is one clear indication as to where the forces of destruction, and the forces of the New Arab Nation are heading: The former, downward to extinction, the latter upward to a new rebirth. It is Easter time. Like in the bible, the Quran provides that **"Christ is Risen." "The Arabs want to be in that number, when the saints**

139

come marching in."

# In the Grip of Middle Eastern Chaos, Even Lying Becomes a Challenge!!

Friday, April 24, 2015

A lie is an intentional false statement.

This is not in praise of lying. It is in demonstrating that the Arabs, while in the grip of total chaos, cannot even lie well. The examples are endless. So we shall offer here limited samples. Samples of both lies and chaos.

**"The Houthis in Yemen are Iranian agents." A lie!!** The war in Yemen is an inter-tribal event. The north is tribal and Houthi dominated. The south is developed and wants to split from the north. I authored for the World Bank a study on Yemen and judicial reform.

**"Islam is of two kinds: Sunni and Shii." A lie!!** There is a difference between faith and ice cream. Faith is in the heart; ice cream is on the tongue. Faith does not come in flavors: Sunni and Shii. Ice cream comes in many flavors. The Sunni-Shii thing is a mere cover for a fight 1400 years ago on who is the rightful successor (Khalifa) of Muhammad. My present authorship of a biography in English on Ali evidences that his partisans (Shiis) have a logical claim. Does such a claim in regard to succession make of the Shias apostates? Nonsense.

**"Iran has claimed for itself Baghdad, Damascus, Beirut and Sanaa, not as Arab capitals of independent Arab States, but as under Tehran hegemony." A lie!!** That statement was never uttered by Tehran as an official statement. It was a statement by an unofficial person who felt a bit of Persian triumphalism which means nothing.

**"Hezbollah is a credible counter-weight to Israel's military might." A lie!!** Yes Hezbollah stood its ground in 2006 in spite of Israeli huge pounding. But standing its ground, and gaining grounds are two different proposals. I wonder with amazement how the intervention by Hezbollah on the side of a killer called Al-Assad can help the cause of Hezbollah in either Lebanon or in the Palestinian/Israeli confrontation.

**"Saddam should have been left to rule over Iraq securing its territorial unity." A lie!!** Like Bashar of today, killer Saddam merely kept the lid on a boiling pot through resort to genocide against both the Kurds and the Shias. I was in Iraq six times after the American war of choice on Iraq. I have never met either a Kurd or a Shia or a Sunni who lamented his disappearance.

**"The Egypt of El-Sisi, in its closure of the Rafah Crossing, is depriving the Gazans from even breathing." A lie!!** Rafah is not a toll booth on a highway between Gaza and El-Arish in Sinai. If the Gazans want access to Sinai, let them convince Hamas to abandon its Charter. Egypt has a peace treaty with Israel, while Hamas claims that not one grain of sand in historic Palestine should be claimed by the Jews.

**"The Yemen war is a trap manufactured by the US to weaken Saudi Arabia." A lie!!** Who in his right mind would expect the U.S. to encourage the Houthis to threaten Saudi Arabia and the security of the sea lanes to and from Suez? And please make up your mind: Are the Houthis pawns of Iran or pawns of America? They cannot be both. Why? Because they are neither.

**"The Arab United Armed Forces has little support in the Arab world." A lie!! First,** at the Arab Summit in Sharm El-Sheikh in late March, reservations were made about it by only four Arab States: Iraq, Qatar, Lebanon, and Algeria. That is four out of a total of 21 States. **Second:** No poll has been conducted in the Arab world about that. **Third:** The Arabs have been hungering for a rebirth of the League of Arab States. The coalition, as led by Saudi Arabia, is voluntary and its sphere of action is confined to limited engagements.

**"ISIS is everywhere and its territorial gains are increasing, covering an area from Nigeria to Pakistan." A lie!!** Just look at the map. No territorial contiguity for ISIS. Except in the no-man lands north-east of Syria and north-west of Iraq. I was in Anbar, Iraq. No border markers in that open desert. Pledges of fealty to ISIS from various corners of the Arab/Muslim huge expanse are largely video fantasies intended for psychological warfare.

**"El-Sisi is losing the adulation of large sectors of the Egyptian public." A lie!!** The popular bang at the beginning of his presidency is now translated to nation-building inside Egypt. Thanks God, there are no high profile Nasser-like excursions about Egypt being **"the leader of the Arab world."** Egypt should always be pre-occupied with Egypt. The enormous mountains of need have to gradually come down in terms of meeting the basic needs of 100 millions. Nearly a third of the Arab world.

**"The Muslim Brotherhood has a huge influence over Washington, D.C." A lie!!** One photo op at the U.S. State Department does not arise to the level of a Brotherhood lobby in the U.S. Capital. The fact remains that US media, thanks to correspondents like David Kirkpatrick of the **New York Times** in Cairo, has kept a drumbeat regarding the June 30 Revolution being a coup. But the recent actions by the Obama administration which released lethal armament to Egypt shows a disconnect. Except in the case of Israel, US media and policy considerations in America are mostly not directly related.

**"The Egyptian judiciary, in dealing with cases of detainees, whether Egyptian or non-Egyptian, is a political tool of El-Sisi government." A lie!!** Egypt's judiciary is immunized from such pressures. Admittedly, mass sentences do not usually accord with the proper law of evidence. But as a whole, if you are caught even as a bystander at an illegal demonstration (no license), you might be presumed guilty. After all, presence is a form of participation.

**"The use of Egyptian armed forces outside of Egypt is contrary to the Constitution of 2014." A lie!!** First, read that Constitution. No such provisions in it. Second, national defense does not stop at the national border. Third, there is the Arab Defense Pact of 1950, an inter-Arab treaty without Arab borders.

**"For Egypt, the present Yemen War is a repeat of the Yemen War of 1962-1968." A lie!!** In the 1960's, Nasser acted on his own, by throwing Egypt's armed forces in the oven of an inter-tribal civil war. The goal was to vanquish Arab monarchies in favor of Arab republicanism. Egypt suffered massive defeat and further antagonized Saudi Arabia, the other Gulf States, Jordan and Iran of the Shah. This time, in 2015, Egypt's involvement is through a decision of the Sharm El-Sheikh Arab Summit. And clear Egyptian national interest in the security of the Suez and the Gulf are implicated.

**"Iran has always been an enemy of America." A lie!!** The U.S. intervened in Iranian internal affairs by toppling Prime Minister Mossadeq in 1953. In his place, America helped re-install the Shah against popular will. The lesson to be learnt by all, including Iran and the U.S. of today, is:

**intervention in the internal affairs of other States shall always backfire.** Under international law, Iran of the Ayatollahs is entitled to freely manage its own internal affairs. But no revolution for hegemony is exportable.

**"The Secretary-General of "Khorasan," a terrorist militia organization active in Iraq, announced that they recognize only Ali Khamenei, the Supreme Guide of the Islamic Republic of Iran."** A compounded lie. **First:** Khorasan confuses between shiism and **"the Rule by the Jurist" (Wilayet Al-Faqih).** The Rule by the Jurist came into vogue only with **Khomenei** in 1979. **Second:** Khorasan, which claims that the Islamic world is borderless, manifests utter ignorance. Admission to UN membership and regional organization is one of many indications of border legitimation. **Third:** Khorasan manifests ignorance of the term **"Islamic Umma."** In Islamic jurisprudence, **"Umma"** does not mean **"nation."** It means **"community."**

*Conclusion: In the midst of massive chaos in the Arab world, even lying becomes a challenge!! These lies must have been produced by amateurs!! Engaged in hashish smoking!!*

# 12 MAY 2015

## Combatting the Brotherhood's Ideology Through the Use of Authentic Terminology

Friday, May 1, 2015

Lies need more than one dictionary. One for the faithful; one for the unfaithful; and one for those in between. The importance of dictionaries lies in their being reflexively believable. One never argues with them. With the **Muslim Brotherhood,** of which there are several varieties, the falsehood of words is a powerful and less costly recruitment tool.

Let us have a look at key terms. Let us see how the various MB brands understand them; package them for sale; advocate them; highlight them in various languages for various ever-changing needs and audiences.

**(1) "Allahu Akbar:"** The MBs creed begins by **"Allah is our Objective."** **Correction:** But they treat Allah (God) as if He were patented in their name. If so, which is ridiculous, the patent in intellectual property expires in about 17 years. They, the MBs, forget that we, the 7 billion of humanity, are His.

He is not ours except in the context of our being His. In Islamic jurisprudence, **"Allahu Akbar,"** means that we are all equal before God. Regardless of our faith or even of non-faith. Its use by the MBs, like its ISIS offshoot, as they sever the head of a hostage, or burn alive the

145

Jordanian pilot Moaz Al-Kassassbah, is an outrage.

**(2) Authority:** In the **Quran** it is provided that public order is the essence of harmonious development. It is the opposite of **fitna** (insurrection; chaos; mayhem). Hence the Quran calls on the faithful to: **"Obey God and obey the Messenger, and those entrusted with authority over you."** (Chapter IV, verse 5-9).

But the MBs would not have any of this. Especially as regards El-Sisi administration which they describe as **"a coup"** against the so-called Islamist regime of Morsi. This selectivity ignores the fact that Morsi was handed a trust (I voted for him) only to have him engage in the brotherhoodization of Egypt. An exclusive rule by the long beards which produced an Islamic Constitution (now abandoned). That Constitution put women, Copts, Shiis, and liberals outside the pale of the law. The result: Popular recall of that regime through the public square on June 30, 2013. The Islamic Constitution had no recall or impeachment provisions.

**(3) "Constitution:"** As part of their creed, the MBs declares that **"The Quran Is Our Constitution."**
**Correction:** For a Muslim, the **Quran** is the word of God (in Arabic - Allah). You take it on faith. You don't vote for it; you don't amend it; you don't litigate by the use of its literal provisions (only 200 legal rules within 6400 verses). That is with the exception of personal status matters. If you believe in the Quran, you must also believe in the sanctity of other revealed books. The **Old Testament,** and the **New Testament.** That is because faith is primarily a matter of the heart. Non-negotiable.

**(4) Cooperation:** The Quran provides parameters for international cooperation. In Chapter V, verse 2, it states: **"Cooperate with all in what is good and pious, and do not cooperate in what is sinful and aggressive."** The MBs active cooperation is with **Hamas, Ansar Beit Al-Maqdis,** and such terror varieties which they regard as **"brothers in Islam."** However, that brotherhood is underpinned by criminality and acts violating public order. It is the brotherhood of a Mafia. Only the Mafia does not base its acts on religion.

**(5) "Copt."** For the MBs, the term denotes a trespasser on Muslim lands.
**Correction:** The Copt is Egypt, in both belonging, history, faith, and law. The MBs expansion on that term is **"infidel."**
**Correction:** In Islamic law, **"an infidel"** denotes someone devoid of values. It is God who judges; other humans have no business judging. This is because the **Almighty** has created humanity on the basis of equality.

146

Thus there is no **"heavenly apartheid."** You exist through according to others what you claim for yourself.

**(6) "Coup."** The MBs have changed the meaning of that term. Before January 25, 2011, it meant an uprising against Mubarak. So they sat out the Tahrir uprising from January 25, 2011 until **"the Camel Battle"** of January 28. Seeing the Mubarak regime wobble, and **Field Marshal Tantawi** instructing the armed forces to protect, not to shoot, they jumped on the band wagon to own the Revolution which they had invoked God's wrath against it.
**Correction:** The MBs rule in 2012-2013 was the real coup against the popular will.

**(7) "Egypt."** For the MBs, it does not exist. Except as a territorial expanse, with provincial characteristics. When it matures, it becomes an **"Emirate."** Its recognition in their dictionaries can only be found in the geographic world of Islam. Its boundaries are not sovereign.
**Correction:** Egypt has been a State for 10,000 years -**8,500 years before Islam.** A State is defined by four criteria: fixed boundary; fixed population; a functioning government; and competence to conduct foreign affairs. Egypt, as a State, has met these conditions for millenia. No, says the MBs; the population is supplantable. Bring the Gazans to Sinai, no big deal!! Have Qatar or Turkey interfere in Egyptian internal affairs -that is normalcy!! Ridiculous!!

**(8) "Fatwa."** The **MBs** franchises use it as a double tool of both obfuscation and mind control. They spew fatwas as a torrent in every direction, clothing their pronouncements in the garb of the unalterable sacred. **You deviate, you go to hell.**
**Correction:** A fatwa is a legal advice, unenforceable, and issues from highly trained specialists, under the guidance of **Al-Azhar. The Mufti,** in this regard, is a religious authority who, through the proper understanding of the Quran and the Sunna, fills in the gaps created by changing circumstances. There is an entire area of **Fiqh** (sources of Islamic Law) which is called **"Jurisdiction Based on No-Text -Textless Fiqh. Can you imagine that a mass killer like Osama Bin Laden had issued Fatwas?"** The blind leading the blind.

**(9) "Ijtihad:"** Ijtihad is the application of mind to the text of the Quran or the Hadith (the tradition of the Prophet Muhammad). Desirous of rigidity, the MBs claim that ijtihad is closed.
**Correction:** Sharia is applicable to every place and every time. The essence here is not that Sharia is international law. The essence is its adaptability to

147

changing circumstances, and its capability of evolution. In fact, there is a dynamic branch of Islamic Law (Sharia) called **"The fiqh of Maslahah"** (the **Law of Public Interest**).

**(10) "Jihad:"** The MBs creed states that **"Jihad is Our Way of Life."**
**Correction:** Who is **"our."** Count me and nearly a billion and a half other Muslims out. We have seen the MBs jihad: butchering; sectarianism; destruction; foreign occupations; **fornication jihad** through female abductions and recruitment; and black flags of ISIS.

Following the ouster of the Brotherhood in Egypt from power, their resort to terrorism needed a change of slogans. Today's slogans are **"No dignity without jihad; No jihad without armament."** In Islamic Law, jihad is self-policing and defense against foreign invasion. The term **"Holy War"** does not exist in Islam. It is a pet term used by Islamophobes whose hate for Islam is fed by the MB gone crazy.

**(11) "Martyr:"** The MBs creed provides for **"martyrdom (death for the sake of Allah) is our cherished hope."**
**Correction:** In Islamic Law, the martyr (or shaheed in Arabic) is one who dies fighting territorial aggression against his homeland. **It does not apply to suicide bombers who kill innocent civilians.** It does not apply to Al-Qaeda operatives. **It does not apply to those who inflicted 9/11.** In Islamic Law, the martyrs of 9/11 are not the attackers who perished. They are the 3000 persons who perished as a result of that criminal act. **Bin Laden** had called those attackers **"The Great Nineteen."**

**(12) "Minaret."** The MBs variety regards it as an architectural requirement and an obligatory Islamic monument.
**Correction:** Where does it say this in the Quran? A Saudi national, residing in Switzerland, took the federal authorities to court on this one. They had required him to conform to zoning laws in regard to its height. He lost; and a plebiscite ensued resulting in the banning of minarets in Switzerland.

**And if the MBs varieties are so enamored with monuments, why destroy the monuments in Afghanistan, Iraq and Syria?**

**(13) "Muslim."** For the MBs, it is not enough to say and believe that **"God is one, and Muhammad is His Messenger."** You also need physical characteristics: A long beard, a big raisin-like skin impression on your forehead, and a scull cap over your head.
**Correction:** A Muslim is defined as someone who submits to the will of God. No mention in the Quran about those other outward manifestations.

**To the MBs, a female in jeans and without a hijab is a sinner.** But where in the Quran is this stated? The Quran says **"be modest"** in dress. It does not go beyond this. Personal freedom, within the accepted norms of each society, is a hallmark of Islamic jurisprudence.

**(14) "Shiis."** The MBs regard the Shiis, who are over 10% of the Muslim population, as **"apostates."**
**Correction:** The wayward Brothers who in Cairo killed and dragged Shii corpses in the streets, believe that only the Sunnis are Muslims. Who decreed that stupid notion?! The Sunnis and Shiis confess the same faith, follow the same precepts, and face toward Mecca, not Tehran, in prayer.

There is no takfeer (apostasy) in Islamic law. **Otherwise, Sunnism shall be taken as replacing Allah.** Because He alone is the only judge. **He** has not retained the MBs as his exclusive brokers. In fact, it is the Sunnis who invented the criminal practice of suicide bombing. The Shiis, as my late Azhari father who was a Sunni scholar taught me, are the Islamic branch which taught the **Umma** (The Islamic Nation) the veneration of Muhammad, and love for **"Aal El-Beit Muhammad's family."**

I am at present authoring the first biography of **Ali Ibn Abi-Taleb** in English as based on Arabic primary sources. **Imam Ali** was Muhammad's foster child; the **First Muslim;** and the icon who, among other historic deeds, put Muhammad in his grave. Ali's partisans (Shiis) are entitled to equal treatment as the Sunnis. Read **"Hadith"** (Muhammad's pronouncements about Ali). Accordingly, you could then gauge how ignorant, indeed catastrophic, is the alienation of the Shiis!! **The problem of succession to Muhammad is not a religious issue. It is a political struggle for succession long gone.**

**(15) "Shura:"** In Arabic, it means communal consultations leading to decision-making through consensus **(ijmaa).** Shura is one of the main pillars of democracy in **Fiqh** (jurisprudence). The other pillars are: (a) equality before the law (meaning **Adl** -justice); (b) transparency (denoting **Sidq** -truthfulness in transactions); and (c) denial of discrimination on any basis (symbolized by the Islamic adage: **"There is no difference between an Arab and a non-Arab except through the performance of good societal deeds."** Expressed in two words **"no discrimination"** (in Arabic -LA FARQ).

But the MBs made a mockery of **"shura."** Only to come back through the back door of July 3, 2013 and claim that their odious regime was illegally toppled. **Really?** In office, Morsi was a front for **El-Shatter, his money**

149

**bags;** Al-Azhar's Rector was downgraded and was on the verge of removal; Christianity was deemed so un-Islamic that a fatwa was issued that it was forbidden to say **"Merry Christmas!!"**

Under the Islamic fascist year in governance, **"shura"** was the preserve of the **"Supreme Guide"** and his politburo called **"The Office of Guidance."** Some guidance, folks!! You have even transgressed against the Quran (which you define as your Constitution) where it says: **"And those who respond to their Lord and establish prayer, and who on matters other than those God has decreed, conduct them by mutual consultation..."** (Chapter 42, entitled Ash Shura, verse 38). There exists no Islamic democracy, and non-Islamic democracy. It is universal even if practiced differently in different cultures.

**(16) "Tawheed:"** The onness of God; the ideological pillar of Islam. It eliminated worship of the idols -the multiplicity of gods which prevailed in Arabia, including Mecca and the Kaabah before Islam. The MBs are so mixed up in their heads that their franchises advocate **a stupid myth: The Pyramids, the Sphinx,** and the now-destroyed great historical city of **Nemrod,** as Idols.

Now ask these obscurantists: **"Have you seen someone pray facing the Sphinx and asking it for the forgiveness of sins?"**

A monument is a cultural icon, not a deity. Even the ancient Egyptians knew that. **They created a space between the monuments and the temples.** The Egyptians, 5000 years ago, separated between the State and its cultural IDs, and worship. In this, they were even ahead of the U.S. Constitution in separating between religion and the State.

**Conclusion:** I have selected from among 100 terms only some. But a war of ideas has to be buttressed by a more comprehensive and authentic vocabulary. It is high time to correct the false dictionaries produced by the Muslim Brotherhood varieties. This is as **important as the use of arms against global jihadism.** Thus the call by **El-Sisi** on Al-Azhar to wage **"a religious revolt"** is a call for denying the Muslim Brotherhood and their terror varieties the illegal free run which they have so far enjoyed.

*In an interview in early March 2015 with Al-Ahram newspaper, the former Mufti of Egypt, Dr. Ali Gomaa, offered the best ever characterization of the abuse by Jihadis of Islam, as both a faith and a culture. He told his lady interviewer that ISIS and other jihadis "have conjured up a parallel religion that has nothing to do with*

*Islam."*

# Why Did Egypt's Train Depart, With the Brotherhood Still Standing on the Platform?

Saturday, May 16, 2015

Because the Brotherhood were standing on a false platform.

Because the great majority of the passengers saw in the Brotherhood a clear and present danger. Boarding that train would have meant inclusiveness. Well!! **The Brotherhood wished to travel alone.** Their **"Guidance Bureau"** decreed that.

Because the train did not segregate men from women; veiled women from the unveiled; lots of Copts and some Shiis exercised their right to board; and the train had changed its course, from going east towards Hamas, to going west in a grand opening **towards a broader and more interactive world.**

Yet, even when abandoned by themselves on that empty platform, the Brotherhood still nurtures the dream that the passengers will rebel. Their dream is based on their assumed right to have the train turn back to have them board. Thus their spokesman, like **Ahmed Darrag,** addresses over the BBC airwaves on May 11, 2015, these fancy hopes of return. He claims that:

- We are more popular inside Egypt than **El-Sisi;**
- The **"deep State"** of **Mubarak** and the Armed Forces engineered our ouster;
- Our ouster did not come about through the will of the people;
- Fuel was made scarce through conspiracy;
- We are but a broad **"social movement,"** not a political organization;
- Morsi's mandate was cut short, and should be allowed to resume;
- We have been around for 80 years and we are everywhere in the Arab and Muslim worlds;
- We stand for democracy. But shall not take part in any parliamentary elections;
- Democracy is not **"elections"** only; and
- We committed no mistakes while governing Egypt.

**A total farce.** An enveloping self-delusion. Typical Brotherhood contradictions. No need to rebut every argument advanced by **Darrag,** even if you dignify all his points above as **"arguments."** However an **overall rebuttal is called for.**

Even after two years of being thrown out of governance, the Brotherhood remains **unrepentant.** They don't believe in admitting errors **-grave national errors:**

- Looking upon Egypt only as a launching pad for **islamization;**
- Egypt is only a province within a vast **Muslim Nation (Ummah);**
- Having their **"Guidance Bureau"** as a super-sovereign decision-maker, with Morsi as a junior partner;
- Engineering the election of a President before the promulgation of a Constitution;
- Rail-roading that **Islamic Constitution of 2013** through Egyptian polity. That is after chasing out Copts, women, and secularists from the Constituent Assembly;
- Having **Morsi** declare that he was above the law one month prior to the plebiscite on the Islamic Constitution;
- Attempting to create a militia and a Brotherhood Presidential Guard to parallel these iconic State institutions, a la Iran;
- Harassing the **judiciary** and downgrading **Al-Azhar** and the **Coptic Church;** and
- Opening the Sinai gateways for **Hamas** and its war on Israel.

In spite of all these Brotherhood calamities, they looked upon the Second Egyptian Revolution of June 30, 2013 as a rebellion against their **"law and order."** And termed their non-responsiveness to peaceful political re-integration, through appeals by El-Sisi from June 30 to July 3, 2013, as a sacred right to exclusive governance. Then launched bloody sit-ins at **Rabaa** and **Al-Nahda** squares in Cairo as **"a peaceful exercise of the right to dissent."**

After 6 full weeks of refusal to peacefully disperse from their declared **"Rabaa and Al-Nahda Emirates,"** their obstructionism and criminal actions of murder and hostage-taking necessitated State action. Hundreds were killed, including some State security elements. So now self-victimization became a battle cry -a cry that openly invited foreign intervention and foreign funding.

**No, Mr. Darrag!!** Your arguments are vacuous; your **Valhallas** (mythical palaces in which so-called slain heroes are thought to feast) are pure fantasies; and your inattention to God's words is patently manifest. Especially when it comes to your non-recognition of your mistakes about which the Brotherhood remains unrepentant. The Quran says: **"But as for the one who repents and believes, and does righteous deeds, he may be one of the prosperous."** (Chapter 28, Verse 67).

**You and the rest of your Brothers are waiting in vain for the Egyptian train,** standing alone on a non-promising platform. Your station has been re-named **"Terrorville!!"**

I now have an admission. For a long time, I thought that the Brotherhood was always at its best when they lied. **To them lying has been an industry.** And it comes in various forms. From suppression of the truth, to the invention of facts. From evading to answer directly, to reinterpretation of what you or they have said.

Where was I wrong about giving the Brotherhood the **Devil's World Prize for Lying?** When they last week surpassed their lying metrics with reports claiming to be secret recordings. Done of conversations among senior Egyptian army commanders. These were reported in **The New York Times** of May 13, by David Kirkpatrick, known for his bias toward the Brothers. You read those so-called **"unflattering leaks"** about the upper echelons of the mighty Egyptian armed forces. Then you say: **"Wow!! How stupid!! I thought the Brothers were much better liars than that!!"** Why?

The reports on the supposed leaks are the product of an interested party. **The lawyers representing the political party of ousted President Morsi.** They are supposed to be **"evidence in a criminal case in Britain."** Against whom, and what is the basis of action? Against the alleged illegality of ousting Morsi, and **"the take-over's leaders (being charged) with torture and other human rights violations."**

Now let us first stick to the underlying issues. That is before coming to the great vista of the Brotherhood specialization in not honoring facts. Those lawyers instituting that frivolous case **must be dumb.** Sovereign political issues are not justifiable. The principle of universal jurisdiction does not apply. Evidence based on unauthorized recording is inadmissible for its being hearsay. Also the plaintiffs (the Brotherhood's lawyers) must prove either legal representation of their clients, or prove that they were directly injured (tortured). Even if they prove appropriate lawyer/client relationship, the client (the Brotherhood) has been declared a terrorist organization by sovereign authorities. Open rebellion against Egypt's security forces on August 14, 2013 vitiates any claims against those forces and/or their commanders. There is no subsidiarity in the relationships between the Egyptian judiciary, a party aggrieved by the Brotherhood, and any non-Egyptian court system.

Should I say more about what a **"loser case"** this is? Oh, yes!! **Who are the presumed defendants in that Brotherhood case which is forum-shopping in London?** The reports say **"the take-over leaders!!"**

But El-Sisi was never **"a take-over"** leader. His actions from June 30 to July 3, 2013 were prompted by **35 million Egyptians rising in a massive human wave** in a second revolution against the Brotherhood's take-over of Egypt's identity. He, in that regard, was a go-between between an Egypt angered by the brotherhoodization of their country and Morsi. Morsi had refused for 3 days a consensual solution **-an exit from a civil war.** That refusal transformed El-Sisi's role, as Defense Minister, into an actor for protecting the country from a lurch into Civil War. El-Sisi did not seek that role. The Brotherhood's obducracy imposed on the Armed Forces the duty to act.

Turning now to whatever substance there might be in those presumed leaks. I see in them Brotherhood's desperate attempts to tarnish the legitimate El-Sisi administration. But even if those recordings were authentic, **their value seems to serve the present Egyptian administration.** For banter is a common sport in international relationships. **None of that banter amounted to serving personal needs, nor is it any** indication of selling Egypt short.

On the other hand, miles of such tapes can never amount to Brotherhood's callous underestimation of Egypt. **The Brotherhood's former Supreme Guide openly said "To Hell with Egypt" (Toz Fi Masr)!!** And the Brotherhood's agent, Morsi, allowed a participant in one of his conferences in November 2012 to call for war on Ethiopia in order to keep alive an outdated treaty on Nile water allocation. These were not secret recordings of doubtful authenticity. **The whole world heard them.**

By comparison, El-Sisi's greeting is **"Tahia Masr"** (Long Live Egypt). Then he, as the present leader of **"a strong Egypt,"** went to Ethiopia earlier this year. Starting a participatory **Pax Nilotica** between Addis, Khartoum and Cairo.

Well said, **Mr. Michael Morell,** the author of the recently published book **"The Great War of Our Time."** In an interview with **Charlie Rose** of PBS (Public Broadcasting System) on May 12, 2015, he was asked a question about Egypt. His answer was clear, short and illuminating.

**"Morsi was taking Egypt to ruins. El-Sisi's Egypt looks good for the future."**

To me, **Morell is more believable than Morsi and his hordes.** Morell was Deputy Director of the CIA under both Bush II and Obama. His task for decades was to be the first person every morning to have the ear of two presidents. Briefing them on facts and analysis relating to the state of the world.

**Mike Morell,** 53 years old, is still in play as possibly returning to the White House in 2016. That is regardless of who wins. The value of truth in reporting. **Hardly to be found within the ranks of the Brotherhood.**

# Kicking Arab Allies, Out of Their American Nest; To Fly On Their Own Wings, In Their Own Raging Tempest!!

Friday, May 22, 2015

The diagnosis is positive. And the symptoms keep on multiplying!!
- King Salman did not attend the Camp David Summit. America shrugs it off.
- ISIS retakes Ramadi. America: **"So What."**
- The Houthis attack Saudi territory from Saada. America: a big yawn.
- Netanyahu fulminates against a possible US/Iran deal. America: **"We are not there yet."**
- The Gulf might go nuclear. America: **"It cannot threaten us."**
- France is busy planning for a UN resolution in Palestine. America: **"Nothing to worry about."**
- Multi-Billion dollar contracts for armament from Europe to the Arabs. America: **"It is their money."**
- China and Russia are gaining influence in the Arab Middle East. America: **"Good Luck."**

The Obama administration has prepared America for a Hillary administration in 2016. It shall take a miracle to have a Republican President in 2016. And Barack is bequeathing to Hillary a solid new foreign policy framework for the US through at least 2020. No more American breast-feeding of the Arabs. In fact none to any others.

Back to the Future, America!! Back to President Washington's advice: **"No entangling alliances."** Well - How about the Monroe Doctrine of gunboat diplomacy in South America? No more. Obama buried it in Panama in April, 2015 at the Summit of the Americas. His Panama statement reflected the new principle of **"America First."**

As America reconciled with Cuba after 55 years of enmity and sanctions, Obama postulated a new global Obama doctrine. He said:
**"So often, when we insert ourselves in ways that go beyond persuasion, it's counterproductive; it backfires. That is why countries keep on trying to use us as an excuse for their own governance failures. Let's take away the excuse."**
Whether as an American you are a democrat, a republican, or an independent, this, in our age of chaos, makes sense. It has made sense for Canada and Scandinavia and the rest of Europe for a long time. How do we know? They are not a constant target for terror and adverse propaganda. Subject to hit and miss, yes. But we see no banners proclaiming, **"Death to Europe,"** or **"Canada is Satan,"** or **"Go Home Swedes."**

How does this apply to the Arabs? Plenty. Dependency on America is no longer acceptable. It is costly; America no longer needs Arab oil as it now produces 85% of its energy needs. **The U.S. of today is the new OPEC.** And none is going to challenge American naval supremacy guaranteeing the freedom of navigation. **The Arabs are free to sulk.** They have to do in defense and diplomacy with the precious little America can afford to give them.

This is clearly reflected in Obama's policy positions at the **Camp David Gulf Summit.** No strategic defense alliances or guarantees. The U.S. shall help on a case by case basis. The Arabs are neither Japan nor Israel. Washington shall offer arms and logistics. That is it. No American shall die fighting another war in the Middle East. And America shall select its own type of involvement in the war on terror.

These are not my views, nor are they my early warning signals. These are positions which are now in place. They are elucidated by those who have the ears of the Obama administration, and damn whatever the Republicans might scream about in opposition.

Clear demonstrations were offered early this week by **Robert Gates,** former CIA Director, and former Defense Secretary under both Bush II and Obama. Interviewed on May 19 on MSNBC, a progressive channel, here are selections of the questions by a panel and Gates responses:

**"Who created ISIS?" Answer: "The Syrian civil war and Maliki's sectarianism." "So why did the US, during your tenure, support Maliki for the post of Iraq's Prime Minister?" Answer: "Because we felt that his weakness will force him to work inclusively with all other sectors: Sunnis, Kurds, and Shiis. But when we left, he showed his true colors as an extreme Shii." "What are your expectations about the present turmoil in the Arab World?" Answer: "It shall go on for a very long time." "What is the expected outcome?" Answer: "Possibly the fate of Yugoslavia, especially as regards Syria and Iraq. These two are artificial States." "Whom should we support in the Arab World?" Answer: "Our traditional friends."**

Does this mean America is back to isolation? **No.** It means that America, while unburdening itself from the chaos in the Middle East, is finding in Asia, through trade, better alternatives. **It still regards itself as indispensable. Even in the absence of a coherent global policy.** So it is pivoting toward its interior, concerned about being number 24 in the world in infra-structure modernization. **Pivoting toward Asia and the Pacific is a part of the solution.**

In pivoting toward Asia and the Pacific, America shall not be too critical about issues of human rights in China or Russia. Its primary concerns are that its economic ranking might become number two after China's. And if America may appear weak to its detractors **(no US action on Assad crossing Obama's red lines),** the fact remains that America is still the only super power on the world stage. **Even with Putin not budging from his position on the Ukraine, or his schemes regarding Latvia.**

Its exercise of military power abroad shall be both limited and selective. Its number one priority is the **Trans Pacific Partnership (TPP).** Republican opposition to the TPP has been shredded. That opposition had nothing to do with the issue of American jobs. **It had to do with Republican hatred of China which, by all measures, is more than their hatred of Obama.**

America's ideology toward Europe has become at variance with that of Europe. **The difference lies mainly in America leaving the leadership role to Germany.** Thus America is lessening its emphasis on philosophical questions of how best to enhance human rights and how to boost the ideals of western democracy.

To America, the South China Sea has more priority economically than the North Sea. It is not even pre-occupied with the **possible break-up of the**

**United Kingdom.** On a bilateral basis, the number one priority for America is its relationships with China and India. The present framework of that relationship is **"the weaponization of trade and finance."** A freshly-minted American term.

How about the issues of the Gulf? America is now defanging its sanctions weapon everywhere. This has been done in the case of Cuba. **Iran's next.** But wouldn't this anger Saudi Arabia? Well, Washington's approach, as guided by the principle of **"America First,"** is to balance its relationships between Tehran and Riyadh.

**The expectation is a split between Washington and Riyadh.**
Washington seems now to be resigned to a greater Iranian role in Iraq, which is expected to see no Iraqi territorial unity. Washington sees in the recent fall of Ramadi again to ISIS, the advantage of Shii forces footprint. Better for America than US footprint.

**And what captivates America now about the New Egypt?** Cairo's activism in the economic reconstruction of the New Egypt; its persistent confrontation of terrorism in Sinai and the interior, and Western Sahara; and above all, El-Sisi's call for **"a religious revolution."** America regards that call as a possible turning point in the containment of jihadism.

**Hence the repeated criticism in America of the non-responsiveness by other Arab and Muslim States in support of a reinvigorated role by Al-Azhar to make that historic call a reality.**

Reflecting the behind the moment thinking, an Arab writer opines in an article from Paris a faulty advice on **"The Gulf-US Alliance."** Mr. **Mutaa Safadi** counsels: **"After the Camp David Summit, it is high time for Gulf leaders to liberate themselves from the bondage of friendship with America."** This happens to be the prevailing theme in Arab media. **It is a faulty theme because the only reality is the reverse. It is the U.S. which is now liberating itself from the bondage of a suffocating friendship with the Arabs.**

Iraq was a slow though huge turning point in that strategic change in America's outlook. An American analyst, **David Brooks,** puts it succinctly in his op. ed. column in the **New York Times** of May 19. Under the title of **"Learning from Mistakes,"** Brooks says: **"Iraq teaches us to be suspicious of leaders who try to force revolutionary, transformative change. It teaches us to have respect for trimmers, leaders who pay minute attention to context, who try to lead gradual but constant** change."

**This is a seismic shift in US strategy towards the unbrave new world.**
Watching it nearly daily, as I do, I find its birth certificate. **The year 2007.**
That is when I was in Iraq. Asking 4 marines at Camp Victory, separately:
**"What is your most cherished wish?"** Their answers were uniform.
**"Sir!!" "To go home!!"** It was not a yearning for simply going home.
Those were members of the best fighting machine in the world saying: **"I
am no longer for wars in the Middle East."**

Obama won his campaign of 2007 largely on this promise: **"I shall end
these wars!!"** It was a reformulation of: **"Our long national nightmare
is over!!"** A new patriotic American adage. Obama is satisfying those
marines' best held wish. **Semper Fi. "Always Loyal."** A marine oath.
Loyalty now is to **"America First."**

The Camp David Summit was the notarization of **"America shall no
longer fight the wars of others."** Even if Saudi Arabia might continue to
sulk. **The American bald eagle wants its nest all for itself.**

To some extent, the same applies to Israel. **Netanyahu** is frothing at the
mouth in anger. **His memory is dulled by his own anti-peace policies.**
Otherwise, he would have benefited by what **Hillary,** as Secretary of State,
told him about Iran. In effect, she is reported to convey to the Israelis: **"If
you strike Iran, we cannot help you."**

**Bad news for the Republicans.** That war party is out of touch. And
Hillary is expected to be the first female American president. **Semper Fi**
for **"America First."**

It is high time for the Arabs to see the writing on the wall.

Apparently Cairo has been ahead in deciphering that message. As of 2014,
it adopted El-Sisi's call for **"A Strong Egypt" (Al-Dawlah Al-
Qawiyyah).** Regardless of the carping of the under-educated Egyptian
media wondering in vain: **"What have we accomplished in two years!!"**
Leaning forward to steer the Egyptian ship across the **60-year old
cataracts takes time.**

Now is the time for the Arabs to abide by the wisdom of their great poem:
**"For Scratching Your Skin; The Best Tool is Your Finger Nail; For
none Can Mind Your Business; Like Yourself Minding Your Store!!"
(In Arabic: Ma Hakka Jildaka Methlo Zofrek; Fa Tawalla Anta**

**Jameea Amrek).**

# 13 JUNE 2015

## On The Freedom of Speech, There Are Two Models: Pope Francis and Pamela Geller

Friday, June 5, 2015

What a broad spectrum!! Between **Pope Francis** (Sky Above), and **Pamela Geller** (Mud Below). The two levels have to do with faith. The Islamic faith in the sanctity of Muhammad. And the Zionist faith in the sanctity of obfuscation.

Following the **Charlie Hebdo** massacre in January, Pope Francis was asked by reporters about his views. Seventeen people were killed at the satirical home of that magazine by two deranged Muslim brothers. Avenging the satirical cartoons about the Prophet Muhammad. So the Pope was asked about his views: **"Isn't the freedom of expression deserving of protection?"**

Here is Pope Francis' balanced response: **"Freedom of expression is a basic human right. But it had to be exercised without insulting the faith of others."** His Holiness did not stop at that. He is an Argentine, the first Latin American to be elected Pope. So in a gaucho (Argentine cowboy) style, he felt the need to be clear.

So he said: **"If a friend of mine speaks ill of my mother, he should be prepared to get a punch from me."** Then, in his white papal robes, he gestured with a closed fist as if he was delivering that punch.

To the startled reporters, Francis went on to amplify: **"This is natural. It is unacceptable to provoke others by insulting their beliefs. There are lots of people who speak ill of other religions. They are provocateurs."**

We now turn to a provocateur par excellence. Pamela Geller, a committed Zionist, with millions of dollars to spend on making Muslims and Arabs **"savages."** That was her chosen epithet. In all cars in the New York City subway system, a hate campaign was launched in 2014.

Posters placed by Geller for millions of subway riders to read. The posters, in effect, proclaimed: **"If there is a conflict between the civilized and the savage, support the civilized. Support Israel."**

The Muslim community tried hard to get the administration of Michael Bloomberg, the then Mayor of New York City, to get these hate posters removed. **But in vain.**

The New York City executive claimed that that was **"protected speech."** It is not. And it is not I who is judging it as **"unprotected speech."** It is the U.S. Constitution and U.S. case law that say so. The theory of **"speech regulation based on content"** is abundantly clear.

That non-controverted constitutional theory imposes speech regulation under the principle of public law and order. Thus regulation comes in through the door of **"Inciting Imminent Lawless Action."** Its legal formulation is as follows:

**"Speech can be burdened if it creates a clear and present danger of imminent lawless action. It must be shown that imminent illegal conduct is likely, and that the speaker intended to cause it."**

**Pamela Geller** is calling Arabs and Muslims and others opposed to Israeli practices **"savage."** In both fact and effect, she has intentionally engaged in **"inciting imminent lawless action,"** and got away with it. Her unprotected speech is not only **"unconstitutional."** It is an anti-American act which exposes the country to retaliation.

But **"non-adjudicated felons"** like Pam Geller have a habit of revisiting the scene of their crimes. In early May of this year, Geller did just that. Propelled by her millions of dollars, she struck again. Goading Muslim extremists in the U.S. and abroad, she ventured into Texas. This is a State where one of its two Senators, Ted Cruz, a Republican now running for President in 2016, is calling for having U.S. troops re-invade Iraq.

Using her freedom to engage in unprotected speech, Geller took her organization **"The American Freedom Defense Initiative" (AFDI)** to Garland, Texas. Described by **The New York Times** as **"an anti-Islam organization based in New York,"** the Geller organization was organizing an anti-Islamic event. It included **a contest for the best caricature of the Prophet Muhammad, with a $10,000 top prize.**

Now with Pam Geller back to her criminal forays, so were two irate Muslims who, on May 3, shot at a security officer guarding the **Curtis Culwell Center.** That is where the Muhammad vilification event was held by AFDI. Both assailants were shot and killed by Garland police officers in response. Material evidence of what Geller's American Freedom Defense Initiative can accomplish in the service of unprotected hate speech.

Our age is one of rage. Facts are few; knowledge is even less; and comprehension is dulled by retrograde educational systems, especially in the Arab and Muslim worlds.

In the midst of these overwhelming contradictions, especially as regards to freedom of expression, let us take a tally of these contradictions. Learning begins with a listing of easily recognizable episodes. And episodes are more assimilable when put in contrasting positions.

- Geller calls the Arabs and the Muslims **"savages."** And Hamas denies Israel the mere right of existence.
- Netanyahu has just appointed **Dore Gold** to his ultra-right cabinet. Born in Connecticut, USA, Gold's **Jerusalem Center for Public Affairs** opposes Israeli withdrawal form the occupied West Bank. Saeb Erekat, the so-called **"Chief Palestinian negotiator"** calls that appointment **"an internal Israeli matter."** How muted can you get?
- Compare Erekat's utterance with those of Israeli pundits denouncing those appointments as **"farcical or worse."** In the meantime, one of Gold's six published books is entitled: **Hatred's Kingdom: How Saudi Arabia Supports the New Global Terrorism.** Isn't occupation a casus belli?
- The New York Muslims could not assert a legal claim against Geller's Islamophobic campaign. Yet **The American Civil Liberties Union (ACLU)** instituted in August 2013 a suit against the New York Police Department (NYPD) on behalf of Muslims.

The suit challenged the constitutionality of the NYPD **"Muslim Surveillance Program."**

- Compare this action on behalf of Muslims, with Geller's mouthing off about Islam. She shrieks on TV shows that **"Islam is the problem,"** and **"stand up for free speech."**
- As a committed ideologue, Geller does not differentiate between ISIS and the broad demographics of Muslims. Closer home where she stands, she does not differentiate between Judaism, a recognizable faith, and Zionism, a political ideology of assertive territorial claims. In late May, the new Deputy Foreign Minister **Tzipi Hotovely** counseled the diplomatic corps. He advised that they **"should use the Bible as a tool for telling the world that the entire land between the Mediterranean Sea and the Jordan River belongs to the Jews." (The New York Times, May 26, 2015)**
- Mixing faith with politics puts such declarations at par with those of Muslim extremists and committed terrorists. The new Egypt is engaged in a new revolution, a **"Religious Revolution."** Under the leadership of Al-Azhar, the term **"jihad"** is being redefined in textbooks. **In accordance with the notion of accepting the other.** Israel's new leadership is opting for a greater Israel dressed in a religious garb.

In today's world of rage and non-sensical assumptions, only the course of putting yourself in the shoes of the other shall ultimately prevail. Hate mongers, and those who do not see the other in their midst as equals and deserving, are doomed to failure.

That is why Pope Francis represents **"The Sky Above,"** while Pamela Geller stands for **"The Mud Below."** No wonder that the **Holy See** has just recognized **"The State of Palestine."** For Francis is a peace recruiter. Geller is a jihadi enabler.

Other jihadi enablers, though perhaps unwittingly, are:
- Netanyahu's advocacy of the elimination of the 2-State solution of the Israeli-Palestinian conflict;
- Republicans campaigning for the US presidency, calling for **"slipping a State of Palestine into Egyptian territory;"**
- **The Likud** characterization of criticism of Israeli practices in the occupied territories as efforts for the delegitimation of Israel;
- **Hamas** denial of the right of Israel to exist within agreed borders;
- **The holocaust deniers.** They are worse than history fabricatiors. Because they are blind to a human calamity which, among other things, changed the entire history of the Middle East and beyond.

*As in the mold of Pam Geller, such calls are grist for the ISIS mill of barbarism and obfuscation. In spite of the chaos now gripping the Middle East, the use of religion for political ends, or as a cover for hate, shall have very limited shelf life.*

# Studying American-Arab Relationships From Unexpected Angles. This Time It Is the American Supreme Court on Jerusalem

Friday, June 12, 2015

America is complex. Because it speaks with thousands of voices. Voices that come from myriad of sources. Not necessarily from the Oval office or the Pentagon or the State Department. **Voices also from the American street.**

Because I live and work in America, I study American-Arab relationships. Especially those with one-third of the Arab world which call themselves **Egypt.** One or two hours a day of such study are enough. I have other things to do.

Consequently, I was struck by a most important piece of news on **June 9.** The thundering voice of the U.S. Supreme Court on the explosive question of Jerusalem. I am a member of the Bar of that august Court. But was unaware of the case against **Secretary of State John Kerry** which reached the Court through an appeal by **Mr. and Mrs. Zivotofsky** on behalf of their son **Menachem.**

These are American Israeli citizens, who wanted the U.S. passport of their son, who was born 13 years ago in Jerusalem, to reflect Menachem's place of birth. They wanted that passport notation to say **"Place of Birth: Israel."** And the American Supreme Court, by a majority of 6 to 3, said **"No."** Answering why, is the heart of this blog posting. It also reveals the importance of systematic study of American-Arab relationships, especially from unexpected angles. For the sake of knowledge. And knowledge is power.

The case **Zivotofsky v. Kerry** is all about the power of the U.S. President, under the Constitution, to recognize foreign governments. In defiance of that presidential power, Congress in 2003 had adopted a politically-based law.

That law instructed the State Department to **"record the place of birth as Israel"** in the passports of American children born in Jerusalem. Of course providing that their parents requested that designation. That is in spite the fact that since Ben Gurion declared Israel a State in 1948, no American president has ever issued a declaration acknowledging any country's sovereignty over Jerusalem.

This is evidenced by the fact that the U.S. embassy for Israel is **still located in Tel Aviv, not in Jerusalem.** That was the principal argument before the Supreme Court by the U.S. Solicitor General, Donald Verrilli, in the case of **Zivotofsky v. Kerry.**

The Solicitor General characterized the neutrality of the U.S. Government in regard to the status of Jerusalem as **"prudent."** Why? Because the issue has been **"the most vexing and volatile and difficult diplomatic issue that this nation has faced for decades."**

For listing **"Israel"** as the place of a birth which happened in Jerusalem would have negative effects for the system of governance in the U.S. The most important would be subjecting the Presidential powers of **foreign States recognition** to a Congressional act violative of those powers.

This is the heart of the U.S. Constitutional system **-separation of powers.** The status of Jerusalem and the U.S. recognition of Israel as a State are two separate issues in which the powers of the President are supreme. Recognition of the State of Israel is an active application of presidential power. Recognition of Jerusalem as **"Israel"** is a negative application of that power.

For that reason, **U.S. neutrality toward the status of Jerusalem** has nothing to do with America's strategic relationships with the State of Israel. A unique distinction which the Arabs, especially in Ramallah, should comprehend. Mixing between these issues is like mixing palm dates with desert pebbles.

Looking at the arguments of the Supreme Court's majority of 6 to 3 is immensely instructive for issue-spotting and issue-analysis.
- The Court is divided between liberals and conservatives. The liberal wing consists of **Justices Breyer, Ginsburg, Sotomayor, and Kegan** (the last three are women). In this judgment, that

liberal wing was joined by **Justice Kennedy** (known as **the swing vote;** he wrote the opinion). Unexpectedly, those 5 votes were joined by **Justice Thomas,** a die-hard conservative. The dissenting justices were **Roberts, the Chief Justice, Scalia and Alito.**

- In support of dismissing the Zivotofsky's claim, the six justices affirmed that **"the power of recognition"** rested exclusively with the President. It cited Article II of the Constitution, case precedents, and historical practice **"from the first administration (of George Washington) going forward."**
- That was not all. The Court also struck down the provocative law of 2003. By doing so, the Supreme Court stressed another related principle that had to do with the unity of **"the American Nation."** It said that:

**(i)** the president has **"the exclusive power to recognize foreign nations and governments;"**

**(ii)** the President alone could **"receive ambassadors,"** an indication of recognition of the sovereignty of the sending State; and

**(iii)** only the President could have **"the characteristic of unity at all times"** as it was **"necessary for the Nation to speak with one voice with respect to recognition."**

That is the beauty of the separation of powers. It should also be noted that the judicial power in the Zivotofsky decision did accomplish a historic task: shredding the **Foreign Relations Authorization Act (FRAA).** Here the Court, **while not in any way deciding the future status of Jerusalem or the territorial outcome of the Arab-Israeli conflict,** blocked the back door for a creeping recognition that Israel and Jerusalem were one single issue.

There is a plaintive tone in **Chief Justice Roberts'** opposition to the Zivotofsky decision. He said: **"Today's opposition is a first. Never before has this Court accepted a president's direct defiance of an act of Congress in the field of foreign affairs."**

Of course that is indicative of the tilt to the right in the highest court in America. For here again, **Roberts** is acting as a spokesman for what **President Woodrow Wilson** was warning against: **Congressional government.**

The majority found fault with that position. It upheld the argument for exclusive presidential powers in the conduct of foreign affairs. That was the constitutional side of the coin.

Relying on long practice since 1948, the Executive, in its brief, told the Court: US policy since Harry Truman's presidency **"has been to recognize no State as having sovereignty over Jerusalem, leaving the issue to be decided by negotiation between the parties to the Arab-Israeli dispute."**

At this point, I go back to what this blog advocates: **Studying American-Arab relationships, not only from the conventional angles. But also from the unexpected ones.** Here are examples of what the Arabs have so far ignored as sources of knowledge about America. A country which is in constant change:

- In early June, the U.S. Supreme Court ruled for the **right of a Muslim woman to wear her hijab in public.** This is contrary to the legal position adopted by major European countries. **Zahra Sheema,** a Pakistani lawyer of 25 years of age was denied a job by the company **Abercrombie and Fitch.** The Court ruled that that company had violated a federal ban on religious discrimination. The decision, said the **New York Times "elevated the profile of Muslim women and the challenges some face when they choose to cover their heads as a sign of piety."**

- The primary issue in the presidential elections of 2016 are **the inequality of economic fortunes within American society.** It goes by the name of **"the income gap."** The democrats are accusing the republicans of focusing on the top 1% of the population (the super rich). The republicans are countering by saying that the democrats are class-minded and are dividing the nation. They call Obama **"the divisive President."**

- **Hillary Clinton** is shifting to the left as she battles for the Oval Office. This is while all of the slate of 18 republican hopefuls are appealing to their base in white conservative and evangelical circles.

- America is fast becoming a nation where 45% of its population are **minorities from non-white countries.** Wouldn't be smart for the Arabs to learn how to influence America through cultivating positive relationships with the mother countries from which those minorities have hailed?

- The free trade agreement, on which Obama had worked so hard, **was defeated today in Congress (June 12). Not by his opponents, the republicans,** but by his own party -the **democrats.** A big defeat for the president for whom June 12 was a bad day. **It was due to fears from the labor unions, the back bone of the democratic party.** This is a major defeat for globalization and the shift toward Asia inflicted by U.S. Congress. Ironically, it was the democrats who had originally lobbied for that bill called the **Trade Adjustment Assistance (TAA) bill!!** Thus it makes sense for those studying U.S.-Arab relations to study those relations not only from the top level of American decision-makers. But also from the grass roots level **-the labor unions.** The America of today is a super power which is largely focused on **JOBS!!** Not different from Egypt and the rest of the Arab world.

- Of course the new Egypt should take note, for whatever it is worth, of the **U.S. administration's report on Egypt to Congress dated June 8.** While ignoring the long history of American support for the Mubarak regime, the report represents the new Egypt from a **dogmatic angle.** It says, without due reference to Egypt's war on terror, **"the overall trajectory for rights and democracy has been negative."**

- But the same report presents also a **pragmatic facet** of the new Egypt. It credits Egypt with beginning to overhaul its economy **"by cutting subsidies, increasing taxes and improving the business climate including for U.S. businesses."**

- So the Egyptian media, rather than howling about **"intervention in our internal affairs,"** should also analyze that routine statutory report from its most unexpected angle!! What is that? It is that **"Egypt's success or failure impacts the prospects of peace, stability, democracy and economic growth across the Middle East."** The very language of that report.

Time for the Arabs to study their relationships with America from its unexpected angles. As I said above, **"America is complex."** A reason why I like what **Ambassador Abdel-Raouf El-Reedy** has recently advocated in an article in **Al-Ahram** newspaper.

That experienced diplomat and scholar, **the honorary chairman of the Egyptian Council for Foreign Affairs,** has called for the formation of study groups to track the arguments and the developments of the on-coming competition for the Oval Office between democrats and republicans. An angle which should take the Arab thinking about America **"out of the box."**

**Income inequality and student loans (a trillion dollars) in America, not the sanctions on Russia, shall hold sway in the competition between the party of war** (the republicans) and the party for **"the little people" (the democrats).** The republicans are expected to lose. They have no policy on economic opportunity. The old party of Lincoln is now the party of the rich. And republican Senator **John McCain,** that old war horse, is now chairman of the Senate Armed Services Committee. With an annual military budget of more than **$600 billions.** In a country tired of war.

**McCain,** a former prisoner of war, is opposing Obama's advocacy of closing Guantanamo.  **If only closed minds came with closed mouths!!**

No reason under the sun for me to vote in 2016 for a republican president.  The competition is now intensifying.  In my mailbox, I find an electioneering pamphlet from the democratic party.  It is titled **"Will the Koch Brothers' billions decide the next election?  It's up to you!"**

This is an allusion to another unexpected angle for studying America.  A few years ago, the **U.S. Supreme Court** decided that money is free speech.  The case was **Citizens United**.  A terrible setback for democracy.  For it allowed the rich to pour unlimited funds in support of their favored electoral candidates.  The American rich is pouring zillions of dollars to support the party of the rich -the Republican Party.

*As an American citizen, I choose to remain unattached to either party.  But my vote in 2016 shall go to Hillary.  And as an Egyptian, I voted in 2014 for El-Sisi.  Nice to have the best of the two worlds.  Two worlds which should get to know each other in more effective ways.  Particularly from unexpected angles.*

# The Youssef Al-Qaradawi Phenomena As Measured By the Scales of Egyptophobia
Friday, June 19, 2015

How can one person represent more than one phenomenon, so as to become phenomena?  It is possible if you are **Youssef Al-Qaradawi.  No title of Sheikh.**  He does not live up to that lofty standard.  Sheikh means Islamic scholar.

He is a graduate of Al-Azhar, the citadel of moderate Islam.  Now expelled from its ranks.  He was born in Egypt, thus an Egyptian citizen by birth.  But has now been denied that citizenship.  He is supposed to be a man of faith and peace.  Yet he is on the lam, hiding from the arm of Egyptian laws on terrorism and tucked away in Qatar.  In fact, he was recently tried in absentia in Egypt and is now under a death sentence.

**What happened?** In late 2012, during the one year of Islamic oppressive rule in Egypt, he was offered the rare accolade of preaching from the pulpit of Al-Azhar. A true Muslim Brotherhood voice of doom. When the Egyptian masses rose up in a companion revolution on June 30, 2013, **Youssef Al-Qaradawi,** once more, fled into the open arms of Qatar. Another pair of open arms were awaiting this turbaned man of 85 years of age -his Moroccan bride, who is six decades his junior.

Youssef Al-Qaradawi heads a shell organization, **"The Global Union of Muslim Scholars" (GUMS).** I could not find GUMS origins, nor where it was chartered, nor its organigram, nor its mission statement. **Nor how Youssef Al-Qaradawi has become the head of that shadowy corporation.** What I found was a Qaradawi call for violence in Egypt to avenge the deposition of the Morsi regime in July 2013.

The Qaradawi call for insurrection was adorned by its inclusion in a public manifesto. Outwardly impressive. Practically hollow. Bearing the signatures of what is claimed to be 150 **"scholars and preachers."** What does this Qaradawi manifesto call for?

**"Revenge should be enacted. Against all decision-makers; judges; army and police officers and other personnel; all those who issue fatwas (religious interpretation of the Quran and of Muhammad traditions); media people; politicians."** Not many were left off that death list.

In the name of GUMS, the crazy Qaradawi manifesto has a no escape clause. It even adds on: **"And everyone who might have participated, or conspired or abetted in the..."**

Here the manifesto dips below the belt. In it, there is also the standard charge of **"defiling the honor of women, spilling of innocent blood, and snuffing the lives of their victims without legal sanction of Sharia."** The non-Sheikh Al-Qaradawi resorts to the scare tactic of: All of you secularists are going to hell!!

Advocating for mayhem in Egypt is the heart of that manifesto issued in late May 2015. Posted on the Internet as **"Nida Al-Kinaneh"** by Qaradawi's blood brothers, that **"Nida"** could be translated in two ways: **"The Call from Paradise,"** or **"The Call for Egypt."** Take your pick. Its presumed 150 scholars from 20 countries (what happened to the rest of the membership of the Organization of Islamic Cooperation of 57 States?) grandly tweets: **"This is our faith. These are our scholars."** I am a bit relieved that he called his cabal **"our"** not **"your"** scholars.

The **"faith"** and **"the scholarship"** of Al-Qaradawi **GUMS** call El-Sisi Administration the **"result of a military coup in Egypt in 2013."** This administration, the Qaradawi manifesto claims, is **"a criminal gang which, by deposing the Morsi rule, subverted the popular will of the Nation."**

Now which **"Nation"** is Al-Qaradawi talking about? And what rule of Islamic jurisprudence is he calling on? And on what legal Islamic premise is he basing **his idiotic fatwa on?** And what credibility does he have, being a well paid agent by a foreign power -**Qatar?**

- Like his parent organization, **the Muslim Brotherhood,** Al-Qaradawi regards Egypt, **not as a sovereign State.** But **as an Emirate** within the broad expanse of the Muslim Nation of 1.5 billion people.
- **Like ISIS and Al-Qaeda and Al-Nusra and Boko Haram,** national borders do not exist. To them, Islam is a nationality whose precepts are defined in terms of excluding all other faiths. The Copts of Egypt; Christians of Lebanon; Jews of Morocco; Indians of Pakistan, have no equal rights in these Muslim societies. Why? **They are non-Muslims!!**
- So are the Shiis. Whether in Iran or Iraq or Syria or Yemen or Lebanon, or Egypt. **"Sunnism Uber Alles." "Sunnism is above all."** a historic Nazi odious call.
- How about the **will of 35 million Egyptians** who rose up on June 30, 2013 demanding an end to the Islamic dictatorship **(a veritable coup)** of the Brotherhood? No, says Al-Qaradawi and his cohorts. Only the call from the Muslim Brotherhood minarets are the authentic voice of the people.

So historically secular Egypt had to strike back.

- The Minister for Religious Affairs, **Dr. Mokhtar Gomaa,** called for adding GUMS and its putative president, Youssef Al-Qaradawi to the list of terrorist organizations. A justifiable addition to the listing of the Muslim Brotherhood as a **"terrorist organization."**
- The Egyptian Fatwa Administration described the Qaradawi manifesto as **"a desperate attempt to destabilize Egypt."** Its **"Observatory of Extremism"** cited that call for a coup in Egypt as **"FASAD."** Translated from the Arabic as **"corruption."** But in Islamic jurisprudence, FASAD is the Number One criminal offense.
- **Condemnation of FASAD occurs in 50 verses in the Quran.**

Spread over no less than 25 Chapters in a total of 114 Chapters.
**"The Observatory"** cited several of these verses accusing Al-
Qaradawi and his cabal of FASAD.

- Including: **"... do not work corruption on the earth, after it has
been set right. This is better for you if you are believers."
(Chapter VII; Verse 85). The weight of Quranic
condemnation of FASAD is seen from making it tantamount
to "insurrection" and "mayhem."**

From an Islamic perspective, these are the acids that dissolve the social
contract between government and society. Thus the Quran assigns for it
capital punishment as a deterrent.

At this juncture, the war within the Muslim world is on several fronts. It is
between Islam as a faith and Islam as a cover for hate and terrorism.
Calling the latter **"extreme Islam"** is a misnomer. **It is a labelling error.**
Akin to calling the crusaders **"extreme Christianity."**

There is no such thing. Crusaderism was an acute military-religious
conflict. Raising the Cross, a symbol of love, in the way ISIS raises the
black banner emblazoned with **"God Is Great and Muhammad Is His
Prophet."** A flag of butcherism, barbarity and a **hocus-pocus Caliphate.**
With **Abu-Bakr Al-Baghdadi,** a thug from Anbar, as its head.

The terrorist phalanxes have an ideological auxiliary. In the latter category
falls **Al-Qaradawi and his minions of GUMS (The Global Union of
Muslim Scholars).** Their danger to world peace and to Islam is more
lasting. Because it is an insidious slow-acting weapon of brainwashing.
**With the Goebbels effect of recruitment.** You can bomb ISIS. You
cannot cleanse sick minds by military means.

Al-Qaradawi is now being confronted in Egypt head-on by **"the Religious
Revolution."** Called for by El-Sisi with implementation by Al-Azhar. **The
Arab summit of Sharm El-Sheikh** of late March 2015 provided a historic
endorsement.

The battle against Al-Qaradawi **"Helter-Skelter"** (with nominal apology to
madman **Charlie Manson**) has begun. Its starting point is logical -
**revamping textbooks.** All references to exclusion of **"the other,"** and to
defining Jihad as a broad lawless battle by self-appointed free lancers are
being expunged.

By the end of May, **Al-Azhar, together with the Egyptian ministries of
Education and Religious Affairs (AWKAF),** joined by specialists in

173

various fields, were ready to welcome El-Sisi. It was on May 27, 2015 that **Al-Azhar's Rector, Imam Ahmed Al-Taiyeb,** was ready to share with the Egyptian President the blue print for the counter-attack against ISIS, **its franchises and its enablers like Qaradawi and his GUMS.**

For the first time we now have 13 recommendations for that counter-attack. They begin by the defining **"the Religious Discourse."** It says: **"Its cleansing from superstitions and misconceptions which are counter the mission of Islam: Its tolerance, humanity, common sense, care for the common interest of humanity in accordance with changing circumstances. In service of country without infringement of other faiths or beliefs of established moral codes."**

No wonder that **Leon Pannetta, former US CIA Director and Defense Secretary,** had this to say in Cairo on May 28, 2015: **"Having met with President El-Sisi and members of the cabinet, I regard all efforts to support Egypt's counter-terrorism efforts are deserving of unremitting support."**

So, Mr. Al-Qaradawi, **get a life.** You and GUMS, in your vain attempts to gum-up the new **"Religious Revolution,"** are heading for the garbage can of history. **So is your Egyptophobia.**

Like in the case of the Muslim Brotherhood, the Qaradawi ideology seems to fit better with a theme song in an Egyptian comic TV soap opera. **Zohra,** a beautiful young Tunisian woman, is the screen name of its star. In the title role of **"Zohra and Her Five Husbands."** Per my translation, the first verses bemoan Zohra's fate:

*"Going through the ocean of my life; dreaming of finding a landing!!*
*And see the day of deliverance; from afar a distant line!!*
*From the day of wading in the ocean of life; have never found safety!!*
*All my life episodes; start with ecstasy!!*
*But never even once; their ending is not a catastrophe."*

# In the Yemen War: It Is Not Sunni vs. Shii!! It

# Is Tribalism vs. The National State Concept

Friday, June 26, 2015

It could be very confusing. There is only one way to steer clear from the entanglement of the multiple cobwebs of historical layers.

With this said, let us avoid the facile characterization of the Yemen war. **Sunni vs. Shii reflects a mental fatigue which tries to quickly package Islam as two kinds.** Sunni and Shii is like having two sons, **Omar and Ali.** Or two daughters, **Aisha and Fatima.** The resilience of Islam lies in its simplicity, together with its unreserved acceptance of other faiths. **Strange? Not at all.** The Jihadi dictionary has infected our understanding of Islam and of Islamic jurisprudence.

Back to the war in Yemen. **Utter confusion about its genesis.** Not only in official policies. But also in media confirmation of the errors of these policies. This is especially so in Arab media, which **in most cases lack research, public opinion polls, presence at the fields of battle, and writing creativity** which asserts the truth of opinion, not the durability of ascertained facts.

What we have in Yemen today is what we had in Yemen yesterday. The tribal flag flies higher than the national flag.

**I was in Yemen from 1999 to 2001.** Commissioned by both the World Bank and the Government of Yemen to do a field study. It was on legal and judicial reform and how to enhance the capacity of the two twin areas. The study was done; some of its recommendations were implemented.

It is impossible to judge the pulse of any polity or political environment, especially without physical field experiences. Get the pulse of the patient, not from a chart. But from being physically with the patient -with the subject.

So in order to bestow credibility on my arguments below, in regard to the present Yemen war, I feel the need to cite other field experiences with Arab areas of armed conflict.

In **Algeria** during the war of independence in the early sixties, as UN spokesman. In **Syria,** in 1962, to assess for the UN the status of the United Arab Republic. In July of that year, I predicted collapse. In September it

175

did collapse.  In 1964 in **Gaza,** to assess the status of peace-keeping under the command of my able Indian friend, **general Rikhe.**

In the mid-70's, lecturing at New York University on counter-insurgency.  And much later, commissioned by the U.N. Security Council in 2006 for a mission in **Darfour,** the Sudan.

Why is this personal recitation of relevance to the present war in **Yemen?**  It confirms a non-changing fact about inter-Arab conflicts.  **Lack of recognition of their cultural under-pinnings.**

In most Arab areas, war and politics reflect various shades of tribalism.  The cohesive national State **(the Egyptian model)** is still on the way.  Let us look at Yemen:

- The movement of the **Houthis is a North vs. South.  Shii v. Sunni is pure rubbish.**  Islam does not come in two flavors or two packages: One marked Sunni; the other marked Shii.  **Imam Ali,** on whom I am now authoring a book in Arabic, was neither Sunni nor Shii.  He was simply the **First Muslim; the foster child of his cousin, the Prophet Muhammad.**
- The South **(Aden) is progressive.**  The North **(Sanaa)** is a museum for the middle ages.
- In the south, you find **women judges on the bench.**  In the north, you cannot serve litigation papers on someone.  There are **no addresses outside of Sanaa.**  To help the Yemeni prosecutorial system, I recommended a simple system for the problem of serving court notices:  **Provide bicycles or donkeys** for the server, and a guide from the tribal area.  It worked.
- In the north, the Emirates built up the Supreme Court in Sanaa, with **"Lady Justice"** symbol on top.  It was shot down by a Kalashnikov held up to its head by a tribesman.  **He did not like a judgment issued against him.**
- In the south, I found **courts ruling for a Spanish mother to have her son back.**  His father, a German, had kidnapped him and fled to Aden after pretending to adopt Islam.  Some one had told him: If you adopt Islam, no court in an Islamic country would ever rule for the return of a son to his Christian mother.  The court ruled against the so so Muslim father, stating: **"Dad adopted Islam as a cover for a crime!!"**  The Spanish mother returned back to Spain clutching the hand of her son.
- From the north, **Yemenis immigrate to Saudi Arabia for work,** handing their passports to a Saudi **"Kafeel."**  Without the consent of that Kafeel, the worker cannot leave, **even if the employer is**

**oppressive.** In the south, there are syndicates and labor unions. Protecting fair employer-worker contractual relationships. Observing the rules of the UN-related International Labor Organization (ILO).

- **In the north, Al-Qaeda thrives.** It, like ISIS, lives by the oxygen of tribalism and unevolved sunnism. In the south, your identity, as a southern Yemeni national, trumps Islamism in case of conflict.

Yemenis, until recently, have been the most preferred laborers in Saudi Arabia. They are not only neighbors. They are very focused workers. The **Bin Laden Construction Company,** now based in Saudi Arabia, had its origin in **Hadramaut, southern Yemen.** The souring of relationships between Saudi Arabia and Yemen is **due to political, not religious reasons.**

**Where does Egypt stand in the face of these controversies?**

Riyadh had opposed Nasser's intervention in the Yemen revolt against the imamate in 1962. **It was the gravest mistake of the Nasser rule** -the use of Egypt's huge armed forces to prop up a nascent republic. It signalled the beginning of the decline of Nasserism, which became **more of a memory than a movement.**

For millennia, Egypt has been a security State. Stability is its base. Just look at the Pyramids: twin symbols for State and for stability. A basic premise for understanding Egypt. A premise grossly misunderstood by the Muslim Brotherhood resulting in their collapse.

Within this unalterable framework, the call by **President El-Sisi** for Egypt becoming **"a strong State"** resonates with the country's cherished history.

The present buildup of the Egyptian navy reflects a basic concern for the security of the very long Egyptian coastline. Stretching from **El-Salloum** near the Libyan border, to **Rafah** on the Mediterranean, then looping south to the Sudanese border on the Red Sea.

By this August, with the inauguration of the second Suez Canal, 85% of the world trade between the Americas, Europe and Afro-Asia will transit Egypt. Transit fees are expected to surpass tourism revenue.

The exit from the southern Red Sea to the Indian ocean is at **Aden (Bab El-Mandab).** Threatening it, whether by the Houthis or other parties, is a security threat to the Suez expanded regime. An unacceptable challenge to Egypt's transitioning to prosperity. This is a primary reason for Egypt being in the **Arab coalition led by Saudi Arabia.** The aim is to slow down the Houthis surge beyond Sanaa to **Aden and Al-Hodaiyedah,** both ports on the southern Red Sea.

But there shall be no Egyptian footprint in Yemen. **Not again!!** And the framework for the new Arab defense force, which is being constructed by the League of Arab States, is both defensive and voluntary. The new axis between Egypt, Jordan and the Gulf, as led by Saudi Arabia, is a reflection, not of ideology, but of common defense interests. Its present front is Yemen. Its other fronts are left to be managed by each Arab country on its own.

The **Houthis, Shiis of the north, are not Iran's agents. Nor are the Sunnis of Aden Saudi catpaws.** The two parts of Yemen were united through war in 1994. They were never united in one common nationalism.

**Saleh,** ruled over a republic held together by the equivalent of scotch tape. **A dictator (a Shii)** who played the sectarian game for his own end - **dictator forever.** With the help of the hurricane of the Arab Spring. **The Gulf Cooperation Council** mediated his peaceful departure, and a successor, **Hadi (a southern Sunni)** was installed in his place.

**But leaving Saleh in Yemen was a big mistake.** The snake moves. Saleh, was still moving to undo what he had ostensibly accepted. So the Houthi resurgence was propelled by: southern agitation for separation; the Iran/Saudi Arabia rivalry for preeminence in the Gulf; the general chaos of the sputtering Arab Spring in Syria, and Libya; and **the rise of the fiction of Sunni vs. Shii, resuscitated by the disastrous US invasion of Iraq in 2003.**

In **Tehran,** there is a false sense of **triumphalism.** Very short-sighted. The same spirit pervades the **Ordogan regime in Turkey,** presumably on behalf of Sunni Islam. That is until the Kurds, now in the Turkish parliament, put the brakes on Ordoganism. Its retreat has begun. Or so it seems!!

In the Middle East, there are crazy notions amounting to what I may call **"religious imperialism;" ethnic imperialism; and ideological imperialism.**

Examples of **"religious imperialism" are the calls for internationalizing Mecca and Medina.** These are iconic cities within Saudi territory wherein lies the holiest of Islamic shrines. **Same calls by**

**Iran in respect of Karbala, Najaf and Kufa.** Iraqi territory wherein lies holy Islamic locations, especially revered by the Shiis.

**"Ethnic imperialism"** was manifest in Saddam laying false claims to **"Khozistan"** (Arabistan), Iranian territory. Iraqi maps of the 1980s showed the boundaries of Iraq jumping over the Gulf into that **Abadan area** of Iran.

**"Ideological hegemony"** applies to Turkey's support of the murderous ideology of the Muslim Brotherhood. **The mother lode of jihadism in Egypt and beyond.**

**So what are the lessons to be learnt from the present Yemen war?**
The war is not a Sunni vs. Shii conflict. It is the tribalized north versus the politically-developed south.
Regardless of the outcome of that war, Yemen is most likely to split again into Yemen and Southern Yemen.
The Arab coalition of the willing is a reassertion of Arabism vs. Iranian and Turkish transnational assertions.
Thus talk and policy are now about **"The Arab Nation."** Unified militarily on a voluntary basis, and culturally, as a riposte to both Turkish and Iranian espousal of causes which go beyond their geographic boundaries.
*The Houthis are not putting their Arabism as a door mat for Tehran.*
*Like in Afghanistan, the Houthis find in endless war a tenured contract. If they lose today, there will always be a tomorrow.*
*Tribalism shall always be alive and well in Yemen's great strategically-located geographic space.*

# 14 JULY 2015

## In the Global War On Jihadism, May God Save Egypt Also From Its So-Called Journalism

Friday, July 10, 2015

I asked a veteran guru of Egyptian journalism, Mr. Galal Dowidar, formerly the editor of **Al-Akhbar** of Cairo. **"Why is today's standard so debased?"** His answer was: **"After the two revolutions of January and June, they have no material."** An honest and crisp response.

Now that anti-terrorism has been **declared by Prime Minister Mahlab as war,** it is time for another revolution. **A Public Information Revolution.** Based on an enforceable code. Its aim is to create a credible civilian face for the Sinai war. Its components are: In depth research; credible evidence; deep penetration of Egyptian society; teach-ins on anti-jihadism; recruiting youth as intern reporters; putting national security ahead of the ingrained Egyptian desire to be funny; and becoming a tool of mass mobilization. **Other components: When to publish. And when to shut up.**

The army, the police, other security institutions, the judiciary, the executive of all branches, **Al-Azhar and the Coptic Church,** and all other educational institutions are all participants in weeding out terrorism.

**For the Information Revolution is primarily an ideological response** to the massive online rubbish spewing out daily from the **Brotherhood/ISIS franchises.** In essence, those cabals are reminders of the **"Wizard of Oz."** Fear is artificially generated by a mad person turning the wheel of panic. From behind **the black curtain of a mythical caliphate.**

With selected targets, foreign or laundered internal funds, captured war materiel, and video games reflecting barbarism, they have aimed at **employing fear hypnosis.** Encircled from the outside and from within, the jihadists keep alive **the myth of invincibility.**

They have no future. **Terrorism has never established a State.** Anywhere, Islamic or non-Islamic. Putting up a sign and receiving endorsements **(they call these Baiaa)** are mere props for the theater of the absurd. **Butcherism combined with "jihadi fornication"** are in-stock tools. For them, Islam is a convenient cover for genocide.

Assassinating **Egypt's Attorney-General Hisham Barakat.** Detonating deadly charges against the Sinai army defenders. Using Bedouin grievances as incentives. These are all proof of one verity: Jihadi forces of various stripes, including the Brotherhood, have coalesced. **Making of the holy month of Ramadan, a month of blood, not of charity.** Fomenting a Sunni/Shii split, a Muslim/Coptic conflict, or a Bedouin/nationalist cleavage. All of these are **the tools of dead-enders.**

**A case in point is the recent attack in Kuwait on the Mosque of Imam Jaafar Al-Ssadeq. The Emir of Kuwait, descendant of nation-builders, has the appropriate response. He prayed at the scene of the crime.**

In the Arab homelands, national borders shall always stand tall. Even if the national entity is geographically split. As in Syria, or Yemen. **Statelets shall be defined by their future borders.**

40,000 tweets by ISIS on a daily basis are no indicator of longevity. It is only **"the Wizard of Oz"** syndrome. Turning his sound machine to **frighten Scarecrow and Tin Man. But not Dorothy or her little dog Toto!!**

So the Sinai war, being the Egyptian front on the global war on terror, urgently needs a **reformed Egyptian journalism.** Those journalists should either shape up or ship out. The list of examples of their banality and triteness is endless.

**Claiming that El-Sisi is not a decisive decision-maker.** I don't work for him. I am a mere employee of **her majesty the truth.** A volunteer for **"the Strong State,"** the New Egypt. Thus I feel the sting of what is published in the newspaper **"Al-Masriyoon."** It claims: **"El-Sisi declarations about terrorism are contradictory."** They should know better. The fight against jihadism is a daily changing nasty affair. The **Head of State is entitled to reflect that changing reality.**

**Claiming that every statement by El-Sisi should be fully-documented. Time, place and manner.** Al-Watan newspaper downgrades El-Sisi declaration after the Sinai massacre of July 1. He has said: **"The armed forces shall conduct these attacks...The perpetrators shall know that Egyptian blood is not cheap."** What is wrong with that? But **Al-Watan** finds fault with El-Sisi words. **"Nobody knows where El-Sisi said that and when?"** Is this the main issue?

**Claiming that the new anti-terror law which is yet to be promulgated is obnoxious as it restricts freedom of expression.** All because of one article (Article 33) which is now being re-examined. **Al-Ahram** newspaper writes: **"This is a call for ignoring human rights. It is contrary to the aims of the anti-terror campaign."** Oh, really? In times of war, security considerations trump. **The great American emancipator, President Lincoln, suspended parts of the US Constitution.** The American civil war, in which 850,000 American troops perished, was on. The survival of the U.S. was at stake. And the slave owners were being assisted by Great Britain. The same situation with the Brotherhood in Egypt being bolstered from abroad. **And the new Egyptian law is intended to replace the existing State of Emergency laws.**

**Claiming that the Sinai armies are not entitled to exhibit the bodies of the dead terrorists.** **"Al Maqal"** newspaper decries that action as **"triumphalism unbecoming of the armed forces."** Amazing. How about the jihadi daily massive of barbaric butcherism to keep us all hiding like rabbits in our holes? The burning alive of the Jordanian pilot, Moaz Al-Kasasbeh, in a cage should sear the mind of humanity for a long time. Telecast by ISIS repeatedly.

**Claiming that the Government is derelict in divulging how the weapons of the jihadis have penetrated Egypt.** So **"Al-Masri Al-**

Youm" writes: "Every Egyptian is entitled to know how these weapons entered Egypt; what kinds of weapons; and when have these weapons arrived?" Then it adds: "Apparently all who raise these questions are attacked as unpatriotic." But the whole world knows that the **events in Libya and in Gaza** have created points of entry for these weapons. Does that newspaper put the priority at investigations of the weaponization of the present war, when the State institutions, including the judiciary, are overburdened with all types of investigations? And haven't the armed forces bombed the Libyan borders and created a **"cordon sanitaire"** at the Gaza/Sinai borders? Doesn't the whole world know that today Egypt is buying from us ultra-modern surviellance equipment? Where is that technology going to be placed? At the Libyan border!! For decoration? No!! For border protection on the west (Libya).

**Claiming that the State should not use the term "liquidation" in its anti-terror statements. "Al-Shorook"** newspaper writes: **"The State establishes justice not vengeance and revenge."** Well!! What is the difference between **"containment, degrading, and ending jihadism,"** and **"liquidation?"** Is this a war of combat for rescuing the homeland or a war of words?

The list goes on and on. **Ad nauseam.** Some of the same commentators described the status of journalism in Egypt as **"the public information chaos."** Amen!! Time for an **"Information Revolution."** If it is a war, it should be fought like a war. **On all fronts. By all means. Akin to general mobilization.** May God save Egypt from jihadism and its inane journalism!!

The shallowness of present-day journalism in Egypt makes me **over-nostalgic to its golden age.** Established in the 19th century **by Lebanese Christians,** it was the home of great essayists. One of them was our neighbor in **Sharqia Province -Zaki Abdel-Qader.** A few years later it was **Ahmed Bahaul-Din and the twins, Ali and Mustafa Amin.** How about **Fikry Abaza and El-Zayyat?** Today, these stalwarts are terribly missed.

There is strong evidence that the **hallow carping of present-day journalists in Egypt leads the US press to draw absurd conclusions.** One of these is the perpetuation of the **myth that the June 30, 2013 Revolution was a coup.** Witness the stupid conclusions in the Egyptian press about El-Sisi donning his military uniform during his visit with the Sinai troops following the treacherous attacks by the ISIS branch called **"The Sinai Province."** And remember how Bush Jr. as president, who has never been in military service, was applauded when he donned a military uniform, parading himself on a battleship. Falsely declaring about the American invasion of Iraq: **"Mission Accomplished."**

One of the side benefits of the **two companion revolutions (January 2011 and June 2013)** is that the average Egyptian has found his or her voice. So did Egypt's journalism. But with one difference in the case of the latter. **Most of their contributions seem to equate between democracy and a constant barrage against the government.**

Credible statistics show that since January 2011, the army and the police in Egypt **lost 258 martyred in the course of the war in jihadism in Sinai.** The bloody results of **74 attacks.** Over various periods of post-Mubarak rule. The SCAF (Supreme Council of Armed Forces) from February 11, 2011 to June 30, 2012. The Morsi rule, the Mansour rule, and the present El-Sisi rule.

**All the while, the New Egypt is a building.** From the expected opening of the Second Suez Canal in early August, to ensuring the safety of its tourists, to combating the income inequality in the land of the Nile. **So enough is enough with spilling of ink to fill empty pages in Egypt's newspapers.**

Aside from efforts for economic recovery and anti-terrorism, the **main pending issue is the holding of elections for the lower house of parliament.** Egyptian journalism paid scant attention to the march of Egypt toward those parliamentary elections later this year. The Egyptian Supreme Constitutional Court has approved the draft bill on electoral districts **(a total of 209),** paving the way for its promulgation, following presidential approval. The daily moan and groan is: **"Nothing is OK with the New Egypt."** Their monument is a permanent wailing wall.

What a great free ride for the **Brotherhood/ISIS/Sinai Province** criminal consortium to read that headline in Egypt's so-call press:
**"The disappearance of the President from view increases the public's fear of a tsunami of decisions. The unknown envelopes Egypt. And fear pervades the majority of its population."**
*In any country in a state of war, such fear-mongering would have prompted the authorities to prosecute the offending outlet. The legal grounds are: "Aiding and abetting the State's enemies through falsely and maliciously causing public panic during wartime."*

# Islamophobia Degenerating Into Anti-Islamism: An Advocacy By Ayaan Hirsi Ali For "Reforming" Islam Through Editing the Quran!!

Friday, July 17, 2015

Ayaan Hirsi Ali **- a young woman; an ex-Muslim; an ex-Somali.** A victim of Somali tribalism: genital mutilation, and an escapee from a pre-arranged marriage. Her pain, we understand. But her advocacy is Islamophobia that has crossed even the line of the most vehement anti-Islamist.

Her understanding of Islam is framed through her tribal experiences. **Islam, as a faith, has nothing to do with Ayaan.** Yet, in the West, she has become the poster child of virulent anti-Islamism. Blaming what her tribe did to her on the religion of others. **1.5 billion Muslims.** For she has never met that faith, face to face. Has never met young Egyptian women pilots. Has never met Saudi women lawyers. Nor Lebanese beauties who sing and dance.

**Has never comprehended the Quranic vocabulary:** The word **"Read"** means **"Learn;"** the term **"Ayah"** (verse) does not mean the words; it means **"evidence"** or **"proof."** She is not an Islamic scholar. **Unfortunately she made the West see the rich Islamic culture through the parched land of her ignorance.**

Because of predisposition to Islamophobia, the West has been using her as an excuse. In return, she has used western pulpits to vent her grievance. She has been regaled by membership in the Dutch Parliament. And now she is described in the prestigious US magazine, **Foreign Affairs**

as **"a public intellectual."** Presently occupying a post of distinction at Harvard as a **Fellow at the Kennedy School of Government.** Her writings, whether of books or articles, such as the recent one in **Foreign Affairs** (July/August 2015), are celebrated. **Yet their context and content are part of the oxygen that jihadism is gasping for.**

Emboldened by that misplaced attention, Ayaan has embarked on a journey for which her anti-Islamism is her only guide.

186

**Calling for world peace through reformation of Islam. How? By editing the Quran.** She must know from her Somali wretched days that under Islamic dogma, the Quran is taken as the word of God. It is not authored. It is revealed. This has to do with faith. **And faith is non-negotiable.**

Moreover, the Quran and the tradition of the Prophet Muhammad are subject to interpretation by Muslim qualified scholars. **In order to meet changing circumstances.** Ayaan Hirsi Ali is no faqih. Otherwise she would have known that neither genital mutilation nor pre-arranged marriages are to be found in the Quran.

She had renounced Islam. **No big deal.** Contrary to Pakistani's anti-apostasy laws, Islam accepts apostasy. **It accepts Ayaan's decision to opt out.** The Quran says: **"Surely those who disbelieve...cannot harm God in any way"** (Chapter 47; verse 32).

**So, Ayaan: if you are out of the game, stay out of the game.** Your pontification about **"reforming"** Islam through editing its **primary pillar, the Qura,** leads to a one-way street: recruitment of idiots to fight for ISIS, endangering global security.

Here are the Ayaan arguments in her article in **Foreign Affairs** entitled **"A Problem From Heaven,"** she starts off by: **"We have a problem -not a problem from hell, but one that claims to come from heaven."** Believe what you wish Ayaan. **"In faith, there is no compulsion,"** so says the Quran -the Bible of Islam. **So why poke your stick into a hornets nest leading to more human tragedies?** Unless it is your way of victimization for validation.

- She is critical of Obama's statement before the UN General Assembly last September. Why? Because the U.S. President stated that **"Islam teaches peace."** Well, Obama had voiced a fact. Islam means **"the submission to God's will;"** advocates peace; and accepts every faith, revealed or non-revealed. What is the basis? **Tawheed** (the Oneness of God). **Tawheed means that there is no special God for every faith.** In fact the God that you, Ayaan, think that you have abandoned is the same one which you have now espoused.
- She claims to be a **"Muslim dissident."** How far from the truth. And she is unaware of her own contradiction as she reports: **"A few, including myself, have been forced by experience to conclude that we cannot continue to be believers. Yet we**

187

remain deeply engaged in the debate about Islam's future."

- I cannot find your **"few."** The **"few"** is you. And being **"an unbeliever"** by your choice is an automatic disqualification for an engagement **"in the debate about Islam's future."** Reason: You cannot reform what you don't understand. A pitchfork marauder like you, Ayaan, has no audience. The Arab adage says: **"You cannot give what you don't have."**

- Ayaan then moves to the heart of her thesis. A thesis of hallucination bred out not from the Quran and the Hadith (Muhammad's verified words and conduct.) **But from her own personal nightmare in Somalia.** Somalia the capital of Al-Shabab -a franchise of global terrorism.

**First:** In her misdirection, she attacks these two pillars of Islam: The Quran and the Sunna. Saying: **"the majority of otherwise peaceful and law-abiding Muslims are unwilling to acknowledge much less repudiate the theological warrants for intolerance and violence embedded in their own religious texts."**

**Second:** She also attacks **Al-Azhar.** Citing one source in a statement published in the Belgian newspaper **De Standaard** in March 2015. Her source, **Sufyan Al-Omari** blames Al-Azhar for the rise of ISIS. He, as quoted by a very receptive Ayaan, says: **"The Islamic State does not fall from the sky...The texts to which (ISIS) appeals for support are exactly what we learnt at Al-Azhar. The difference is that (ISIS) truly puts the texts into practice."**

**Third:** She quotes individuals whom she describes as **"Islamic thinkers"** as dreaming of **"a version of their religion that no longer exalts holy war, martyrdom, and life in the hereafter."**

**Fourth:** Ayaan cites an Iraqi cleric as arguing that **"the Koran was created by the Prophet Muhammad, but was driven by Allah"** (Whatever **"driven"** means). This, she says, was part of a report from **"the Middle East Media Research Institute.** In that report, Ayaan's source **"proposes a modifiable religious ruling based on fiqh al-maqasid, or the juris prudence of the meaning."**

**Fifth:** She calls for US intervention in support of those bogus claims. In her words in that article, she makes this ludicrous appeal: **"American presidents and Secretaries of State need not give lectures on the finer points of Islamic orthodoxy. But it is not too much to ask them to support Islamic reform and make the fate of Muslim dissidents and reformers part of their negotiations with allies such as Saudi Arabia**

**and foes such as Iran alike."**

**Now for my rebuttal.**

- The U.S. Government, especially since 9/11, has committed to the advocacy that **America was not at war with Islam, but with terrorism** which wears a false mask emblazoned with the word **"Islamic"** on it. In view of this sane policy, **no intervention in religious beliefs by America could be envisioned.** This is particularly so in the light of the US constitutional provision for separation between State and church.

- Ayaan's call for US intervention in the core of Islamic faith and beliefs is based on the wrong analogy. For she, in her article, refers to the impact of **Radio Free Europe,** an American medium, on the collapse of the USSR. She is obviously oblivious of the difference between the Muslim world and the world of communism. With the exception of the bands of terrorists, from Al-Qaeda to ISIS, the **Muslim community** of **57 States has never threatened US security. The USSR did.** Two vastly different situations.

- A recent report in the **New York Times** headlined: **"Most U.S. Attacks Are Homegrown And Not Jihadist."** And the **Christian Century** of May 27, 2015, in its review of a new book entitled **Europe and the Islamic World** concluded as follows: **"Readers will come away from the book profoundly suspicious of simplistic narratives about Muslim aggression and endless jihad. Ideally, they will also be skeptical of any claims about what Islam does, as opposed to particular States or communities."**

- It is clear that Ayaan anti-Islamism, aside **from deriving from her tribal experience now elevated to a whole industry,** does not know: That the term **holy war** is a crusader term, never an Islamic term. That jihad in Islamic jurisprudence means **"personal self-improvement"** and **"self-defense."** That in Islam, **there is no aggressive war waged beyond your borders.** That self-sacrifice is forbidden by the very terms of the Quran. That those terms equate between male and female. And that Islam bestowed on women the right to choose their spouses, the right to own property, and the right to unilaterally divorce an abusive husband.

- The list of misconceptions, intentional or out of ignorance, can go on and on. But her attack on the texts of the Quran and the Hadith are so outrageous and uninformed. They have the imprint of total insensitivity that I should leave the rebuttal to someone else. As so could be found below.

189

To the credit of **Foreign Affairs,** Ayaan's article was followed by another, authored by **William Mc Cants, Fellow at the Center for Middle East Policy at the Brookings Institution.** Mc Cants, in his opening paragraph, states: **"Hirsi Ali is profoundly wrong when she argues that Islamic Scripture causes Muslim terrorism and thus that the U.S. government should fund Muslim dissidents to reform Islam."**

Appropriately Mc Cants article is entitled: **"Islamic Scripture Is Not the Problem."**

Ayaan also attacks Al-Azhar. If she were **"a public intellectual,"** and concerned about her so-called Islamic reform, she seems not to know, or chooses to ignore, that the **Religious Revolution advocated by El-Sisi is spearheaded by Al-Azhar.** In this context, it should be noted that **Al-Azhar's document of August, 2011** remains a primary framework for that revolution. One of its eleven principles provides as follows: **"Islam does not recognize a State solely based on religion."** The Coptic Church has fully endorsed that document. Witness the disbarment by Egyptian authorities of Imams who use their mosques as arenas for jihadi preaching.

As for the essential role of interpretation in Islamic jurisprudence, Ayaan does not even once refer to **"ijtihad." It is the application of the mind to the text.** One of its primary products is that **public interest trumps.** It is called **"Fiqh Al-Maslahah."**

In my research in 2006 for the **American Bar Association,** I found that there is **80% commonality between Islamic jurisprudence and the U.S. Constitution.** I teach the subject as a law professor in New York City. My late Al-Azhari father has blessed my marriage to a Catholic American woman. He was on sound grounds. Islam fully acknowledges diversity and the full right of others to their creed.

It is a shame that Ayaan Hirsi Ali does not accord the same diversity to her former Muslim co-religionists. For she does not realize that **Allahu Akbar** is not a war scream as per ISIS. It means **"we are all equal before God."**

Hirsi Ali's ignorance is not surprising. **She has made of it a real industry.** In her authorship of that book entitled **"Infidel"** -an incredible diatribe against Islam, she does not realize that the term does not mean **"a Non-Muslim."** It means **"a person who has no values."** An apt characterization of Ayaan and her campaign. Her **primary beneficiaries** are the **ISIS franchises.** They use her arguments against Islam as a war cry for jihadi recruitment. **In this regard, you, Ayaan are one of their enablers.**

Ayaan: I judge you by your words. By analysing them, I find you to be **intellectually depraved.** You call for Islamic reformation a la reformation undertaken by **Martin Luther.** His was a rebellion against central authority which made of faith a **trade in the indulgences.** And a return to the holy scriptures. Islam is a different setting. **There are no payment for coupon to go** to paradise; no central authority, and a full adherence to text, modifiable by ijtihad (by common sense and changing circumstances).

Then you call yourself a **"Muslim dissident."** But you have already opted out of Islam. Enjoy your conversion. **Who cares?** The Quran says: **"Whoever wishes to believe, let it be. And whoever wishes to disbelieve, let it be."** Terming yourself a dissident is an obfuscation. For dissidence does not mean anti-Islamism which has become your mission and your industry.

Your call for US intervention in support of your ridiculous theory is **a clear call for cultural imperialism.** This means endless wars. But you describe it as a path to peace. How obscene!!

Through your ignorance about and antipathy about Islam, you regard Sharia as a frozen unevolved legal system. A threat to individual human rights and friendly relations among nations. Utterly insane. With the exception of few Islamic States, **the legal system is a hybrid. Sharia plus legislated law.** The former is a family law jurisdiction. The latter is everything else.

The **poor treatment of women in Somalia has nothing to do with Islam.** It has to do with arcane practices elevated to the levels of law by ignorant imams.

The Quran and Hadith call for shura (consultations), which is institutionalized in today's parliaments. Those two pillars of Islam call for **the removal of an unjust ruler.** The only limitation is avoidance of **mayhem (FITNA)** resulting from such populist action.

The judicial system, in Islamic jurisprudence, encourages the **judge to be defendant oriented.** Punishment for a proven guilt does not follow the literality of the Quran. It is modifiable by legislated law.

Ayaan: Under your misguided notions, you look upon the Quran as if it was a textbook in need of revision. Nearly two billion Muslims regard it as **revealed. It is a faith, regardless of poor Islamic practices.** A heavenly road map which all modern legal systems respect.

So enjoy your notoriety. I pity those who, at the **Harvard Kennedy School of Government, sit to hear you expound on your anti-Islamism.** The only winners are those in the ranks of murderous terrorism who take your attacks on Islam as a justification for their conviction that Islam is under attack.

You have elevated your personal vendetta against Islam to the level of an international cause. The Hirsi Ali cause is a hopeless one. It exists only in her **tribally traumatized** head.

From the foregoing, you, Hirsi Ali, could see the depth of my rejection of what you stand for. Denigration of Islam and stirring up of inter-faith conflict.

Yet there is one thing that you have said correctly. Unintentionally. You titled one of your books **"Infidel."** This is because you have adopted the western error that **"infidel"** means **"non-Muslim."** It doesn't mean this at all. In Islamic jurisprudence, **"infidel"** means **"a person who has no values."** Without realization, **you have chosen the correct term. An omnibus description of yourself.**

*The Muslims abide by this verse from the Quran: "So woe to those who write the scripture with their hands, then say, 'This is from God,' to trade with it for a pitiful price!" (Chapter 2, verse 79). This is the Muslim faith. And Pope Francis said it all when he declared that freedom of expression does not include attacking the faith of others.*

# 15 AUGUST 2015

## Why Is the Republican Party (The Grand Old Party - GOP) Deserving of My Grand Contempt?

Friday, August 7, 2015

Mainly for two reasons: Subjecting US sovereignty to foreign interference, and to the power of special interests. And, in the process, downgrading the majesty of the Office of the US President, for ideological reasons of the evangelical right wing.

Now to evidentiary details:

Starting with the downgrading of the majesty of the Office of the President. It is impossible not to link between the constant attacks on Obama and his being black. Racism in the US is a cancer in that body politic since the introduction of slavery. Cures that have been developed, especially with the civil rights movement of the 1960s, have dealt with the outward symptoms, not with the roots.

Yes the Voting Rights Act was signed by Democratic President Lyndon Johnson in 1965. But today, several States, called **"red States"** for being under Republican administrations, are chipping off at those rights. Measures intended to make it ever harder for minorities (Blacks and

Latinos) to exercise those rights. The alarm bells sounded as of 2008. The percentage of whites eligible to vote in the presidential elections, won by Obama that year, was 66% of the aggregate voters. **Guess what?** Same percentage of Black and Latino voters who rushed to the polling stations to have a man of color win.

This trend had to be obstructed, so reasoned the GOP in several states. How could this be done without the appearance of violating the law? Under the 10th Amendment of the US Constitution, **"the powers not delegated to the United States by the Constitution, nor prohibited by it to the States, are reserved to the States respectively, or to the people."** It is called **the supremacy clause.**

This is **"The United States,"** 50 of them; a federal system, where the states have all powers except for a few. The few powers of the federal government are: to declare war, to collect taxes, to regulate interstate commerce, and others. Those **"other"** powers are listed. Whatever is not listed, belongs to the states.

As stated above, voting rights are governed by the 1965 Act. But how to exercise those rights is decided by the states. In order to make that exercise difficult, regardless of the principle of **"equality before the law,"** the **"red"** states have been very busy: Gerrymandering of electoral districts, intended to unfairly secure disproportionate influence at elections for non-minorities. Shortening the hours for voting. Placing polling stations at geographically far locations. Requiring photo identification cards. Closing polling stations on Sunday.

Yet this is the heart of the democratic process. A process which the US is eager to have other countries adopt. Vigorously calling for **"respect for the right of dissent."**

Such roll back of minority rights is not a mere assertion of states rights. To understand its dimension in full must include **the rejection by the neo-racists of the President.** Never has a US President been more subjected to personal slurs and affronts by the right, the Tea party, the evangelists and Republicans. **The list is endless and truly disgusting. More importantly, un-American.**

Here are samples, and attribution to specific Republicans in search of nomination for the presidency in 2016:
- Marco Rubio: **"The President has no class."**
- Donald Trump: **"I don't know who he is."**

- Lindsey Graham: **"I don't know whether he is Christian."**
- Scott Walker: **"I presume he is, because he says he is."**
- Mitch Mc Connell: **"We shall make sure that he is a one term President. (On Obama's inauguration day in January 2009).**
- Ted Cruz: **"He is the worst President in the history of the United States."**
- A congressional member yelling at the President during his delivery of the State of the Union message: **"You are a liar."** Obama's restrained response: **"Thank you."**

How can such affronts to the present occupant of the Oval Office not be demeaning to the majesty of that Office? How can it not affect the credibility of the U.S. world-wide when its Head-of-State is called names (including, **"he is a closet Muslim"**) as a civil polity? How can the principle of separation of powers, underpinned by constitutional checks and balances, maintain its efficacy in a system where the Republicans have shut down the federal government earlier. **Now, they are threatening to do the same again.**

Obama is also threatened by empty Congressional proposals for impeachment. Faced with Republican majorities in both houses of Congress, he has resorted to **using his constitutional instruments in defense of the executive branch.** These are: his resort to issuance of executive orders, and of the use of his veto power. Yet as a constitutional scholar, he had sought these mechanisms sparingly.

Obama's signature accomplishment of the **"Affordable Care Act"** was challenged by this Republican Congress more than 40 times. Extending health insurance to millions of uninsured Americans, largely the poor and the elderly, it has been divisively called by his opponents **"The Obama Care Act."** All Republican aspirants to succeed Obama have pledged collapsing that historic Act as of **"Day One in the Oval Office."**

Same totally negative attitude towards Obama's repeated attempts to fix the broken system of immigration; of tax reform; of bank regulation, of income inequality, of education reform (an area reserved for the states), of gun control, and of reforming the criminal justice system.

Even the historic trade pact with Asia was about to be killed if not for a brief moment of bipartisan support. In Singapore, Secretary of State Kerry on August 5 voiced the obvious. **"No country can expect its economy to grow simply by buying and selling to its own people."**

More glaringly is Congressional blocking of Obama's attempts to close down Guantanamo. That is where more than a hundred Muslim detainees are still languishing in legal limbo since 9/11.

They are neither charged. Nor are they released. Several states of the U.S. do not want them loose in their neighborhood. And foreign States do not want them either, largely for reasons of radicalization through prolonged incarceration. **An ugly relic of the party of war -the Republican Party, which has lurched into** xenophobia since the criminal acts of destruction of 9/11.

Moving along into the area of foreign policy and its reflection on war and peace, one reaches the depth of Republican Party conversion. From the party of Lincoln, the great emancipator, to the party of endless wars. Especially in the Middle East.

It is well-known that sovereignty is an essential requirement for the ability of a State to conduct its own foreign policy. Thus the US Constitution has assigned to the President the following powers: **"He shall have the Power, by and with the advice and consent of the Senate, to make treaties, provided two-thirds of the Senators present concur."**

Clear enough!! So let us examine the chaotic situation in Congress with regard to a present issue of war and peace in the Middle East. **I am not referring to the Israeli-Palestinian conflict where no sane leadership exists on either side:** of Israel, a brutal occupier, with no regard for international law or common sense fairness. Nor on the side of the Palestinians, forever divided, habitually corrupt, and deeply committed to the falsehood of the UN creating their State for them, rather than the State, when in being, applying for UN membership.

**I am examining the Iran nuclear deal** where US sovereignty and Obama's commitment to disengaging America from the endless wars in the Muslim world are implicated.

Here we have a deal reflecting the coming together of 6 States with Iran's moderate leadership. A historic agreement, reached after 16 months of arduous negotiations. Its only goal is to prevent Iran from weaponizing its enriched uranium, and be rewarded with the lifting of sanctions and reintegration into the international community. Iran said **"yes;"** Russia, China, France, Britain and Germany said **"yes."** The UN Secretary Council, usually a dysfunctional body because of the veto, unanimously said **"YES."**

**Not yet America:** In US Congress, the deal has become the latest version of a football game with no rules. Here are the unbelievable details:
The majority of both houses cried **"foul."** Claimed that Obama was **"fleeced"** (as per the Republican Chairman of the Senate Foreign Relations Committee.) Even prior to digesting that 159 page report, they were asking for a better deal!!
Obama, Secretary Kerry, and the great nuclear physicist, Moniz, Secretary of Energy, responded: **(a)** What is your **"better deal;" (b)** Your **"disapproval"** shall be vetoed by the President; **(c)** scuttling the deal will cause the sanctions regime to unravel; **(d)** Iran could be then forced to proceed to the development of a nuclear bomb; and **(e)** America's credibility is in the balance.
Seventeen Republicans aspiring to occupy the Oval Office in 2017 gave these responses short shrift. Called the deal **"an appeasement"** a la Munich in 1938; considered war against Iran a viable option; **bought into the Netanyahu alarmist propaganda that the deal was an existential threat, not only to Israel, but to the whole world.**
Then came Obama's definitive response to these falsehoods. In his historic speech at American University in Washington, D.C. on August 5, Obama reminded the Republican Party of **its horrific war misadventures in both Afghanistan and Iraq.**

Against the calls of out-of-control war-crazed John Bolton of **"bomb Iran now,"** the President chuckled in derisive amazement: **"Those people were wrong yesterday. They are wrong today."** The party of war, bereft of any logical response, began to froth at the mouth:
**"The U.S. has become the main supporter of terrorism"** -said Senator Ted Cruz;
**"Obama is marching the Israelis to the door of the oven."** -said former Governor Mike Huckabee;
**"This is the worst President the U.S. has ever seen."** -said Donald Trump.
With money pouring in for daily ads against the deal with Iran, the opposition had two very powerful backers. The U.S. Supreme Court's decision in **"Citizens United"** which considered money gifted to electoral candidates as a form of **"free speech."** And AIPAC (the American Israeli Political Action Committee). AIPAC is funding **"Citizens for a Nuclear Free Iran"** which is planning to spend $25 million to defeat that historic deal. Of course there is no likelihood of **"Citizens for a Nuclear Free Israel."**

As the President met with 20 leaders of Jewish groups to win their support, Netanyahu had a packaged response to Obama's arguments about **"no**

**alternative other than war."** In blatant interference in US sovereign decisions, Israeli's Prime Minister called Obama's arguments as **"utterly false."**

For these reasons, the **"Grand Old Party"** deserves my grand contempt. The President of the US is the constitutional manager of America's foreign affairs. **Israel is a foreign power, regardless of the degree of its strategic relationships with the US.**

I have not seen Obama pursuing Israel in regard to **ending its colonist settlerism in Palestinian territories.** By the same same token, Israel should have no legitimate business in interfering blatantly in US sovereign decisions regarding what defines America's national interests.

Nothing in the annals of diplomacy is found to permit the Israeli ambassador to America to openly delve into an internal conflict between Congress and the President. Were it the Ambassador of, say, Turkey (a NATO ally of the US), he or she would have been promptly thrown out as **persona non grata.**

In his speech on August 5 at American University, the US President reminded the Republican hordes of their lying to the country as they led it to the disastrous war in Iraq. Without mincing his words, he bluntly chided their unending beating of the war drums. Said he: **"Many of the same people who argued for the war in Iraq are now making the case against the Iran nuclear deal."**

But AIPAC's director of communication, **Marshall Wittman,** responded to President Obama on the same day. Lying through his teeth, he said: **"To remove any misinformation or confusion, AIPAC took no position whatsoever on the Iraq war."**

Then, parroting his real Master's Voice (Netanyahu's), he felt obliged to insult the American President in nearly the same words. So Wittman added: **"This is an entirely false and misleading argument."** This is not mere lobbying. This is being **"an agent of a foreign power -Israel."**

Watching the first televised Republican debate among the 17 Republican aspirants for the presidential office on August 6, I turned off that miserable show with one impression: Truly pathetic!! Felt even sorrier for America when **Michele Bachman,** standing on the sidelines, was interviewed.

Though she was not one of the 17, Bachman seemed to speak for all of them in regard to the Iran deal. Her insane solution was: **"Bomb Iran now because the window of opportunity is fast closing."** Bachman, the queen of Islamophobia in the U.S. had claimed that God speaks to her!!

Does she have a private God who also communicates with other select Republican war lords like **Dick Cheney and Donald Rumsfeld?** Two unindicted war criminals, afraid to leave the US for fear of being bagged to the Hague to stand trial before the International Criminal Court.

**Isn't America's sovereignty worthy of support?!**

In the avalanche of these acrimonious diatribes, it is uplifting to discover some sane voices. **Particularly those issuing from American Jewish leaders.** In a letter to the Editor of the New York Times of August 7, one such voice said: **"I believe that Netanyahu's address to American Jews on Tuesday (August 4) and his in person speech to Congress in March were wholly inappropriate, insulting to the American president and people, and constituted an intrusion by a foreign leader into American domestic politics."**

The author of that letter added: **"It is up to the United States to make a decision on this deal on its merits."** Well said, **Mr. Seymour Reich, former Chairman of the Conference of Presidents of Major American Jewish Organizations.**

**Is America's sovereignty for sale?**

*What we have in America today is nothing other than a power grab by Congress of presidential prerogatives; a distortion by money and lobbyists of the popular will through fair national elections, and the demeaning spectacle of a foreign power jumping over the high fence of American sovereignty to subvert an international deal seen by the Obama Administration as in the best interest of the American people and of world peace. Let each State define by itself, and for itself, the requirements of its own security.*

*Yes, American sovereignty matters!!*

# Egypt's "Field of Dreams": Connecting the Seas Began in 1380 B.C.

Friday, August 14, 2015

That great American film, **"Field of Dreams,"** captures the imagination by one sentence. **"If you build it, they will come."** The reference was to a mid western hope in the future of a corn field. A corn field from which the ghosts of great baseball players, long departed, appear to the field owner. Playing, then disappearing in the thick of corn stalks. Wondering if it was a signal for carving out a baseball arena on his farm. Yet afraid that no spectators would come, he was advised: **"If you build it, they will come."**

So it was the case with Egypt's field of dreams. Connecting the Mediterranean and the Red Seas. A dream that began in Ancient Egypt in 1380 B.C. A canal that shows Egypt as a world crossroads. Making of commerce a rational substitute for conflict. Yet when the dream became a reality with the opening of the first Suez Canal in 1869, it brought both commerce and conflict.

The Suez Canal of 1869 was the successor regime of all the prior efforts. Beginning with **Pharaoh Sitti I** (1380 B.C.) through **Amre Ibn Elass** in the 7th Century A.D. It was the latter who led the Arab and Islam into Egypt during the Second Caliphate of **Omar Ibn Al-Khattab.** Amre wanted to link the two seas.

But Omar, with his clear Bedouin cum legal mind, vetoed the connection. Allowed only a link from the Nile to the Timsah Lake to the Red Sea. **Omar** feared foreign intervention if the two great seas were linked. **Amre,** a successful military leader, didn't mind courting that challenge. But Amre was over-ruled by his boss in **Madina.**

Amre couldn't play circles around Omar again. He had done it before and gotten away with it. Omar had instructed Amre not to march into Egypt - at least not yet. Quick over-expansion of Islamized territory was not an acceptable formula for the Omar Khalifate. But Amre, nonetheless, crossed over into Egypt with his armies. Pretended that Omar's instructions arrived a bit too late. Resulted in Omar keeping his **"General Mac Arthur" (Amre Ibn Elass)** under constant watch. The first instance in history of civilian control over the military.

A digression intended to link the name of Suez to the inner core of the Egyptian psyche, and spirit. Not with numbers. But with symbols often missed by Egyptian media for lack of connection to the Suez connectedness. Lack of **"Egyptianess!!"**

**Now Egypt has Suez I and Suez II.** A whale of a difference between the two symbols. Though tied at the hip, implicating Egypt's sovereignty.

Suez I was a project spearheaded by **Ferdinand de Lesseps,** a French Vice-Consul in Alexandria. Received from **Khedive Said Pasha,** a son of Muhammad Ali, the great founder of a strong Egypt, permission to dig the canal in 1854. The hesitant Khedive needed England's view. Though France and England were allies during the Crimean war, the British Consul offered no clear opinion. Resulting in the signing of an agreement dated January, 1856.

An unconscionable agreement as far as Egypt was concerned. An **"adhesion contract,"** so heavily restrictive of one party, Egypt, while non-restrictive of another, the Canal Company. This grave inequality of bargaining power is manifest in the following:

- The Company builds a feeder canal drawing fresh water from the Nile, covering all needs for work on the Suez Canal;
- In return, **Egypt donates all land for work and construction, tax-free;**
- The Company has the right to charge all Egyptian users of that fresh water. **Together with the free use of Egyptian mines and quarries;**
- Egypt provides for free, **four-fifth of the labor needed,** with new shifts of manpower every three months;
- All dues of passage in the Suez Canal, whether for human or cargo per tonnage to be collected by the Canal Company;
- Profits are to be debited 10% as interest on investment. The balance is then **divided between Egypt 15%; 10% for the foreign Canal founders; 75% for the canal administrators and upkeep.**

So for 15% of the **net profits, Egypt provides land, labor, fresh water, natural resources, and security. For 99 years, a colonial regime was established by a foreign company** on lands deducted from Egyptian sovereignty. What an imperial bargain!! The nominal suzerain, the High Porte of the Ottoman Empire responded: **"Hell, No!!"**

Ignoring that refusal, de Lesseps, went ahead with open bids for subscription, in November 1858. Nearly half a million shares were snapped up at 500 francs per share all over western Europe.

**Egypt did not own the Company. The Company owned Egypt.** And 1 million of its peasants (25000 each 3 months for 10 years), most of whom perished for lack of care. While slavery was outlawed in Africa south of the Sahara, indentured slavery was instituted in Egypt by a contract with a Government which existed in name only.

**British Prime Minister Palmerstone** protested to Istanbul the loss of Egyptian lives. Not primarily for humanitarian reasons. But for fear of growing French influence in Egypt, the gateway through Suez to India where rebellion was seething. Anglo-French rivalry in Egypt focused on the Canal.

That was **Said Pasha.** But with **Ismail Pasha** succeeding him in **1863, Egypt acquired new claws. The strong State was back,** clawing at the illegally gotten advantages. Attacking the enslavement of its citizens, to the applause of Great Britain. Paying the avaricious Company two million Egyptian pounds for 177,642 shares bought by the weakling Said, but had remained unpaid.

Then Ismail labored for the reduction of the number of Egyptian Canal diggers; forced the Company to disgorge State land sequestered by the Company through machinations and bribes. And with approval of the **Ottoman High Porte, the Company received an eviction notice: Accept the reformation of that stupid contract or get the hell out!!**

**De Lesseps** nearly had a heart attack; the astute Ismail agreed to have **Napoleon III** arbitrate; **decision for Egypt on July 6, 1864:** No enslavement; no crack of the whip on Egyptian backs; restitution of the huge swathe of land to the sovereign owner -Egypt.

**The Company was left with only 200 meters on the two sides of the Canal.** The price was steep: **Nearly 3.3 million Egyptian pounds;** an enormous price to retrieve what Egypt owns. But Ismail paid up, saying: **"I want the canal to be for Egypt, not Egypt for the Canal."** The Ottoman Empire issued the firman (Imperial Executive Order) approving the deal in March 1866.

And with a big bang, the Suez Canal was inaugurated in 1869. Monarchs were personally invited by Ismail who travelled to Europe, personally carrying to them invitations. **All expenses paid from his personal funds. Ismailia, the city on the Canal, which was appropriately named after**

**the patriotic Khedive,** was bathed in light and splendor.

The **French Empress, Eugenie, danced all night,** and still asked for more. A palace in Cairo by the Nile was built in her honor **(now the Marriott Hotel).** Roads were paved to the Pyramids. And the Opera Theatre was built at Opera Square, in the heart of Cairo.

By the standards of 1869, the cost of the party was huge, **1.5 million Egyptian pounds - i.e. pounds sterling.** Ismail, like the U.S. of today, was well practiced in deficit funding!! The debts led to the British occupation of Egypt in 1882. The Sudan also came under British hegemony.

The Canal continued to be the lighting rod for Egyptian nationalism; Sinai was ceded by the Ottoman Empire to Egypt in 1906; with the collapse of the Ottomans in World War I, Great Britain's creeping annexation leaped over the Canal and Sinai into Palestine.

From the records of the Canal Company, the **aggregate cost of the Suez Canal was 17.5 million pounds. Of that amount, Egypt paid the staggering amount of 16 million pounds. Not counting the huge human cost** and Egypt's exposure during times of weakness, to foreign intervention. But with the end of World War II, Egypt, thanks to the impetus of the Canal, rediscovered its sinews of power: location, demography, diversity, cultural cohesion, and **national fervor to wipe out any vestiges of past humiliation.**

By 1956, the British occupation of the Canal Zone was gone; and **Nasser**, the new strong man of Egypt, nationalized the Suez Canal Company. Egypt's adversaries cried foul; propagated in policy, media and foreign affairs, that **"Egypt has nationalized the Canal!!" Utterly stupid. You don't nationalize what you own.** The nationalization was for the Canal Company which had been chartered under Egyptian laws. **And every shareholder was paid in full.**

But the myth was propagated in order to **"cut Nasser to size."** A prelude for the Israeli, French and British vicious aggression of 1956 against a country, Egypt, for daring to exercise its inherent sovereignty. With the cessation of hostilities, peace-keeping by the UN was born. But for a life of only 10 years.

For in 1967, Israel struck again in the so-called **6-day war.** Sinai was reoccupied; thousands of Egyptian military lives were lost in both Sinai and at the Canal. **Yet Egypt, under Sadat, burst again across the Canal in October 1973, destroying** a newer myth: Israel's invincibility.

**Now in little over than 40 years, a second Suez Canal has been dug.** Inaugurated on August 6, 2015 by El-Sisi, the present-day advocate of **"the Strong State."**

But what a difference between the environment of building **Suez Canal I** and building its younger sister **Suez Canal II.**

We have seen from the above, the miserable circumstances surrounding the de Lesseps project (Suez Canal I). **Suez Canal II is the concretizatoin of the New Egypt:**

- A historic symbol of washing away the oppression meted out to the Egypt of the 19th century;
- An abashed declaration of an Egyptian equivalent of **"Yes, We Can;"**
- Dug by the armed forces, under the command of **Vice Admiral Mohab Mameesh,** in less than one year;
- Funded in mere 8 days **by totally -Egyptian subscriptions** induced by the spirit of **Egypt of January 25, 2011 and June 30, 2013;**
- An impetus for China to build the **Kra Canal in Thailand** to bypass the **Malacca Strait.** A new maritime silk road shortening the voyage by 1200 kilometers. Ending up in Suez welcoming two arms;
- China is also planning road and rail routes through Pakistan. All ending up in Suez **"aller et retour;"**
- **85% of world trade carried** expeditiously by the giants of canal containers plying their cargo **"24/7;"** from Port Said to Suez, and vice-versa.
- Seventy kilometers of daily transit from 49 to 85 crossings over the next 10 years. The volume of world trade moved by sea is expected to double in the next 20 years.
- CNN described Suez II, the new companion of Suez I, as a **"game changer for the future of world trade;" "the most strategic waterway in the world;" "a vital lifeline connecting the East and West;"**
- **MAERSK,** the largest shipping company in the world declared: **"It is more profitable for us to use the Suez Canals. We shall stop using the Panama Canal;"**
- Suez II was projected to be dug and operational over a period of 5 years. Shortened at El-Sisi's insistence to only one year. **"We**

**don't have the luxury of time,"** declared the Egyptian President.
- And in short order, a Presidential decree was issued creating **"The Suez Canal Economic Zone."** From ship repairs to rest and recreation, to training in maritime commerce, to amusement parks.

**Washing away the shame of yesterday: the slavery, foreign manipulation, and the arrogance of power. Now all gone!!**

Still doomsayers predict less financial and economic returns. No proof on that. Only to fulfil a self-induced prophecy of unfulfilled expectations. But the **Suez Canals are primarily about:**
- National resurgence; and Arab achievement in the midst of the cyclone of destruction of the Arab Spring;
- **An Arab symbol of hope and restored strength,** dissecting the Arab homeland by flags of all nations parading on ships on water in the heart of the Eastern Desert.

Commented **Judge and Senator, Mrs. Taghreed Hikmet** of Jordan: **"It is a gift from the nation to the world."** In its present hour of peril, the Arab Nation is in sore need of boosters. That historic Nation could always count on its big sister, Egypt, to faithfully provide.

In a way, the Suez project is an Arab iconic project. Protected by armed might from **Port Said in the North to the Gulf of Aden in the South.** Defending the freedom of navigation, world commerce, and, above all, the sovereignty of the host and owner -Egypt of 100 million Arabs.

All of this is while combating terrorism, jihadism, and anti-Islamism. And at the same time singing the *new lyrics inaugurating Suez II: "Tomorrow Egypt Shall Be Sweeter!!"*

# In a Broken Democratic System, Donald Trump, An American Billionaire Clown, Is Bidding for the Presidential Crown!!

Friday, August 28, 2015

Here is a buffoon with billions of dollars. Running on his riches with 25% approval rating. Talking like a thug, yet aiming at the U.S. presidency on a Republican ticket. Calling his other 15 contenders all kinds of nasty names. With none of them standing up to him. Including **Jeb Bush** about whom he said: **"He cannot negotiate himself out of a paper bag!!"**

On Donald Trump's head, a cap reads: **"Make America Great Again."** Now none of his crowded field of opponents can use this phrase in their campaigns. He has copyrighted it. **How?!** It is difficult in the law of patents (intellectual property) to protect such a common phrase. You cannot patent **"Hello!!" But he did.**

Trump, a real estate developer, is riding the wave of discontent of the general public. People are weary of Washington, D.C.; of sluggish economic recovery; of partisan feuding between the Democrats and the Republicans; of economic inequality; of illegal immigration; and of the rise of China whose economy is today's second only to America's. The words **"establishment politics,"** evoke mistrust and anger across party lines. **On the scale of political respect, local measures are at the top; federal measures are well below them.**

Several years ago, I read Trump's book **"The Art of the Deal."** There is nothing exciting about that book. With this publication, Donald Trump makes it sound as if it were the yellow brick road to richness. And in the age of super commitment to riches, Trump peddles his persona along the line: **"I can make you rich too. I know how to make deals."**

So **what deals is he promising America if ever he became president** -a very doubtful proposition?
- He will vanquish ISIS! How?! He says: **"I can't tell you;"**
- He will stop Mexican and other illegal immigrants from coming to America! How: By building a wall between the U.S. and Mexico. Then insanely he adds: **"I shall have Mexico pay for it;"**
- As to **China,** Trump claims that he, if president, will force China to open up its markets to US products. **"They buy my condos!!"**
- How about **Russia?!** Trump will rebuild American military might that would scare off Putin from challenging the U.S.; **no specifics;**
- Thousands gather to hear him. After insulting a woman anchor on **Fox News**, his popularity with women jumped in numbers. His being foul-mouthed makes the public like him. **"He talks like any one of us,"** they say.

**"Make America Great Again"** is repeated by that man who has never before run for any public office. Through sneers, bombast, vulgar sound bites, Trump has shaken the system. On both the Republican side (especially **Jeb Bush**), and the Democratic side (especially **Hillary Clinton**). Diagnosing American democracy, one spots cancer. **Money has subverted this great constitutional system, primarily through one**

**fateful decision of the U.S. Supreme Court.**

In the case of **"Citizens United,"** the Court, by 5 to 4, made a bad judgment. Decided that spending money on electioneering is constitutionally valid. **Why? A form of Free Speech!!** We know that **"money talks."** But that is a saying applicable to transactions. Not applicable to controlling the outcome of elections **-the expression by the citizen of his or her choice as to who represent them in the enactment of legislation.**

To American democracy, **Citizens United** is a cancer whose diagnosis is not hard to find. That diagnosis is learnt from its impact whose best illustration is the **Koch brothers.**

- **Charles and David Koch,** the famous private billionaire brothers are, in the words of **Time Magazine** of August 17, 2015, **"Power Brokers Recharging To Elect a Republican in 2016."** In a brilliant article by **Philip Elliott,** the brothers, through their unlimited funding of conservative candidates to Congress, **"have retooled with more money, better strategy and a new plan for victory."**

- **How do they subvert the free will of the American people through their massive wealth?** One recent example: They convened for dinner a seaside summit for 450 like-minded conservative donors. And Charles Koch welcomed his guests by triumphantly declaring: **"we grew up with every advantage."**

- Their institutional mechanisms include: **The Freedom Partners Chamber of Commerce; Americans for Prosperity; Generation Opportunity; and Concerned Women for America.** Their philosophy is limited government; their biggest focus for the next two years is on four States **(Florida, Ohio, North Carolina and Virginia).** Without winning these States, no Republican nominee can win the White House.

- **Transparency is not required of this conservative enclave which plans to spend $889 million before Election Day in 2016.** Obama is their political adversary. While conservative Republican nominees like **Marco Rubio, Scott Walker,** and **Ted Cruz** are their favorites. Said one of the loyal Koch donors, a lawyer by the name of **Tim Busch: "These guys are using business principles to create political solutions."**

So you can shout **"one person one vote"** all you want. But the high dam of dollars lets through the sleuths (openings) selective publicity for or against candidates whose backgrounds may not be widely known. TV ads are very expensive; massive mailings add to the cost, and the average citizen is caught in the web of hearsay that an enlightened decision on election day is quite difficult. For this is an electorate as culturally diverse as the American pool of voters. **That is not democracy, but plutocracy -the rule of the wealthy.**

Juxtaposing Trump with the Koch brothers yield the same undemocratic results. For Trump prides himself on being his own funder to accomplish the defeat of the Democrats in 2016. Thus trying to bring all three branches of government under the low stifling ceiling of conservatism. Congress, the Executive, and a right-leaning U.S. Supreme Court. Mixing extreme language with rudeness, he, in a search for **"Make America Great Again,"** yells:

- **"I am rich;"** and he brags about his prior donations to his very Republican opponents; for the purpose of embarrassing them into silence;
- On the wings of his private **Boeing 757 plane,** and his $7 million **Sikorsky helicopter,** he swaggers like a prize fighter wading into adoring crowds;
- **Trump vulgarly mocks the modesty of Jimmy Carter, a Nobel Peace Prize Laureate.** He spreads his hands, curls sneeringly his lips as he says: **"Carter had it wrong when he would walk off Air Force One carrying his own suit bag in a show of solidarity with regular folk... They don't want that. They want someone who's going to beat China, beat Japan;"**
- With untethered megalomania, he looks upon dealing with the world as if he is selling condos. In his words: **"Trump gets things done. I know how to get things done." "Jeb Bush (one of his 15 opponents) shall be unable to get things done with China, with Mexico;"**
- He claims that other world leaders are **"more cunning"** than American leaders. Proof: **"The U.S. cannot get its products in China."** And Trump blames American indebtedness to China in the amount of $1.4 trillion, on the claim that **"Our people are babies."**
- **"When was the last time that you saw this country have a victory? We don't have victories. What things am I going to do different? Almost everything."**
- **Regarding ISIS,** Trump has a solution: **"We are going to have to do something very strong... One of the elements of what I said is that we go and take over that oil. We just go in there and we blast the hell out of them, we take over that oil."**
- **On the Iran deal,** he denigrates the expertise of **Secretary of State John Kerry,** plus that of the foreign ministers of the US

other five partners. **"There are things in the deal that I'm sure (Kerry) doesn't even know about that I will find. And if they make a mistake they've got big problems."**
In the present broken democratic system in America, Trump flaunts his billions as a sure way of aspiring to the U.S. presidency. On the unregulated campaign funding, he dismisses his need for outside donations. **"I'll take your money, if you insist. But I shall spend a billion dollars of my own money to fund my campaign."**

**Unfortunately, the present system has availed idiots like Trump a hospitable environment.** His approval rating stands at **25%.** That of Congress is a miserable **9%.** In a recent survey, participants were asked to provide the first word that comes to their minds upon hearing specific names. The result: **"Liar,"** for Hillary Clinton; **"Killer,"** for Jeb Bush; and **"Arrogant,"** for Trump.

No wonder, **David Duke,** head of the **Ku Klux Klan** (anti-blacks), has supported Trump. Trump's racism has been glaringly manifest. Calling Mexican immigrants **"rapists, criminals, and drug users."** White supremacist feelings are back. People are, as per the description of **The New Yorker magazine** dated August 31, 2015 **"fearful and frustrated."** By 2030, the Latino population shall be a full one-third of all Americans. And by 2050, the whites in America are expected to be a minority.

**Again to money as a determinant of electoral victory.** With Jeb Bush having raised **$140 million,** and Hillary Clinton **$100 million,** for their respective campaigns, the public sees in these figures, an early indication of pre-eminence. Add to the mix what another Republican contestant, **Senator Ted Cruz of Texas,** the darling of **The Tea Party,** proclaims. **"All politicians are liars and thieves."**

In support of that perception, a former political consultant for Trump, Roger Stone, adds his voice. **"There are two things going on. One is the total revulsion of American voters with politicians and the entire political system. And secondarily, just the belief that he (Trump) can't be bought."**

As a decisive judgment by the Supreme Court, **Citizens United** has enhanced the **cracks in the facade of the representativeness of the American system.** The power of that Court to impact the presidential election system was manifest in putting **George Bush II ahead of Albert Gore in 2000.** A disastrous presidency in both birth and war-like approach to foreign policy. Especially in warring on Afghanistan (2001) and on Iraq

(2003). **Both losing wars.**

In his new book on the need to amend the Constitution, **retired Supreme Court Justice, John Paul Stevens,** put in perspective the central issue of the dangerous absence of regulating campaign financing. Said that venerable Justice: **"I shall explain why it is unwise to allow persons who are not qualified to vote -whether they be corporations or nonresident individuals -to have a potentially greater power to affect the outcome of elections than eligible voters have."**

Centuries before Justice Stevens, the Romans defined the primary motivation for good governance. In two words: **"Liberum arbitrium"** **(Free will, free choice).** So with the present enfeebled democratic system in America, where clowns like Trump is now bidding for the presidential crown, we should ask ourselves: **"Is America entitled to advise other nations on how to practise democracy?"**

*To me, the answer is No. Why? When your own door is broken and left un-repaired, you have no credibility telling someone else to fix their broken windows.*

# 16 SEPTEMBER 2015

## How Appalling To See a Mainstream Writer Like David Brooks, Seemingly Legitimating The ISIS Mega Crooks!!

Friday, September 4, 2015

He is an admired Op Ed page writer employed by the **New York Times.** When I buy that paper, I begin reading it not from the front. But from the back. Looking to learn something new from **Paul Krugman** on economics. He is a Nobel Prize Laureate at Princeton University. And from **David Brooks,** a distinguished commentator on American social trends and values.

Being a creature of habit, I did the same on August 28. Both **Krugman** and **Brooks** were on the same Op Ed page. What a jolt from reading Brooks!! Under the title of **"When Rapists Win."**

To his credit, he begins, in his inimitable style, to assess ISIS as we all know it. His first line sums it in a few words: **"The ISIS atrocities have descended like distant nightmares upon the conscious of the world."** Yet, amazingly, his column proceeds, unpredictably, to **an abyss of illogic.** Seemingly to legitimate the **ISIS mega-crooks,** by conceding to them their grounds. On what basis, if I am reading him correctly?: **On the basis of a**

**fait accompli.**

Herein lies the roots of my disgust with one of my favorite writers.
Samples raising red flags:

- **"(ISIS) offers a confident vision of the future. It fills the
  vacuum left by decaying nationalist ideologies;"**
- **(Its) intent is to use this as a wedge with which to expand
  beyond its base in Iraq and Syria and weaken secular
  nationalist borders in Lebanon, Jordan and in even more
  innately nationalist countries like Egypt;"**
- **"This is a war about a vision of history. ISIS have legitimacy
  because it controls territory and has a place to enact them."**

Mr. Brooks: **"A confident vision of the future?!"** Does jihadism have **"a
future,"** or **"a vision?"** Only because they marched in and occupied **land
where no government existed?** Where the Sunni population, crushed by
the Maliki sectarian rule, which had been propped up by America's crazy
invasion of Iraq in 2003, sided temporarily with the ISIS hordes? And in
Syria, **Bashar had to vacate the northeast** to hold his crumbling lines
around Damascus?

Mr. Brooks: You are theorizing imaginatively about the issue of territorial
control, illegally achieved, as if it were irreversible. You are claiming for
ISIS a pasture which our own government, the U.S., does not concede. Let
alone, the international coalition of 40 other countries. **Not even the
Kurdish Pesh Merga which has pushed ISIS out of Kobani and other
areas.**

Your expression of defeatism is not only unsupported by the facts on the
present ground of battle against that paper tiger, called the Baghdadi
Caliphate. It flies rudely in the face of two historical facts, not of the type
of your depressing **"vision of history."**

**Your first fallacy** is that ISIS is **"weakening secular nationalist
borders."** It is the Arab Spring, wherever it has overcome the resultant
civil wars, that is redrawing **"the secular nationalist borders."** This is the
start of nullification of the colonial borders forced upon the Arabs by the
victors of the First World War. **The Arabs are now in the process of
burying Mr. Sykes and M. Picot. Two conspirators who nullified
promises given to the Arabs in return for turning against Ottoman
oppresive rule.** Post-Assad Syria may witness the rise of three states,
replacing one unified Syria.

**Your second fallacy** is your unthinking statement about Arab nationalism.

For your claim: **"For the past many decades the Middle East has been defined by nation-states and the Arab mind has been influenced by nationalism. But these nation-States have been weakened (Egypt) or destroyed (Iraq and Syria). Nationalism no longer mobilizes popular passion or provides convincing historical narrative."**

Mr. Brooks: **From where did you get that?** Surely, at least in the case of Egypt, you did not get it from the Egyptian street. **My proof on your distance from objective reality:** The U.S. government and media still overlook the significance of 35 million Egyptians rising in a historical **"Egyptian Intifadah,"** on June 30, 2013. Calling on now deposed Islamist President Morsi, **"IRHAL" (Begone!!).** In spite of these realities, **the Brotherhood is still looked upon in many American quarters as a legitimate opposition** whose removal constituted a coup by the Armed Forces. A continuous affront to the free will of the overwhelming majority of the Egyptian people.

On these grounds alone, I doubt it, Mr. Brooks, that you are as familiar with Egyptian history as I am. I am not in competition with you. You have **The New York Times** as your vehicle. I have the facts about the history of modern Egypt as mine. And facts are more supreme and durable than media. **Especially when those media are either biased or uninformed.**

As a teacher of Egyptian history, let me share with you a bit of that history:
- For the past 7000 years, **Egyptian nationalism** has been the glue that binds the nation;
- **Never has Egypt witnessed civil war,** nor, in spite of colonial British attempts, has it been split between North and South;
- The only army in the Arab homeland, whose recruits and officer corps owe allegiance only to the State, not to provinces, is **the Egyptian army;**
- In 1952, **Colonel Nasser** ousted **King Farouk** by staging an army coup. Upon the King's departure from Alexandria, the front man of the coup, **Muhammad Naguib** saluted his monarch with a 21-gun salute. Farouk's last words to **General Naguib** were: **"Take care of Egypt's army."** That is nationalism at its best, Mr. Brooks.
- In spite of modest economic means, Egyptian women surrendered repeatedly since the 1870s, their golden ornaments to shore up state finances. **The first women revolt against the hijab, was in Egypt in the early 20th century;** an assertion of Egyptian secularism;
- Egypt is the only Arab State which **officially celebrates**

**Christmas** as a national holiday. **That is on January 7,** which marks the Eastern Orthodox Christmas. And the only mass political party in Egypt whose symbol is the **Crescent with the Cross within it replacing the star -the Wafd party,** established in 1919;

- In homage to the roots of the faith of its majority, Islam, the only Arab flag which is adorned by **the falcon of Quarish,** the Arabian tribe of which the **Prophet Muhammad** was a member of its main branch **(the great Hashemites)** is Egypt's flag.

And I hope that your argument, David Brooks, about the weakening of Arab nationalism, **especially by a phantom called ISIS,** had found its inanity (silliness) on August 6, 2015. That is the date on which Egypt inaugurated Suez Canal II. Built within less than one year by subscriptions from only Egyptian citizens.

With Suez Canal II yesterday, and now with the **discovery of huge gas reserves off Egyptian territorial waters,** Egyptian nationalism shall continue to express itself in the new song: **"Tomorrow, Egypt Shall Be Sweeter."**

Finally, and in regard to the assertions of **The New York Times** of August 18, 2015 which headlined **"Egypt Expands State Power With a New Security Law,"** I have the following rebuttal:

**State power in Egypt does not expand through the promulgation of security laws.** Laws are invariably an external result of internal developments. That power expands through nationalist fervor. **Uncomplicated by the resort to the total denial of due process manifest in our American phenomenon of "Guantanamo."** Shameful, yet falsely trumpeted as a security measure.

*Mr. Brooks: Guantanamo has "become (one of the) recruiting tools "for jihadism. Quoting the words of none other than President Obama. His efforts over the past 7 years to close that abysmal institution of horror and torture have failed. Due to the obstructionism of the Republican-dominated Congress of the U.S.*

# Thousands of Arabs Are Fleeing!! From What? From a Disastrous Arab System!!

Friday, September 18, 2015

**Aylan Kurdi,** a Syrian of 3 years of age. Lying lifeless, face down, on a Turkish beach. Washed by the sea waves as dead fish. Nearby were the bodies of his brother and mother. Emblematic of a disastrous Arab system. Those bodies graphically depicted a lifeless Arab State system. In fact a non-system, except in name only.

And across those merciless waves of the Mediterranean, thousands upon thousands of Syrians and Iraqis were in full flight. With their babies and meager belongings, braving barbed wire, fences, and inclement weather. All running from the horrors of misrule, butchery, and hunger in their countries of origin. Mostly Muslim, running into the welcoming arms of Germany and Austria, facilitated by Greece and Italy. Seeking refuge in Christian countries; in total fear of Muslim countries where death is everywhere.

Anomalies, yet realities. Arab refugees, by the thousands, lost faith in their flags, traditions, symbols, and religious incantations. To them, the words of Arab leaders were mere lies. And they were lies. In Damascus, the capital city of death, banners proclaimed that the Arabs were **"One Nation, with an eternal message!!"** How cynical!! As you raise your head to read that banner, you are greeted by a barrel bomb whistling its way to you from above. With a clear warning: **"Are you still here?!!"**

Arab flags are mostly of three colors (red, white and black). Representing a famed Arab poem. That is when the Arabs truly believed in the words of their focal points, from rulers to poets. The poet had meant red, for liberational struggle; white, for pure intentions; and black, for victory over an unjust past. But the millions of refugees have come to see in their national flags only doom and gloom. Trust in Arab governments is gone. Trust in the often maligned West is the new creed.

ISIS, Bashar, sectarianism, and jihadism are now all one. Yes, Islam is a faith of tolerance, collective care, and rescue for the downtrodden. This is what the **Book (the Quran)** says. But is there much generalized faith in the great Quranic instruction which abhors senseless death, extra-judicial executions, car bombs, human suicide, and arcane interpretation of Islam?

If there is, show me.

Show me where is **verse 32 of Chapter V** of the **Quran** is observed.  Read it and judge for yourself.  If follows:
**"...We prescribed to the Children of Israel that whoever kills a soul, unless it be for retaliation or because of spreading corruption on earth, it would be as if he had killed all mankind.  And whoever saves a life, it would be as if he had saved the life of all Mankind..."**

Where is **Bashar** from that heavenly standard?  Where is **Maliki**, who as Prime Minister of Iraq, openly practiced sectarianism?  Did **Qaddafi** of Libya, or **Saleh** of Yemen abide by it?  We are not talking about lax observance of basic human rights!!  We are here dealing with genocidal acts against citizens!!

**Most of the Arab geographic area now looks like a cesspool of brazen untruths, and unbelievable inequities.**  Splashed over billions of screens of social media.  While Europe getting together to host Arab and other refugees, Arab petro-dollars are gearing up to  refurbish images of their leaders.  Through very costly western public relations firms.  Funding for image, not for substance.  Including fancy speeches about human rights in the halls of the UN General Assembly later this September.  Image, image, image!!

And speaking of **"inter-faith!!"**  The Arabs still regard it as **"a dialogue."**  A conversation.  A kind of a composition.  A statement in flowery words meant to enhance the standing of those who utter them.  Not the importance of the message, which is only honored in the breach.

**Action?  The main action is in the West.**  That is where compassion towards Muslim refugees is flowing beyond bounds.  **Pope Francis** has called for opening monasteries and the Vatican itself, to shelter that Muslim stampede.  **Germany** has allocated nearly $5 Billions to care for those arrivals in Munich.  **Austrians** have stood for hours to say to those immigrants: **"Welcome to your new home."**  Even an individual, **a young woman lawyer in Florida, Carolina Maluje.**  Partly Syrian, partly Chilean.  Told me recently: **"I must do something for those Syrian immigrants."**

An Arab foreign minister from a petro-dollar country was asked: **"What has your country done for the Syrian refugees?"**  His answer was an example of obscurity.  **"Many of my countrymen are married to Syrian women,"** said he proudly.  How impenetrable to sight this can be!!  Thanks

God, there arose Arab exceptions. **Mr. Naguib Sawiris,** an Egyptian Copt and a billionaire, rose up to purchase a Greek or an Italian island to house those refugees.

The flood of Arab immigrants has revealed where the rule of the law is observed by only a minority of 22 Arab governments. Arab advocacy of one common history, and one common language has remained only aspirational. Non-supported by a broad culture. A culture illuminating a road map drawn by the intersection of common interests. As a result, the **League of Arab States** has been frozen in paralysis since the adoption of its Alexandria Charter in 1944.

No way could an Arab Union, similar to the European Union, emerge in the foreseeable future. For loyalty, in the majority of Arab States, remains confined to the tribe, or the region, or the province. That is unless you are in a country like **Egypt or Tunisia. Reason:** national cohesiveness is a reflection of a historical continuum which began centuries ago. The fate of a divided Sudan, a divided Yemen, a divided Syria may travel to cover other Arab States beyond these unhappy examples.

In spite of these disheartening contradictions, the migration catastrophe has evoked in the Arab homeland a sense of shame. Acted upon individually, by each sovereign State as an act of charity.

**Amr Musa,** former Secretary-General of the League of Arab States, made a high-ringing statement on September 9 in Austria. The occasion was the annual meeting of the **International Peace Institute** which was convened to discuss challenges to the present international legal system. As usual, his emphasis was on hope for solidarity in regard to the immigration catastrophe affecting the Syrians and the Iraqis.

You read it, then ask the humorous American advertising question: **"Where Is the Beef?"** Proposals on top of proposals. Who will implement? Who will pay? Who will evaluate the performance? And who will remove the root causes? Questions dancing over the horizon of hope. Soon to be forgotten. A high-level meeting. But with a low-level energy!!

Nonetheless, **Aylan Kurdi's** lifeless body has, in its own way, convulsed the Arab State lifeless body to twitch. A short spastic contraction of the fibers of the Arab muscle:
- **Jordan** is now a host of more than a million Syrians. The only Arab State with historically open borders to all Arabs;
- Same numbers in **Lebanon and Iraq;**

- **Egypt** hosts a quarter of a million;

Of course, numbers do change. What does not change may be presented succinctly hereunder:

- Europe had started a coordinated policy. It is based on future quotas of Syrian and Iraqi immigrants. With Germany taking the most. While other members of the 28 Member States of the European Union, like Greece, may take the least;
- The Arab world, where the Syrian killing fields exist, has no coordinated policy in this regard. **Each State is on its own.** However the Arabs are bound together, through the League of Arab States.
- Those binding ties are focused on the League's image. **Ambassador Ahmed Bin Hilli,** Under-Secretary-General of the League, on September 8 rose to defend the League against European criticism of weak Arab action. The issue, he fulminated, will be discussed at the forthcoming 144th session of the League at the ambassadorial level. Again the image is in the forefront; the real action, coordinated or not, remains in the realm of eternal hope.

*In the meantime, policies, plans, and implementing mechanisms are being set-up elsewhere in Europe and the Americas. Said the lady President of Brazil, "the image of that dead toddler, Aylan Kurdi has shocked us all as a challenge to the whole world." A whale of a difference between Arab paralysis, and non-Arab actions. Primary reason why the Arabs are fleeing from most of their homeland. In droves. They are not heading East. They are heading West in a massive Hijrah!!*

Running away from an Arab State system whose nominal faith is the great Islam whose Book advocates: **"Cooperate with all in what is good and pious. And do not cooperate in what is sinful and aggressive." (Chapter V, Verse 2).**

And since God is One under the principle of **Tawheed** (God's oneness), the castaways, mostly Muslim, are seeking the certitude of safety provided by Christian governments. For there is action on the belief of **"The Peace Prayer"** of St. Francis of Assisi. In part it says: **"For it is in giving that we receive; it is in pardoning that we are pardoned."**

All this is happening under the dark shadow of 9/11 where men, covering their box cutters under the cloth of Islam, caused the murder of 3000 innocent victims.

That faith in murder has been passed on to phantom governments like Syria's, and phantom caliphates like ISIS.

**The Arab code of old was superior to the Arab code of today.** Because the older code regarded the admission of failure as the road to reform. In his instructions to the Arab judiciary, **Omar, the second Caliph to succeed the Prophet Muhammad** in leading the nascent Muslim State said it all. **"Never hesitate to reflect on your judgment of yesterday. For nullifying a bad judgment is better by far than perpetuating an error."**

Alas!! That was 1400 years ago. **Today's Mr. Hilli, the Under-Secretary-General of the League of the Arab States does not abide by that golden rule.** To him, admission of the shortcomings of the League is a sign of weakness. Forgetting that the whole world is witnessing leaks in the plumbing of the Arab system. Leaking millions of horrified millions of Arabs of all denominations. Running away from what used to be a Homeland, but no more.

*That broken system needs an army of plumbers. For fixing the leaks in the moral infra-structure of Arab lands can never be done by pretending that it does not exist. Reason why Omar, though a Bedouin, was, by all accounts, the real "Arab Profile in Courage!!" Ignoring his Code shall result in a million Syrians expected to flee their country by the end of 2015.*

# **17** OCTOBER 2015

## In Fending Off Its Attackers, What Does Egypt Need to Master? The Art of Response!!

Friday, October 2, 2015

In national life, the most critical juncture is transitioning. From chaos to stability. From poverty to development. From dictatorship to democracy. From the Rule by One, to participation.

The New Egypt is now at this critical juncture. Transitioning from a have-not country to a have country. From the dependent State under **Mubarak,** to the strong State under **El-Sisi.** From borrowing and foreign aid, to being self-sufficient. **From a country concerned with the affairs of other Arab States, to one concerned primarily with its own improvement.**

That is why the great Egyptian educator, **Loutfi El-Sayed,** advocated one essential principle for Egyptian development. He cried out **"Build Fences Around Egypt!!"** That is the essence of **"charity starts at home."** But Egyptian leaders did not heed that call. Examples from the Nasser period:

- **Did Egypt need to unite with Syria from 1958 to 1961: No.** To Syria, Egypt exported a stern military intelligence governance. From Syria, Egypt got a deluge of nonsensical rhetoric about socialism and Arabism.

- **Did Egypt need to be immersed in the Palestinian problem to the extend of losing its unity with the Sudan? No!!** The plebiscite of 1954 in the Sudan resulted in 7 to 1. Seven for unity, from Damietta on the Mediterranean to Lake Albert at the source of the Nile. **Water is power.**
- An Egyptian/Sudanese union would have been the strongest backbone for the Nilotic population in dealing with the outside world. Instead, of bringing in the Sudanese leadership, beginning with **Ismail El-Azhari,** to co-rule the Nile Valley, North and South, Egypt sent **Salah Salem** to perform a tribal dance in southern Sudan.
- To southern Sudan, an intelligent leadership in Egypt should have sent **Coptic leadership.** From ages immemorial, the Coptic Church had been advocating a **federation between the Egypt/the Sudan and Uganda and Ethiopia.** But the wise voice of the Copts were inaudible to the ears of Egypt's strong man, Nasser.
- **Did Egypt need to rush headlong into the Yemeni civil war of 1962, following the disastrous dissolution in 1961 of the artificial union between Egypt and Syria? No.** That was a tribal coup, leading to a mountain warfare for which the Egyptian army has never been trained. It caused rupture with Saudi Arabia, depleted Egypt's meager resources, forced **Nasser's** Egypt to use napalm against the tribes supporting the Imam (the present day Houthis).
- That involvement also whetted Israel's appetite to attack Egypt in 1967. **Resulting in the greatest catastrophe in the history of the modern Arabs. Resulting in the second Israeli occupation of Sinai, on Nasser's watch, the occupation of Gaza, the West Bank, Jerusalem and the Golan Heights. Namely the rise of Greater Israel.** Only Sinai was returned to Egypt, thanks to Sadat's vision of **"let us first take care of Egypt."**
- For that liberation, **Sadat** was assassinated. The first Egyptian head of State to exit life in that fashion since **Mameluke** days. And as Sadat was breathing his last on October 6, 1981, and paving the way to an inept **Mubarak** as President, the PLO issued a statement of treachery. **"May the hand that pulled the trigger be blessed,"** the Arafat organization intoned.

The Arab system which produced the present **League of Arab States in 1944 has a birth defect.** It unites the Arab States peripherally. You can only see the outer field of vision. But enhances their division substantially.

Since its establishment, the League of Arab States (LAS) has convened 144 regular sessions. This is without mentioning the new mechanism of Arab summits. **At that rate, and by simple math, LAS has met 2.5 times each year of its lazy existence.** And not much to show for it.

Just consider the role of LAS in the present Syrian horrific genocidal conflict. With 11 million Syrians either in full flight or trapped inside as internally displaced. **Who is acting on this mammoth Arab catastrophe?** Not LAS. But Russia, the US, Iran and Assad the butcher of Syria. **Suspending Syria's membership of LAS had zero impact on Assad.**

**So why keep what doesn't work?** Unless the Arabs are eternally wedded to the concept of LAS as a talisman. An object held to act as a charm to avert evil and bring good fortune. Most of Arab North African States have more commercial, financial and trade agreements with Europe than with other members of LAS.

From all the above, there are objective lessons: **The only useful mechanisms in LAS** are its functional adjuncts -its sub-agencies working on trade, education, health...etc. **The least useful in the LAS mechanisms are those dealing with political and sovereignty issues.**

**The Arab system should learn from the Organization of American States (OAS). Reason:** The inter-American system does not allow for interference in internal affairs. The Arab system is diseased by that interventionary germ. **Illuminating examples:** splintered Hamas, and petro-dollar puffed-up Qatar supporting the terroristic rebellion of the so-called Muslim Brotherhood inside big Egypt. A hopeless endeavor which the New Egypt is robustly confronting.

Now back to the need for this New Egypt, re-emerging into **"the strong State"** to practise the **Art of Response.** Just focusing on one recent report by **David Kirkpatrick, New York Times correspondent in Cairo,** and a consistent attacker of the policies of post-Islamist Egypt: His article is dated September 22, 2015, and its parsing (analytical examination) should serve as **a sample for the need to learn the Art of Response.**

In my view, the David Kirkpatrick article is a model of what appears to be deliberate animus toward post-Islamist Egypt. It is headed: **"Egypt Destroying Far More Homes Than Buffer-Zone Plan Called For."**

I shall use it as a sample illustrating the art of response as a demolition tool. Here is a suggested technique honed through my practise as a defense attorney.

**First: Find consistency of bias by his paper - The New York Times.** And show how that consistency is in violation of the obvious facts. Bias is basically an irrational smothering of the facts. **The New York Times** has nearly always attacked post-Islamist Egypt through its editorials and its reporters based in Cairo. It is a bias in favor of **the mother of terrorist organizations called the Muslim Brotherhood.** That paper still regards the Brotherhood as a legal and peaceful opposition.

**Second: Impeach the source or sources of that article.** This one is fairly easy. The sources are invariably the same. **Kirkpatrick invariably seeks out the same poisonous wells.** In the case of this article, these are: **Human Rights Watch,** a non-governmental organization in search of funds. Through attempting to interpret the facts about the New Egypt to fit its own theoretical notions of what constitutes the upholding of human rights. It is a private corporation in search of aggression through **intervening in internal affairs via the human rights pearly gate.** Ignoring that in countries in transition, like Egypt, the collective rights of the populace trump the rights of the individual.

**Third: Parsing the offending text:** This is the coup de grace -the stage of the death blow through correct factual analysis. While doing so, **put a big mirror fronting the faces of the likes of Kirkpatrick.** This is intended to uncover the idiocy of bias through reporting. **Here we cite only 3 excerpts.**

- **(1) "The government has destroyed more than 3,255 homes and other civilian buildings... More than 3,200 families have been displaced... And security forces are still in the process of levelling the entire border town of Rafah, which has a population of 78,000."**
- **Counter-points:** Terrorism in Sinai is an outright warfare. Egypt is acting on the western adage: **"Everything is fair in love and war." Sovereign Egypt cannot wage that war with its hands tied behind its back.** Its military commanders are in no need of consulting before acting. US pilotless drones over Afghanistan, Pakistan and Yemen do not pre-warn their victims. I, have seen the huge devastation in **Falluja, Iraq,** during two US demolition operations. Following the total defeat of Nazi Germany, the allies in 1945 **levelled the city of Dresden** for no obvious defensive reasons.
- **(2) "The government has produced no public evidence that militants have ever received weapons or aid through the tunnels."**

- **Counter-points:** This is the abyss of idiocy. No need to cite instances of **"public evidence,"** which Kirkpatrick himself ignores in making his mythical case. Common sense is sufficient evidence, when asking: **"From where did the Gazan and other terrorists gotten their weapons? But thanks, David, for at least admitting that the tunnels exist or existed."** But for what purpose? Please also note that when a weapon is smuggled through the tunnels dug by Gazans, the weapon is not stamped **"Tunnel-Procured."**

- On the very date of that offending Kirkpatrick article, **US Congress heard testimony on the role of those tunnels in terror warfare.** In a hearing for 2 hours before the Senate Armed Services committee. The witness was **General David Petraeus, former CIA Director (2011-2012) and former Commander in Iraq and Afghanistan.** So please hear him declare to the approbation of all committee members. **"The Egyptian Government has done an excellent job in destroying those tunnels through which weapons flowed."**

- **(3) After a militant attack on a checkpoint killed 28 soldiers, the Sisi government announced plans for a buffer zone in October.**

- **Counter-points:** At long last, Kirkpatrick sets forth the legitimate reason for Egypt's need to create that buffer zone. But what he concedes by one hand, he, without shame, takes away by the other. That is particularly where he describes those legitimate actions by Cairo as **"scorched-earth tactics."** He conveniently forgets that Sinai was earth-scorched only twice, in 1956 and in 1967. During two wars of aggression by Israel against Egypt.

A buffer zone in Sinai to keep ISIS affiliates in Gaza, including the murderous terrorists of the so-called **"the Province of Sinai"** cannot compare in magnitude with US actions in 1941/42 against American citizens of Japanese descent. Remember the concentration campus established by the Roosevelt administration in which thousands of citizens were herded. Ostensible justification: **national security in the aftermath of the sneaky attack by imperial Japan against Pearl Harbor in December 1941.**

This is although Kirkpatrick is not the only example which could be used to demonstrate the art of response in rebuttal.

For we have other examples taken from the present campaign for nomination by the Republican party for US President in 2016. One of these is **Dr. Ben Carson.** An Afro-American physician who made a most egregious declaration against Islam and Muslims during a debate in Las Vegas.

**Carson said that he regarded Islam as incompatible with the principles of the U.S. Constitution. Then added that therefore no Muslim could ever be president of the U.S.** Yet contrary to Carson's demagogic assertion, my research in 2016 for the American Bar Association proved that **Islamic Law and the U.S. Constitution have 80% of their principles in common.**

So when the Carson campaign called me recently for a contribution, I fully employed my art of response. In my refusal to make a financial contribution, I could not possibly dwell on the virtues of Islam. **Not to, a confirmed bigot.** Therefore, I simply reminded that caller that **Carson, through his racism, was endangering US security.** By providing jihadists with ammunition for their claim that Islam was disrespected, denigrated. Worse still, that Islam was under attack.

*Because of their idiocy, shameless individuals, like Kirkpatrick and Carson, deserve to be objects of the Arab proverb: "Those without shame have no limits to what they do or say!!"*

# The Post-Obama Oval Office and the New Egypt

Thursday, October 15, 2015

After Obama, America will never be the same. For he has shifted the country's center of gravity from war to negotiations in foreign dealings. And from economic inequality to economic egalitarianism in domestic matters. By egalitarianism, I mean a belief in human equality. Especially with respect to social, political, and economic rights and privileges.

When Obama leaves the Oval Office in January 2017, his replacement shall be a democrat, whether Hillary or Biden. No Republican is expected to win the presidential race in November 2016. The Republican party has been hijacked by the right. That right is an amalgam of the Tea Party, the evangelists, the crazies-for-war, like Trump, and the addicts of American exceptionalism, like Dick Cheney.

All brash characters, adept at theatrics and political theater. Their focus is on a rear-view mirror in which they see an America ascendant. Not an America bewildered by a continuously changing world environment. A black President destined for high marks from history.

Before entry into specifics, especially with regard to Egypt, let us have a bird's eye-view of the differences between the Democratic Party of today and it's contestant, the Republican Party.

The Democrats are for a strong central government capable of delivering federal services; the Republicans are for a shrunk government, relying on the States to do limited services. This said, the Democrats seek experience; the Republicans search for the apolitical outsider who excels in image-building. The Democrats adhere to an orderly political process; the Republicans see in that process a curtailment of the freedom of the individual and of the market forces.

Therefore, I shall have to predict that the next President shall try to live up to the Obama legacy. A legacy shaped by the war scars caused by Republican adventurism under Bush Jr. It shall also be shaped by the words of the former chief of British intelligence, John Sawers. On CNN on September 12, Sawers described Obama as <u>"calm, steady, and reliable,"</u> and <u>"with a focus on the domestic side."</u>

The next administration in Washington, D.C. shall see in Egypt a reliable partner, not a dependency. That partnership has already been through fighting a common enemy: jihadism. Egypt is the only entity in the Arab world which is capable of hitting at jihadism on two fronts, Sinai and the western desert.

Egypt is also bringing to the fight its own brand of "a religious revolution" as called for by President El-Sisi. But with an extra flavor: A coptic endorsement. People think that the Obama speech at Cairo University in 2009 has lost its impact on Democratic decision-making. It has not, though its reverberations have been muted by the aftershocks of the Brotherhood's coup d'etat of 2012-2013.

The flow of US arms to Egypt is not expected to be interrupted, nor shall aid provided for it by the obligations of the 1979 Treaty. Rather than ebbing, it is expanding: the "Bright Star" joint military exercises, suspended in 2013, have been resumed; and the American military contingent at the Egyptian/Israeli line of control has been bolstered. This recent development has come about as a result of the terrorist attack perpetrated by a combined force of Hamas renegades and Ansar Beit Al-Iraqdis -now renamed vaingloriously "The Sinai Province." A putative adjunct of the so-called Islamic State, under a hopeless loser from Anbar, self-named Calipha Al-Baghdadi.

In studying America, one has to look into many corners of that powerful and complex entity. They call it connecting the dots. I call it looking at the joints. Being a world power, its foreign policies may look contradictory. So it turns out that the nuclear deal with Iran has widened the rupture in foreign policy practices. But no in strategic relationships, between the U.S. and Israel. Netanyahu was stupid to embarrass Obama by addressing Congress in March. His aim of sabotaging that international agreement backfired. It revealed the Republicans to be beholden to the Jewish vote and funds. But it also ignited a sense of "America First" throughout the body-politic.

Israel, for its own purposes, is trying hard to paper over this rift. It calls it "a family quarrel." But this quarrel, from which Egyptian foreign policy can draw no benefit, goes to the heart of a post-Obama America. That new America is tired of the Arab/Israeli question. Except for any threat to Israel's existence. It is also tired of foreign issues where the locals cannot take charge of their solutions to their own problems. Only through a concert of powers can America be re-involved.

Another important reason why a post-Obama democratic administration shall quickly be pleased by the emergence in Egypt of "the strong State." American human rights organizations and correspondents, like those of the New York Times based in Egypt, may grumble about the status of individual human rights in Egypt. The U.S. executive branch does not see it this way. Congress, from the lesson of the Iran deal, has been taught a harsh constitutional lesson: Let the President do his or her job of running foreign policy.

And the New Egypt is bolstering that thinking which shall continue to prevail during the reign of the incoming Administration. Economically, Egypt is putting its house in order. Its new prospects of prosperity from the new duality of the Suez Canal, and the new gas discoveries, and the new laws impacting on terrorism and public demonstrations. All these developments support local solutions to global problems. Music to the American ears.

America is pivoting toward Asia in search of commerce not conflict. So is the new Egypt. New contracts between Cairo and Russia, India, Singapore and China. New weapons technology from Russia, and upgraded rockets technology whose products are being exported to the Syrian regime. New sea and air armaments from France, flexibility of foreign policy which may lead to a new Egyptian opening. Not only to Syria, but also to Iran where every Gulf state has an embassy.

These are important signs of robust Egyptian sovereignty. Seen by America as parallelling Washington's appreciation of local solutions. And tracking Washington's renewed relations with Cuba, and soon with Venezuela. And a bit later with Iran.

American concern about Russia's military build-up in Syria shall continue. It is muted for three basic reasons: the priority of defeating ISIS an effort in which the New Egypt is pulling its weight; American militarization of both Japan and Australia; and American mishandling of Putin in the Crimea, Ukraine crises.

In a new book by Marc Lynch entitled "The New Arab Wars," the author posits what I have set forth earlier in this presentation: America of the future is reducing its material presence abroad, exercising restraint, and stepping back challenging allies to take greater responsibility for their own future."

The Republican Party lament of "if only the U.S. was stronger," is going nowhere. And when Jeb Bush, now running for President on the Republican ticket, says that he would consider waterboarding of detainees, his voice finds no echo. The book by Dick Cheney and his daughter, Liz Cheney, entitled "Exceptional" has been given the cold shoulder by the majority of Americans. It called Obama a hater of America, and vainly tried to have Dick Cheney refurbish his name.

America of Dick Cheney is the now despised past. America of Obama and his democratic successor is the wave of the future. Egypt and its Arab allies cannot lose from these developments.

For this is the new Oval Office as of 2017 where its occupant shall for a long time heed this assessment. An assessment made by no other than Obama. He said something that I expect to resonate with the next President. He said: "At this moment, the greatest threats come from the Middle East and North Africa, where radical groups exploit grievances for their own gain." So what can the Oval Office's occupant in 2017 do about it?

Answering this question, we have the voice of the top military officer of the U.S., now retired. He is General Martin Dempsey, the former Chairman of the Joint Chiefs of Staff. He gave the best description of what he called "today's global security environment." "It is the most unpredictable I have seen in 40 years." (The New York Times, August 12, 2015).

In conclusion, I say that Egypt, vis-a-vis the US executive of 2017, should stay its present course. Internal strength at home, militarily, economically. Though the Brotherhood pretends to have American legitimation, I am finding that the earlier misconception about the Brotherhood, as a bona fide political opposition, is fading away. The noise they, the Brotherhood, produces in Times Square, New York City, benefits only theoretically from the protection of the First Amendment of the US Constitution. But no structural or policy value, in terms of official recognition.

The harder Egypt fights terrorism, the higher it shall go up in the American index of respectability. US/Israel strategic relationship is not destined to be converted into a mutual defense pact with America. That Israeli hope is now dead.

And Egyptian aid from America is not that huge. It might be better to consider converting it, in due course, into income from US investments in Egypt.

Under no circumstances can Egyptian sovereignty be for hire. And the occupancy of the post-Obama White House shall find it impossible to attempt it. The proof: It ended in failure with the departure of Mubarak. It goes again the grain of the huge shifts in American interests abroad.

# The Obama Doctrine On Middle East Conflicts

Sunday, October 18, 2015

You judge a doctrine by its opposite. Diametrically opposed to Obama is Dick Cheney, who in effect is a warlord. And a member of the war party, called the Republican Party.

For a book recently published by Dick Cheney, who ruled America for 8 years as a Vice President to the hapless George Bush Jr., the chosen title was Exceptional.

The authors, Dick Cheney and his daughter Liz, postulated that Obama has weakened America. Therefore, they arrogantly argued, Obama was, in their words: "A villain, ineffectual, America hating, destroyer of the military, soft on terrorism, an appeaser, and damaged America's standing in the world community."

These are epithets thrown at Obama by a war criminal, and an unindicted felon. This is judging by his thrusting America in a losing war in Iraq - a war of choice. For Obama, the first black President in American history, has, since his days in the Senate, opposed the war in Iraq. From that point, he continued to evolve his peace approach into a coherent theory. A theory put in practice becomes a doctrine. Our topic this evening.

I began by quoting Cheney. Now I must put this presentation in context. A most recent context - the deal with Iran on its nuclear portfolio, reached in July. This is a signal concretization of the Obama doctrine on Middle East Conflicts. That doctrine is working. And I expect it to continue under a presidency by the democrats, being it Hillary Clinton or someone else like Joseph Biden.

Evidence of the success of this doctrine which consists of many parts is manifest. In a Republican dominated Congress, the Iran Agreement, with seven signatories on it (the Five Permanent Members of the UN Security Council, plus Germany, plus Iran), has survived. It was not even put to a vote in either house of Congress. Obama won, without the Agreement reaching his desk for a certain veto. The war mongers, including Netanyahu, lost in spite of $25 million funding attack ads and a visit by 36 US Congressmen to Israel.

This was a victory not only for the Obama doctrine on Middle East conflicts. It was a resounding win for American sovereignty over an overwhelming Israeli intrusion in internal American politics. Now Israel wants to compensate for its defeat in Washington, D.C.

The compensation is too high that no American administration could agree to it. Israel wants a mutual defense pact with America. Meaning that an attack, real or fabricated, on Israel would be regarded as an attack on America. Washington is staying in a strategic relationship with Israel. But not to the point of converting that relationship into a mutual defense pact.

This shall avoid the tail, Israel, wagging the dog, America. It has been the failed goal of Israel, the American right, and the American neoconservatives. A lost hope. America is not returning to war anywhere in the Middle East.

Returning back to the Iran deal, now a <u>fait acompli,</u> it could now be said with certitude, that that deal is a part of "a new grand strategy for America in the Middle East." Here I am quoting Robert Satloff, the Director of the Washington Institute for Near East Policy.

A strategy is the concretization of a doctrine, on whose specifics I now embark.

Since the Second World War, America had no military victories. When the Cold War ended in 1990, America has repeatedly turned to outside powers and the UN for any large scale military or enforcement action. That super-power has, by necessity, turned into a super-coalition builder. Thus the report card on America, in spite of its unparalleled military power, reads as follows:

The Gulf War of 1991 registered one success; the wars in Korea and Afghanistan were a draw; the wars in Vietnam and Iraq were losing wars, with huge defeats for the American economy, especially the middle class. Why?

Even with a budget surpassing all military budgets of the European Union, the American military is poorly suited to the non-conventional conflicts now raging in the Middle East. With the borders being either porous or non-existing like in Syria/Iraq. The globalization of those asymmetric conflicts has been ironically facilitated by American technology. America's so-called war on terror lacked a focus, as I personally discovered in Iraq. Even the Cheney War on Iraq, which toppled Saddam was a boon to the empowerment of Iran. It also resulted in the rise of devastating sectarianism.

This is not to mention the huge rise of China which has become a global rule-maker, not a rule-taker. Add to this the violent military response of Putin's Russia to the western effort to bring NATO's boundary to the heartland of Russian nationalism -the Ukraine and Crimea.

Today, young Russians believe that, and I quote, "America is trying to encircle us. We have finally risen out of chaos, and you, Americans, don't like it." Russia's Czarist strategy to reach the warm waters of the

Mediterranean is, at long last succeeding. A foothold in Syria, at a Russian naval base at Latakia and Tartous. Propping Assad is a dual Russian strategy: Appearing to assist a formal Government against rebels turned terrorists. While breaking out of Western imposed isolation as a king-maker in the Arab Spring.

These moves are factored into the Obama calculus of staying engaged in the Middle East without American military footprint. And at the same time keeping wary eyes on Russian military moves in the same geographic space. Obama, aside from US airstrikes on ISIS in Iraq and now also in Syria, is responding through diplomacy. Putin is going about in a dual fashion: diplomacy and Russian military footprint.

In doing so, Putin has no fear of militarily colliding with Yankee troops. In the meantime, these Russian moves are causing Israel concern, whether real or pretended. Under the Obama doctrine, American troops have returned home. Leaving only technologists to operate their drones and to train whomever they can find around in Sunni Iraq and Sunni Syria to battle ISIS.

In this context, we have Putin suddenly and openly declaring Russian provision of military aid to Damascus. This is while the Pentagon is struggling to find native recruits to fight ISIS without also battling Assad. In the meantime, ISIS is reported to have doubled the number of its foreign recruits. From 15,000 in 2014 to 30,000 in 2015.

Again looking at the Obama doctrine of limited engagement in Middle East conflicts, from the prism of its global environment. That environment includes primarily both China and Russia. We have seen China celebrating in August its military might in Tiananmen Square. Real awesome hardware being reviewed by President Xi in a world message that say: Don't mess with China!!

China's traditional silence about its global power is over. Its resurgence is noted through its militarization of uninhabited Pacific islands, its strategic inroads in Pakistan to counter the US/India new strategic relationships, its diesel-powered submarines, and its state of the arts nuclear aircraft carriers. That might shall rebound to the benefit of crossing from sea to sea through Egypt's dual Suez Canals.

In a similar fashion, the consequences of the Obama doctrine about Middle East conflicts, can be seen through the strong men surrounding Putin today. These Kremlin hard liners are called Siloviki, "men of force." They are a coterie of generals and KGB veterans. For the past two and a half years, they have dominated. Their loyalty is to Putin personally who continues to lament the collapse of the USSR. The Siloviki have been calling the shots in the undeclared war in the Ukraine. Crimea is their prize. And ethnic Russians in the east and the south of the Ukraine are their active and open fifth column. They are sworn to stopping NATO enveloping the Ukraine.

Let us also throw in the mix Russia's exhibiting its opening of new mosques in Moscow and elsewhere; their expanding their beachhead in Syria; their creation of an alliance with Iran, Iraq, and Syria; and their wooing of the New Egypt, as a strong State.

Here we need to realize that the Obama doctrine on Middle East conflicts was born in the Libyan Arab Spring. And it reached its maturity in the Syrian Arab Spring. The doctrine gets its historic oxygen from the Reagan days of the 80's. That is when Hezbollah operatives, through suicide bombing, attacked US marine barracks in Beirut killing nearly 300.

That was an American tragedy which compelled the Republicans at that time to say about the ongoing conflict of Arab vs. Arab: "If these jackassess want to kill one another, who are we to keep them apart?!"

So the first chapter of the Obama doctrine of disengagement from war in general, especially in the world of Islam, went by the deceptive name of "leading from behind." That was in March 2011. Arab leaders, previously cuddled by Washington, were falling down in the Spring of 2011. Ben Ali, Mubarak, and Qaddafi were gone within only 3 months. Saleh in Yemen was losing the South. And Syria, at that time, began disappearing as a unitary State. This is while Maliki in Iraq was refusing to sign with the Americans a status of forces agreement. Biden tried, Maliki balked, and, from the sidelines, Iran cheered Maliki on.

In the US, there are 47,000 bridges in need of repairs. The Ford Motor Company is building its cars in Mexico. The great American highway system is lagging behind its European counterpart. In the country that ushered the technology of railway systems, linking Boston in the east to Los Angeles in the west, now needs foreign assistance. Boston, at present, needs to upgrade its railway transit system. So who does Boston call upon for help? The China Railway Rolling Stock Company (the CRRC). That company has been awarded a $60 million contract in September to build a plant in Massachusetts to supply cars for Boston Transit.

Iraq has cost America nearly 3 Trillion dollars. This is taxpayers money, and there is nothing to show for it. Except for the great American recession of 2008, and the collapse of great financial institutions like Merrill Lynch and Lehman Brothers. Job creation and middle class resuscitation became the Obama battle cry of "Yes We Can."

For these reasons among others, the American public is saying: Down with further involvement in proxy wars in the Middle East and terror franchises and jihadism. Up with America, whose great potential of innovation and its huge military are the real props of the new American dream.

No wonder that when Assad used chemical weapons against his own citizens, America, now bound by new rules of non-engagement, silently watched. That is in spite of prior Obama declarations of such brutal measures as "redlines" not to be crossed, Assad seemed to know better. He flagrantly crossed them, and Congress showed no desire to back an Obama intervention. Especially that the British parliament had already denied Prime Minister Cameron any authority to involve Britain in the Syrian civil war. Obama was able to blame that failure on Congress; and his promise of "no more antagonizing of the Muslim world" held firm.

The Obama doctrine seeks coalitions abroad. Going it alone is not a part of its make-up. Leaders like John Kerry have seen war in Vietnam. They are the pillars of diplomacy and soft power as means of protecting American interests. NATO is therefore now refurbished as a component of the new ideology. That ideology is expressed in: "We cannot fix all the world's problems. We are not the world's gendarmes."

It has become a "yes" for supporting local forces for local ends. A "no" for doing it for them. That doctrine sees in ISIS no equivalency to Al-Qaeda. ISIS is busy holding and ruling territory. Its parent body, Al-Qaeda, remains a force that only strikes and varnishes.

Those who say regular ground American forces shall be back on Arab soil should recognize that that day is over. Even the Republicans, the Party of War, wants to build the US military to the point of countervailing strength that it may not need to be used.

If you wish to build a line connecting the various stages by which the Obama doctrine has matured, I suggest that you do it mentally this way: From war, to military withdrawals, to the use of isolation tactics on the adversary, to the imposition of sanctions, to a dialogue on specific issues.

Throughout these steps, Obama is not afraid to appear weak. He, as a constitutional scholar who, I predict, might one day become a Supreme Court Justice, is after results. He is ready to meet Putin, and did at the UN, and even go to Tehran one day. After all, his middle name is Hussein.

He sees his doctrine as forcing the Kurds and the Saudis to build their own forces. No more total reliance on "mother America." Defeating ISIS has to come from within the area directly threatened. Another reason why America's halls of power are now warmer towards the New Egypt.

It is noteworthy that Russian planes and American planes are today conducting airstrikes in Syria. The former, in support of Assad; the latter in an attempt to degrade and defeat ISIS. A prime example of Russian antipathy to regime change in Syria, and of American commitment to see Assad eased out of power.

Of course America can keep both Saudi Arabia and Iran engaged with Washington. The proof: The Iran Deal. King Salman has protested and shunned an Obama summit for Gulf leaders at Camp David. But then came to Washington to declare his approval of that deal. And Iranian mobs may shout "Death to America." But this is only noise from the Iranian street. The Supreme Leader had called on Parliament to approve that deal. Now the Iranian street has changed its chant about America: From "the Great Satan," to "the Small Satan."

This has been the crowning success of the Obama doctrine on Middle East conflicts. It has all the elements of US power in the 21st Century. At the Pentagon, in July, Obama, praised patriotic American Muslims; called on them to discredit the ISIS ideology; and said that terrorists distort Islam.

As he says these things, he is looking for the success of "the Religious Revolution" of Egypt. The battle for the hearts and minds of moderate Islam has always found its citadel in Al-Azhar. Right under the shadow of secular Egypt represented east of Cairo by the Muhammad Ali Mosque. And west of Cairo by the great monuments of Ancient Egypt.

These monuments shall never have the fate of Palmyra monuments in Syria. History has spoken about this. At the beginning of the Nasser coup of 1952, one of the "Free Officers" ordered the great Egyptian singer, Um Kalthoum, to stop her concerts. She had sung for King Farouk before he was deposed. Nasser was told. He picked up the phone and gave an order to that officer. "Go and destroy the pyramids." In total disbelief, that officer responded: "Afandem?!!" (Sir?!!) Nasser's reproachful response was:

"If you can silence an Egyptian monument like Um Kalthoum, why not finish the job by destroying the Pyramids!!"

Now the Obama doctrine has another important side effect on the Middle East: The amazing build-up of local Kurdish forces; simultaneously, the bringing up of Turkey into the ISIS fight through the use of its airbases for American for launching air attacks; and the Saudi realization that military strength starts from within, together with an alliance of the willing in the Arab world, manifested in the creation at the Sharm El-Sheikh summit of a United Arab force.

This is the immediate background of what a close aide to Obama said a few weeks ago. That was Ben Rhodes declaring, undoubtedly reflecting the mindset of his boss: "We are not going to chase every rabbit in every hole in the Middle East."

A colleague of mine asked me about the title of tonight's lecture. He is a professor of law at Fordham Law, New York City, where I also teach. When I told him, he responded: "I have never heard before about an Obama doctrine on conflicts." I replied: "I made up that term." For out of daily observation over a period of seven years of Obama's presidency, you discover that behind the changes, there is a thread; a consistency. After all, a doctrine is defined as "the body of principles in a branch of knowledge or system of belief."

So here, in conclusion, is the lexicon of the Obama doctrine: A huge defense budget of more than $600 billion for deterrence; slimming down the military into smaller but technologically efficient units; more focus on the art of knowledge and the gathering of intelligence; improved economic equality; more drones in the sky and less military footprint; stronger emphasis on coalition-building and multilateral diplomacy through the UN; talk about human rights abroad, but refusal of direct interference in internal affairs; and finally, respect for the strong State like the New Egypt of June 30, 2013. TAHIA MASSR!!

# Interfaith Transitioning From Dialogue To Action

Saturday, October 31, 2015

Today is not like yesterday. And tomorrow shall be different. Time is galloping forward bypassing most of us. For **God** owns time, enjoining us to own ourselves. The **Quran** says: **"Surely God does not change the condition of a people unless they change what is in themselves."** (Chapter 13, verse 11). The best popular song I heard in Cairo 10 days ago was titled: **"I Am the Ruler of a Republic Called Nafsi (Myself)."**

Herein lies the essence of sovereignty. The sovereignty of the individual under the mercy of the Creator. The essence of the need to change, to improve, to abandon the ways of yesterday for the sake of today. To realize that faith is one; faith is non-negotiable; faith is not a fad; faith is an inner quality seeking to burst out to commune and to communicate. With whom?

With others with faith, without trying to change their faith. Your faith becomes stronger when it reaches out to others through their faiths. That is when you recognize that your God-given sovereignty is separable but interdependent on allowing the other to pursue peacefully their path to their own faith.

That is interfaith, which needs to transition from dialogue to action. Here I am expressing an abandonment of the method of **"conference"** of mere words. In favor of an espousal of **"interfaith in action."** Action at the level of the individual, the repository of God's grace, God's implanted sovereignty, the invisible power to move us to the celestial sphere of goodness and compassion. Each chapter of the Quran, and each action by a Muslim begins with **"In the Name of God, The Merciful, the Compassionate."**

The holocaust did not occur by itself. ISIS did not start by itself. The wars, both just and unjust, do not start by themselves. The butchering by ISIS of others of every faith does not occur in a vacuum. Millions, now running away from the lands of Islam to the welcoming arms of western communities, do not simply get up and flee. In all of these situations, the hand of darkness is casting the shadow of annihilation over them.

Now interfaith has a decided role. A role of action. Thus faith must first begin by evolving into conceptional directions.

Through new concepts, through ijtihad - the application of the mind to the non-changing text. Creating new institutions, new media, new leadership, new civility. Civility which, for example, would frown on insulting a sitting president of the US, by calling him **"a closet Muslim."** As if Islam and

Ebola are one and the same.
The sins of the bad few should not be transferred to millions upon millions whose hands are free from shedding the blood of others.

And if we are serious about putting interfaith in action, let us forget about the need for an intergovernmental organization, like the UN to do it for us. Why? Because the Charter of the UN, which was celebrated on October 24, adores only national sovereignty. It celebrates the sovereignty of the State, leaving the sovereignty of the individual behind. It makes of the veto a tool for obstruction, not a medium for good change.

Just think about it!! Non-governmental organizations, like Catholic Charities, or Doctors Without Borders, or the thousands of Jewish and Islamic charitable organizations, are more effective than the UN. They, through putting interfaith into action, are eclipsing the UN Economic and Social Council and the World Health Organization combined. Non-Governmental Organizations are what the UN Charter, in its preamble, calls **"We the People."**

Today, the weakest human organization is government. In fact, America's neoconservatives today call for the destruction of federal government. Let us face it: Today's effective actor is the individual. Functioning through the great marble halls of interfaith festooned by the chandeliers of collective action.

As we seek that interfaith action, we need new vehicles. New vehicles are motored by a new vocabulary to express them, to carry them out. We need to know, for example, that in Islam **"Allahu Akbar"** is not a battle cry. Terrorism must be forced to disgorge that manipulation of religious vocabulary. Its real meaning is: **"We are all equal before God."**

And **"Tawheed"** (meaning the Oneness of God) is the glue that binds our God-given sovereignties to one another. Elohim and Allah are holy names of the same Creator.

And for vehicles, we need to launch or refurbish or support institutions which systematically put interfaith into practice. The Sophia Center of the Huntington Seminary of the Immaculate Conception was a beacon for interfaith in action. I served there. But with the passing of its founder, Father Bob Smith, it died with him. What a loss!!

For 40 years, Temple Emanuel has been one of my fora. Its banner, held aloft, became the vehicle for events like this one. And the iconic Al-Azhar of Cairo, the citadel of moderate Islam, since the year 975 AD, is now leading **"the Religious Revolution"** to counter jihadism.

From vocabulary to vocation. In secular Egypt which I visited earlier this month, I saw a progression. From the horrible year of Islamic rule by the Muslim Brotherhood (2012-2013) to action through interfaith. Represented by millions of Muslims cheering on the Coptic church.

And in 2011, Al-Azhar has been calling for a huge change of concepts. It advocated that **"Islam does not recognize a State based solely on religion."** The world outside of Egypt did not hear that historic call. Reason: it was in Arabic.

The Wahhabis of Saudi Arabia intone the myth of a Sunni Islam vs. Shii Islam. But **Pope Francesco,** the Jesuit in white robes, the Pope of the Poor, is a better defender of Islam than the Wahhabis in their keffiyehs and white robes. For a long time, the Jesuits have immersed themselves in the study of the Quran and Islam.

The second successor of the prophet Muhammad was **Omar**. Omar gave specific orders to the Muslim armies upon their arrival at Jerusalem in the middle of the 8th centuries. I teach his legal decrees at Fordham Law. He prohibited the sequestration of churches and temples. That was interfaith in action.

Four centuries later, **St. Francis of Asisi** put his interfaith into practice. That was nine centuries before the Wahhabis co-ruled Saudi Arabia. He tried to mediate the conflict between the Crusaders and Saladin -a Kurd.

In the New Egypt, the secular Constitution of 2014 provides for the official recognition of the Torah and the Bible. All Jewish temples in Egypt are now being refurbished.

This is the new age of the individual -sovereign, rebellions, suspect of authority, has the social media at his or her fingertips.

But that individual does not know what to do -except scream. Let us heed the call of that sovereign and work toward changing that scream into a symphony of putting interfaith into action.

# 18 NOVEMBER 2015

## ISIS Kicking Sand In the Eyes of the Truth - Losers!!

Friday, November 6, 2015

Even in catastrophic tragedies, ISIS hurries to reap the wind of evil. The Russian airbus plummets from 31,000 feet down to the Sinai mountainous floor. More than 200 hundred Russian and Ukrainian tourists and crew head to a fiery death. Instead of heading home with lungs refreshed from the iconic resort of Sharm El-Sheik. The alternative capital of Egypt during Mubarak days.

So the world grieves for the human loss. Egyptian groups gather before the Russian Embassy in Cairo with flowers, candles and songs of condolences. Putin declares a national day of mourning. Egyptian-led teams of investigators descend upon the floor of tragedy seeking the inner secrets of the black box to reveal the actual cause of the tragedy. A hundred Egyptian ambulances carry the body bags to awaiting Russian planes to fly the victims home.

Everyone on the face of the earth bow their heads in a prayerful gesture of accepting the fate of that airbus and its occupants.

**Except for ISIS!! Evil celebrates evil.** In a transparent attempt to grab the headlines for publicity of a false victory. Even before the investigations by Egyptian, Russian, French and American reveal the real cause of that enormous human tragedy. ISIS celebrates: **"We did it. Victory for our Sinai campaign."** Yet no such celebration and **"high five"** are in order. The fact belies the ISIS premature claims of victory of evil over good. For at 31,000 feet high up over the Sinai sky, no ground to air missile is known to climb more than 20,000 feet. An airbus in flight at that altitude is not akin to a low flying helicopter, easily reached by a powerful and well aimed Kalashnikov.

These are facts. Not a barrage of lies spread by ISIS and its affiliates in the Sinai/Hamas regions. That is where the combined strength of the mighty Egyptian Second and Third Armies, concentrated by El-Sisi in the hands of one brilliant and battle-tested commander, is pummeling that evil. **Gradually out of viable existence whatever time it takes.**

Thus to ISIS and its so-called Caliphate at Raqqa, Syria, the Holy Quran, in Chapter VIII, seems to address itself to the anti-Islamic **"Islamic State."** Verse 37 is on point: **"So that God may distinguish the corrupt from the Good, and pile the corrupt one upon another. And so heap them up together, and throw them into Hell. Those are the losers."**

**The losers keep on kicking sand in the eyes of the truth.** The truth is that ISIS moves where there is no opposing movement on the ground. Moves into empty spaces; into where loyalties are split by **the fiction of a Sunni Islam and a Shii Islam;** into the void of authority; into the void of jobs taken away from half a million mighty Iraqi army, officered mainly by Sunnis during the reign of Saddam terror. That was a void created by an **American lunatic called Bremmer** at the outset of the great American war debacle of the Bush/Cheney war on Iraq.

**We are still in an age of several voids exploited by the phantom Caliphate of an Anbar thug called Al-Baghdadi.** Let us have a recitation of these voids on the US side, enabling ISIS to temporarily prosper on the oxygen of these voids which have to be likened to the underground tunnels. Previously dug by Hamsawis in an attempted underground invasion by the renegade Gaza enclave of mighty Egypt.
- No US coherent policy in regard to US war effort against ISIS;
- The US Secretary of Defense, **Ashton Carter,** is wedded to three R's:
  **Raqqa/Ramadi/Raids.** But from the air. An air campaign cannot secure timely victory for on the ground campaign.

- Only **50 US special forces for Syria, and 3500 for Iraq.** To do what?: **"Advise and Assist!!"** What does this mean in regard to ISIS in Syria? It means that the US has no reliable partner on the ground in Syria. But in Iraq, there is the **Pesh Merga of Kurdistan,** seeking through their collaboration to secure from within Iraq, the State of Kurdistan.

- But would Sunni Arabs of Syria acquiesce to a Kurdish occupation of Raqqa, following the expected defeat of ISIS? **Of course no.**
- So here we go again: A complicated battlefield. Lines keep on shifting; loyalties are measured only by the day. Your friend of today is your enemy of tomorrow. Thus the concept of **"command and control"** goes to hell.
- Add to this, the general policy, in fact doctrine of Obama of **"no more US involvement in Middle East wars."** This is the prevailing doctrine at the very time when ISIS needs a strong response.
- On top of that, add the absence of a legal framework for any robust US involvement. **There is no declaration of war by Congress.** Because? Against whom? Against the foes of selected bands. But how do you know that that selection endures? Especially when the US has no informants on the ground!!
- Have I just said **"the absence of a legal framework for any robust US involvement?"** Yes. But attorneys like myself have to be both credible and circumspect. So, OK!! There is one legal framework. It is a Congressional authorization that **dates back to the tragedy of 9/11!!** Thus it is no good for the age of ISIS. Obsolete. And in law, **whatever is obsolete cannot be cited as credible.**
- Also bear in mind that **"an authorization"** cannot be legally equated with **"a declaration."** You usually authorize another branch of Government, after its action has begun. And you **"declare,"** no **ipso facto.** You legislate. And your legislation is upon request of either the legislature (Congress) or the Executive (the President in the Oval Office). **And you fund what you legislate.**
- And your legislation, when unfounded, becomes a dead letter. Unless stopped by a Presidential veto or an executive order. Provided that executive action can survive a Congressional over-ride of a super majority. **Complicated? Yes. The story of the American system, especially when it comes to war.** This is what we do as legal counsel in US constitutional issues: **The process of unscrambling,** which drives our students sometimes to mental exhaustion!!
- The pile-up of uncertainties is not yet complete when it comes to

the **US vs. ISIS.** Because?

- There is a lack of attainable goals. **The best result is to prevent the occurrence of the worst scenario.**
- There are no clear limits of authority between Congress (where the Republicans have a majority in both houses), and the President who is passionately hated by the Republicans -the war party.
- Why not **"a no fly zone?!"** You must be kidding. No fly zone (NFZ) could protect those on the ground whose loyalties you don't know. NFZ needs to be defended. NFZ infringes sovereignty. Sovereignty which is still claimed by **present-day super-killer Bashar.** Who is supported by Russian military might, Iranian Al-Quds Revolutionary Guards, and Hezbollah, the only discernible ruler of Lebanon. **So instead of Syria occupying Lebanon, we now have Lebanon occupying Syria!!**

I still have more bad news, about the efficacy of America's war in Syria: the terms that have wavering meaning, or no consensual meaning whatever. Here are some: **"The broader war;" "Boots on the Ground;" "War improvisation;" "Guiding Local Fighters;" "Covert Training and Equipping by the CIA;" "Ideological Spectrum;"** and **"Downward Slope."**

**I hope that the reader has not concluded from the above that ISIS shall eventually prevail!!** They don't have the long breath, the enduring bond between themselves and their subjects, **the mammoth weight of Islam as a faith,** and their reliance on incidents of panic-creation not on the Rule of Law -any law. **They are the proverbial losers!!**

Back to the Quran: **"Say, 'The pure and impure are not equal, though the abundance of the impure may allure you much.' So be God fearing, O people who possess minds, that you may be successful."**

Thus with the US and Russia or without, ISIS and Al-Nusra and their nominal franchises wherever they may be, **shall be proven to be the proverbial losers.** For they are like bats, flying at night -the night of present-day Islam.

**Soon there shall be dawn!!** Yes, ISIS for now can kick sand in the eyes of the truth. But truth is more durable than sand. Sand that falls apart with a good dose of cleansing water.

# Idiotic Claims on the Giza Pyramids By the Most Ignorant of Today's Stupids!!

Friday, November 13, 2015

The claimants cover the three Ibrahamic faiths: Jews, Christians, and Muslims. The democratization of insane ignorance.

Some Jews claim that they built those pyramids. A Christian running for the U.S. presidency, Ben Carson, claims that the pyramids were used by biblical Joseph to store grains. And the Muslim Brotherhood saw in the Giza pyramids idolic symbols that should be destroyed.

All idiotic claims by the most ignorant of today's stupids; the crazy revisionists of world history. Under the guise of giving themselves a leg up on the ladder of legitimacy. **And the evidence is clear through the following facts.** Facts that are stubborn enough to make those claimants the world's laughing stock!!

As students in Egypt, our curriculum included **"Ancient Egypt."** At both the primary and secondary levels. And all history majors at the university level are required to pass that course before graduation. I was one of them. This is the DNA of Egyptian education. It has a basic pedagogical reason: **The modern Egyptian is thought of as an amalgam of ancient Egyptians and Arabs.**

That genealogical link is the back bone of never-ceasing Egyptian nationalism. **It has served Egypt well. No foreign occupation of Egypt went unpunished.** From the days of the Hyksos to the days of the Zionists.

Now to the historical facts about the Giza pyramids. And down with the myth information maintained by some of the Jews; by an Afro-American Christian brain surgeon who should get his own brain operated on; and the un-Islamic Muslim Brotherhood whose leader one day said: **"To Hell With Egypt." (Toz Fi Massr)!!**

- The age of the pyramid builders began with **"The Old Kingdom."** It lasted for **500 years.** A united regime with a firm throne, occupied by a great pharaoh worshiped as God or God's representation by a pious population.
- The entire history of **"The Old Kingdom"** was characterized by

self reliance and self sufficiency. Through those Egyptian masses which believed in the sanctity of the Pharaonic system. Underpinned, not by the small group of Israelites, Moses adherents. But by an indigenous faith. **Hard work by these masses was a subsidiary religion.**

- The age of the pyramid builders separated between those **residents** who were outside the faith of Ancient Egypt, and those who were immersed in it. **The ruler was a God; the public was his congregation; and his plans to build the pyramids was to concretize the stability of the State.** In this grand endeavor, the public, as pyramid builders, during 3 months annually **(the Nile flood period),** was engaged in a second mission. No outsider was to lift a stone in that nationwide Egyptian declaration of greatness. The sacred had no place for those who looked for God outside the official faith of the State.

- That huge sacred endeavors stretched west of the Nile from near Luxor in the south, to Memphis, the great capital near which the **3 great pyramids arose.**

- **The overseers were engineers; the advisors were the priests** of **"The Old Kingdom;"** the peasants, now in the employ of the Pharoah, moved tons of stones; the boats moved the granite over flowing Nile waters from south to north; and the peasants, turned laborers, sang as they slid the stones in place. **No mortar. But air suction to keep the stones tightly in place.**

- The stepped pyramid of **Saqqarah was considered an old model.** Now the pyramids have to rise up with one solid face to remind the whole world that the **stability, faith, economic prosperity, and mighty armed forces, are the four corners of Ancient Egypt.**

- The gravitas of Egypt, its capital, moved from the south to the north, at where the great Nile split in two branches. Pouring its waters rich with silt, into the Mediterranean. **From the first Nubian cataract south of Aswan to where Alexandria stands today.**

- The great engineering genius of the Giza Pyramids was **Imhotep, Pharao's priest, his prime minister, and his great architect.** Imhotep was a northerner; was later regarded by the Greeks as **"the genius of stone engineering."** A graduate of the ancient Egyptian schools of science, religion, and politics. **Faith was in the Sun (Raa). Not beyond. Heliopolis** became, at that dawn of history, the Mecca of ancient Egypt.

- That was five thousand years ago. **Faith and governance were one. The Giza pyramids were to be the burial places of the**

**pharaohs.** Their greatness lies in their being the first stone structures in the world: **durable; perfect angels; standing aloft** at the edge of the desert; peering over the temples and the burial places of personalities lesser than the mighty Pharaohs.

- **Khyops, Khafraa and Mankaraa, were the respective occupants of the Big Pyramid, the Middle Pyramid, and the Small Pyramid.**

**Case closed.** History speaks louder than the Jewish myth of taking part in pyramid building. In that regard, those false claimants are akin to saying that non-Muslims could participate in the washing of the Kaabah.

**So is Ben Carson** who believes in the apocalypse and the end of time. If he had been to the pyramids only once, he would have seen that the pyramids are **no silos for grain storage.**

**So is the crazy Brotherhood that regards the pyramids as idols which should be destroyed.** Why? Diversion from the Muslim faith of the oneness of God, and the exclusion of statues and images as distraction from Muslim worship. **Real idiocy!!**

Sorry, fellows!! **You can go home now.** See whether you had something to dream about the leaning **Tower of Pisa (Italy).** Or the **Arch of Triumph of Paris (France).** Or the **Statue of Liberty in New York.** Do yourselves a favor and leave the Giza Pyramids alone. Your claims are as bogus as those who try to sell the Brooklyn Bridge to the fool.

And if you have free time, see the comic Egyptian film starring Muhammad Al-Heneidy, who stars in **"Hamam In Amsterdam."** See the depth of his spontaneous revulsion at something **"an Israeli"** starring in the film told him. **"The pyramids are ours!!"** Prompting Hamam not to shake hands with that offending usurper. Usurper of basic historical facts. Repeating to himself in amazement, **"Can you imagine him saying: 'The Pyramids are ours'?!!"**

The basic context of the pyramids project of Ancient Egypt is this: **It was the first equivalent in human history of the State taking care of the needs of its citizens.** Especially at times of agricultural paralysis due to the Nile floods. **Citizens were defined by faith.** Worshippers of the sun (Raa) were the only recognized faithful. Everyone else, including the Israelites, were mere residents.

At that dawn of history, **the State launched the equivalent of the first Social Security scheme in world's history.** If you are a citizen, not a mere resident, you were entitled to be covered by that scheme. That is when you could not farm.

So you get on **"the food stamp scheme"** of that time. **Build the pyramids, and get your ration** of wheat, maize, and oil to feed your family. On top of that you get the heavenly stamp of indulgence after death. That stamp, in essence, might have read **"A Participant In Pyramid Building."** No one else got it. If you were a mere resident unacknowledging the pledge of allegiance to Pharaoh.

You see, **knowledge is light. And information is power.** No amount of hallucination about **"the Giza Pyramids"** is of any use. Because you are merely whistling in the wind. The wind of the Western Desert which hugs the Pyramids from every angle. **With the Sphinx keeping close watch as a royal guardsman. A heritage for all mankind!!**

I love **Sadat.** Yet I have been critical of his allowing **Menachem Begin** to get away with saying at the Pyramids: **"We built these. But we are not going to claim them."** Instead of a well-deserved retort, Sadat laughed. For diplomatic reasons.

But one should always keep in mind that **diplomacy cannot trump history. History must always trump diplomacy.**

# In Paris, The Bells of Notre Dame Cathedral Have Tolled - Their Ring Has Ushered In a Just War

Friday, November 20, 2015

November 13 should signal the start of a revolution. A new type with a global perspective. Against global terrorism which, as it sputters, murders the innocent in its wake.

Liberty, equality, Fraternity!! All of these should be reborn. Out of the martyrdom of more than 120 human beings. They died in Paris. But shall be reborn in our world action that strikes without mercy, without a holiday.

To call this despicable tragedy **"jihadism"** is to elevate the humanly abnormal to the level of normalcy. If terrorism knows no boundary, so should be the global pre-emptive response. No boundary; no mercy; no shedding of crocodile tears by the so-called **"human rights"** organizations, reminding us of due process.

France has, in the immediate aftermath, closed its borders. Like in Sinai, there cannot be freedom of movement to allow the assassins the freedom of butchery. (How laughable to hear Hamas leaders calling the Rafah Crossing the Gaza lungs. Resuscitating the Gaza lungs is in the hands of Hamas, not in the hands of Egypt).

From France, the land of **"The Social Contract"** should emerge a new version of **"Le contract social:"**
- A new global World War Council to coordinate the global moves against all and every terror outfit;
- A new system of intelligence sharing to help that **"World Defense Council"** to strike pre-emptively. Not to await reactively;
- A global **"Situation Room"** that oversees the 24/7 pounding of the nests of evil. Regardless of what they call themselves;
- A massive world information system to inform the world citizenry of the progress of that **"War Without Borders;"**
- To the maximum extent possible, a protective shield against **"collateral damage,"** whereby the innocent perishes as the wicked is attacked;
- A constant interpretation of the terrorist chatter across the globe to be fed to those who, in the War on Terror, are flying planes, staffing war ships, parachuting on the dens of evil, or rescuing hostages;
- Screening by modern technology the attendance at mass events whether sportive or artistic;
- Replacing the international and civil codes of civil and political rights, such as those of the 1960s of the moribund UN; and
- Assisting those who are fighting for securing a viable life of independence in geographic areas which they can call **"a homeland,"** such as in the Middle East.

From the Russian plane crashing in Sinai, to the murdering of innocent civilians by hooded criminals in El-Arish (Egypt), to the bombing of Syrian civilians by a murderous Assad regime, to the attacks in Kenya, and Somalia against hotels, to the stoning of women for alleged adultery, to the kidnappings by **Boko Haram,** to the assistance extended to the Muslim Brotherhood, to the claims that the New Egypt is smothering dissent...!!

All of the above are various symptoms of the **new Ebola of global terror.** That world terror:

- **Has no faith;**
- **Knows no mercy;**
- **Has no plans for an orderly society;**
- **Bears no resemblance to the ordinary human being;**
- **Respects no charter, no reconciliation, no orderly progression to integration within global society;**
- **Uses open borders and freedom of movement as means for reaching nameless and non-suspecting victims;**
- **Hides behind veils of secrecy and shields of trumped up interpretations of faith to satisfy its appetite for human chaos.**

It needs war stratagems, globally coordinated, with each nation doing its part. Especially the Member States of the Organization of Islamic Cooperation.

For after November 13, 2015, our world has become one. **A unity for survival.** No more need for empty denunciations a la **Ban Ky Moon. The U.N. Sermonizing General,"** instead of **"The U.N. Secretary-General."** Who from the 38th floor of his glass house on the East River in New York City, does not see his real world beyond Long Island across that River.

Time for action for whatever time it takes on all fronts, and by all means.

For those who gloated over their social media that **"Paris is burning,"** should be made to count their days. That cry of satisfaction at mass slaughter should now be heard through a **globalized war command and control.**

Evil is the same. Even when it uses **"God"** as a part of its odious name!! **ISIS (The Insane Satan In Iraq and Syria)** pompously declares **"responsibility"** for killing in cold blood. Killing 129, and injuring multiples of that number in Paris. **"Responsibility?"**

This is a word denoting high morality. **"Responsibility"** refers to values which **Al-Baghdadi,** the thug from Anbar, has never known.

President Hollande of France got it right. **"An Act of War,"** he described the dastardly attacks of November 13, in the **City of Light - Paris.** So did **Hillary Clinton,** who is expected to be the first female President of the U.S. as of January 2017. She said: **"ISIS should not only be contained. It should be defeated."**

**The martyrs (Shaheeds)** of Paris are not the eight stealth killers who perished to hell wrapped in their explosive belts. The martyrs (Shaheeds) are those who perished as they watched a soccer game, a concert, or sat peacefully for a pleasant dinner. This is what Islamic Law calls them!! **Shaeeds.**

Yes, Al-Baghdadi. It was a Friday. The Muslim day of prayers, reflection, and constructive interaction with all other human beings. Thus calling you a **"Muslim" is like calling a poisonous snake a "bird of paradise."** May you and your gangs perish in hell. Wrapped in your black turbans and your other garments whose blackness points directly to the true color of your heart.

Paris shall always be full of light. **Al-Raqqa,** in Syria, now under daily bombardment by the French air force, shall, in time, become the mass grave for the worst perpetrators of criminality against Islam.

The global menace of ISIS has an ideological sideon which it feeds. ISIS is enabled, though unwittingly, by **Islamophobes.** You can find them especially among those who speak or write about that faith without ever having studied it. Or even understood it.

A prime example of such ISIS-enablers can be found in a **book recently published by Ayaan Hirsi Ali.** A Somali young woman with terrible tribal experiences. Genital mutilation and a forced arranged marriage. Issues whose only link to Islam is that they were visited upon Hirsi Ali in a country which, though Islamic, yet socially dysfunctional. The capital country of the murderous **Al-Shabab.**

Ayaan's ignorance of Islam, a faith which she has renounced, became to her a substantial source of undeserved fame, and an ill-gotten fortune. In both Europe, particularly in the Netherlands where she was made a parliamentarian, and now in the U.S., a guest so-called scholar at Harvard and in Washington, D.C.

Ayaan, out of deep ignorance, has previously in an article, called for **"the rewriting of the Quran."** As if the Quran is another terrorism manifesto, not, as per Islamic dogma, the word of God revealed to the Prophet Muhammad. Her recent book is entitled: **"Heretic: Why Islam Needs a Reformation Now."** Published by Harper, she boldly declares in the introduction: **"To make many people - not only Muslims but also Western apologists for Islam - uncomfortable."**

Her conclusion is that **"Islam is not a religion of peace."** With such a conclusion, repeated also in her three previous books, ISIS draws the oxygen of its barbarity under the pretext that Islam was under attack. Under attack, not only by you, Ayaan. But by the West whose circles are providing you with encouragement. An encouragement to propagate hate and contempt for the faith of 1.5 billion Muslims. So when **"Paris"** happens, you and your entourage of hate-mongers find justification for the lies which gush constantly from the deep well of your ignorance.

**In essence, Ayaan Hirsi Ali, you and ISIS feed on one another.** You need ISIS criminality to sell your books of Islamophobia. And Al-Baghdadi, the thug from Anbar, needs you as an un-witting enabler/recruit to bolster his nihilistic ideology.

**It was your tribe, Ayaan, that attacked you. Islam did not.** When you opted out of Islam, that faith looked the other way. Under its humane principle of **"In matters of faith, there is no compulsion."**

Perceiving yourself as a scholar, especially in matters of Islam, has been devastatingly rebutted by **Max Rodenbeck, the Middle East Bureau Chief of the Economist.** In his review of your book **"Heretic"** in **The New York Review of Books** dated December 3, 2015, he posed a central question on the cover of this forthcoming issue: **"Can Ayaan Hirsi Ali Change Islam?"**

**His resounding response was a big "No!!"** Here is a quote from his review, covering from page 35 to page 37:
**"But there are several problems with her approach. These include such troubling aspects as her use of unsound terminology, a surprisingly shaky grasp of how Muslims actually practice their faith, and a questionable understanding of the history and political background not only of Islam, but of the world at large."**

So Ayaan, go find a respectable way to make your living. Your barrage of rantings against Islam have the effects of a **big horned ram repeatedly attacking a mountain.** That mountain shall not move. But the ram shall soon lose its attacking horns!!

One of the tragic aspects of the Paris massacres is that similar outrageous calamities in southern Beirut do not get the same world attention. Call it **"citizen's fatigue,"** or **"differentiated treatment."** It is both. When we have a quarter million Syrians killed over 4 years of civil war, overall numbness takes over. Paris, by comparison, is expected to be safe. Safe enough for one million migrants aspiring to head toward it.

In this regard, the ISIS Satan has proved capable, at least for now, to force us to think differently about the same human tragedies. A global focus on Paris, as it should be. Less attention to southern Beirut, as it should not be. Beirut is thus entitled to feel, by comparison, forgotten.

Summing up the moral depravity of the eight suicide bombers who attacked Paris, I would say to their ISIS masters:

- **Your ideology is nihilistic - the burning wish to die;**
- **Your desire to kill and your desire to die are the clearest indication of your futile search for clarity;**
- **Your search for violence as an end in itself is foredoomed as dead-end;**
- **Your program, if one may charitably call it that, is based on a faulty premise: divide our world between Muslims and non-Muslims; between Muslim Sunnis and Muslim Shiis, and between Muslim Sunnis who submit to your enslavement and Muslim Sunnis who are yearning to leave your hell hole;**
- **Your riding the migration wave which you have caused is sure to close that escape hatch. But will surely serve the ranks of those who want you dead;**
- **Your genocidal ideology' shall boomerang and justifiably turn it into a sword for your eventual annihilation.**

Your targeting the **Bataclan arena,** where a soccer match between France and Germany, and which was attended by President Hollande, had a response of defiance: a piano with its player, moving his fingers deftly and sounding music about peace.

That song is by **John Lennon of the Beatles.** It begins by **"Imagine All the People!!"** An apt response of resilience in the face of barbarity. Within an unshakable refrain: **Vive La France!!**

The Arab and Muslim star is composed of eight angles. Angles of light, referring to all kinds of learning. The savage executioners in Paris were eight. Each angle pointing to all kinds of evil for which they, and their so-called **Emirs, stand clothed in infamy.**

Now here is another clear indicator of the gulf in values between the wicked (the Paris terrorists), and the good (the innocent Parisians). The mastermind of the Paris attacks of Nov. 13, **Abaaoud,** gloated about how easy it was for him to get from Syria to Paris to plan that massacre. That was before he perished a few days later north of Paris at the hands of the French police.

253

Scum like Abaaoud shall never know that their ease at inflicting harm on humanity is rooted in a higher value. **The openness of borders, the freedom of movement, and the trust in the decency of other humans not to use these universal values for subversion and criminality.**

A real gulf in values which can only now be bridged by a globalized effort, led perhaps by boots on the ground, through the creation of an **Arab/Muslim NATO** to erase the so-called Islamic Caliphate from the face of the earth.

They do not belong with other humans as sharers of this planet. Because they have come from Hell, to which they are surely returning. Their presumed express passports, through imagined martyrdom, to paradise have, especially since 9/11, been stamped **"CANCELLED."**

# 19 DECEMBER 2015

## In the Voice of the Baby of the San Bernardino Killers

Friday, December 4, 2015

Mom and Dad
Wherever You Both Are Now
Maybe In a Bad Place
After You Killed the Innocent

oooo

You Left Me With Grandma
Who Awaited Your Joyous Return
To Pick Me Up, Change Me
And Feed Me

oooo

But You Never Did
Only Your Images
On the Somber TV
When You Moved Among the Living

oooo

255

Why Did You Do It?
All That San Bernardino Killing
Of Moms and Dads
Whose Families Are In Mourning

oooo

Your Names Are Deceptive
For Rizwan Means God's Blessing
And Malik Is One Name
For God Almighty

oooo

Neither Malik Nor Rizwan
Shall Be On Your Side
Especially That Farook
Means Separating Right From Wrong

oooo

These Are Muslim Names
Intended To Glorify
The Oneness of God
Whom You Have Grossly Deceived

oooo

I See All Those Faces
Whose Bodies are Lifeless
Cause You Acted As Life-Enders
While We Worship Life-Givers

oooo

Life-Givers Like Robert, Bennetta
Aurora, Sierra, and Shannon
And Daniel, Damian, and Tin
And Nicholas, Yvette and Michel

oooo

They Trusted You, Your Co-Workers
As Did America, the Giver,
Treated You As All Others
Your Faith Was No Problem

oooo

Where is Pakistan
And Where Is Saudi Arabia
I Only Know The USA
As My Birthplace, My Birthright

oooo

My Home Where When I Grow
I Can Be Equal To Men
I Can Learn and Endear
All Others Under Our Flag

oooo

Now With Your Victims Gone
To A Place Better Than Yours
I Am Here Left Behind
Baring The Shame of Being Yours

oooo

Of What Can I Be Proud
With Whom Shall I Play
Your Pictures Are Not Glorified
Your Faith is Tainted

oooo

Those Flowers, Those Candles
Those Moans Of The Injured
Those Vigils Are But Cursing You
And Blurring My Future

oooo

I Did Nothing Except Being Born

To Parents With a Pact
A Pact With Those Far Away
From The Sacred Bond of Mercy

oooo

Your ISIS, Your Bullets
Your Guns, Your Grenades
Have Taken Over My Space
Space of Toys, Love and Light

oooo

How Dark It Is To Peer
Into A Future I Don't Know
Filled Of Fog and Doubt
About Whatever Follows Thereafter

oooo

On Your Epitaph,
What Shall I Place
Your Inscription On A Tomb
Would It Be Like A Curse
Of All Jihadis Like You

oooo

And What Should I Be Called
The Unloved Issue Of Killers
Who Turned Their Blooded Backs
On Those Who Gave Them Life

# In North America, Two Outlooks on Muslims: Canada is Kinder , America is Weary!!

Saturday, December 19, 2015

His appearance at the airport in Toronto in December carried an entire message. Young photogenic Prime Minister **Justin Trudeau** hugging the Syrian refugees. Putting warm jackets on their backs. Declaring to them and to the whole world: **"Welcome to Canada. You are at home now!!"** They, have reached a safe harbor.

Contrast this to the bluster of **America's Trump.** He, a fool, does not speak for America. But he is the poster idiot of a mean America. And no one in the Republican establishment dealt harshly with his profane calls for: **A database for American citizens who happen to be Muslims; a non-return to America of those citizens; a total ban on the entry of other Muslims to America, even for study or family reunification.**

Trump (or Chump) glories in anti-Islamism. And in anti-Latinos. And in anti-women. And in anti-peace. His mantra, which is a call for an American Sparta, is **"Make America Great Again."**

A demented buffoon who is exposing America to the wrath of 1.6 Billion Muslims. Daring to fight the world from fictitious citadels called **"The Trump Towers."** Punching the air with his fists, saying: **"I am rich"** -a **stupid qualification for ruling a super-power.**

Now to Canada. That is where you find its Prime Minister on hand at the Toronto airport welcoming Syrian refugees. But that was one aspect of Canada's kinder outlook on Muslims and non-Muslims. Fleeing their countries westward in search for safety.

That phenomenon was best described by **Obama**. Standing on December 15 in Washington, D.C. delivering an address at a citizenship ceremony, he graphically summed up the migrants dilemma. **He likened Syrians fleeing the civil war in their native country to the Jews who fled the Nazis.**

But in America these words do not compare to actions and public campaigns in Canada. A gulf of differences between two outlooks.

**For in Canada:**
- Prime Minister Justin Trudeau keeps on repeating: **"Extending the sins of the Islamic State group to all Muslims is irresponsible,"**
- He also adds: **"There shouldn't be a contradiction between what it takes to keep us safe and what it takes to keep us Canadian.;"**
- At the provincial level, political leaders, like **Andrea Horwath** calls on the **Ontario government** to face up to racial issues. This is to

be accomplished through action on legislation providing for setting up a secretariat to conduct **public education and research on racism.**

- The hallmark of schools in the **Greater Toronto Area (GTA)** is extra help provided by teachers to immigrant children. These are traumatized kids of very diverse backgrounds;

- During the Christmas season, front page newspaper articles project the beginning of the healing process for new immigrant arrivals. **Photos are splashed for toddlers lighting prayer candles at the St. Mary Armenian Apostolic Church;**

- A chorus of hundreds of children of different faiths singing the greeting extended to the **Prophet Muhammad** by the residents of **Medina** upon his arrival, fleeing persecution in **Mecca** 1437 years ago;

- The Canadian Government, through its **Minister of Immigration,** keeps on increasing the figures of migrants from Islamic lands fleeing into **the welcoming arms of non-Muslim western countries.**

- By contrast, **Saudi Arabia** which prides itself on being the **Custodian of the holiest of Islamic shrines in Mecca and Medina,** had an obtuse response to this humanitarian calamity. Its foreign minister's response was: **"Many Saudis are married to Syrian women."** Four million Syrians have fled their war-ravaged country since its slide into civil war in 2011.

- During the Canadian elections of October 2015, the majority of Canadian voters showed their disgust for what the **Toronto Star** of December 15, 2015 described in graphic terms. It attributed the defeat of the conservative government of **Stephen Harper** to Canada's **"own version of ugly Muslim-baiting by politicians desperate for votes."**

- One of the top columnists of the same newspaper had his column in the same issue headlined: **"Would Trump flourish here? Unlikely."** The columnist **Irvin Studin** explained why. Here is what he opined:

- **"The recent call by US presidential candidate Donald Trump for the wholesale exclusion of Muslims from entry into the United States can only give thinking Canadians some degree of comfort that our founders created Canada, in constitutional terms, as the negation of the American project."**

Of course, in America, the Trump voice is rather negated by liberal editorial writings in **The New York Times.** In its issue of December 5, 2015, one such editorial was titled: **"Fear Ignorance, Not Muslims."** Following the San Bernardino massacre, the editorial commented as follows:

**"Wherever the investigation leads, Americans must guard against overreacting, and subdue the panicked reflex of distrust and hatred towards the Americans among us who are Muslims. This has been a problem at least since 9/11 and will remain one as long as ignorance about Islam remains deep and widespread."**

Wise words. But American public opinion continues to give the lunacy of Trump thumbs up. **No less than 65% of Americans recently polled supported Trump's advocacy for a ban on Muslims.** This is not only unconstitutional under several US constitutional provisions. It is also a clear violation of international law principles dealing with **"freedom of movement"** as a human right.

But here we must keep in mind the individual instances in Canada of a bias against some Muslims. Reference here is made to putting a woman teacher on leave for wearing the hijab.

That teacher undoubtedly believes that hijab is decreed by the Quran for Muslim females. **She is wrong,** as such an injunction cannot be textually proven by the Quran to be an obligation. The most charitable description of the hijab phenomenon is to say that only after the **Khomeini Islamic revolution** in 1979 was that **fad** elevated to a **fareedha** (obligation).

This issue is ironically further compounded by brutal enforcement in Wahhabi lands by a religious police called, for obfuscation: **"The Volunteers" (Al-Mottaween).** Storm troops with canes ready to strike without legal sanction.

These are lands which are **divorced from the spirit of Islam as a faith continually evolving** to accommodate changing circumstances. Particularly **in regard to integration with** legislated laws and customary practices in countries to which Muslims emigrate. This is the essence of what **the Quran** states 21 times as **HEKMAH** (the reasoning based on common sense).

We all recall how **The Muslim Brotherhood,** during its fascist one year rule in Egypt (2012-2013) terrorized **the Copts.** A lesson which the New Egypt, under **El-Sisi,** is not likely to forget anytime soon. It was a violation of the DNA of historic Egypt of 7000 years as a State.

Thus in regard to anti-Islamism, the issue is multi-faceted. Both Muslims as well as non-Muslims still have a way to go before mutual accommodation.

**But the efforts at such accommodation seem to be more manageable, more promising, in Canada than in the U.S.A.**

*A Very Merry Christmas and a Happy New Year to All!*

# A Crazy Call For America To Sanction The New Egypt

Thursday, December 24, 2015

Hard to believe, but true. A Michael Wahid Hanna writes in the latest issue of **Foreign Affairs** that Egypt is **"an unreliable partner"** of the U.S.

His crazy call for sanctioning the New Egypt comes wrapped in Egyptophobia. As a **"Senior Fellow at the Century Foundation"** and **"an adjunct at New York University School of Law,"** Hanna has plenty of room to hallucinate in that article titled **"Time to Rethink Relations."**

**How?** Primarily through **"lowering the total of the annual amount (of U.S. military aid) from $1.3 billion to around $500 million."** For what reason? **"To alter Egypt's negative trajectory"** through **"expressing U.S. displeasure with the status quo."**

But what **"status quo"** is that **Michael Wahid Hanna** referring to? The Peace Treaty between Egypt and Israel concluded in 1979 and is still observed by the two sides. That is in spite of the howling hurricane of the so-called Arab Spring.

How would tampering by America, who is the guarantor of that peace between Israel and one-third of the Arab world which calls itself Egypt, affect that historic peace? **Hanna** skirts that crucial issue of cause and effect. He offers no gems of wisdom on that matter. That is not his concern. His concern is to drum up Egyptophobia at whatever cost. Hanna's demons cannot be silenced.

Suppose Washington, D.C. acts on Michael Wahid Hanna's muddled day dreams of sanctioning the New Egypt. Where would those fictitious savings garnered from U.S. military aid go?

Ah!! Our Michael has a plan for where those illegal cuts go. He howls his solution. **"The United States should consider diverting future military assistance to more reliable allies"** in the area. Like whom, Michael? **"Such as Jordan."**

And supposed Jordan, a valiant Arab sister State of Egypt, but with a fraction of the size of the Egyptian military, cannot absorb those savings? Then to who else, Mr. Hanna?

**"To partners that need help far more urgently than Egypt, such as Iraq."** Did you say **"Iraq,"** Mr. Hanna? Where is that? Hasn't Iraq, outside of Kurdistan, spurned a security arrangement with America, in order to accommodate Iran?

OK!! Details trouble Wahid Hanna. So he shifts directions in the same breath. Which directions: **"Or to States in the region that are transitioning to democracy more successfully, such as Tunisia."**

Oh, my God, Michael!! You make me a bit dizzy by your zigs and zags all over the Arab area. Of course Egypt wishes Tunisia, her sister Arab State, well. But I must admit to my slow thinking. **Where is the Tunisian successful transitioning to democracy?** Hasn't a prolonged state of emergency been declared in Tunisia by **President El-Sibsi** (not to be confused with the name of El-Sisi of Egypt)?

Now we reach **the root cause** of what ails the brain of Michael Wahid Hanna about Egypt of June 30, 2013. **The ouster of the diabolic Muslim Brotherhood from power.** Not by the army supported by popular demand, as our Hanna, with a defective bull horn, is screaming his head off. **But by popular demand supported by the army. The Egyptians, 35 million of them, were the prime movers. The army simply protected them!!**

Please Michael. Those, like you and your friend, **David Kirkpatrick,** another Egyptphobe writing in the **New York Times,** are not **"aficionados"** of history. So it behooves you not to try to revise it.

Mr. Hanna: You begin your 7 page article in **Foreign Affairs** of November/December 2015 by a provocative paragraph. In it, you make a bogus claim stating: **"There are no longer any compelling reasons for Washington to sustain especially close ties with Cairo."**

Then you compound that mystery by unabashedly saying without any proof: **"What was once a powerfully symbolic alliance with clear advantages for both sides has become a nakedly transactional relationship."** Sir: Are there any alliances which are not transactional? Name just one, if you can.

In America, we teach in law and political science that alliances are **predicated upon mutuality of interest. That alliances are generally based on parity of sovereignty.** That alliances need to be perceived, and are in fact of mutual benefit to the two sides. That is unless they are based on duress. In this case, they are colonial contracts between an imperial power and its protectorate.

So where do you draw your learning about alliances, Mr. Hanna? And how do you substantiate your naked claim that the Cairo/Washington, D.C. present relationship **"benefits the Egyptians more than the Americans?"** Nuts!!

If that is the case, and it is imaginary, or at best a hypothetical case, **why does the U.S. Secretary of State, John Kerry, keep on having a stop in Egypt a near permanent feature of his shuttle diplomacy in the Middle East?** Even to the point of attending recently in Sharm El-Sheikh, a mammoth Economic Conference organized by President El-Sisi!!

Let us now look for even a scintilla of logic to justify any of your claims, Michael, in that issue of **Foreign Affairs.**

You, seemingly inexpertly in the art of logical argumentation and presentation, lump disjointedly three different issues. A compounded and an inarticulate compendium of situations affecting the New Egypt with which you contemptuously deal. Here it comes:

**"After a popular uprising followed by an authoritarian relapse in Cairo, and with the peace process moribund, and jihadism now a chronic condition, the U.S. - Egyptian relationship has become an anachronism that distorts American policy in the region."**

Allow me to help out in disentangling the disparate elements of that overburdened paragraphic sentence.
  - Your charge of authoritarianism is totally unfounded. **El-Sisi became president through open and fair elections held in June 2014; his elevation came in accordance with a Constitution adopted in a popular referendum held that year;**

and the consensual Road Map has now been implemented by a free and open popular elections.

- In those elections, the Islamist party of **"Al-Noor"** suffered defeat, and the secularists, as evidenced by **"The Free Egyptians"** party of the **Coptic entrepreneur Naguib Sawiris,** triumphed. So if you happen to be an Egyptian Copt, as your name leads me to suspect, you should be dancing in the aisle.

- Where do you find **"the peace process moribund?"** I hope that you know some Latin to realize that **"moribund"** comes from the Latin **"moribundus,"** meaning **"at the point of death."** In fact Hamas and its terror-supported organizations such as **"The Friends of Beit Al-Maqdis,"** has kept Egypt in their cross-hairs. Their declared reason: **Cooperation with Israel** through blocking the terrorists attempts to transfer the conflict with Israel from Gaza to Sinai. **A well-known ISIS tactic.**

- As for jihadism being **"now a chronic condition,"** you are right, Mr. Hanna. But only on the surface. Making jihadism a chronic condition attaching only to Egypt is an insult to the innocent victims of jihadism in **Paris, Brussels, California, Turkey, Mali, Russia, Syria and Iraq.**

- And how is that situation causing **"the U.S. - Egyptian relationship"** become a factor that **"distorts American policy in the region?"** Your claim has an appropriate term in American contract law. It goes by the name of **"nudum factum."** Meaning bereft of facts justifying your claim. To elaborate: A bare contract or agreement that amounts to merely a naked promise. **Sorry, Michael, your argument has no leg to stand upon.**

Of course, Mr. Hanna, there is a distinct possibility that you, with your senior position at **"The Century Foundation,"** are not keen on the facts of this Century. Otherwise how are the following known facts **"distorting American policy in the region?" The reverse is the only reality:**

- Allowing American military aircraft to fly over Egyptian airspace;
- Egyptian provision to U.S. naval ships of fast track access to the Two Suez Canals;
- Provision by Cairo of diplomatic support for American regional policies, with regard to the Gulf region;
- Egyptian American resumed joint military exercises;
- Provision of eight F-16 U.S. aircraft to the Egyptian air force;
- Continued training of Egyptian elements of the armed forces in the U.S.;
- Military Egyptian involvement with Saudi Arabia, the Emirates, and the U.S. in the present conflict in Yemen;

- The U.S. opening to Egypt of the alliance with other Arab States in combating ISIS;
- The recognition, in fact the praise, of Egypt's massive contribution to the fight against ISIS on two priority fronts, Sinai and the Libyan border;
- The expected stationing of the two Egyptian aircraft carriers recently purchased by Egyptian funds from France at the Libyan border and opposite the troubled Gaza coastline near the northern terminus to the Suez Canals.

**The list can go on and on.** Including the involvement by Egypt of U.S. energy companies in the exploration of the newly discovered natural gas reserves in the Western Desert and the Delta.

Mr. Hanna: Please get it in your head that what we have today is a **new Middle East where America, through the Obama doctrine on Middle East conflicts, wants the Arabs to take care of their defense needs.**

You must be comatose when you allege in your article that **"Egypt has an interest in pursuing counter terrorism for its own reasons."** Anti-jihadism has eliminated your outdated fiction of each State should combat jihadism only for **"its own reasons." Jihadism knows no boundaries. So should anti-jihadism.**

And if anti-jihadism requires **"a religious counter-attack,"** where would you find the rich ideological resources for that lethal weapon in places which are better than **Al-Azhar of more than a thousand years?**

Could you also please help me understand this foolish assertion of yours: **"In short, the regional landscape has been transformed, and Egypt has been left behind. Egypt is no longer an influential regional player. Instead, it is a problem to be managed."** Is it because Egypt is turning from chaos to the strong State? A problem to be managed?! **I haven't heard that term since the publication of my book in 1971 on "decolonization."**

How laughable!! The only problem to hopefully be managed is **your Egyptophobia.** Compounded by your **approbation of the reign of Islamic hegemony in Egypt** for one year (2012-2013) by the Muslim Brotherhood.

*You seem to regard Egyptian sovereignty as either for sale, or as a legitimate target for unilateral U.S. sanctions.* Whatever you believe, you, Michael Wahid Hanna, are on the wrong side of history.

And were you to find a magic cure for your myopia, you would see that **a focus on internal affairs following upheavals, is not equivalent to becoming a marginal player either regionally or globally.** Both America, following its five losing wars, and Egypt, following four years of upheavals preceded by 32 years of stagnation, are doing the same. Each of them are rebuilding their infrastructure, creating jobs, improving their educational systems. All acts of fusion of internal energy. **Because national salvation begins from within.**

*So keep on whistling in the wind, Michael!! You wouldn't even get the benefit of an echo chamber!!*

**Reason:** From your writings and your responses to Egyptophobes in **The New York Times,** you have stayed the course of the equivalent of **"Uncle Tom"** in regard to the New Egypt. Under the guise of freedom of expression, you seem to have made of your anti-Egyptian phobias a lucrative industry. **Your neo-colonialism revival is sure to fail.**

*Michael Wahid Hanna: You have a bullhorn and an audience. Instruments which you are using in support of your merchantilist approach to the New Egypt. But please note an undisputed fact regarding your success in spreading mythology about Egypt -a rising strong State. You are operating in a Post-Fact America.*

# 20 JANUARY 2016

## America Now Says: "Old Ways of Military Intervention Don't Pay!!"

Saturday, January 2, 2016

Its first President and liberator has said it. **"No entangling alliances,"** It was George Washington's wise counsel to the U.S. More than 200 years later, another great American general, an Afro-American, also said it. Colin Powell as Secretary of State said: **"Before we get militarily involved, we must have an exit strategy."**

**But then America lost its way.** Duped by the war lords into attacking Iraq in 2003. **Cheney, Rumsfeld, Wolfowitz and Feith,** coalesced around the idea of war on Iraq would be a bonanza for the U.S. Intelligence assessments were tampered with. Expert reports were commissioned to produce desired conclusions. **First:** that Saddam was in league with Al-Qaeda. **Second:** Saddam's lie about possessing weapons of mass destruction should be manipulated.

**Results:** Colin Powell appeared before the UN Security Council advocating the necessity of war on Iraq. Presenting false evidence, **a pack of lies given to him by the CIA,** on Saddam's possession of weapons of mass destruction. **Lies within lies.** America attacked. When those WMD could not be found, the war lords had a stupid answer: **"We shall eventually find them."** None could be found.

So from 2003 to 2011, when US troops had to leave Iraq (a raging Sunni rebellion, and Maliki's refusal to extend American military stay), Iraq was left earth-scorched. **Rampant sectarianism; destroyed infra-structure; non-trained Iraqi army;** and calls by Vice President Biden for splitting Iraq in 3 statelets.

The voids were quickly filled. In Erbil, **Kurdistan,** with oil emerging to challenge Baghdad. **Musab Al-Zarqawi,** a thuggish jihadi in Anbar split from Al-Qaeda. After his liquidation by an American predator air strike, his successor was a more brutal thug - **Abu-Bakr Al-Baghdadi.**

With Syria in flames, as of March 2011, against Bashar, ISIS, now split from Al-Qaeda, acquired a new **"capital." Raqqa** in northeastern Syria, became an ISIS hub. A hub with oil, money, propaganda, and welcoming Sunni allies in Anbari Iraq.

And with a huge arsenal of American war materiel left behind, the highly trained **Saddam's war generals found a new employer: ISIS.** Mosul, the second largest Iraqi city, a ripe low hanging fruit, fell to ISIS. Nearly without a shot being fired.

**America did not create ISIS. But America's war on Iraq did.** As ISIS gained foreign recruits, nearly 3000 from Europe and America, it finds its criminal jihadis ready to strike. Inside and outside of the Arab world. **Paris and San Bernardino, California were wake-up calls for America.** One jihadi-directed; the other jihadi-inspired. Same result.

And as America packages its commercial products, so does it engage in collective punishment. **Branding Muslims as potential jihadis.** Producing calls from seekers of the US presidency in 2016, such as **Donald Trump,** for sanctioning 1.6 billion Muslims. Demented claims that **"Islam Is Jihadism."**

A lunacy gone too far -as declared especially by Republicans. A dilemma between going too far, and protecting America from Jihadism. So now we have the pendulum swinging again towards a middle ground.
- Tightening visa requirements with regard to applicants **from mostly Muslim countries;**
- Acknowledging that American intervention abroad negates the wisdom of **"no entangling alliances;"**
- Abandoning the myth of **"nation-building"** abroad, as a formula proving **"non-working"** in both Iraq and Afghanistan;

- Tacit approval of the **Obama doctrine on Middle East conflicts** -basically no American ground troops fighting those wars. **The locals should do it;**
- Focusing on nation-building in America: the economy; jobs; banking regulation; health care; the middle class needs. And a focus on technology, including a smaller but highly tech armed forces.

Now we have in America a civilian side to the Obama doctrine. **"No nation-Building" abroad is complementary to no military footprint in the Middle East.** Leading from behind militarily. A laserbeam focus on internal American issues. **Including gun control through executive action.**

In essence, the **"civilianization"** of the Obama military doctrine. Of course it has its opponents among the Republican neo-conservatives, the Tea Party, the evangelicals, and the war lords of the Bush Jr. administration.

Which side will win? I am betting on the success of those who espouse **"no-intervention."** The exigencies of the economy and the cost of monitoring jihadism through intelligence-sharing, mainly with NATO allies are crucial factors.

**What does this mean to the Arab and Muslim worlds?**
- Dictatorships are not a problem for America. They are the problem of the locals;
- Human rights throughout the world should be respected. But they should not be defended by the force of American arms;
- In fact the consequences of the fall from power of Saddam and Qaddafi are now being re-interpreted in America. **"America would have been safer from jihadism if Saddam and Qaddafi were still in power. They were America's first lines of defense. Terrible dictators for Iraqis and Libyans. But America's safety is American's concern."**
- Music to the ears of Bashar, the Syrian killer. But to the present American thinking: **"Better Bashar than the unknown."**

A near perfect alignment with American attempts to work with Russia, Iran and Turkey. And if Riyadh is upset, so be it.

It is now common knowledge that outside intervention is costly to the intervener in both blood and treasure. This is while those losses are usually compounded by uncertainties: Would the intervener gain at home from the intervention abroad? Of course Russia's intervention in the Syrian war by conventional weapons guarantees Moscow no net benefits.

By contrast, America's caution in regard to that very complex war arena carries with it its own benefits. Obama's Republican detractors are left in the dust howling: **"Obama is weak."**

**How can he be weak when he has turned the negatives of American footprint intervention into a positive?** Primarily through enhanced arms sales to **Qatar, Saudi Arabia and Iraq.** Let the natives fight their wars with American arms, under multibillion dollar sales, supplies, continuous modernization, and constant training.

On this issue, the annual report by the **Congressional Research Services,** a division of the **Library of Congress,** has astounding revelations. It reports that the U.S. now controls over half of the global arms trade.

This is great economic, strategic and political news. Their delivery to Congress seems to command symbolic, if not statutory, timing. With an imaginary ribbon on top, that annual report came to Congress at **Christmas, 2015.**

**American weapons receipts rose to $36.2 billion in 2014 from $26.7 billion the year before.** A jump of 35%. Even as the lucrative weapons market was adversely affected by the free fall in oil prices. Russia was a distant second (only $10.2 billion in arms sale); Sweden was third ($5.5 billion); France was fourth ($4.4 billion); and China was fifth ($2.2 billion).

Connecting the dots, you would find a **logical relation between America's opting to stay out of direct intervention, while enhancing its lucrative arms sales.**

In a lecture at the American University in Cairo (AUC), delivered on October 18, 2015, I presented **"The Obama Doctrine on Middle East conflicts."** Its heart was the avoidance of intervention. But its main background was the calamitous American war adventurism in Iraq from 2003 to 2011. Calamitous for the following reasons:

- Its faulty motivation was 9/11. But Saddam had nothing to do with Al-Qaeda, the perpetrator of that heinous crime;
- The Bush Jr. presidency was largely in the grip of **four war mongers: Cheney, Rumsfeld, Wolfowitz, and Feith.** This gang of four set aside sober CIA analysis. Replaced it by fabricated reports on Iraqi weapons of mass destruction;
- **As said above,** that fabricated intelligence was fed to the UN Security Council. In February 2003. Colin Powell, as Secretary of State, presented imaginary evidence on biological weapons. A total

lie; the war mongers called those fabrications **"alternative intelligence;"**

- With massive US military force slamming into Iraq in March 2003, **Baghdad fell in less than 3 weeks.** Saddam and his two sons fled. Later to be found and killed;
- Within weeks after Saddam, Iraq was in total chaos. Symbolized by a young Iraqi student crying: **"My destiny is lost;"**
- Yet Rumsfeld gloated in his press conferences that **"America brought freedom to Iraq. And freedom is untidy."**
- **Paul Bremmer** was dispatched to Iraq in May 2003. **A total idiot** who presided over de-Baathification and over the firing of a mighty Iraqi army, largely officered by Sunnis; he knew no Arabic; he had no inkling about Arab/Iraqi tribal culture;
- The Sunni massive rebellion in the north against the occupation, was the **incubator of ISIS** that in 2014 controlled one-third of Iraq, including Mosul.
- Said **Richard Clarke,** a former US presidential advisor on anti-terrorism: **"If there was no American invasion, no ISIS would have emerged;"** and
- Aside from ISIS, the Iraq war resulted in the **death of 150,000 Iraqis and 5,000 Americans;** in the massive loss of trillions of dollars; in entrenching sectarianism which is now tearing Iraq apart; and in the **flood of migrants heading toward the West.**

Not one of the gang of four perpetrators of that calamitous war, named above, even apologized for their actions. Actions which may be considered war crimes.

America's war on Iraq was aptly described by **Fareed Zakaria, on CNN** on December 27, 2015: **"The Long Road to Hell."** The Bush Jr. administration was drunk with power.

Now sits in the Oval Office, **"a sober president,"** **Obama,** who now has laid a firm foundation for non-intervention. The cherished calm, relatively speaking, after a war-infected hurricane period.

This new commitment is also expected to catapult into the Oval Office, the **first woman president -Hillary Clinton.** Even calamities, like the war on Iraq, could become historical game-changers.

As for the New Egypt, these consequences are largely of no direct consequence. Except for more American respect for **"the Strong State."** The victory in Egypt of the secularists over the Islamists of **"Al-Noor,"** in the recent Egyptian parliamentary elections should augur well for a

**refurbished Cairo-Washington reconnection.**

History seems to be on the side of this evolution. To America of today, **fluidity of alliances with Middle Eastern States is the norm.** The magnetism of Middle Eastern oil is now gone as a glue to such alliances. Selectivity and temporariness of these old alliances are now dictated by two factors operating in the New America: **Need and cost.**

The deal with Iran on the nuclear file is pervasively instructive: Delay the day of a nuclear Iran at the cost of making Saudi Arabia jittery. And punish an Iranian challenge of missile development which will not be stopping it **(President Rouhani is pushing for more).** Yet America is bound to release $55 billion to Iran, which is Iranian money deposited in non-American banks. And continue to support Riyadh's war on Yemen!!

These are highly nuanced American foreign policies which may be difficult for Riyadh to absorb. **A situation which gives Riyadh palpitations, but offers Washington internally some relief from the onus of an association with a State** which greets the New Year with the execution of 26 persons accused, without evidentiary support, of terrorism.

Reflecting this pervasive trend toward avoidance by America of intervention in Middle East conflicts is to be found also in the **omnibus spending bill passed by Congress in December 2015.**

The bill allocated for the Pentagon **$58.7 billion to continue fighting ISIS.** But mainly only from the air. With Congress thereby abdicating its exclusive constitutional responsibility to declare war, the White House is left to implement the Obama doctrine of war avoidance.

*It is not that Obama is weak. He draws more strength from being in his last year as President. No more worries regarding re-election. His executive pen is at the ready. Even in regard to closing Guantanamo. It is Congress that is weakened by its partisan conflicts. And ideological paralysis.*

*Happy New Year To All Readers!!*

# It Is Truly Uncommon!! But Between ISIS and Trump, There Are Certain Things In Common!!

Friday, January 8, 2016

Incredible. The super rich **Trump** and the super rich **ISIS.** In America, **the Donald** is running for President, so far as a Republican. In Syria and Iraq, **Al-Baghdadi** is running as a terrorist for the **Caliphate.**

In America, Trump has 14 other competitors saying **"he is no good."** In Syria and Iraq, there is a fractured international coalition, saying **"ISIS is no good."** But Trump has his own plane, his own helicopter. ISIS has its own tunnels and human shields to protect its forces from the coalition's air strikes.

Since June 2015, all American pundits assured their audiences that the Trump bubble would soon burst. But the Trump **"bubble,"** if it is a bubble, has now expanded. Became a tent for its adherents. Same with ISIS. Predictions of its disappearance soon proved pre-mature. Like the **Mark Twain** famous saying: **"News of my demise are greatly exaggerated."**

But the real commonality between Trump and ISIS is akin to a domain previously reserved for the Nazi propagandist Goebbels. The big lie technique. The bravado!! The blustering swaggering conduct. The pretense of bravery. The slate of being foolhardy.

Here are the elements in common between those two phenomena: **Trump and ISIS,** the inhabitants of fool's paradise. Gleaned over a period of time from what they say.

- **"I'll Make America Great Again."** Says Trump. **"I'll Make Islam Great Again!!"** Says ISIS. But how? **"When I become President, I shall make our military so powerful, so strong, nobody shall dare mess with us."** In Trump's words. **"We shall fight on either to victory or to martyrdom."** Declares the ISIS propaganda machine.
- **"I, Donald J. Trump, hereby call for banning all Muslims from entering America. See what happened in Paris, in California."** Trump intones. Great fodder for the ISIS propaganda department. Picked up by an affiliate -**Al-Shabab** in Somalia and

Kenya. A video on Trump played over and over and over again. Affiliates of ISIS rush in with reinforcements. Declaring that all non-Muslims hate Islam. Islam, they claim, is at war. Especially with America.

- And Trump is ready to oblige. **"Obama is a Muslim. He is not even born in America. Obama is Kenyan. I'm not at all sure who he is. But one thing I know: He is the worst President in the history of this country,"** Declared Trump. Al-Baghdadi of ISIS and his goons are ready to recruit, especially from among Muslims in Europe and America. **"We call on all Muslims to come to the Islamic State. That is where you will be safe. Will be respected."** An inducement beamed by all social media controlled by ISIS. A million tweets daily, luring the disaffected to the dungeons of ISIS. To its dark underground vaults.

- **"If we want to defeat ISIS, let us take all oil in the Middle East. You take the oil, you defund ISIS."** Implores Trump. **"Arab oil is Muslim oil. It belongs in Bait Al-Mal (The Islamic Exchequer). Our natural and national resources. It is to be sold to fund jihad."** An ISIS stance whereby oil flows for sale through Turkey. Black gold, not under Trump's thumb. But under ISIS control.

- On the stump, and to the wild cheers of supporters in Burlington, Vermont, Trump declares that Iran is a mortal enemy. **"The worst deal was the Iran nuclear deal. They get $150 billion from US (in fact it is Iran's money), and keep their nuclear program as well. We are very stupid."** And thousands of Vermont citizens go wild. Cheering repeatedly: **"Trump!! Trump!! Trump!!"** ISIS is also on board there. But from a different angle. **"Shii Iran is the enemy of all Sunnis. They want to take over the gulf. The Saudis cannot stop Iran. But ISIS can."** Blares unthinkingly the bullhorns of ISIS.

- **"Yes, yes..."** cried Trump. **"Iran has taken over Iraq. It now controls the second largest oil reserves in the world. Next only to Saudi Arabia. So now they are fixing their gaze on Saudi Arabia. That Kingdom is Iran's next victim. And Washington will do nothing about the Ayatollahs."** From Trump's declarations. Again ISIS is on board. **"Jihadism is the answer. Shiism is apostasy. We are the troops of true Islam."** An ISIS propaganda tack. Used for legitimating their barbarism. Their butchery.

- **"What? A guy over there is protesting?! Take him out. He does not belong here. He is nobody. Kick him out. But keep his jacket. Don't give him his coat. It is 10 degrees below zero**

**outside. Yes. Keep his coat."** So orders Trump his security bouncers. ISIS has its goons as well. They do not kick their opponents out. They need them as human shields, as female comfort for their operatives (fornication jihad), or for huge ransoms if allowed to migrate. ISIS does not keep the coats of their opponents. They keep their heads. Severed from their bodies.

- **"I fund my own campaign."** So says Trump. **"I am smart, rich, and I am not part of the establishment. I don't know what 'political correctness' is all about."** Trump's political ID. ISIS, too, is proud of its self-sufficiency. Tired of the establishment. To them Islamic scholars are the **"Sultan's scholars."** Hirelings for authority. Persons who serve for hire. Especially for purely mercenary motives.

- **"My rallies are attended by thousands upon thousands. From all kinds of classes. They love me. Because I am successful, independent. Even ashamed of my own Republican party. My Republican opponents?! Ha!! They are falling down one by one. They have no energy. Look at Jeb Bush. He is a loser. I opposed the war on Iraq."** Well, guess what?! So claims ISIS regarding its opponents. Whether Sunnis or Shiis. The stridency of ISIS is getting louder, especially when they are losing ground. **"God is on our side!!"** Shout the ISIS media. **"Our energy is unlimited. The war on Iraq was a war on Islam. Also for oil."** An ISIS persistent claim.

- Both Trump and ISIS are presently surfing the same dark waves. Waves of discontent, resentment, frustration, and lack of education and opportunity.

- And the hordes of each of the two, Trump and ISIS, are hungry for non-sensical rhetoric (the old art of empty oratory) pleasing to the ear, non-penetrating of closed minds.

- Anti-feminism is also a common denominator between Trump and ISIS. Admittedly not in the same degree or on the same grounds. For Trump, a woman TV anchor, when tough in questioning him, **"has blood oozing from her everywhere."** And Hillary Clinton, the anticipated Democratic rival of Trump for the presidency **"cannot be a commander-in-chief. She lacks stamina"** - declared the Donald of multiple divorces. For ISIS, women are not equal to men. They belong behind the niqab (covering the entire face, except for the eyes). This is Sharia -claims the ISIS platform. Forgetting that women sat with the Prophet Muhammad at his decision-making councils. And at times, their advice prevailed over his.

- Both Trump and ISIS claim total fidelity to God. Though God is one, one for all faiths, Trump, in a play towards the evangelicals of Iowa declares **"I am a true Christian, a protestant."**

- Of course, for ISIS, Islam is a trade. It is a bargaining chip -used to demonize Christians, Jews, and all other religions. Even non-sympathetic Sunnis are mortal enemies to ISIS. For both Trump and ISIS, God is an item for sale. A stock in trade.
- A final crazy refrain from Don Quixote, now back to life as Don Trump. **"I'll bomb everywhere!! I don't care."** This is what ISIS does. Same threatening language. As they manipulate social media in the most insane social ways.
- Both Trump and ISIS have also one feature in common: They both are headed toward failure. Their calls are false; their cause is transient; their adversaries are closing on; their rhetoric shall soon be forgotten; their promises are unattainable.

*Their advocacy is reminiscent of the fearsome Wizard of Oz. -An empty shell. At the end of it, comes the famous call: "There is no place like home."*

*Home is a sane America. And a sane Muslim world. Neither one is an enemy of the other. Trump's towers are not real towers. And Al-Baghdadi caliphate is only a mirage. The commonality between the two is merely transitory.*

# America The Durable!! Why? Its System Has Several Backup Systems!!

Friday, January 15, 2016

They sing **"Oh Beautiful America...!!"** I write: **"Oh Durable America."** Lived in it and learnt from it as an Egyptian American since 1952. Without losing sight of the rich and diverse culture I came from. That was Egypt the beautiful of pre-1952. Which I see it returning in the durable form of the post-Islamist regime of 2012-2013.

**What makes America durable?** Its system has more than one back-up system. You can almost touch that durability in Obama's last State of the Union message. Delivered with passion to a joint session of Congress on January 12, 2016. Delivered to the Democrats who rose up to their feet repeatedly to cheer him.

Also delivered to the Republicans who largely remained seated out of political distancing. The variables in those reactions did not seem to trouble the first black president of the U.S.A.

**Where does that durability lie?**

Its Constitution has lasted for more than 200 years. Albeit with 27 Amendments. **"We the People"** in its Preamble means what it says. All the people in America, whether citizens, residents, newly-arrived immigrants, or visitors. Underpinning the hallowed principle of **"quality before the law."** Infractions like **Guantanamo** are a glaring exception. But technically, Guantanamo is not American sovereign soil. It is a stain on the fabric. Not the fabric itself.

**Its separation of powers.** Yet not really separate. But overlapping for balance. **Congress** is the federal legislature. But it has executive powers such as in treaty-making. And judicial powers, such as in appointing federal judges including to the Supreme Court. **The Executive,** in turn, has powers to veto legislation, unless that veto is over-ridden by a super majority in Congress. The **federal judiciary,** the creation of both the Executive which nominates, and Congress which affirms or denies, has the task of judging. Among other things, the constitutionality of laws. And other disputes.

All of this represents the Olympic circles - overlapping to represent unity of action, focus on purpose, and toning down of the tendencies of the other two circles of power. The durability of the American system is enhanced by its built-in checks and balances.

But this is not the end of the checks and balances labyrinth. Full of intricate passageways. Difficult at times to navigate, but once comprehended, its rationale is luminous. **The federal government is one of limited powers.**

Limitation here does not spell weakness. You can read it as delimitation. There are essentially two governments in the U.S. One federal, to keep the fifty states together - **"The United States."** And one for each state. These states are sovereign in exercising powers over issues not specified for handling by the federal government.

**How does this duality enhance the durability?** The 10th Amendment of the Constitution provides for the regulation of that relationship between Washington, D.C. and the capitals of all States. D.C. specifically has the power to declare war, collect taxes, and regulate interstate commerce. A truck travelling from New York to New Jersey is engaged in interstate commerce once it crosses the George Washington bridge.

**Everything else is within each state's power to regulate.** Nearly everything, because if there is conflict between federal and state in a matter affecting other states, Washington wins. So the American union continues to strive for what the Constitution's preamble calls **"a more perfect union."**

With a view to delimitation of powers between the federal government and the states, the Supreme Court has ruled in favor of the states in matters directly affecting the people. Family relations, internal state commerce, and local law enforcement fall, under that ruling, within state jurisdiction.

Licenses for marriage, or grants of divorce, or a will are state-based. Attorneys are authorized to practise law by the state. Yet they can practice in any other state (as I do) upon declaring or proving in the court of **"the other state,"** where they are licensed.

At the state level, law enforcement is carried out not only by state courts. But also by the **"police power"** of the state which extends to the national guard (originally state militias). These forces are also available to the federal government at times of national emergencies. **"Federalization"** of these forces is another power to be exercised by the federal government.

The Tenth Amendment of the US Constitution is the last of the ten Amendments called the **Bill of Rights.** That Bill begins with the much debated **First Amendment** which introduces basic provisions including those affecting the state and religion. Because of its centrality to the durability of the American system, it bears quoting:

**"Congress shall make no law respecting an establishment of religion, or prohibiting the free exercise thereof; or abridging the freedom of speech, or the press; or the right of the people peaceably to assemble, and to petition the Government for a redress of grievances."**

Note that that Amendment, as regards religion, does not establish a state religion; but allows for **"the free exercise"** of what any American may regard as a religion. **(An interesting point of commonality between the U.S. Constitution and Islamic Law. For Sharia does not establish a faith and a State. It establishes a faith and a community).**

Also note that new rights are continually created by the Supreme Court, such as **the right to have an abortion.** Thus changing circumstances are accommodated without having to resort to the nearly-impossible procedure of amending the Constitution. The **"Law of the Land"** is whatever is federally legislated, or is integrated through treaties approved by the Senate and signed by the President. These are other forms of back-up systems whose flexibility is intended as a means for durability.

The above is obviously not the entire or even the rigorously academic presentation of all aspects of the durability of the American system. This is because these features are always open to challenge through both interpretation and the evolution of globalization.

Nonetheless it is my way of highlighting what makes America sail relatively smoothly through various types of crises. A brief look at the State of the Union message delivered by Obama on January 12, 2016 sheds further light on how **America navigates its status as a durable super power.**

But before doing so, let us sum up and supplement the above as regards federal powers.

**First:** The union is held together by a Constitution which keeps on evolving through interpretation. **(In the Muslim world, it is called ijtihad: evolving a rule where the text is unclear, or does not exist).** Every exercise of federal power must be traced to the Constitution.

**Second:** There are constitutional and self-imposed limitations on the exercise of federal jurisdiction. This is the theory of **"strict necessity."** Political questions will not be decided by the courts.

**Third:** The **"We the People"** is in action constantly, at all levels of government. That is from the federal, to the state, to even the smallest community. (The water authority in Suffolk County, New York State where I live, is a form of local government. Its school system is supported largely by taxes paid by us residents. Even if we have no children attending those schools).

**Fourth: "We the People"** is the basis for voting, for the organization of political parties (both the Democrats and the Republicans, plus splinter groups). Demographically, it continues to grow and diversify through birth and immigration.

**Fifth:** If there is a conflict between a congressional act and a valid treaty, it is resolved by the order of adoption. **The last in time prevails. (The Iran nuclear deal is not a treaty).**

**Sixth:** Under executive privilege/immunity, the President has a privilege to keep certain communications secret. **National Security secrets are given deference by the courts.** From that flows the State Department rulings on matters of foreign affairs. Also given judicial deference by the judiciary; and

**Seventh:** The U.S. may sue any of the fifty states without its consent. But public policy forbids a state from suing the U.S. without its consent. That is unless Congress passes legislation that permits the U.S. to be sued by a state in given situations. On the other hand, one state may sue another state without its consent. **The Supreme Court has exclusive jurisdiction in a state v. another state litigation.**

In his last State of the Union message, Obama declared:

- **"We will build... We do not give up... Government is a shared responsibility."**
- America's power is credible, he asserted. Debunking the view expressed in the **Wall Street Journal** to the effect that 70% of Americans think that the U.S. **"is moving in the wrong direction."** (So do most of the Egyptians without cause in regard to their country now recovering from 65 years of stagnation).
- Obama defined his legacy in the **context of economic recovery** (from the ravages of wars of choice); health insurance for all; opening to Cuba, Iran and to Pacific trade; energy self-sufficiency; criminal justice reform; environment and climate change measures; support for the middle and lower classes; and equal pay for equal work.
- He **attacked the politics of fear;** islamophobia; curtailment of voting rights; gun ownership without proper control (a **Second Amendment problem**).
- Declared his determination to close Guantanamo; and laughed at those peddling the fiction that ISIS poses a direct threat to the U.S. **"Just ask Bin Laden!!"** he challenged the nay-sayers. Called on congress to grant him authorization to **"use the military against ISIS."** Not satisfied with a coalition of 60 states and 10,000 air strikes;
- He **presented America's priorities in four points:** How to provide every American with equality of opportunity; how to make technology work for America; how to keep America safe; how to align U.S. policies with **"what is best in us, not with what is the worst."**

**This is America the durable.** Its durability is anchored on constant change, constant innovation; **"the spirit of discovery,"** Obama called it.

**"The U.S. is the most powerful nation on earth,"** Obama intoned. Predicted instability in the Middle East and southern Asia for a long time to come.

**Now for a general comparison between the American system and its Egyptian counterpart.** A broad brush, without elaboration. With the usual pitfalls of any comparative presentation:

**(1) On Exceptionalism:** In their different ways, both the Americans and the Egyptian peoples consider their countries, in its environs, **"exceptional."**

**(2) On Their Constitutions:** America amends (27 Amendments); Egypt starts anew -without too many variations. **Its first Constitution of 1923 was fine.** But the lore of opening a new page is an Egyptian constitutional trait.

**(3) On Obama and El-Sisi as President:** In America, Obama is the first Afro-American to occupy the White House. In Egypt, El-Sisi is the first President with a military background to occupy **"Al-Itihadiyyah" after open and fair popular elections.**

**(4) On Congress and Parliament:** The first Egyptian parliament was held in 1860s. Less than a hundred years following the first U.S. Congress. The present Egyptian Parliament has just been convened in **fulfilment of the Road Map of 2013.**

**(5) On Diversity:** America prides itself on it. A nation of immigrants. In Egypt, once the secularists prevailed over the Islamists as of June 30, 2013, diversity was restored. In terms of Muslim/Christian harmony; women in high places; and other areas guaranteed by the 2014 secularist Constitution.

**(6) On Foreign Policy:** Both America and Egypt are pivoting in new directions. **America towards the Asia/Pacific area.** Egypt **towards a balance between east, attention to the Gulf, and south, attention to the greater Nile region.** Now what Egypt needs is to **open up to Iran.** America has done it through the nuclear deal.

**(7) On the Armed Forces:** Hallowed in both countries as bulwarks of security, sovereignty, and national pride. The essential differences are compulsory draft in Egypt, and the existence of national guards in every one of the 50 American states.

**(8) On Religion and the State:** The defeat of the Muslim Brotherhood in Egypt in 2013 signaled the end of the lurch towards the islamization of the State. Keeping religion out of politics is constitutionally guaranteed in both countries.

**(9) On the Media:** In Egypt, media analysis is largely not supported by facts. In America, analysis is largely devoid of on in-depth knowledge of the Egyptian/Arab street.

**(10) On Love of Country:** Nearly the same in both countries. Different tributes. In America **"God Save the United States of America."** In Egypt **"Tahya Misr" (Long Live Egypt)**.

**(11) On War:** Both countries now value staying out of war adventures. Result of war has been now seen in both Washington and Cairo as destructive of nation-building at home.

**(12) On Terrorism:** The fight is one. Different fronts. Different means. Same goal.

*The durability of America relies on multiple back-up systems. In Egypt, the back-up system is a long continuous history going back to the days of the Pharaohs!!*

*Happy 5th Anniversary for the Egyptian Revolution of January 25, 2011. It ushered in the New Egypt. Where Tomorrow Starts Today.*

# Roadsigns On the New Autobahn To and From Tehran

Friday, January 29, 2016

That autobahn to Tehran has been inaugurated. Not only through mountains of hurdles. But also through other higher cliffs of enmity. Primarily between Washington and Tehran. This enmity between the two had its first roots in the CIA. Acting as a parallel US government, the CIA was instrumental in toppling the Iranian popular democratic regime of

Muhammad Mossadeq in 1953. Brought the Shah back from Rome to rule with a westernized but iron fist.

The cause of that outside intervention was one: oil. The Anglo-Iranian oil company was nationalized. After the Shah was sacked in 1979, America to Iran became **"the Great Satan."** And Iran, with **Ruhollah Khomeini** heading an Islamic Republic became to Washington a **"state supporting terrorism."**

The gulf between the two was so poisonous, that it hardened into a creed. So for nearly four decades, punctuated in the 1980's by **Saddam** attacking Iran with US and Arab support, Iran was made an outcast.

But the international wheel of fortune never stops turning. **Khomeini** failed to export his austere form of Shia papacy to the Gulf. He assumed the title of **"Imam,"** while converting the Shia scholars (ulama) into a ruling class. The cleavage created between the ulama of **Karbala, Iraq,** and some of the ulama of **Qom, Iran,** became greater.

And in 1981 the Khomeini brand of Shiism further alienated the demographically largest Arab State, Egypt. Egypt whose capital, **Cairo,** and its historic citadel of Islamic learning, **Al-Azhar,** were built by Shiis. That was more than 1000 years ago when the **Fatimidis** ruled supreme. Before they were replaced by **Saladin** -a Kurd and a Sunni.

Yet **"the conversion"** of Egypt to Sunnism has remained formalistic. Egyptian reverence for the **House of the Prophet Muhammad (Al-Bait)** is a shared quality between historic Persia and historic Egypt. Two States, going back into history for thousands of years, could not be easily alienated from one another.

But **Khomeini** gave that historic bridge a shock. Upon **Sadat's** assassination, Tehran named one of its main thoroughfares after his assassin. Sadat had granted the Shah asylum, and concluded a peace treaty with Israel in 1979. The rift fossilized.

Now fast forward to the new Iran. With the moderate President **Hassan Rouhani,** and the new Egypt, with the pragmatic President **El-Sisi.** Sanctions were imposed on Iran by both the the US and the UN for its nuclear portfolio. But Egypt has never been in favor of sanctions. Except for those imposed on apartheid South Africa. Even during the **Libya of Qaddafi,** Egypt led the charge, choreographed by **Nabil El-Arabi** at the UN Security Council, for lifting those sanctions. Egypt, upon signing its peace treaty with Israel, had the bitter taste of regional isolation.

But reformers, like **Rouhani,** read the pulse of his nation as desirous to rejoin the international community. In US-educated **Jawad Zarif** as foreign minister, Rouhani found a superb negotiator. **"Get us out of sanctions, and in with the world."** So the decision was made to allay international fears from the perception of an Iran armed with an atom bomb.

Over more than two years, negotiations between Tehran and the five permanent members of the Security Council and Germany proceeded along a bumpy road of reaching an accord on the nuclear file. In July 2015, **the energy of diplomacy, unleashed, won the day. The sword of demagoguery, unsheathed, was blunted.**

And by late January 2016, the **International Atomic Energy Agency** testified that Iran has carried out its side of that historic bargain. Even before that awaited certification was made public, non-American business representatives were descending upon Tehran to be signed up. **The autobahn to Tehran was now agog with international traffic.**

But the season of disruption was not yet over. **Sheikh Al-Nimr,** a Saudi Shii leader was judicially, but injudiciously, executed. Incensed, the Tehran mobs attacked the Saudi Embassy in Tehran.

That attack on those diplomatically-protected premises, was condemned by **Ayatollah Khamenei,** Iran's highest leader. He was joined by Mohammad Javad Zarif who lamented: **"This was an act that we were not proud of... I think our Saudi neighbors need to realize that confrontation is in the interest of nobody."**

But the shrill voices of confrontation were not to be easily stifled. Especially in America. That is where the Republican Party keeps on emitting the piercing sounds of hostility toward Tehran. Their voice was amplified by **Foreign Affairs** of January-February 2016. **"Time to Get Tough on Iran,"** shrieked the title of a pugnacious article by **Eliot Cohen, Eric Edelman, and Ray Takeyh.**

Their thesis is that **"the Islamic Republic is not a conventional State making pragmatic estimates of its national interests, but a revolutionary regime."** The shrill then gets louder. **"Iran is an exceptionally dangerous State -to its neighbors, to close US allies such as Israel, and to the broader stability of the Middle East."** And: **"The agreement recognizes Iran's right to enrich uranium and**

**eventually to industralize that capacity."**

Well, Iran does not require an international agreement to recognize its sovereign right to enrich uranium under **IAEA** guidelines. It is also a State which has now proved its pragmatism by demonstrating its readiness to rejoin the world community.

In regard to its Arab neighbors, the Syrian issue for Iran, cannot be framed only in a **Shii vs. Sunni context.** Regime change by outside intervention is anathema to Iran. Since 1953, it had a bitter taste to that proud nation.

This was plainly manifest in its tough stands during negotiations on its nuclear file. The result was a win-win result for all parties. Even American critics of Iran such as Nicholas Burns, a US former under-secretary of State, saw in it a historic shift. He described it as **"a potential turning point in the modern history of the Middle East."** In his **op ed** page in the **New York Times** of January 19, he also interjected: **"But Iran remains a powerful adversary of America across nearly all the conflicts of the Middle East."**

True, though reflecting a sweeping conclusion. Belied by the present negotiations on a political exit from the Syrian quagmire. Such an exit cannot be found without the cooperation of **Tehran and Moscow.**

Unfortunately, the language of Nicholas Burns is mirrored by the language about Iran used by Saudi Arabia's Foreign Minister. In the **New York Times** of January 20, 2016, **Adel Al-Jubeir** vehemently asserted that **"The world is watching Iran for signs of change, hoping it will evolve from a rogue revolutionary State into a respectable member of the international community."**

On various levels, that is utterly wrong:
- Within Iran there is more give and take between the rulers and the ruled than in Saudi Arabia;
- His claim that Iran **"helps the Islamic State flourish"** is patently bogus;
- So is his reliance on **"We are not the country designated a State sponsor of terrorism. Iran is."** Mr. Al-Jubeir should be aware of the politicization of such designations, and the reasons for selectively applying them;
- It is in the nature of exercising national sovereignty for Al-Jubeir to warn: **"Saudi Arabia will not allow Iran to undermine our security or the security of our allies."** In the context of

sovereign equality, the same argument should also be marshaled by Iran.

**The fact remains that both Riyadh and Tehran are engaged in an unseemly ideological battle world-wide. Riyadh supports Sunnism; and Tehran supports Shiism.**

Petrowealth has been liberally employed by the two antagonistic capitals in the illiberal cause of splitting Islam in two genres. **A fiction that has no Islamic jurisprudential basis whatsoever. There is no Sunni Islam, nor Shii Islam.**

However, within this seemingly endless battle for the soul of Islam, one finds roots of that ailment: the super imposition by both capitals of their brand of Islam on the affairs of State. Reason why **Al-Azhar's** position should be applauded as it declares that **"Islam does not recognize a State based solely on religion."**

One of the many problems with faith and State in the Arab and Muslim worlds is the absence of analytical reasoning. An ignorance that leads to direct copying from others without due scrutiny. This is a black hole that is exemplified by an article in Arabic in **Al-Ahram,** the official newspaper of Egypt. **Hani Imarah,** an op ed page writer, states in it without evidence that **"Iran, like cancer, has expanded for tens of years in the Arab body."** Where? When? He does not say.

This is imagination born of ignorance. As such, impossible to prove. Unless relying upon unofficial Iranian hot air talk about controlling Arab capitals. The **New Egypt deserves** better media. **Egypt, by its culture and civilization, should immerse itself in repairing the gulf between Iran and the western shores of the Gulf.**

Obviously, Iran could not be comfortable with decades of cooperation between the intelligence services of Riyadh and Washington, D.C. **That relationship heightens Tehran's mistrust of both.** Even after blessing the Iran nuclear deal, the Iranian supreme leader warned against placing trust in America. It was a message which can only be read in Riyadh as also aiming at the Kingdom. **The friend of my enemy is my enemy.**

A restored **Cairo/Tehran entente** would be the most suitable vehicle for that political and religious reconciliation. My present research for a book in English on the Sunni-Shii rift finds no evidence of an Islamic religious foundation for that fiction.

And as we speed along the autobahn to Tehran, let us forget about a non-substantiated **fatwa by the Grand Mufti of Saudi Arabia.** He recently declared that **"chess is the work of Satan."** On what basis did that gentleman anchor his fatwa? The Quran refers to **"Satan's handiwork"** in the context of **"intoxicants and gambling and idol worship and fortune telling"** (Chapter V/90). None of the above applies to chess.

A fatwa is only a non-binding opinion on a matter of religion. **Sheikh Al-Sheikh, the Grand Mufti of Saudi Arabia: Your fatwa doesn't advance the cause of Islam.** A faith that values science and ijtihad (application of common sense to the text). Your fatwa can only contribute to Islamophobia. As does your banning of dance, music and gender equality.

Chess is a cerebral game of strategy and mental agility. **Originally developed in Persia.** The grand civilization which has hugely contributed to Islam through emphasis on science, math, and technology. Iran's nuclear advances are a natural by-product.

The **New York Times of January 29, 2016** states:

**"Despite lingering animosities and the United States' designation of Iran as a sponsor of terrorist groups, European governments and corporations have made it clear that economic opportunity is going to trump concerns over human rights, security and politics for now."**

Tehran is now bringing in the Airbus manufacturer to deliver 118 of new aircraft. President Rouhani is consorting not only with Italian and French leaders but also with Pope Francis. *A very welcome dividend of peace secured through the dignity of equality of sovereignty between nations. Another cold war seems to be coming to an end.*

# 21 FEBRUARY 2016

## A Mini Interpretive Dictionary of American Elections Vocabulary. Here Follow A Text As Well As A Sub-Text

Friday, February 5, 2016

There is nothing more boring than dictionaries. They are not for bedtime reading. Learners reach for them only when obliged to verify a word. This blog posting is **ipso facto** boring. But necessary to explain, selectively, the American lexicon in this year of electioneering. Here follows my mini political dictionary of American elections oratory.

**"Live Free or Die:"** It is the motto of the State of **New Hampshire.** A liberal state, known as a **"blue color State."** Were it conservative, it would have been categorized **"a red color State."** Like most of the southern states which still call **"the Civil war,"** the **"war between the States,"** with a capital letter (S).

**"The Hawkeye State:"** Reference is made here to the state of **Iowa.** A rural state in the Midwest. Where 64% of its inhabitants are **evangelicals.** You might as well call the evangelicals the near equivalent of the **Muslim Brotherhood.** Except that they do not engage in physical violence. That is where the primary elections for both the Democrats and the Republicans are first waged.

**"The Primaries:"** Are intended as boxing matches and are held between the multiple candidates of the two main parties. Determining the viability, meaning **"the electability"** of a candidate. Leading the winner to be the party nominee. Weeding out the political chaff from the wheat. Like giving the American voter a test run of a new car before committing to buying it.

**"An Establishment Candidate:"** Is someone who had prior political experience. As a senator, a governor, or an ambassador. This year, if you are an **establishment candidate,** you are not a favorite of those newly - participating in the elections process. Call it a generational gap; an educational gap; or a regional gap. Gaps here are the sluices (sliding gates) where rage about government pours out. This year in America, is definitely **a year of rage.**

**"A Future To Believe In:"** A mantra by Senator **Bernie Sanders** of Vermont. Fashioned after Obama's winning political motto of 2008 **"Yes We Can,"** and **"Change You Can Trust."** Reference is to the general perception that **"Government lies."** An innuendo about the **CIA fabricating the news about Saddam's** ownership of Weapons of Mass Destruction.

**"Projecting High Turn Out:"** Refers to total uncertainty about the percentage of those eligible to vote casting their ballots. **In Iowa,** the percentage of youth **(defined in America as between the ages of 18 and 30)** who stayed at home in recent elections ((caucus) days) was a whopping **84%.**

**"A Razor-Edge Margin:"** In the American system, a fraction of one percentage of voters for a candidate satisfies for putting the winner on top. **Winner takes all.** Avoids the Italian or French fractional representation. At the Iowa caucuses, **Hillary Clinton** won by **49.8%** caucus-chosen delegates; her opponent, Senator Bernie Sanders, got **49.6%.** A razor thin difference. To cover that defeat, Sanders called it **"virtual tie."** Made the Hillary camp laugh saying: **"There is no such term. A win is a win is a win."**

**"Caucusing:"** A special form of politically choosing through a meeting of an elective party committee. **Caucuses are all about local politics.** Giving the nation a pre-warning of what might emerge through national elections for president this November. A form of **participatory democracy.**

**More on "Caucusing:"** Is it fit for the Arab world? Such as in Egypt of

Tunisia? **No!!** Primary reason: America began from localities; the Arab States began from centralism.

**"Identity Politics:"** Refer primarily to age, not race. Identity is with issues, not with minority interest and majority interest. Determination by age keeps America on a consistent political course, **regardless of the changing demographics.** This helps political stability, since by 2030, the whites in America shall slide downward to **45%** of the populace. **"Equality Before the Law,"** as based on the enduring Constitution with its amendments, is America's governance safety net.

**"Conservative versus Liberal:"** Terms primarily used by contenders for the Democratic Party nomination. Now, with the elimination process, it is **between Hillary and Bernie.** Pushed Hillary to the left, forcing her to call herself **"progressive centrist."** Whatever this means. Her new appellations are not in her favor. Sanders has stayed, for the past 20 years, his ideological course for **"a socialist revolution."** But causing the Clinton camp to accuse him of **"sloganeering."** Bill Clinton came to his wife's rescue saying: **"Talk is cheap. America needs Hillary. She gets things done."**

**"A Socialist Revolution:"** A political description of Sander's political message. Used against him by the Clinton campaign. In essence, the Sanders message is nothing but **continuity from the days of Franklin Roosevelt.** It means no turning away from the system of social security and of strict banking regulation. But Sanders pushes the envelope further. In the direction of free education for all. (In Egypt, this is called the **Taha Hussein philosophy: "Education is as essential as water and air."**

**"Robotic:"** A robot is pre-programmed. Nothing comes out except what is put in. **An insult addressed to Hillary** (by the Republicans), and to **Marco Rubio** (by his Republican opponents, and democratic haters).

**"From Day One:"** A cliche promise by Republican contenders, promising swift action once in the Oval Office. **Too impractical for implementation;** provides high expectations which threaten the credibility of a new president. The occupant of the Oval Office is not a push-button executive. Hemmed in by checks and balances and by precedents.

**"With all due respect:"** Watch out!! Your opponent is about to **tear your views apart.** It is only a facilitator to a determined denial of the accuracy of what that political opponent stands for.

**"My competitor would make a great vice president:"** A put down by an opponent seeking the presidency. Wanting to say: **"My adversary comes below me in authority and stature. I am way ahead."**

**"This is an awesome non-answer:"** A description of the alleged stupidity of an opponent. Generally used in political debates, or for a refusal to answer a question from the media.

**"Make America Great Again:"** A mantra used by **Trump** to explain that he is ready to use non-conventional means to conventional American ends of supremacy in a turbulent world. So even when defeated in the Iowa caucus, he **prided himself on being new to the game of politics,** but ready to rule the U.S. as an accomplished **"deal maker."** His book, **"The Art of the Deal"** has been made by his campaign as equivalent to **Chairman Mao's Red Book.** Yet when defeated in Iowa, the Iowa newspapers headlined: **"Dead Clown Walking."**

**"Donald Trump Isn't Real:"** Headlined **David Brooks,** a nationally-acclaimed **New York Times** writer. Here are his words against Trump, the champion of banning Muslims from America:

*"Trump's whole campaign was based on success breeding success, the citing of self-referential poll victories to justify his own candidacy. How does he justify a campaign built entirely around his own mastery? Can an aggressor like him respond gracefully in the days ahead to self-created failure? His concession speech was an act of pathetic self-delusion."*

**"You Can't Be a Moderate and a Progressive:"** Personally I don't perceive a big difference between **the meaning of** these two terms. But this is what was said by **Sanders** in an attack on **Hillary Clinton's** political philosophy. In the now contested state for a primary win in the liberal state of New Hampshire. Sander's territory where he has what is called in American political lingo **"neighborly advantage, home state advantage."** Sanders is from **Vermont,** but his home state borders **New Hampshire** to the west. Constituting one of **"the blue states"** of the great region north east of the US, called **"New England."** With a city in New Hampshire called **"Lebanon."**

**"I am not a politician:"** Stands for freshness, innocent of grid-lock chaos in Washington, D.C., and of lying to the public. Fury against the so-called establishment politics has shaken the 2016 races. The **New York Times** of February 2, headlined: **"Electorate Divided in deep disaffection."**

**"Some of my friends are Muslims:"** watch out for what follows. **Islamophobia.** That is where leadership steps in. For the protection of American values of diversity, and also for concern for American security. On February 3, **President Obama visited the Islamic Society of Baltimore mosque.** Warned Americans not to be **"bystanders of bigotry."**

**What Does All the Above Mean?** Democracy has no universally agreed definition. It is a product, that sprouts in various flavors out of the soil of culture. Hence the variables in its political expressions. **As evidenced by the foregoing.** By the way: Iowa is an American State. **Not equivalent to the Egyptian word meaning OK!!**

These are doctrinal differences. But there are other differences of a structural nature between an American model of democracy, and, say, an Egyptian model.

In Iowa, **Jeb Bush spent $5200, per elector.** These are not direct payments. They are largely the cost of staff by the thousands and of media ads.

It is impossible for an Egyptian candidate for public office to spend that kind of money. An Egyptian candidate might offer a pound of fresh meat or of sugar. And for that little gift to a needy public, his Egyptian opponents and media would scream **"corruption."**

Furthermore, it is unthinkable for an Egyptian candidate to have his family, including wife and mother to join him or her publicly on the stump. Again to Jeb. His mother does, to the point of the media spelling his **"momentum"** as **"momENTUM."** And Hillary has her husband, **former President Bill Clinton** next to her behind a microphone.

Which of the two *parties are expected to get the Oval Office as of January 2017? The Democrats. Hillary, not Sanders. He is too shrill, a bit too far to the left. The American electorate tends to be at the center. Hillary, a woman who is expected to follow Obama. From the first ever black President, to the first ever woman President. The voice of both experience and continuity.*

Why did I embark on the perilous journey of putting together this mini dictionary? Perilous, because every paragraph **supra** is subject to challenge.

**But it is worth it.** Because it has an ideological sub-text. Namely that **"democracy"** cannot be one single paradigm.

Like **"The Seven Veils of Eve,"** you cannot measure democracy outside America by an American yardstick. Applicable also to measuring the observance of human rights in the New Egypt. For the New Egypt is still at: **"Sorry For Your Inconvenience, We Are Under Construction."** Democracy, including various forms of respect for human rights, is the **product of its own environment.**

For the purpose of **understanding through the study of contrasts.** Here are two examples: American media has for long become enamored with severely criticizing Egypt's security forces clearing the sit-ins in public squares in Cairo **(Rabaa and Al-Nahdha).**

That was in August 2013, following the removal **(in fact the recall)** of the **Muslim Brotherhood reign of Islamic fascism.** Compare this to the removal by American federal forces of the illegal occupants of the prairies of Oregon. And remember that **Rabaa and Al-Nahdha are not prairies.** They are public squares in a very crowded capital of 12 million citizens.

And while you are it, **why not examine the way the Egyptian prosecution and judiciary are handling the opposition to the State of law and order of El-Sisi government?** In that examination, compare it to an America rightly stressed by **9/11. Erecting the infamous Guantanamo,** where the Muslim victims of that dragnet benefited by no due process!!

As Americans, let us never forget: At **Guantanamo, the great American values were submerged under the flood waters of two contrived fictions:** That Guantanamo is not American soil!! **Really?** So why do I see on it flying high, not the Cuban flag, but **our American flag?**

And that at Guantanamo, the **Geneva Conventions are considered obsolete** and, in any case, not applicable to those Muslim detainees!! You **must be kidding!!** So why do we recall those conventions when a **group of American sailors lost their way** recently in the Gulf, were arrested in Iranian waters, and videotaped by their Iranian captors, prior to their release?

**Please get real!! The world is one!! So should be the word!!** Because words have consequences!! Globally speaking!!

*Life lessons are recalled if taught through contrasts and comparisons. Someone said: "The evil in this world is the creation of those who make a distinction between the self and other." Quoted by David Brooks from a nameless another.*

# Thinking Out of the Box: Framing A Theory On "The Egyptian Mind"

Friday, February 12, 2016

Political Theory is a unique specialization. One of my areas of concentrations. Primarily it teaches you two things: Thinking **"out of the box;"** and framing your arguments for possible durability. People remember ideas longer than they remember events.

With this said, here is the framing of a theory. A theory on **"The Egyptian Mind."** Like all theories, it cannot be perfectly encompassing. And it usually provokes lots of pros and of cons. The grist that may in future produce better flour.

I begin with an apology to the great Greek historian **Herodote (or Herodotus).** Born in 485 B.C., and died in 425 B.C. That is nearly five centuries before **Christ.** Visiting Egypt, he coined a memorable phrase. **"Egypt Is the Gift of the Nile."** True. But, from my perspective, and on my way to a possible theory on **"The Egyptian Mind,"** this is only one side of the coin.

The other side is: **"The Nile Is the Gift of Egypt."** Through worship of natural resources; great engineering throughout its 6500 kilometers length from **Lake Victoria** to **Damietta** and **Rosetta;** unity of its people, especially from the Sudanese borders to the Mediterranean; and ready acceptance of what tomorrow will bring, either a high flood or a low flood. The most important predictors of 10,000 years of Egyptian recorded history is not **"weather forecasting,"** but **Nile forecasting.**

Noting the above, I was galvanized to embark on this theory, because of one recent historic event. **I heard that Egypt is concerned about the beard of King Tut.**

In August 2014, someone touched King Tut's beard. At the Egyptian

Museum in Cairo, the mausoleum of Egypt's DNA. The King's gold mask suffered. The beard detached. Panic struck. **The soul of Egypt was bruised.** Egyptian museum officials, incompetently tried to glue it back on. A botched repair. Eight Egyptian museum officials were carted off to appear before Egypt's Administrative Prosecutor.

A trial is expected. With direct testimony from Egypt's **Heritage Task Force** -an initiative to protect the nation's cultural heritage. A heritage for which a mammoth Grand Egyptian Museum, under construction near the Giza pyramids, shall in 2018 replace the Museum at Tahrir. To the cost of nearly **$1 Billion.**

This is an aspect of **"The Egyptian Mind"** at work. Egypt is not Syria, where Palmyra is destroyed. Not **Iraq,** where the mobs in 2003 carted off the treasures of great **Mesopotamia.** Is not **Afghanistan,** where the **Taliban** destroyed the **Bamian Buddhist temples.**

When the January 25 Revolution ignited from Tahrir in 2011, calling on **Mubarak** to leave, the Egyptian Museum was about to be attacked by the mobs.

Egged on by the **Muslim Brotherhood** after the **Camel Battle** of January 28. For the Brotherhood, Egyptian antiquities are mere idols, non-Islamic. Then we saw the Egyptian mind in full drive: The army which stood silently to protect the Revolution swung into action at the Museum. So did the Museum's employees. For that was the **House of Egypt** -a gift to the whole world.

**So what makes Egypt tick?** What is the make-up of **"The Egyptian Mind?"** What goes into it, and what comes out of it? What are the tentative elements of this attempt at a theory? Let us here try the **notion of a rectangle** -with all four sides equal.

**First:** Belief in a Super Being, without exclusions;
**Second:** A spontaneous commitment to the State and its security;
**Third:** An ingrained belief that adversity can only be temporary; and
**Fourth:** An ethos of **"Egyptianness,"** not to be commingled with Arabism. -a sense of exceptionalism reflected in national folklore.

**First: Belief in the Almighty is the first fabric** in Egypt's historical tapestry. As a tapestry, it is woven from multi-color threads. Reflecting the unique geography of Egypt as a connector between 3 continents. When that fabric is disturbed, Egypt goes back to smooth it all over again.

The hand that smooths that fabric is guided by the principle of the **oneness of God.** In Islamic terminology, it is **"Tawheed."** Didn't begin with Islam, but with **Akhenaton -Father of King Tut.** The multiplicity of deities was replaced by one. How did this faith reflect itself? In the monuments. The obelisk, that monolithic pillar that terminates in a pyramid, tells us something about **The Egyptian Mind.** Though the pyramid building age was gone, the pyramid could not be abandoned. The soul of Egypt lives on, though in a different manifestation.

**For Egypt, eternity is not a hope. It is a creed. Moses** was an Egyptian; the holy family of Jesus, Mary and Joseph sought refuge for four years in Egypt. **From the Delta to Cairo to Wadi el-Natroun. Then up the Nile, south to Mallawi and Asyut.** With the arrival of the Muslims in the middle of the 7th century, the first Executive Order was issued from **Medina** by the **Caliph Omar,** to his general, Amr. **"Don't touch their churches. Don't seek conversion."**

Those instructions held fast. The Amr capital in the Cairo area was called **Fustat,** founded in 641 AD. Fragments from Fustat give glimpses of a cosmopolitan old Cairo. **Polyglot, multi-confessional, and prosperous.**

Centuries later, the **Muslim Brotherhood (2012-2013)** toyed with that fabric. Under the guise of Islamism, they **caused the Copts great anxiety.** They lost, and **El-Sisi,** as President, was seen, on January 7, at the **St. Mark Cathedral** celebrating the Orthodox Christmas. In 2015 and again in 2016. How assuring!!

Contrast this to the Islamists injunction: **"Don't even say Merry Christmas!!"** This is while the **Quran** refers to Jesus as born of immaculate conception. **And the only woman glorified in the Quran is the Virgin Mary.** Her apparitions continue to attract thousands of Egyptians, of whatever faith, to inspirational moments of adoration.

**Except for Lebanon,** Egypt is the only country in the Middle East which has the Coptic Christmas a national holiday. The only country in the world which has a mass political party, **Al-Wafd,** hoisting its symbol of a **Crescent hugging the Cross.**

Even the name of the country has its origins in faith. Tradition holds that its origins are Greek. With due respect and love for Graeco Egypt, **it is not the case.** The term **"Copt"** originated from the soil of ancient Egypt before passing into Greek.

It refers to the temple for the ancient Egyptian god, **Petah.** The most revered among all other deities. Petah had a location. The **city of Manf,** the first capital of ancient Egypt. Th term **"Copt"** was later given to the whole country. The Europeans read it as **"Agyptus."** Guided by the Greeks, the Arabs chose the shortened, but authentic, term **"Copt."**

**Second:** The second side of the rectangle of **"The Egyptian Mind"** is a **spontaneous commitment to the State and its security.** With the multiplicity of religious roots comes a secular faith called **"The State."** The slogan **"Tahya Misr" (Long Live Egypt)** was not born as of January 25, 2011. It goes back 10,000 years ago, though at that dawn of Egyptian history, not voiced in Arabic.

The **pyramids** stand today for the concept of **State stability. Not an epitaph for the Pharaohs.** But as eternalizing the State as a builder, an innovator. Hard stone structures, the first of their kind in the world, stood and continue to stand for durability. The sun always sets on them. But rises again. Also symbolizing the first social welfare in the world (the peasants engaged in construction received daily rations); the technologists (the **engineer was the royal consultant**); and the temples stand below - **separating between the State and religion.**

With Egypt located between three continents, **security became paramount.** The country's armed forces are revered: standing for cohesion, safety, security, and individual sacrifice for the nation. Especially when engaged on national soil, such as in the **October war of 1973, and in combating today's terrorism.** Can't forget the last words of a dying soldier in Sinai: **"This is for you Egypt!!" (Alashaaik Ya Misr).**

These very words are a decisive rebuttal to those who have made a name for themselves attacking the armed forces. The social media did not make the two revolutions of January 25 and June 30 a success. The armed forces did. Under the leadership of SCAF, the Supreme Council of Armed Forces, headed by **Field Marshal Tantawi** and **General Anan,** the military guns in Tahrir stayed silent. A silence that roared higher than the chants of a million civilians.

And in June 2014, **El-Sisi came to power, not on top of a tank. But through the ballot box.** That is after failing to convince **Morsi** in **June 2013** to abide by the national will and face new elections. Reason why **The Egyptian Mind** discards attacks on the authenticity of Egypt's choice of leaders. As it rejects the falsehood that the armed forces have their **parallel**

**economy** -imputing unaccountability.

My words here are borrowed from the World Bank as corroborated by other sources of fact-checked statistics:

- The military's economic share is less than 4% of the gross national product. In Egypt, the **farm land** is mostly private ownership. But most desert land is owned by the State. In food production, the military have a limited role, mainly **confined to subsidized handouts to the poor.** An Egyptian version of America's food stamps for the needy. In construction, publicly-owned firms hold **11.5%** market share. The private sector holds **88.84%.**
- Of course, there are, as should be, **strategic exceptions.** Connected to security and national stability considerations. The prime example is the construction of **the second Suez Canal.** Inaugurated in August 2015, but funded entirely by subscriptions for shares spreading the ownership throughout the populace.
- And under the stewardship of former **Prime Minister Hazem Al-Beblawi,** certain infrastructure projects were allocated to the military. For reasons of quick execution at a low cost. **Total value reached 5.5 billion Egyptian pounds ($1=LEG 7.83)** A figure constituting only 10% of public investment in fiscal 2014-2015.

No wonder that **"The Egyptian Mind"** values a security State. Not that it is ruled by a security apparatus, but its peace is guaranteed by the army, the police, a diplomacy of peace, and a new leadership which exalts **development over ideology.** After America was attacked in **9/11,** it created the **Department of Homeland Security (180,000 employees),** nurtured 50,000 security companies; created **Guantanamo** and suspended the **Geneva Conventions.** Egypt is targeted by hostile acts from outside at nearly all times.

**Third:** The Third side of the rectangle of The Egyptian Mind is an **ingrained belief that adversity can only be temporary.** Resilience, not advocated, but deeply felt. National catastrophes, like the war of 1967 when Egypt's air force was totally destroyed by the Israeli attack, was recorded as **"a setback."** Six years later, the score were made even. And when the food riots erupted in **February 1977,** as a result of withdrawal of government subsidies for basics, the **International Monetary Fund was debunked.** And nearly 20 years earlier, when the U.S. and the World Bank reneged on premises to fund the **Aswan Dam project, Nasser** nationalized the Suez Canal company.

On the matter of the Aswan Dam funding, Egypt did not nationalize the Canal as uninformed world press asserted. The Canal is sovereign territory, meaning that you do not nationalize what you own. The company was a different matter. Yet nationalization of the company cost the share holders, mostly foreign, nothing. Those shares were fully compensated by Egypt at their fair market value.

And here emerges another facet of resilience as an impulse of **"The Egyptian Mind." Respect of treaties.** In March 1979, a peace treaty was concluded in Washington, D.C. between Egypt (one third of all Arabs) and Israel. Nearly all Arab States retaliated by isolating Egypt. **The League of Arab States,** moved its headquarters from Cairo to Tunis. But Egyptian resilience had a voice. In Sadat's voice, the response was **"Egypt is a country which isolates; it is not subject to isolation."** A few years later, the Egyptian peace theory prevailed. And the League was back to its birthplace.

It is challenging to attempt a listing of factors for that belief that **adversity can only be a passing cloud.** But a few of these factors may be highlighted as a framework for resilience:
  - An ancient cradle of civilization
  - **Many Egypts** from the Mediterranean to the aquatic Red Sea; to the sacred heart of Egypt at Luxor; to Egypt's front garden at the **Fayoum oasis**
  - Moderate climate
  - Vast desserts east and west ready for reclamation
  - Readiness to do with fewer amenities. Lunch could be a loaf of bread, a piece of cheese, an onion, and a glass of sweet tea
  - **And the Nile shall always flow** regardless of hydropolitics in eastern Africa. If not the Blue Nile, then the White Nile in cooperation with the Sudan. **What can go wrong?!**

  **Fourth:** Completing the rectangle encompassing **"The Egyptian Mind"** (with spaces to be filled by the reader) **we have Egyptianness.** A living mode of exceptionalism. Not haughty, but seductively humble and urbane, and smiling.

Four Egyptian languages: **Arabic, Coptic, Nubian and Berber (in Siwa).** An early children teaching that **"you are part ancient Egyptian, part Arab."** An educational system, though ineffectual, but still clings to teaching **English, French, German, Italian, Spanish, and as of late, Russian. Farsi and Hebrew** are also taught. Diverse cuisines, from **Molokhiyyah** (green soup), eaten by Ancient Egypt, to grilled meat kebabs and kofta, and of course, falafel.

And a bewildering array of dress, from that of a mayor **(Omdah)** to a western-looking **young woman pilot of Egyptair.** Together with a focus on protecting the most vulnerable borders -the **coastline, of 1555 miles on the Mediterranean and the Red Sea.**

**Exceptionalism** is also prominent in song, dance, films, the theater and the arts. All protected by constitutional provisions of the **secular document of 2014.** Including the popular song for the Armed Forces on July 3, 2013: **"May God Bless the Hands of Our Armed Forces."** A failing attempt to negate it by the Muslim Brotherhood **"May the Hands of Our Armed Forces Be Paralyzed."** Antagonism and non-belonging to **"The Egyptian Mind."**

And the head of the Coptic Church, **Pope Theododros II** of Alexandria was a pharmacist. While the Grand Imam of Al-Azhar, **Sheikh Ahmed El-Tayeb,** is a graduate of the Sorbonne in France.

We cannot exit this text without reference to the sense of Egyptian humor. Especially when quoted from a President and an Egyptian Coptic Pope:

- Sadat was once told that Israeli Prime Minister **Golda Meir** was hurling accusations at Egypt. His laughing response: **"What do you expect from an ugly looking woman?"** Later was a topic of laughter in 1977 between the two leaders.
- The great scholar, the **late Pope Shenouda III,** and hailing from southern Egypt **(Al-Ssaaeed)** put this question to a group of his listeners (including me): **"Do you know why God created the Egyptians of southern Egypt?"** No answer from the audience. The Pope provided the humorous answer: **"For comic relief!!"**

**"The Egyptian Mind"** encompasses more than the above. The **fact remains** that **Egypt is a special place.** For where else in the Arab and Muslim worlds would you have **"the Prince of Poets,"** Ahmed Shawki **(1868-1932),** a Muslim, writing a poem of praise about **Jesus.** Conveying true inclusiveness, it reads, through my translation from Arabic into English:

*"Upon Jesus birth, so was mercy born;*
*good deeds, heavenly guidance and eternal life.*
*No threats, no temporal might, no revenge;*
*no sword, no invasion, no blood.*
*In his love and adoration;*
*great disciples bowed their heads."*

**"The Egyptian Mind"** retains the adage **"Misr Umm El-Donia"**

**(Egypt Is the World's Mother.)** It also retains the Coptic prayer inherited from the Saints **"Blessed Be My People - Egypt."** And how would it forget that the **Quran mentions Egypt by name 5 times** in no less than 4 Chapters. Including a verse which greets all of arrivals at the Cairo International Airports: **"If God pleases, enter Egypt in safety."** (Chapter 12, from verse 99.)

From faith, we conclude with high diplomacy. Indicative of **"The Egyptian Mind."** An exchange between two giants, not yet reported before anywhere.

Concerned about Egypt's professional representation at the UN Secretariat, the great **Foreign Minister, Dr. Mahmoud Fawzi** went in the early 1950s to see the best-ever UN Secretary General, **Dag Hammarskjold.** The S.G. asked: **"Mahmoud: How do you qualify an Egyptian fit to serve here."** Without hesitation, Fawzi responded: **"Regardless of faith or affiliation, or gender, that individual should intimately reflect Egypt as a unique civilization."**

*An example of "The Egyptian Mind" in full view on the world stage. As defined by Mahmoud Fawzi, the Godfather of the Egyptian School of Diplomacy. A school that suffered no interruption since 1922, come "Hell or High Water!!"*

# By Whose Hands Was Secretary-General Boutros-Ghali Robbed of a Second Term?

Friday, February 26, 2016

This is not investigative reporting. These are legal forensics revealing the hands that robbed him of a second term. And these hands are not what is publicly peddled. **Not by the Clintonites. But by a UN Charter full of gaps and contradictions.**

Looking at the Charter, you discover that it is **not what we teach at law schools.** At Fordham Law (New York) I focus on the words. Analyzing not the provisions. But why those provisions drafted in 1945 belong to a museum. Not to the world of 21st Century. Since 1965, Boutros-Ghali and I discussed this at length.

**First,** the term **"peace-keeping"** does not appear in the Charter, a Second World War document. In San Francisco, the allies of the war were believed to maintain their cooperation in the post-war years. They did not. The cold war inherited that world. Completely nullifying **Article 47** which provides for **"a Military Staff Committee."** You cannot pool your military expertise with your adversary.

That vacuum was provisionally filled by **Dag Hammarskjold.** That was his response to the tripartite aggression on Egypt by Israel, France and Great Britain in 1956. The **"Blue Helmets"** were born not in the Security Council Chamber, but in Port Said. The helmets were painted blue, the UN color, in Italy.

Expanded in the Congo of 1960, **"the Blue Helmets"** was a huge flop. Across one of the rivers, an Italian contingent was massacred by **Lumumba supporters.** Calling for help by an Irish contingent a few miles across that river, the Irish did not respond. Not because of cowardice. But because the Italian signal could not be understood. Why? **No pre-planned training in peace-keeping, including signal unification, could be held.** Until today.

That chaos resulting from **Charter dysfunction** reached the shores of **Yugoslavia** as it was breaking up. It also engulfed **Rwanda.** The Muslims of Bosnia and Herzegovina were ethnically cleansed. A million Tutsis were massacred. Security Council resolutions, as expected, proved to be hollow moralizing.

**Second:** Not only was the Security Council failing in its Charter-outlined duties. It was ironically expanding its jurisdiction in areas prevented to it by other Charter provisions. **Article 2, para. 7** prohibits intervention in **"matters which are essentially within the domestic jurisdiction of any State."** Fine. Although each State decides those matters as it pleases.

Now here comes the kicker!! Later the same provision regarding respect for sovereignty takes a turn to a dead end street. It says: **"But this principle shall not prejudice the application of enforcement measures under Chapter VII (i.e. on sanctions)."**

**Guess who decides on sanctions?!** A no veto by any of the Big Five (US/UK/France/Russia/China) plus 4 non permanents (total non-permanents is 10). So you now have a system where the 5 permanents agree on selecting a State to be sanctioned (couldn't be one of their proteges). **World justice disappears when you have selectivity.** Inequality before the law. Easy to sanction an Iraq or a Libya, or an Iran or a Sudan. No Big Power umbrella. No powerful uncle or Godfather.

With no hope in reforming the Security Council, the Council turned its gaze to individuals within sovereign States. Came up with **"the travel ban"** on individuals without serving advance notices. Also without hopes of reviewing the list of banned individuals. Creating islands of Guantanamo-style preserves without the torture additive.

**So you now have two UN systems in one:** the General Assembly (akin to a House of Commons), and a Security Council (akin to a House of Lords - the Permanents). But the GA resolutions are a mere wish list -no enforcement mechanism. And the House of Five Lords is the only body which can take decisions. **But selectively. Pick and choose.** If there is a tie, say an Afghanistan, then a new non-Charter mechanism called **"a Presidential statement"** has been put in place. Does not even have the teeth of an executive order.

**In the thick of this mess, stands the Secretary-General.** The most neutral body in the world organization is the **UN Secretariat.** I have served there for 32 years. The Secretariat is on duty 24/7, serves all UN Member States on an equal footing, and provides data and mission reports for guidance of the SG and, through him, to the entire membership.

But speaking of the Secretary-General, you have to be careful which SG you mean. There are **two of them in the same body: An executive SG and a political SG.** The former is covered by Article 98; the latter by Article 99.

And within Article 99, I find the problems faced by Boutros-Ghali. That article is the real separator between the **League of Nations,** and its presumed continuity in the UN of the San Francisco Charter. Better to quote here its text:

**"The Secretary-General may bring to the attention of the Security Council any matter which in his opinion may threaten the maintenance of international peace and security."**

Thus the political Secretary-General is born through the **mid-wifery of Article 99.** Armed with the big word **"MAY"** -meaning **"discretion."** Theoretically this is a form of power-sharing. A power sharing expressed by Boutros-Ghali in what he inadvertently called **"The Sixth Veto."** You see, **Boutros-Ghali was not a politician;** he was a lecturer in international law.

Ministering to a collection of rowdy States which, **especially the U.S.** resented his threatened intrusion into their power preserve.

He was conscious of the political pitfalls. But deeply felt that the Charter, though deficient, could be reformed through **"political ijtihad"** - interpreting broadly, through common sense, the existing text which cannot be easily revised.

His **honeymoon with the Clinton administration was brief.** And Afghanistan, not ex-Yugoslavia or Rwanda, was the issue that unleashed the **venom of Albright,** the then America's UN Permanent Representative. Those were the early 1990's. With both Clinton and his rivals, the Republican Robert Dole, finding in the UN an easy target to prove a nationalist point. That America shall not be legislated to by an UN where anti-American feelings ran high.

**French support for Boutros-Ghali could not match a Clinton administration** that saw in Boutros-Ghali an advocate of a UN which is not subservient to Washington's diktat.

The great theoretician Boutros-Ghali who was a close friend of mine for 50 years, lost. Through its fossilized nature, the Charter favored the Clintonite politics. That iconic thinker lost the battle for a second term. And was succeeded by a politician, **Kofi Annan,** who had no problem staying for two terms.

Kofi Annan was chosen to appease African UN membership for jettisoning an African -Boutros-Ghali. From the Big Powers point of view, an appeaser, Annan, instead of a confrontationist Boutros-Ghali. **A manager in the place of a thinker.** A typical play within the play!!

In Boutros-Ghali's failure to gain a second term, I find a strong echo of **Dag Hammarskjold.** Their commonality of approaching the Charter is clear. Hammarskjold stood his ground in 1960; had Khrushchev bang his shoe on the table at the General Assembly. Shouting to the S.G. **"IRHAL"** (Leave). And a year later, in 1961, the white regime of Rhodesia was suspected of causing his plane to fall from the sky.

Boutros-Ghali also stood the same grounds. Advocated reform of the Security Council and ran afoul of Washington. But he kept his promise to his own convictions: idealism not reflected in the political world of rough and tumble in the world of the Glass House by the East River, in New York.

In 1992, in his office on the 38th floor, he privately asked me: **"Do you wish to return to serve? Haven't you enjoyed 6 years of retirement?"** "No, Boutros," I said. **"I have left this cage. Now breathing freedom on the outside. Lots of options."**

His silent but approving smile guided me to the exit. It is difficult, in fact impossible, to forget neither his ideas and ideals. Nor that quiet but knowing smile and innate wisdom. **A second term was a passing episode in a life which shall always enrich the world he left behind.**

And there is more. **More to the Boutros-Ghali saga.** The media say that he lobbied for the post. Dead wrong. Africa lobbied him for the post at an African summit. Mobutu, then Congo (Zaire) President, motioned to him and whispered: **"The Anglo-phone Africans want to nominate one of them. You are our Franco-phone candidate."**

Taken aback, Boutros-Ghali responded: **"What would President Mubarak say?"** Mobuto winked and said: **"I shall call Mubarak!!"** And he did. Then the game was on. **How do I know that?** From the lips of Boutros-Ghali in Mexico City. He had invited me to join him there for personal and confidential consultations. That was before **Mitterand,** as President of France threw in his heavy political weight, tipping the scales for Boutros-Ghali as UN SG.

Yet through the debacle of the Clinton animosity, forged in the crucible of an old and tattered UN Charter, the process of nominating a UN Secretary-General is at long last about to change. The effort is aiming at breaking the strangle hold of the Big Five on that closed medieval method of nomination. A method whereby the General Assembly is a mere rubber stamp for what the Big Five agree upon in private consultations.

That is the process which sank the ship of nominating **Tanzania's Ahmed Salem,** in the early 1980's, to replace **Kurt Waldheim** of Austria. Waldheim, later found to be a former Nazi operative in Greece, was running for an unheard of third term. Salem was his opponent.

America vetoed the Salem nomination. **His sin?** Dancing in the GA aisles upon the the admission of mainland China to its rightful seat at the UN.

**China vetoed Waldheim.** And the deadlock continued. For 16 ballots. Salem, in our frequent meetings, would laughingly say **"Waldheim has no chance. The process is broken."** Finally **De Cuellar** of Peru was called from a beach resort to occupy the post as a final compromise. Boutros-Ghali followed, in spite of early American misgivings.

In his book **"Unvanquished,"** Boutros-Ghali stressed what the Charter could not accommodate: **dedication for being a Secretary-General who dared defy a big power armed with a veto.** And no meaningful reform of the council is at present possible.

If I were to write an epitaph for Boutros-Ghali, I would say: **"HERE LIES A LEADER WHO SACRIFICED A WORLDLY POSITION FOR WORLD'S PRINCIPLES."** Rest in peace, my friend.

*May his soul rest in peace. His Egypt bade him farewell in the most celebrating manner -A military/State funeral. For he was a true combatant for his motherland, and for the cause of a universal Rule of Law.*

Dr. Yassin El-Ayouty, Esq.

# 22 MARCH 2016

## From The Womb of Trump's Fascism Emerges A Chaotic American Spring

Friday, March 4, 2016

The man is an impostor. An impostor in the village. The very title of my novel in Arabic: **An Impostor In The Village.** Published in Cairo twice. Once in 1948; the other in 2014. And **Trump's village is America.**

From his lips gushes bombast and abuse. The adage says **"loose lips sink ships."** Trump's lips has sunk the Republican Party. The Grand Old Party (GOP) of the great liberator, **President Abraham Lincoln.** At the age of 16, I travelled to Lincoln. Spiritually from my Egyptian village, Kanayat, Province of Sharqiah.

That was through trudging in 1944 for 3 miles to the provincial capital, **Zagazig.** Headed to the public library to read in English a thin book on Lincoln. Captivated by that bearded and humble man who managed to free the slaves in America, through a bloody victory of the North over the South. **Then assassinated in 1865.**

**So with his party today.** Where his assassination is repeated, but this time on his party, the party of Lincoln. **By a buffoon called Donald Trump.** Whose fascism is worn on his sleeves. Through:

- calling for the building of a wall between the U.S. and Mexico;

311

- ridiculing blacks, women, and minorities;
- calling for a ban on Muslims from entering the US, even if they were returning citizens;
- using his book **The Art of the Deal**, the way Hitler had used **Mein Kampf**;
- accepting, through avoiding clear disavowal, the endorsement of **David Duke, the former head of the Klu Klux Klan;**
- calling for bombing the families of suspected terrorists to avenge terrorist attacks;
- praising Mussolini as an effective leader; and
- calling Obama an American hater, an alien born outside the U.S., and a non-Christian/a closet Muslim.

The list can be much longer. Trump is a mob inciter whose calls for **"let us make America great again"** is nothing but a call for a Spartan America whose wars are endless, and her grab of the natural resources of other States (oil as an example) is the fruit of **"winners take all."**

Through content analysis, one finds in Trump the making of a dictator, an anti-Republican quasi conservative. And a man who has succeeded in turning his own party against him. Here are samples of his bombast reflective of his sense of vaunted superiority.

- About Hillary Clinton, the prospective Democratic nominee for president: **"She's been there (in Washington) for so long. If she hasn't straightened it by now, she's not going to straighten it out in the next four years."**
- **"Mexico is sending to America its criminals and rapists across the borders;"**
- He wants to torture people accused of terrorism;
- Former Senator Norman Coleman of Minnesota declared: **"You've got a con man and a bully who is moving forward with great speed to grab the party's mantle to be its standard bearer. That's almost incomprehensible."**

A former Republican presidential contender, **Mitt Romney** of Massachusetts went on the attack. Spear-heading a belated Republican effort, to stop the Trump express. Called Trump **"a phony, a fraud, and a con man."** Using the street language of which Trump is a master. Romney was on point:

- Trump University is a fake institution. Graded by its student at **98%**. But by serious evaluators at **D-;**
- Trump resorts are claimed by him to be for everyone. But can everyone afford $100,000 in annual membership dues?;
- Trump's foreign policy is summed up by him in one phrase:

**"military might so great that no one would dare mess with us."** Asked about who advises him on foreign policy, his answer was evasive. Ended up by saying: **"It is I who shall decide;"**

- He was pressed on dealing with foreign leaders if he became president. His response boiled down to the limited language of the real estate broker that he is. **"I deal with all kinds of people. Nobody can close deals like Donald J. Trump."**
- Yet he is oblivious of central facts. Dealing with foreign leaders requires circumspection, in-depth knowledge of the issues on the table, and versatility in the art of compromise. Of all this, the fascist Donald is innocent. Especially in connection with expertise in the art of getting to **"Yes."** An admission unknowingly made by his protruding lips: **"I do not settle;"**

Thus on establishing peace between the Arabs and the Israelis, he looks at it through only one prism: that of Mr. Netanyahu. Largely due to the clear fact that Trump has no expertise in foreign policy. About it, he is not a learner, let alone a practitioner. **Never mind that Trump had made a sizable segment of his fortune in the Gulf.**

Trump's barrage of attacking the problem of America's trade deficit and/or imbalance denies **Japan, China, India, and even Mexico** their sovereign right. The right to put national interest above other considerations, except whatever is required by the rules of free trade.

The Trump bogus claim that the entire world, except the U.S., has leaders who are smarter than Obama. Racism and chauvinism wrapped in one package. **"I shall bring back to America the jobs off-shored back to America!!"** A Trump claim which is not backed by **"How?"**

Calling Trump a fascist is fully vindicated by the very definition of that term. **Fascism defines a political philosophy or a movement or a regime that puts race above the individual and that stands for a centralized autocratic government headed by a dictatorial leader.** One of its basic characteristics is the forcible suppression of opposition. Trump is all of the above:

- He describes his supporters **"a movement;"**
- He calls his opponents like Marco Rubio of Florida **"little Marco"** and **"a liar;"** Ted Cruz of Texas **"a choke artist."**
- To him **Hillary Clinton** might be incarcerated for using a personal server for her emails, some of which **"might have been classified while she was Secretary of State;"**
- He threatens **Paul Ryan, the new Speaker of the House of Representatives,** As President, he, Trump shall **"make him pay**

**a heavy price"** if he stood in the way of his governance. Upon hearing this, the Speaker laughed aloud in his office. And he has reasons for that. **Impeachment proceedings against an errant President begin in the House of Representatives.**

- The Trump supporters are mainly the enraged lower than middle class. Under-educated (**"I love the not-so educated,"** Trump screams to thunderous applause), angry at the **so-called Washington establishment;**
- Anger and rage fueled both fascism and Nazism. Another quote from Trump in this **year of the angry American voter,** aching for the emergence of **"a strong leader."** He claims: **"Our country is being run by incompetent people. And I won't be angry when we fix it. But until we fix it, I'm very very angry."**

On anger, **professor Jennifer Finney Boylan of Barnard College, Columbia University,** hits the nail on its head. She laments **"I see a land where to be a citizen means to specialize in the venting of spleen...Apparently it's vitriol itself, rather than any particular strategy for the future, that's propelling the electorate."** Then she concludes by stating:**"We seem to be mistaking petulance for righteous wrath."**

Coming back to my introducing the theme of **"An Impostor in the Village."**

- Trump plays on the theme of fear. His call for transformation is nothing less than **"TRANSFEARMATION;"**
- Conspiracy is his conduit to presidential politics. He speaks, not the language of establishment politics, but the language of the gutter, a proximity link to the **"Know Nothing"** multitudes. So the theme shifts nearly daily, to whatever the street can absorb. From **"Making America Great Again,"** to placards carried by beautiful young women proclaiming **"The Silent Majority Stands With Trump."**
- He denies **science, climate change.** Even claims that he knows a 2-year old who immediately developed autism from a vaccination."
- His hatred for Muslims is pervasive. Even publicizing gleefully an **Internet false rumor about a U.S. general** executing Muslim insurgents with bullets dipped in pigs' blood.
- So was Trump's false assertion that Muslims in New Jersey cheered from rooftops the fall of the World Trade towers

Such is Trump's danger to the security of the U.S. that the stalwarts of his own party, the party of Lincoln now in the process of collapse, are in a stampede to **"Stop Trump."** The Impostor, in my novel, uses faith for sordid ends. So with Trump. **Using democracy for sordid ends.**

**A showman selling snake oil for healing. A chaotic American Spring is upon us. Results unknown.**

# A Mega Bully In A Mega Pulpit: Trump's Mobocracy In An Annotated Selected Glossary

Friday, March 18, 2016

### A: Anchor
A media person whose quality is determined by the kind of questions he or she addresses in public to the Chairman. If hostile and a woman, such a person has **"blood oozing from everywhere."** Clear reference to the menstrual period. Stamped the Chairman as **"anti-feminist."**

### C: Convention
A formal assembly, usually based, since the 17th century, on tacit consent by its members. When not favoring the Chairman being its nominee for US President, then a hostile take-over is necessary for voiding the popular will as defined by the Chairman.

### D: Debate
An ugly form of verbal warfare in which only profanity, misogyny, vulgarity and dishonesty are permitted. Drowning your opponent's voice and trouncing the moderators for reminding you of your time limitation. For the Chairman, these are debating skills and a propensity to lead.

### Demagogue
A political agitator appealing to the prejudice of the masses. A term fully applicable to Chairman Trump. He has voiced heated opposition to **"political correctness,"** to **"the establishment,"** to organized political practice, and to the principle of compromise. All peaceful tools in the service of the national good. His vain rhetoric is the very language of the **Tea Party,** one of whose symbols is Sarah Palin.

### Deportation
The forceful expulsion by authorities of individuals accused of violation of immigration laws. Chairman Trump is set to deport 11 million persons falling in this category, within 2 years of his presidency. Requiring 30

jumbo-jet flights for 730 days. This explains why Chairman Trump hates media questions about immigration. Such as those posed by **Jorge Ramos,** a Latino spokesman physically removed from his rallies.

## F: Foreign Policy
Generally defined as a State's approach through diplomacy and other means to relationships with other States to maximize national interest. Chairman Trump, nonetheless, has redefined American foreign policy. Made of sound bites typical of his own brand of raucous disparagement of nearly all foreign powers. Examples: **China** is **"ripping off"** America on trade and stealing jobs; **Mexico** is flooding the southern border with migrants and drugs. As to **Japan, "we are getting absolutely crushed on trade."** Salvation is through the Chairman.

## H: Hand
Terminal part of human arm. For the Chairman, its size determines the Chairman's genitalia. In this department, the Chairman has declared that he was **"well endowed."** Nature and destiny are on his side!!

## Hero
An illustrious warrior who has fought for his country or his cause. But if captured, like in the case of **Senator McCain,** loses his luster. Chairman Trump put it succinctly when he declared: **"I like persons who don't get captured."** As if the victim has a say in falling captive.

## I: Immigration
A term which, for the Chairman, refers only to skilled foreign workers. On guest worker visas coded as **H-1B.** Fit for work in Silicon Valley. Chairman Trump is calling for all others to be herded on buses for forcible deportation. But the Latino empire of millions of new Mexican voters is striking back. Denying Chairman Trump, with his blond hairdo, their vote this Fall. The revolt of those vilified are systematically described by Trump as **"drug traffickers and rapists."**

## Islam
The faith of 1.7 billion people, based on two principles: the onness of God, and the surrender to God's will. One of the three Abrahamic faiths: Judaism, Christianity, and Islam. Chairman Trump, in Florida on March 9, intoned another Islamophobic declaration: **"Islam hates us."** A cunning reversal of his Trump coinage of: **"Ban Muslims entry into America."** Even the Florida Governor, **Rick Scott,** endorsed that savage call by Trump.

## M: Marco Rubio

A one-term Senator from Florida with a Cuban ancestry. Now out of the race for Republican nomination for President. Described by Chairman Trump as follows: **"You know that in Florida they hate little Marco Rubio so much because of the fact that he never votes...He has conned the people of Florida into voting for him."** The Chairman, in a humane gesture towards his then opponent **Rubio,** also said: **"I didn't want him to get hurt hitting his head going down."**

## Mobocracy

Originally Latin for **"mobile vulgus,"** meaning excitable crowd. Now refers to the lower order of a promiscuous assemblage of persons whom Chairman Trump targets for his venomous rantings. **Trumpism** has a close proximity to being a **pied piper,** a strolling musician, leading children over a hill to nowhere.

## Muslim

A human being believed by Chairman Trump to be so reviled as a terrorist or potential terrorist. His or her presence in, or admission to America is a clear and present danger to the established Trumpian order. The plan by Chairman Trump to rid the world of ISIS must remain under wraps. It shall be executed by the US military, not in accordance with the laws of war. But by the laws of Trump. **"This is what a leader is all about,"** so declared the Chairman.

## N: New York

A state in the northeast of the U.S. That is where Chairman Trump has multiple towers. Also where he is adored by the New York City Real Estate Board. Winning New York for Trump is declared by the Chairman a foregone conclusion. Thus he forcefully told his supporters in New Orleans: **"We have a shot at winning New York. Can you imagine what would happen if we win New York? New York loves Trump."**

## O: Outsider

A term in the uneducated language of today's American politics. Meaning someone with no political experience. No part of the so-called **"establishment."** Meaning all those chosen through the democratic process to represent the populace. Chairman Trump is riding the wave of rage through pushing the fiction of **"the Outsider." The Tea Party,** the evangelicals who believe in **"the end of time,"** the white blue collar workers are united in the cause of defeating **"experience."** Trump, promises that he, as an outsider, is the answer.

## P: Palin

The last name of Sarah Palin, former governor of the state of Alaska. An empty-headed invention, ill-chosen by **Senator McCain** as his running mate in his failed presidential bid against Obama in 2008. Known for her ridiculing facts and knowledge, now a side kick for Chairman Trump as he seeks to energize his ultra-conservative supporters. Famously described by a French poet as **"a bad joke."**

## Politics

Used to be defined as **"the art of the possible."** Now reversed to be **"the art of appealing to the prejudice of the masses."** Perfected by Chairman Trump in his bid to **"Make America Great Again."** Hence **"a politician,"** which the Chairman is not, is someone who plays by the rules usually ridiculed as **"political correctness."**

## Putin

The man of the hour for Russia whose strength and practices in his country, and in its **"near abroad,"** are admired by Chairman Trump. A reflection of the Chairman's admiration for strong leadership. Now seen by him as the cause of American decline. Reversible only under a president who does not apologize and does not reward America's adversaries, like Iran, by **"very bad deals."**

## R: Rally

To rally is to get together again. Rousing to fresh energy. In the rallies for Chairman Trump, the theme rallying his crowds is to **"get tough,"** to consider a protester an enemy. Thus the Chairman calls on his private army of bouncers to kick out anybody protesting his theme of hate. The emphasis in Trump's message is not on the First Amendment (guaranteeing freedom of speech). It is on magnifying hate into a creed. Forcing the protesters in Chicago to shut down his rally. **"Throw them out,"** yelled Trump to his bouncers. **"Trouble-makers,"** he described protesters. The result: An atmosphere of hate, violence and divisiveness that has become **"the new normal"** for the Chairman's electioneering.

## Rambling

An incoherent, irregularly non-planned speech by the Chairman. Stoking anger of the mobs assembled to watch his show.

## Republican Party

A 162 year old party which should be demolished through either a Trump take-over, or a split through a contested convention intended to deny **the Donald** the historical advantage of being the chosen one to defeat the

Democratic nominee for president in November 2016.

## S: Schizophrenia

A psychotic disorder characterized by loss of contact with the environment. Also contradictory or antagonistic attitudes. Chairman Trump exhibits these symptoms of dysfunction. In his rallies, he calls for his supporters right to free assembly. A First Amendment right. But denies it to those protesters attempting to exercise the same right, by calling them **"villains against whom I shall press charges."** He declares love for the **Chinese,** the **Japanese** and free trade. But simultaneously he calls for 35% surcharge over products imported to the US.

## State Department

The department of the U.S. Government that conducts foreign affairs on behalf of the U.S. President. Under Chairman Trump, the lines are already drawn up. All in terms, not of interaction, but of rage, conflict and enmity. In their turn, those foreign powers are adjusting to a possible Trump presidency. **Mexico's President** says: **"His language is reminiscent of Hitler and Mussolini."** The **British Parliament** debated barring Trump from entry into the UK for his **"hate speech." China** and **Japan** are distressed. **Iran** is laughing at him in its bazaars.

## Swear

**Invoking the name of a sacred being** in an oath. It is the highest form of asserting a promise. Chairman Trump, in Florida, the home state of his then competitor, **Marco Rubio,** resorted to extracting an oath from the enthralled multitude. **"Do you swear to vote for me?"** And their hands and voices were raised **"yes."** Reminiscent of the Nazi **"Sieg Heil" (Victory To the Savior!)** A true mobocracy!!

## T: Taxation

A contribution levied by an established authority on persons, property or business. For the purpose of supporting government's programs on behalf of the entire population. **"No taxation without representation"** was a call to arms by the **13 American colonies** rebelling against Great Britain. So with the position of Chairman Trump. He believes that the conservative and the billionaires causes are not sufficiently represented in American governance. His payment of limited taxes in accordance with the law should not entail making his tax returns public knowledge. The Chairman says: **"It is too complicated."**

## Truth

Truth has consequences. Especially for a billionaire who has captivated

319

millions for being a non-establishment politician. Best characterized by a 60-year old property investor who idolized the Chairman in these words: **"He has no gain in this -he doesn't need the money, he doesn't need the fame, he doesn't need the power."** Because of this, **"the establishment is ganging up on him."** When somebody is being persecuted constantly, that means they're speaking the truth!!

## U: Unifier

An adjective earned by Chairman Trump in his bid for the Republican nomination for president. Part of the process of energizing his base of conservatives, evangelicals, white, black, Latinos, working classes and monied classes. In a massive surge of support for their idol. **Trumpese** is a language springing from the street through which these multitudes surge. Propelling him as the front runner in this brutish campaign between Republicans and Democrats. For the Chairman believes that before you build, you should first demolish, as per his practice in real estate. **The demolisher, to Trump, is the unifier.**

## V: Violence

It is the unlawful exercise of physical force. Also intimidation by the exhibition thereof. The rallies, recently called by Chairman Trump, have begun to be marked by violence. Especially in the industrial Midwest. The Chairman, in a direct way, has nurtured that tendency as his way to **"Making America Great Again."** To him, the protesters against him are **"violent;"** the Muslims, **"most of them hate us;"** **"Mexico shall be forced to pay for a wall"** on the common border; and the US military **"shall do what I tell them to do"** (including torture).

## W: Wall

Not to be confused with **"Wall Street."** It is a beautiful structure projected by President Trump to be built over a 2000 miles length. Between the U.S. and Mexico. **Costing $20 billion.** Chairman Trump has determined that Mexico, which rejects that idiotic concept, shall be forced to pay for it. **How?** As punitive damages for sending Mexicans to America as unvetted illegal immigrants. Through welshing on America's debts to Mexico. The Trump wall, as promised by the Chairman, is expected to surpass in grandeur the **Great Wall of China.**

## War

A state of open hostility between nations, conducted by the force of arms. Waged, in the opinion of Chairman Trump, as the first option to failed negotiations. For the Chairman, the initials U.S. must always stand for **"Unconditional Surrender."** In conformity with the call by **President**

**Franklin Roosevelt,** prolonging World War II against Nazi Germany and Imperial Japan. Chairman Trump has always declared **"I don't settle."**

## White House
The name of the residence of the President of the United States. Located in a federal district, called Washington, D.C. Presently occupied by **Barack Hussein Obama.** Considered by Chairman Trump as **"a closet Muslim,"** with no valid US birth certificate. In the words of Chairman Trump **"Obama is the worst president in the history of the United States."** If Chairman Trump moves into the Oval Office in January 2017, he may attach the name Trump to the facade of the White House. Renaming it **Trump House** may not be out of order.

## Z: Zee End. An Epilogue
A fitting ending, by remembering **President Ronald Reagan.** This is on the sad occasion of the passing on March 6 of First Lady **Nancy Reagan.** She, throughout his tenure as President (1980-1988), was his primary advisor. Though the leader of the Republican party, **Reagan** looked upon the cold war in a diplomatic way. **America's role, he believed, was not to win it. But to end it. And it peacefully ended in 1989.** That was the GOP of Reagan. Not the GOP of Trump.

*From Ronald to Donald?! What a precipitous descent for the Grand Old Party, the party of Lincoln.*

# A Bridge Linking Between Two Bad Shores: Criminality in Brussels And Contradictions In the Muslim World

Friday, March 25, 2016

In Brussels, where terror struck on March 22, there had been words and arms of welcome to the hordes of Muslim refugees. Fleeing the terror in their lands of origin. Hordes harboring in their midst those who are schooled by ISIS to cut the hand and at times the head, of those who shelter them. An unbelievable criminality. And a denial of the essence of humanity: **"Live and Let Live!!"**

In the Muslim world, the origins of that poison are active. In various forms.

From **Wahabbism,** where the **Quran** is given an imperfect interpretation. Especially when it comes to denying legitimate access to worship by adherents of other faiths. Faiths that lie at the roots of Islam itself. To the **Muslim Brotherhood** which hoists a flag bearing two swords. For a faith whose Book, the Quran, does not even contain the word **"sword."**

To the avalanche of spin-offs of criminal gangs. Gangs inspired or led by thugs: from **Bin Laden** (they call him Sheikh), to **Al-Zawahri,** to **Al-Zarqawi,** to **Al-Awlaki,** to the biggest joke of all, the so-called Calipha **Al-Baghdadi** of ISIS.

Passing through the dirt of **Al-Nusra, Boko Haram, Al-Shabab.** Not to mention the **Friends of Jerusalem,** ensconced within Gaza, the run-away Palestinian strip lorded over by **Hamas,** a clear and present danger to the New Egypt. Yet Hamas is vainly calling for easy access to Egypt. Insane!!

This New Egypt, is one third of the Arab world, raising the flag of secularism, fluttering through the gentle winds of **Al-Azhar** in Cairo.

And in the West, the **Muslim Brotherhood,** now and belatedly declared by Egypt a terrorist organization, is being enabled by an absurd public relations campaign. Calling the Brotherhood a victim of an Egyptian military coup led by El-Sisi, -a duly elected President, and a nation-builder.

**Morsi,** from 2012-2013, had sought the glory of a Muslim imperial caliphate. A pipe dream whose only outcome would have been **turning Egypt from a State to a Province.** Where the **Copts** are persecuted, **Hamas** is empowered, and the Muslims who are not in the fold of the Brotherhood are cowed into abject submission. **The seat of power would have shifted to the Guidance Bureau.**

In only one horrible year of failed Islamization of Egypt, Morsi claimed to have accomplished **480 national projects.** Called **"Injazat"** (Accomplishments). Including **a trash conversion factory** in one of Egypt's 27 provinces.

But the **"Injazat"** booklet does not mention that Morsi was elected before the drafting of an Islamic Constitution (now repealed); that in November 2012, Morsi has declared himself above any constitutional limitations; and that for 3 days (June 30 - July 3, 2013) he rejected El-Sisi's attempts to have the Brotherhood respond to the screams of 35 million Egyptians for a new plebiscite.

Adamancy, in the context of Islamic ideologues, is falsely considered **"the Righteous Way" (Al-Sirat Al-Mustaqeem).** But under Islamic jurisprudence, the welfare of the community comes first. Called the **Maslaha jurisprudence.** Whatever is in the interest of the community **(Ma Yanfao El-Nas),** anywhere, and at any time.

In that sense, terrorism in Brussels, or anywhere else, makes a **mockery of Islamic law (Sharia).** And when some rotten apples engage in that type of genocidal warfare, they give Islam a black eye.

So please do not trouble me with **shatter about Islamophobia.** It is terrorism that creates both fear and hate for Muslims everywhere.

And don't trouble world history by tracing the roots of terrorism to the days of colonialism. The colonial period is largely gone. Succeeded by a system of Muslim rulership which puts the perpetuation of its rule ahead of national development and the peaceful transfer of power.

Shifting the blame to what happened decades ago, rather than facing the causes of today's realities, shall not be taken as credible history. This is why I look upon El-Sisi's call for a **"Religious Revolution"** as the right advocacy for moving the New Egypt forward. It is to be here noted that happily **Al-Azhar** is heading that call.

The tangible proof is to be found in a speech in Arabic by **Al-Azhar's Rector, Imam Dr. Ahmed El-Tayieb.** Standing before the **Bundestag in Berlin on March 15,** he addressed many issues of which the following are a selection and a translation of my own. Except for Quranic verses.

- **On the new Muslims in Europe:** "I say to my co-religionists who now live in Europe... Observe the high values of the societies in whose territories you now live."
- **On Islam's Respect for Diversity:** "You ought to present similar perceptions of Islam and its tolerance. Perceptions which respect the other, regardless of religion, sect, or ethnic origin."
- **On Abhorring Combating The New Societies:** He called for the framing of the following Quranic verse: "With regard to those who have not fought you in the cause of Religion, nor expelled you from your homes, God does not forbid you from being considerate and dealing justly with them. Surely God loves the just." (Chapter 60, Verse 8)
- **On the Organic Links Between Islam and Other Faiths:** Dr. El-Tayieb told the Bundestag: **"Islam is a faith with organic**

links to other revealed faiths. As Muslims we believe that the Torah, the Bible, and the Quran are all purveyors of guidance and light."

- **His Quranic Evidence: Quoting from Chapter V, Verse 46):** "And We sent, following in their footsteps, Jesus the son of Mary, confirming what was before him of the Torah, and gave him the Scripture in which was guidance and light, and confirming what was before it of the Torah, and a guidance and an admonition for the pious."

- **On Women In Islam:** He raised Al-Azhar's voice in defense of gender equality. **"In Sharia, women are equal to men in both rights and obligations. So please do not think that the marginalization of women of the East is attributable to Islamic teaching. This is a misconception. In truth, women suffering is the result of divergence from Islamic teaching regarding women. Arcane tradition and worn out custom, with no relation to Islam have been ascendant."**

- **On ISIS and Similar Other Armed Movements:** Dr. El-Tayieb declared: **"ISIS and its affiliates murder, destroy, cut heads off. All in the name of God and of Islamic law... Acts which are antithetical to Islam. Let us bear in mind that no faith would be immune from the charge of violence and terrorism, if it is evaluated from the perspective of the few perpetrators amongst its adherents."**

- **On Al-Azhar's Role In Revamping the Islamic Discourse:** **"Al-Azhar is continuously concerned with revamping its message and educational curricula... Everywhere, its scholars confront wrong concepts. Concepts which distort Islam's message. Exploiting it for the advocacy for a blind insurrection, for blood-letting and countries destruction."**

- **On Inclusiveness Between All Religions:** **"Al-Azhar, in December 2014 held a conference attended by Muslim Sunni and Shii scholars, heads of churches, eastern and western, and representatives of the Yazidis of Iraq. Its final communique condemned all armed sectarian groups and militias which pursue violence, terrorism, and assault the lives of peaceful citizens... Any violence perpetrated against Christians and others in the name of faith is contrary to the ethos of Islam."**

The gulf is indeed wide between the voice of true Islam, as expounded by Al-Azhar's Grand Imam, and the **voice of death heard loudly in Brussels.** Confronting jihadist ideology through the voice of Dr. El-Taiyeb is the starting phase in what promises to be a **protracted struggle.**

For despite the centrality of the voice of Al-Azhar, as the premier citadel for Islamic learning, the divergence in Islamic practices throughout dozens of Muslim countries and cultures makes that voice carry less volume.

But hope springs eternal. The Quran, Muhammad's tradition (Sunnah), and ijtihad, as the brain activated for interpreting those texts should undoubtedly come on top. The **world of today has heard the pain of Belgium!!**

But how could Al-Azhar deal effectively with this **generational battle** against rogues pretending to be Muslims?

The needs of the Al-Azhar's **"Religious Revolution,"** initially called for by President El-Sisi, are myriad.

Among those needs is adequate funding and staffing whose main expertise is communication in main languages to pass on the great message delivered at the Bundestag.

That call for a **"Religious Revolution"** by El-Sisi is a historic game changer in the world of Islam. Still a Cairo TV anchor woman, **Azza Al-Hinnawi** called El-Sisi on the air **"a do-nothing president who speaks like Hitler."** A below the belt stupidity, even for a person like her with a contribution to the New Egypt that does not exceed a **microphone in her hand, coupled with a foul mouth, joined to an empty head that does not even retain the recent inauguration by El-Sisi of Suez Canal II.**

Judging by the follow-up on that message of the Grand Imam of Al-Azhar, I am left with this feeling: The Al-Azhar's counter-attack against the kind of murderous ideology which led to the Brussels massacre, and was about to lead to the possession of **"a dirty nuclear weapon"** is lacking of some basic tools.

*These include good translations from the classic Arabic, which are still woefully lacking. And Al-Azhar points of strategic and effective communication throughout the world. Staffed by experts who do not take a holiday!! Failure in uprooting ISIS and its sister organizations is no longer a viable option. This is a fight to the finish!!*

Let us keep in mind the emblematic treatise by a great predecessor of Sheikh El-Taiyeb, as a Grand Imam of Al-Azhar Al-Shareef. That was **Sheikh Mahmoud Shaltoot.** One of his books is entitled **"Islam: Faith**

325

and Law" **(Al-Islam Aaqeedah We Shareeah),** published in Cairo in more than 24 editions.

Sheikh Shaltoot ends that book by saying:

- **"The fatwas are not binding statements of law;"**
- **"The views of Al-Caliphah, the Imam, or the judge are not immune from being fallible;"**
- **"Interpreting Islam is not the exclusive prerogative of any one;"**
- **"The titles of Sheikh Al-Islam and the Mullah are only but scholarly titles with no binding consequences;"and**
- **"Ijtihad is more authoritative when arrived at, not individually, but collectively."**

*Through this freedom of religious thought there appears, through the present fog, another bridge. Detouring all of us, Muslims and non-Muslims alike, to an existence better than that of a constant fear from a pretended Islam that in fact does not exist!!*

# 23 APRIL 2016

## Reflecting Rage As An American State, The New York Times Calls for Sanctioning Egypt!!

Friday, April 1, 2016

Even a reputable newspaper, like **The New York Times** slips occasionally in the realm of the absurd. The unreasonable, the ridiculous, the war-like. Since its founding in 1851, its motto has been: **"All News That's Fit to Print."**

Judging those words by an editorial dated March 26, 2016, that journalistic promise **induced in me, not concern. But derision, and contempt. Why?..** It was vacuous, unintelligent, and an advocacy for **aggressive meddling in Egypt's internal affairs.**

Under the title of **"Time to Rethink Relations with Egypt,"** the editorial called, not only for the unwise, but for worse. **The unimplementable.** Here are its main false assertions. Followed by rebuttals:

**A Faulty Assertion:** In the summer of 2013, **"the Egyptian military took power in a coup."**

**A Rebuttal:** From June 2012 to June 2013, the **Muslim Brotherhood's**

**reign of Islamization and terror** was leading Egypt precipitously into a bloody civil war.

**El-Sisi's** negotiations with **Morsi,** who presided over that descent, failed to produce a plebiscite. Responding to the call by 35 million Egyptian demonstrators, **"a road map"** agreed by the national civilian forces, **including the Coptic Church,** produced an interim secular administration headed by a venerable jurist, **Adly Mansour.**

By June 2014, **El-Sisi was chosen for the presidency over Hamdain Sabbahi,** a moderate Islamist, in open and internationally-observed elections. The fact that El-Sisi was, at that time, the Defense Minister, does not stamp his selection, by popular will, by the **totalitarian stamp of a military putschist.** El-Sisi ascended to the presidency of Egpyt through **an orderly transfer of power.**

Prior to the instalation of El-Sisi presidency, the Morsi Islamist regime, now recalled by the electorate, clung to the myth of **"legitimacy by the popular choice of June 2012."**

That legitimacy, originally supported by the neutral might of the Armed Forces, was destroyed by the Muslim Brotherhood. Until now, it still clings to the propagandistic myth of **"legitimacy," (Al-Shariyiah).** The Brotherhood's unforgiveable sin was to assume power through democracy. Then to **subvert that vehicle into an instrument of subverting Egypt into an Islamic province.**

*When you board a bus, your ticket of admission as a passenger is not a license for hijacking that vehicle. The terms of your purchase are clear: Ride peacefully, or get off. For you are no longer a rider. You are a criminally offending usurper.*

So was the status of Morsi and his Brotherhood during their one year as **"rough riders."** The bus driver, the Egyptian electorate, threw them out of the national bus. **It was a Brotherhood self-inflicted wound. Not engineered by El-Sisi.** But by the hands of the Brotherhood, presided over by a dictatorial **"Guidance Bureau."**

One of the Brotherhood's **"Supreme Guides"** had once declared **"To Hell With Egypt." (Toz Fi Misr)!!** The nation simply responded: **"To Hell with the Brotherhood." "Tahiya Misr" (Long Live Egypt).**

From an article in Arabic by Egyptian Ambassador **Mohamed Noman**

**Galal,** former Ambassador to China, I quote the following: **"It is Egypt's brave army which assured Egypt's safety and peace; saving the country from collapse. This is by reason of its being a national army which has deep faith in its homeland. Unlike in other several Arab countries, the Egyptian army is not the army of any president, nor is it a sectarian army, battling for either a tribe or a sect."** (Al-Wasat newspaper, March 28, 2016)

**A Second Faulty Assertion: "Egypt's human rights abuses became even harder to overlook."**

**A Rebuttal: And who are you to judge? Egypt is not a US protectorate.** With the exception of the crime of genocide, the question of human rights is essentially a domestic jurisdiction matter. It has been globally manifest that outside uninvited intervention in the internal affairs of other States has always backfired. **Even if, it was done, as in most cases of American unwanted intervention, by proxy.** Proxies either of the internal type, or the external genre calling themselves **"human rights civil society organizations."**

**The New York Times** cites what it calls: **"Egypt's crackdown on peaceful Islamists, independent journalists and human rights activists."** It quotes from **"leading American Middle East experts."** It warns against **"an authoritarian rule, leaving few if any Egyptians free to investigate mounting abuses by the State."** It decries **"arbitrary imprisonment of tens of thousands of Egyptians ... and extrajudicial killings."**

All of the above are reflective of an imperial approach towards the affairs of **outside proud nations like Egypt.** Egypt is not America's burden. America should simply **"Butt Out."** And even falling in line with the colonial interventionist approach of **The New York Times,** the following questions must be raised:

- Were there **"peaceful Islamists"** at the bloody standoffs, lasting for six weeks **(July 3 to August 14, 2013)** between the occupiers of two public squares in the heart of the country's capital? Adamantly refusing the **entreaties of the forces of law and order to peacefully disband? Through well-publicized exists for safe passage?**
- Shouldn't **The New York Times** judge the reactions to such provocation by the standard of the US authorities crackdown on **"The Occupy Wall Street"** movement, or **"The Black Lives Matter"** movement?

329

- Those battles of August 2013 in the Cairo public squares of **"Rabaa,"** and **"Orman"** did not have to occur. **They were avoidable,** except that the overthrown Brotherhood was acting upon its oath which includes **"Death for the Sake of Allah is Our Most Cherished Wish."** In America, we call this **"Suicide By Cop,"** meaning through goading the police to open fire.

**A Third Faulty Assertion: "When President Morsi was overthrown, senior American officials dithered... (hoping) that this would be merely a bump on Cairo's road toward becoming a democracy."**

**A Rebuttal:** Egypt's democracy is on track. **The Road Map of July 2013 has now been fully implemented.** With the inauguration of the new Parliament in March 2016. **It needs no outside evaluator or overseer!!** This monitoring is the most obnoxious form of intervention in the internal affairs of States.

Now I take off my hate as an Egyptian residing in America, to don that of an American naturalized citizen. I find today's American democracy the least suitable model by whose parameters other forms of democracy could be evaluated:

- The American voter does not directly select his or her Congressional representative. Between his/her vote and the final selection is a sieve which **blocks the one person one vote formula.** It is a formula to which Egyptian elections adhere. In effect, since its founding, American democracy is a rule, not by the people, but by a higher oligarchical tier;
- This sieve, now **represented by the electoral college,** still reflects the fear by the Founding Fathers from a rule by the mob, in favor of the rule by the Select. There are voters, then delegates, then super-delegates, then unbound delegates. A dizzying game of numbers, with the primary voter left at the bottom of the formula.
- Thus in 2000, Al Gore, though winning the popular vote in his presidential bid against Bush II, lost to the latter. Becoming a US president whose leadership was overpowered by a war-monger, Dick Cheney, whose vice presidency led to the catastrophic war of Iraq.
- Would the U.S. tolerate Egyptian authorities telling Washington what to do regarding this stratified system?
- At a historic press conference held by **Bush II and Putin of Russia,** the U.S. President spoke of democracy, causing Putin to emit a rare laughter of disbelief. **Bush said something to the effect that the U.S. is a champion of democracy everywhere.**

At which point Putin remarked derisively: **"Like in Iraq?"**

- Money has a determinant voice in the make-up of Congress. In the case **Citizens United**, the U.S. Supreme Court ruled that corporations were entitled to contribute unlimited funds to their chosen congressional candidates. Consequently, a bigger campaign budget makes it possible for a candidate, through ads and the support of special interests, to overwhelm an opponent with a smaller war chest.
- Until today, the US judiciary has, unfortunately failed to effect reform of campaign financing.

Under these circumstances, how can America, as per **The New York Times** editorial qualify for being a paragon of democratic virtues? When its own system is begging for a cure? In fact prompting great American jurists like **Justice John Paul Stevens, now retired from the US Supreme Court,** of whose Bar I am honored to be a member, to call for amending the U.S. Constitution itself.

**A Fourth Faulty Assumption: "Over the next few months, the President should start planning for the possibility of a break in the alliance with Egypt."** A war-like call premised on urging the Obama administration to end military aid to Egypt amounting to $1.3 billion.

**A Rebuttal:** To me, this is the height of absurdity by the so-called opinion-makers of **The New York Times**. Here are my reasons:
- Those funds, which are largely spent on purchasing US weapons, are **integral to the Peace Treaty of 1979 between Egypt and Israel.**
- Though Egypt is not essentially dependent on them for its defense, including defending against terrorism from Gaza and chaotic Libya, that paper is advocating tampering with a treaty. **A treaty is a contract. Sanctioning Egypt by withholding those funds constitutes a breach to perform by the US towards Egypt.** A breach of a covenant that cannot occur without adverse consequences.
- **The New York Times** advocacy for **"Rethinking Relations With Egypt"** goes diametrically counter the paper's own admission to the contrary. The paper concedes that: **"Administration officials... have cautioned against a break with Egypt saying its military and intelligence cooperation is indispensable."**
- Then it pivots away from those expert views to that of a fellow at the **Brookings Institution, Tamar Cofman Wittes.** In an interview, Wittes opines that **"Egypt is neither an anchor of**

**stability nor a reliable partner."**
Here this question arises: If such punitive views become official U.S. policy, **is America a reliable partner of Egypt?** My response is that partnership, if subverted into a master-vassal relationship, shall not stand. There are no American bases in Egypt; only joint exercises and training in the use of US military hardware.

Both the U.S. and Egypt are, in any case, pivoting away from one another. Both of them are eyeing the east: **Egypt, for technology and armament;** America for trade. Obama and presumably his Democratic successor, see America's interest in having a light footprint in the chaotic Middle East. Even calling an old US ally like Saudi Arabia **"a freeloader."** Meaning a defense dependency on the US with adverse implications for the U.S.

**In this context, Egypt cannot be counted within this pejorative description of "a freeloader."** Its economy, though struggling, is not dependent on oil; its defense is native; unlike the U.S., its government is not threatened with partisan shutdowns; and unlike the U.S., its ethos is not racialism which, in the case of America, has been accentuated by the **historic arrival of the first Afro-American to the Oval Office.**

Prudency dictates that America should mind its own internal affairs, which are sorely in need of a fix.

And from its beginning, America has received a historic advice from George Washington, the father of its independence: **"No entangling alliances."**

Hence the shame of **The New York Times** to be giving a boost to the thesis of those who are warring on the honored international rule of **"friendly relations among nations."**

**The very definition of friendship is equality in relationships, giving mutual support to its parties.** As a dual citizen of both America and Egypt, I could see in that relational balance the **very advantage of inclusive bi-culturalism.**

Only the enemies of both America and Egypt can take comfort in that editorial by **The New York Times. Egypt is minding its own business. Shouldn't America also mind its own business?**

**The New York Times** editorial savagely attacks Obama's policy towards Egypt for being **"moored in a series of faulty assumptions."** It is the editorial policy, expounded in that article, that is so hopelessly moored. **Mired in unrealities exposing an unmerited spirit of hegemony.**

**Thumbs up for the Egyptian Council For Foreign Affairs (ECFA).** For its comprehensive response to an **Egyptophobic letter addressed to Obama.** The letter's author is an organization about which I am hearing for the first time. Calling itself **"The Working Group on Egypt."** That organization is in lockstep with that **New York Times** editorial in calling for a US retaliation against Egypt.

**For what?** On the basis of what ECFA described as **"unfounded human rights violations and interference in the independent Egyptian judiciary system."** The ECFA rebuttal also offered me a teaching moment. It highlighted the illegal silence of some civil society organizations regarding **"foreign funding they received, and which domestic social activities they finance... in accordance with Egyptian applicable laws."**

Here ECFA noted that the number of such offending organizations was **"a small minority"** within **"more than 47 thousand"** such organizations in Egypt.

Were I, as an attorney licensed in the U.S. to sue either **The New York Times** or the **so-called Working Group on Egypt, I'd lose. Law and fairness do not always intersect.** If I plead incitement to violence against Egypt, as my hypothetical client, they would defend on the basis of **freedom of expression under the First Amendment of the Constitution.** Even if that freedom of expression is inciteful to violence and, thus, contrary to public policy.

**Throughout history, nations do not die.** But in some of them their civilizations are prone to perish. **America the young, and Egypt the old are of the type where civilization is enduring.** However, in the case of America, there appear early signs of reversible senility. Examples:
- *Storms of rage*
- *Revived nativism through non-acceptance of the other*
- *Return to early Biblical evangelicalism*
- *Glorification of Trumpism where ignorance and bullying are hailed as virtues*
- *Saluting the idea of fences between nations as means of international communication*
- *Replacing diplomacy by a nod to the nuclear option*

- *Insulting feminism through machoism and misogyny*
- *Freezing work wages at the level of 50 years ago*
- *Hailing the equivalent of "America Uber Alles"*
- *Creating from old allies new adversaries*
- *And calling the use of foul language in public "the New Normal"*
- *Shutting down the Government? No problem*
- *Defying the Constitution by the Senate Republicans in not even giving a hearing to a Supreme Court nominee? No problem*
- *Calling for a ban on Muslims or having their neighborhoods in America subjected to police patrols for intimidation in the name of national security? No problem.*
- *Doubly demeaning the US President, as well as 1.7 billion Muslims, by calling Obama "a closet Muslim?" No problem.*

If not in letter but in spirit, most of the above anomalies are reflected in that insulting editorial in **The New York Times.**

Conclusion: The USA is in sore need of a **new national program of cleansing rejuvenation.** Let us call it **"Anger Management." A nation at rage is a nation whose civilizational principles are in disrepair!!** Mindless rage is a paralysis of reason and of what is now defined as **"mindfulness."** An awareness of what you do and of its consequences.

**Another conclusion:** Sadly, a keen observer of the U.S.-Arab relationships will have to regard this phase of American history as regressive. **Regressive into an age of darkness.**

How can America be **"mindful"** when its millions cheer an aspirant to the presidency, **like Trump,** calling for Japan and South Korea to go nuclear? And for getting rid of ISIS through the option of using tactical nuclear weapons!! Trump's version of the **"New World Disorder."**

If the possible Republican nominee for president is envisaging **Rakka (Syria) and Mosul (Iraq)** as possibly the **new Hiroshima and Nagasaki of 1945,** it is a measure of American reversion to the dark ages -Dark Ages II.

With such yardstick, the New Egypt should look upon that editorializing of **The New York Times,** or the mercenary advocacy of **"The Working Group on Egypt"** as as an inflammation in the American body politic.

*Its consequences shall have no more of an effect on Egypt which is presently under construction than that of an annoying fly being swatted to extinction by the frond of a palm tree in Kanayat, Sharqiah, my old Egyptian village.*

# When The Road To Hell Is Paved With Good Intentions: Egypt's Dismissal of An Errant Justice Minister

Friday, April 15, 2016

Beware of the Ides of March!! Last month, the New Egypt engaged in a rare administrative act: The summary dismissal of its Justice Minister. Dated March 13, 2016. Well done!! **Counsellor Ahmed Al-Zind** was a well-meaning person. But he has a disease. Incurable. Is called **"shooting from the hip."** Or diarrhea of the mouth. And Al-Zind shot from the hip, or the mouth, 3 times.

An Arab adage says: **"The third hit hurts the most."** So former Minister Al-Zind met his quota of imbecilities. When the New Egypt, now under reconstruction, hurts, there is little room for **"MAALESH"** (Never Mind).

A license for **"let go,"** well-suited for a permissive environment. Intolerable, when the New Egypt is scrutinized in every step, in any direction it takes.

This is especially so in the realm of the **administration of justice.** Thousands upon thousands of cases are an overload in every court. In a national mood that uses **the Court as a wailing wall.** The newly-found freedoms in Egypt of post-January 25, 2011 have created a highly litigious environment. Creating a near paralysis in moving the legal calendar from **"docket"** to **"judgment."** From **"judgment"** to effective and humane **"execution"** (INFATH).

In such a fluid environment, Al-Zind found his salvation. Even before he had the exalted post of Justice Minister for his country. The very country that exports its justice models to the rest of the Arab World.

Here follow the events that fit the description of: **"the road to hell being paved with good intentions."**

**Big Mouth Salvo No. One:** While he was **President of the Judiciary Council,** Al-Zind, watched in justified horror a spectacle. Hundreds of Muslim Brotherhood bullies besieging the **Supreme Constitutional Court.** Intimidating it for having adopted a legal opinion: One-third of the Islamic lower chamber of Parliament violated election laws. So **Parliament was disbanded. The Brotherhood resorted to its well-practised fascism: intimidation.** Shut that court down!!

A la **Nasser** in 1954. That is when the cry went up: **"Down with the Constitution."** The great jurist **Al-Sanhoury,** head of the **Council of State,** was beaten up in his office.

As judges of the Supreme Constitutional Court sneaked to their offices through back doors, **Al-Zind fumed. And rightly so.** But his good intentions suffered from a dangerous absence. Absence of international judicial knowledge.

Directing a threat at the Brotherhood ring of fire, Al-Zind's fuming produced only derision. For he publicly stated: **"I shall sue the Government (the Islamist Government) before the International Criminal Court."** Alarmed, I sent a word to some members of the Council of State. **"Al-Zind should know that there is no private litigation before the ICC. He has no standing. He does not seem to comprehend the tenets of universal jurisdiction under the 1998 Rome Charter of the ICC."**

In return, **I got an unacceptable response.** It amounted to: **"He didn't meant it!!"** Well, if he didn't mean it, why embarrass himself and the judiciary, and Egypt, by **making that burp in public?**

And if he meant it, he should have known that the ICC litigation is not private. **It is government-anchored; premised upon a decision by the UN Security Council; instituted by a directly damaged party; and to all kinds of other limitations.** Primary among these is **"inability"** of a national judiciary to act. The so-called **"subsidiarity"** principle.

**Big Mount Salvo No. Two:** Al-Zind is now in a different capacity. Now is the time for him as Justice Minister to vent in the name of a Cabinet headed by a technocrat, **Prime Minister Sherif Ismail.** An engineer. The government of Egypt has put on its finishing touches.

**With the new Parliament, you now have three co-equal branches of government.** As per the **Road Map,** produced through consensus of the select national forces, **including Muslims** and **Copts, in July 2013.** Ending the reign of Brotherhood terror.

That Brotherhood had been judiciously declared a **"terror organization."** For its conducting a systemic organizational violence, aimed at cowing the newly regained secularism. **Fronting university students as its shock troops.** Under the false banner of **"public demonstrations."** Freedom of expression and assembly, which were violently prohibited under Islamist (un-Islamic) rule.

The battle ground moved to previously **lawless Sinai.** An **Asian Egypt ceded de facto by Morsi to Hamas.** So north Sinai was infested by Hamas tunnels. But southern Sinai has been blessed by tourism. The armed forces in the North, under the unified command of Field Marshal Askar, took the brunt of armed terror. Casualties resulted.

**With that, Al-Zind's Big Mouth grew bigger.** Shot again out of anger at the casualties inflicted on the defenders of Egyptian security. Good intentions. But stupid performance. Al-Zind's reaction was utterly out of line.

He declared, and I translate from his Arabic: **"I will only be at ease when I retaliate by killing 10,000 Brotherhood supporters in retaliation for each soldier killed."**

The opposition to that injudicious threat was swift. It came from senior members of the Egyptian judiciary. One of them was **Counselor Mahmoud Raslan,** head of the Legislative Unit of Egypt's Council of State. His remarks went as a spear into the heart of Minister Al-Zind's profanity. **"Those words should not be coming from a Justice Minister. He is supposedly aware of the role of the judiciary in these matters."**

Not surprisingly, Al-Zind verbal bomb was a gift to the Brotherhood's propaganda machine. Through Al-Zind, the odious culprit, the Brotherhood, was now playing one of its historic roles: **"Poor Islam is again victim of apostates and usurpers."** Foreign funding poured in; so-called **"human rights organizations"** jumped into the artificial fray.

**And Egyptophobia found another hanger to hang its diatribes:**

337

- Security measures were unjustifiably deemed as anti-human rights measures;
- A murdered young Italian doctoral student was automatically seen as a victim of official Security forces. Even before the Italian-monitored Egyptian investigations of that tragic event;
- The propaganda machine of the Muslim Brotherhood abroad, generously funded by Arab and non-Arab sources, was gleeful at every utterance by Egyptian officialdom which could be interpreted as signs of regression of the Rule of Law;
- Even the so-called indigenous Egyptian media poured oil on the fire. A fire ignited by Minister Al-Zind. Abusing their newly-found freedom to find reason to exhibit false bravery through its own falsehoods.

So by your calculus Mr. Al-Zind, you threaten to kill one million terrorists (10,000 x 100 victims). That is three times the calculated strength of ISIS before its recent losses!! **Bravo for the Zind killing machine!!**

**Enlightened anti-jihadism calls for cooperation of the adversary, ideologically and demographically.** The real task is to peel off from the Muslim Brotherhood the elements which are ready to swear off violence. Integrating such elements and rehabilitating them is not through crazy threats.

The **Prophet Muhammad** had counselled: **"Love thy friend moderately, guarding against his turning one day into a foe. And love thy enemy moderately, hoping for his turning one day into a friend."** The New Egypt cannot hope for ultimately breaking up the Muslim Brotherhood if it denies itself the chance of possibly luring them back into the fold. Particularly at this phase of Brotherhood's internal altercation.

On this, I quote former **President Nixon**. He, the conflict-oriented Republican leader opened, through **Kissinger,** communication with China. His famous adage: **"Sometimes if you hate so much, you may destroy yourself."**

Islamic ethos was fourteen centuries ahead of **Nixon**. The **Quran** put it elegantly and succinctly: **"But if they incline to peace, then incline to it, and trust in God. Indeed, He is the All-Hearing, the All-Knowing"** (Chapter 8/Verse 61).

**Big Mouth Salvo No. Three:** The **Prophet Muhammad** throughout his Mission, suffered enough. And more suffering after his passing. Especially through the murderous campaigns of the **Ummayads.** Killing of **Imam**

**Ali,** and his two sons, **Al-Hassan** and **Al-Hussein.** In our age, **every idiocy by a so-called Muslim has become enough of a pretext to attack Muhammad.** And guess what: No true Muslim could, on religious grounds, attack either **Moses** or **Jesus.**

**Muhammad** has never engaged in any armed conflict, except in self-defence. **"Unholy War"** has never been an Islamic concept. It is a **crusader concept. Concept for power, not for the great Christian faith of love and peace.**

**History is a great lighthouse - A MANAR!!** It teaches unalterable truths:
- Faith is non-negotiable. Buried deep in the heart. A snatching hand of compulsory conversion cannot reach it.
- In Islam there is no proselytizing. No evangelizing. **Muhammad had nothing to do with the barbarity of the Ottomans in the Balkans.** Or with Wahabbism, convoluted from a reform movement into a police theocracy. Or with the fictitious split between Sunni and Shii. Or with Muslim immigrants to Christian Europe abusing their refuge into Islamic Bantustans.
- Nor has **Moses** to do anything with **Netanyahu's** rampant settler occupation of lands allotted under international law and through UN resolutions to a Palestinian State. **Nor has Jesus Christ anything to do with Western occupation of Muslim lands.** He preached **"love."** And imperialism is about suppression.
- So why go to find guilt with the clean hands of heavenly messengers of revealed or non-revealed faiths as systems of human values? **Why mix faith with governance? A combustible formula!!**
- Empires also fall when minority rights are ignored. When the **"Millet System"** was observed, the Ottomans were on the rise. All religions were allowed to be practised. Constantinople was only interested in taxation and army recruitment. But when the so-called Islamic scholars (ulama) assumed ascendancy, minorities became second class citizens, **including the Arabs.**
- Thus was born the **"Great Arab Rebellion."** Not by Lawrence of Arabia, but **Al-Sharif Hussein. He put secular nationalism above an Islam whose golden seat was occupied by a brutal empire on its way to extinction.**

Apparently, Al-Zind was a student of neither law, nor history, nor the role of faith. **"Breach of the Peace"** is an offense which includes acts of destruction or menacing public order and tranquility. Not only violent acts. But also acts and words likely to produce violence in others.

Ex-Minister Al-Zind, had certainly **"breached the peace"** of his country. His Big Mouth is what led him to the exit door for his **"disorderly conduct."**

So why, Mr. Al-Zind, threaten to imprison every malfeasant, **"even if he was the Prophet himself?!"** You are bearing His name **"Ahmed;"** and the name of his cousin **"Ali."** And the name of **Ibrahim** who symbolizes the unity between Judaism, Christianity and Islam. Isn't your full name **"Ahmad Ali Ibrahim Al-Zind?"**

If your real thinking matches your very words, **I have an out for you,** now that you have been kicked out of the Cabinet: Change the spelling of your last name to **"Al-Zinad,"** (the Trigger?) Judges who know you, **Al-Zind,** told me that you don't read!! Good Riddance!!

# In Egypt Under Nasser, Nobody Could Open Their Mouth. But Under El-Sisi, Everyone Is A Big Loud Mouth!!

Sunday, April 24, 2016

This is the case of **"The Islands v. Ignorance."** Ignorance compounded by the herd mentality that seeks in nearly every decision by Cairo authorities a cause for a false **"cry wolf!!"** For **Tiran** and **Sanafir** are as Saudis as Sicily is Italian.

Just look at international maps. Because to study history, you have also to study geography. Study the maritime line in the Gulf of Aqabah: It moves north from the Red Sea to Al-Aqabah.

**Ras Muhammad** to the west; **Ras Nusrani** to the west (Egyptian territorial waters); **Jazirat Tiran** and **Jazirat Sanafir** to the east (Saudi territorial waters); **Ash Shaykh Humayd** to the east (Saudi mainland; end of a long road from **Maan** (Jordan) to the north). Then the maritime line ends at Al-Aqabah, north.

The hordes on the Cairo streets (a few hundreds, big deal) were herded there by another area of ignorance -international law. Maritime lines fall in the midpoint between two littoral sovereignties. Saudi Arabia is east of the Gulf of Aqaba; Egypt is west of that Gulf. With territorial waters filling the geographic space in between.

That principle of delimitation of territorial waters was ignored by Saddam. The dividing line in **Shatt El-Arab** between Iraq and Iran was formalized in **Algiers in 1975.** Between Saddam and the Shah. Then the Shah made a mistake. Asked Saddam to banish an insignificant cleric, by the name of **Khomeini** from Iraq. Saddam obliged. Ended with Khomeini establishing **"The Islamic Republic of Iran"** upon his return from exile in Paris.

Saddam nullified the Algiers treaty; attacked Iran in 1980 with a nod from America; waged a losing battle for 8 years. And in 2003, after the American unjustified invasion, Saddam was caught in an earthen cave and hanged. And prior to that, the Shah died in Cairo, and was buried with honors.

There is a lesson we teach at US law schools: **"Pacta Sunt Servanda." (Pacts Are To Be Kept).** In the Quran: **"O Ye Faithful, Respect Your Obligations"** (Chapter V/Verse 1).

Of course there is a pact between Cairo and Riyadh. The **agreement of 1950:** The two islands, under Saudi sovereignty, were to be administered and defended by Egypt. The danger was Israeli encroachment south in the waterways. **"Administering"** does not transfer sovereignty. It means an **AMANAH (bailment),** entrusted by a **bailor (Riyadh) to a bailee (Cairo)** until the rightful owner returns to claim that bailment.

**Sovereignty is not transferable,** as it does not reside in any government. It resides in the body politic (the corpus), the demographic corporation, called **"The People." King Salman did not come to Cairo to buy territory. He came to witness the signing of the return of the AMAHAH to his country. And El-Sisi did not surrender Egyptian territory to Salman.** Cairo could not keep what it does not own. Otherwise, it would be an occupier, an aggressor against its sister State, Saudi Arabia.

Back to my zones of maximum comfort: **international law, history and diplomacy.** From these disciplines, I raise the following issues. **To the idiots parading their lunacy on Egyptian streets or media, I say:**
- Sinai itself was not Egyptian territory until ceded by the Ottoman Empire to Egypt in 1906. That cession transformed **Egypt from an African country to an Afro-Asian country.** That was only 110 years ago. Just examine the cession agreement. Its delimitation did not jump from Sinai south to the edge of the Arabian peninsula.

- And it does matter that the Saudi State came into being in 1932. Sovereignty does not reside in a regime. The Hashemites, under Ottoman rule, were the regime.
- Tiran and Sanafir, if not for Egyptian military custodial presence have been uninhabited. The absence of any other form of human life did not transform them to **"terra nullius" (land without ownership).** There is an owner -a big visible and important owner **called The Kingdom of Saudi Arabia.** In fact terra nullius, as a term, exists only in imperial parlance to justify illegal land grabbing. Akin to the Zionist fiction about settling Palestine -**"People without land for land without people."**
- Rightful Saudi ownership of the two islands has been repeatedly asserted following the Arab/Israel war of 1948.
- These assertions were manifest as Israel occupied the port of **"Um Rashrash"** (now Eilat); followed by Israeli complaints later at the UN regarding **"Egyptian occupation"** of the islands.

**A mountain of written evidence of Saudi uninterrupted ownership of Tiran and Sanafir is on the record. Including:**

- In the law of the Arab economic boycott of Israel, enacted on October 19, 1955;
- In official Egyptian memoranda to the UK and the US regarding those Arab punitive/defensive measures;
- In the expressed desire later on by Saudi Arabia for the return of its islands to its sovereign fold, as the triggering reason for Egyptian occupation was no more; and
- In the statements by the late **Ambassador Muhammad Awad Al-Koni,** Egypt's Permanent Representative to the UN at the Security Council. It was on **May 27, 1967, a few days before the 1967 war,** when Al-Koni stressed that **"Egypt has never, at any time, claimed that these two islands were part of its sovereign territory." I was there in the Council chamber when the remarkable diplomat, Al-Koni, in his exquisite French language, and gleaming shiny head,** read his historic statement.

So the Saudi/Egyptian agreement of April 2016, regarding a land bridge between the two sister States, was a positive step between two sister-States. Two sovereigns, engaged in inter-Arab economic integration. **The very step which the fragmented Arab world needs today in this darkening age of terrorism and fragmentation.** Caused primarily by ISIS, the Muslim Brotherhood, and their affiliates and terror proxies in Gaza and elsewhere.

The protests raised by Egyptian media qualifying that historic measure of mapping Arab borders on land and in the sea **by Arab hands, are**

**utterly repulsive.** Shrill voices, from which I select the following utter nonsense dated **April 14, 2016:**

- In **Al-Shorook** newspaper, **Fahmi Howreidi** claims: **"The Egyptian side is to blame for national anger. That side is the party which decided to relinquish the two islands and attach them to Saudi sovereignty."**
- In **"Al-Misriyoun,"** its Chief Editor **Mahmoud Sullam** heatedly argues:**"How dare President El-Sisi call on us not to dwell upon the islands matter? Are we his pupils or are we in a military encampment?"**
- In a crescendo of total absurdity, another so-called writer by the name of **Ashraf Al-Barbari** claims the prize of **"Ignorant Cum Laude."** For he attacks the decision on the following idiotic bases: **a)** sovereignty over the islands should have been arbitrated; **b)** Friday, April 8, the date of the Saudi/Egyptian agreement should be called **Black Friday.** Egypt's cession of the islands to Saudi Arabia was a huge shock as it caused young Egyptians to lose their national compass; **c)** For decades our history books have stressed that no Egyptian territory should be given up. **Mr. Al-Barbari: please show us which history books offer this advice which is a total abstraction? Like defining the word "water" by the word "water!!"**
- In **Al-Masri Al-Youm,"** **Hamdy Rizk** calls on the Egyptian Parliament to nullify that agreement in fulfillment of its national obligations. **Mr. Rizk: It behooves you to learn that Parliament has no say in purely administrative matters framed within prior accords.**
- In **"Al-Tahrir,"** **Nasser Arraq** claims that the speed of reaching that agreement, without first engaging the public in it before signing on it, manifests utter disregard for the popular will. **Sir: This is not a plebiscite!;**
- In **"Vito,"Abdel-Qadir Shuhaib** attacks El-Sisi for **"covering up for 8 months"** those negotiations with Saudi Arabia. Dismissively he **tells El-Sisi to treat Egyptian public opinion with respect** as it is unacceptable to conspire against it in a game of deception.

Other media outside of Egypt joined the fray. The **New York Times** of April 16 reported on the Cairo demonstrations gleefully. It said: It was **"an unusual burst of public outrage"** because of **"an unseemly concession to Saudi Arabia in return for billions of dollars in aid, and an unforgivable wound to national pride."**

Egyptophobia and misreading of history in plain sight were also reflected in the **blog by a pro-Nasser Lebanese American.** His name is

**Assad Abu-Khalil,** professor at California State University at Stanislaus. In his **"Angry Arab News Service,"** he promoted a lie connected to **King Salman's** visit to Egypt: **"The statue of Ibrahim Pasha in Cairo was placed under a shroud."** Claimed reason: **He led the Egyptian charge against the Wahabbis in Najd, in the Arabian peninsula in 1819.**

Yet my contacts in Cairo informed me that **"Salman's visit had nothing to do with the renovation work on the statue."** When **Abu-Khalil** was contacted for retraction, he declined. According to the **Los Angeles Times,** that Professor's blog is **"Known for its sarcasm but knowledgeable commentary. Is being consistently pro-Nasser and anti-El-Sisi."**

This is ideological misrepresentation unbecoming an Arab-American professor at a major American university. **For ideology is a partisan advocacy. It is not teaching.** Particularly when it comes to the malady of hate, which is floating hostility. **A form of mental constipation.**

I do my best to judge leaders by their degree of dedication to the national interest. With that measure, and judging by the storm over Tiran and Sanafir, **I raise the following queries about Nasserism in action in foreign affairs:**

Has Nasser ever been elected through the process of **"one person, one vote,"** or by any other democratic formula? **No!! And where were the Egyptian voices which were raised in protest against his policies which led to:**

- The break-up of the Nile Valley, North (Egypt) from the Nile Valley, South (the Sudan); or
- **The authoritarian unification between Egypt and Syria (1958-1961).** And its collapse, largely because Nasser's surrogates in Syria (Amer and Al-Sarraj) **converted Syria into a police State.**
- **And when did Nasser involve the nation in consultation before embarking upon other existential decisions?** Like expelling the **UN Blue Helmets from the Egyptian-Israeli lines of demarcation? Thereby providing Israel with the pretext to strike on June 5, 1967.**
- Then, following that greatest Arab military defeat in modern history, mournfully lamenting: **"We expected the enemy to come from the east, but they came from the west!!"** Historically laughable, especially coming from a military leader!!
- **Nearly the entire Egyptian air force, sitting on the ground, was wiped out in 3 hours! Sinai was occupied - Again!! So**

**were Gaza, the West Bank, Jerusalem, and the Golan Heights.** Until today, with the exception of Sinai, liberated from Israeli occupation by Sadat. The future of these other Arab areas is still in doubt. **Including Jerusalem.**

- And under what Egyptian circumstances was that most humbling of Arab defeats took place?
- Nearly a 100,000 Egyptian army recruits were marched to Yemen by Nasser as of 1962. To be inserted into a Yemeni civil war. **What for?** Not for any reason of Egyptian defense or development. **It was for ideological reasons of Nasser's making.** Pitting in its wake Egypt against Saudi Arabia whose southern cities were bombed by the Egyptian air force.

**With Nasser's gaze upon his personal goal of becoming the paramount Arab hegemon, Israeli's gaze was upon becoming the hegemon of the Arabs.**

It took a leader like Sadat, whose focus was on Egypt, to rescue for Egypt, through war and diplomacy, what belonged to Egypt-**Sinai.** Like in the age of El-Sisi, an Egyptian leadership should first and foremost work towards **The Strong Egypt.**

So I ask again, where were the voices of open and noisy protest against Nasser? Who was aided and abetted by his **"Philosopher of the Revolution," Muhammad Hassanain Heykal.** It was Nasser who was the historic loser of Arab territory!!

In the Tiran-Sanafir issue, Egyptian media uncovered for me an Egyptian perceptional fault line: The dictator who loses territory is reverently called **"The Eternally-Remembered"** (Khalid Al-Zikr). But the openly-elected leader, El-Sisi, is vilified in the post-dictatorship era as **"a sell out."** For respecting Cairo contractual obligations. How ironic!!

**History cannot be invented. It can only be recorded and reported.** So back to the shrill voices within Egypt against El-Sisi. **The leader who saved Egypt from a bloody civil war. The leader who cut Islamist fascism down to size.** I have never met him. He doesn't know me. But I know him through his actions and plans for **"The Strong State."** That is enough for me.

On the issue of water and Al-Nahdha Dam in Ethiopia. **The emboldened but vain voices say that El-Sisi's stand is another sell-out.** Ignorance!! Ethiopia is a sovereign State developing its resources. Same as in the case of the Aswan High Dam. The 1929 water treaty was a colonial creature. Treaties, like contracts, are subject to change. **"The Contracts Theory of Changing Circumstances!!"**

The only voice raised in favor of a **Nilotic alliance** (Egypt, Sudan, Ethiopia, Uganda, Congo) has been **that of the Coptic Church.** Ethiopian clergy were **"created"** in Alexandria. Those Popes looked upon Egypt, and rightly so, as a **"Nilotic State."**

But in the Nasser era, it was **"Hail to the Southern Province"** (the Northern being Syria). And in the Morsi era, **Hamdan Sabbahi called for bombing Ethiopia on the issue of Al-Nahdha Dam. A bravado voice of the insane.** El-Sisi resorted to diplomacy through the modern doctrine of functionalism. Sharing the wealth. Particularly now that the Sudan, as a possible Great South, is no more. **The future lies not in warring on Ethiopia.But on friendship with Addis Ababa. And in hopefully developing the White Nile in cooperation with Khartoum and South Sudan.**

Even an open dialogue by El-Sisi with representatives of civil society, **unimaginable under Nasser,** was the subject of media derision. By the pens which have found their ink only after July 3, 2013.

On April 13, El-Sisi told that conclave:
- **"The military establishment has taught us to fear for our country and its people, respecting every grain of sand in it. We do not sell our territory to anyone, nor do we usurp the rights of anyone."**
- **"I am an honest Egyptian who is not for sale; who did not conspire against anyone; who did not deceive anyone. The Supreme Command of the Armed Services did not conspire against the Muslim Brotherhood. We dealt with former President Muhammad Morsi honorably, with honesty and respect."** Of course they did. For 3 fateful days, from June 30 to July 3, 2013, El-Sisi tried to coax Morsi towards a new beginning. Through a fresh plebiscite. Morsi and the Brotherhood's Guidance Bureau, gave those efforts thumbs down.

Media response to those assurances by El-Sisi on April 13: a truly pathetic campaign by several Egyptian so-called **"opinion-molders."** More protests by **"The Ignorance Brothers"**

The great historian **Jamal Hamdan,** with knowledge and clarity, on April 13 contributed to the undeniable verdict: **"The Islands Belong To Saudi Arabia."** The 3rd of his iconic 4 volumes in Arabic on **"Egypt's**

**Personality"** bears an interesting title. **"The Genius of Geography" (Aabqariyyat Al-Makan).**

In the foolish attacks by Egyptian media persons, one finds total ignorance of that **"genius,"** compounded by falsification.

In a lunatic desire to get the mobs aroused. The very hordes which paralyzed Egypt for months. Besieging, among other establishments **"The Journalists Syndicate."**

All of the journalists named above have a debased auxiliary. Examples: **Adel Al-Sanhouri** in **"Al-Yom Al-Sabee"** (seeing in the agreement of April 11 haste and a cover-up); **Karam Jabr,** also in the same paper (the Government failed in educating the public); and **Muhammad Al-Shebrawi** in **"Al-Shaab"** (What happened to Egypt's independence?). Let alone: **"What was the hurry for concluding the April 11 agreement?"** Al-Shebrawi, you are a rare genius: It was in the making for 18 years!!

Even those who are not advocating an outright falsehood of Egyptian sovereignty over Tiran and Sanafir are espousing **other ridiculous approaches to that non-issue.**

- **Makram Muhammad Ahmed,** in **Al-Watan,** calls for an Egyptian Parliamentary review of the April agreement. His purpose: **delineating the maritime line between Saudi Arabia and Egypt.** A silly argument (in law, meaning **nudum factum** - without factual merit). As it makes Egyptian military presence on those two rocks a nexus to Egyptian sovereignty.

Had holding a territory been tantamount to a conversion to sovereign ownership, then the entire scheme of **decolonization under the UN Charter should be revisited.** If you care to find out how idiotic the Makram Muhammad Ahmed proposal is, read my book: **The United Nations and Decolonization: The Role of Afro-Asia (The Hague: Nijhoff, 1971).**

You find the same absence of legal knowledge or historical facts plainly manifest in **Al-Ahram.** In an article by **Gamal Zahran,** he calls the protests against the Egyptian-Saudi Agreement a **"Fitna"** (insurrection). Claiming in tortured logic that **those protests are not directed towards El-Sisi. But towards the surrender of the islands.** If that is the Zahran defense of El-Sisi, may I never have Gamal Zahran as my defense attorney.

**Real Big Loud Mouths, a deplorable phenomenon of the post-El-Sisi elevation to the presidency. Loud barks never heard during the age of**

**Nasser of imposed silence.**
One more thought: **The recalled President Morsi opened into Sinai** the gates (they call them tunnels) of **Hamsawi occupation of Sinai.** Under the deceptive label of **"Arab brotherhood."** That encroachment upon Egyptian sovereignty lies largely today at the root of terrorism in Sinai.

**Morsi also gave the nod to the Islamist rule in the Sudan: Shalatin and Halayeb.**

No, Dr. Morsi: **Shalatin and Halayeb are north of the 22nd parallel.** A straight line from Libya to the west, to the Red Sea to the east. **Their case is the flip side of Tiran and Sanafir.** The latter were entrusted to Egypt by their sovereign owner for administration. **Shalatin and Halayeb were entrusted by Great Britain,** an occupier of the Nile Valley to **the Sudan for administration.**

**No administrative measure could nullify Egyptian sovereignty over Shalatin and Halayeb.** For these are the same legal principles underpinning the UN Charter provisions regarding international trusteeship.

Sovereignty is **"inherent"** (permanent): Administration is **"temporary."** As in the case of Egyptian administration over Gaza (1949-1967). Does not abrogate Palestinian sovereignty over it. Regardless of the length of an Israeli siege or a Hamas partisan, noisy, and troublesome presence.

Egypt is a sovereign existence for thousands of years. In contrast, its name, **"Egypt"** (MISR) does not even need a qualifier. For no less than 5 times, **the Quran mentions its name as "MISR."** The Bible vouches for Christ uttering prayerfully: **"Blessed Be My People Egypt."** The land and its people are one.

In the Egypt of El-Sisi, the big loud mouths should first learn their country's history. To me it boils down to three sentences: The **Great Pharao Narmer (Mina), 5000 years ago, unified. Muhammad Ali, in the 19th century, modernized. And El-Sisi, in the 21st century, saved from collapse.**

Now, in conclusion, I pose a challenge to those afflicted by a Big Loud Mouth syndrome. **If you truly want to help the New Egypt, shut your mouth and go back to school.** To learn something about Egypt's history.

And take with you **Ahmed Al-Naggar, the Editor-In-Chief of Al-Ahram.** For protesting the rightful reversion of the islands to their Saudi sovereignty. Ignorantly describing that restoration **a treaty of surrender.** The only surrender in play here Mr. Al-Naggar, should be your retirement.

The Chinese say: **"One Learns From the Ear."** And the **Quran,** in its first word of revelation, says: **"Iqraa."** In Islamic jurisprudence, that one word is loaded. It does not only mean **"Read."** Its expansive meaning is **"Learn."**

And about learning through reading. **Officers of Egyptian armed forces read.** How do I know that? My proof here was provided to me in 1974 by the late **Field Marshal Ahmed Ismail.** After the October war, he contacted me with an invitation: **"I need you to present a general lecture at the Cairo Military Academy."** I immediately booked a flight: New York/Cairo.

There were 500 senior officers from all branches of the Armed Forces. Including **Al-Gamassi and Abu-Ghazaleh.** I sat on the rostrum flanked by Ahmed Ismail to the right, and the Academy's commander to the left. My presentation was on **"strategy"** which I had taught in New York to large groups of US Army officers -during Vietnam. Lessons, learnt by me in Algeria during the war for independence. As spokesman for the UN.

When finished with my presentation, **Ahmed Ismail** called for questions to be written, and recruits to collect those pieces of paper. Then instructed the Academy's Commander to organize 74 written questions into 6 themes. Saying: **"Our guest shall answer those themes, because I am escorting him today to our Northern Command in Alexandria."**

Having responded, I requested the Field Marshal if I could keep the texts of the 74 questions. His response: **"Son. Keep them. You are one of us."** On my trip back to New York, I read the 74 questions. **How penetrating? An army that reads!! It fights for Egypt. And also reads for Egypt!!**

That defender of Egypt today is fighting for what belongs to Egypt. And what belongs to Egypt, as far as Sinai is concerned, is **clearly evidenced by the attached map. Delineating the international boundary in the Gulf of Aqaba.** Showing clearly the basis for the Saudi-Egyptian administrative agreement which was signed in 1950. Gave Cairo the privilege of guarding Tiran and Sanafir for the Saudis against the never-ending Zionist thirst for territorial grab.

**That map is Swiss. Produced by a Swiss company in Bern,** from whence my late father-in-law had hailed. Produced by the well-known firm of **Kummerly & Frey,** in 1984, in support of tourism to Egypt. In three languages: Egypt/Egypte/Agypten (English, French and German).

Could the Big Loud Mouths, unleashed only after El-Sisi became president, shut up and read the map. **Maps don't lie. But lying weasels, who have abused their profession as journalists, have perfected the practise of lying.** Including Al-Naggar of Al-Ahram, whose name in English means "Carpenter." The **cure for his incoherence is at hand. A few good nails could fix his trap door -his big loud mouth. Followed by the map that follows!!**

*This is a central issue for the New Egypt. Its importance has prompted me to prepare a longer version of it in Arabic. If you wish to have that version, email to me your request. I could then arrange for its forwarding it to you. Share the knowledge.*

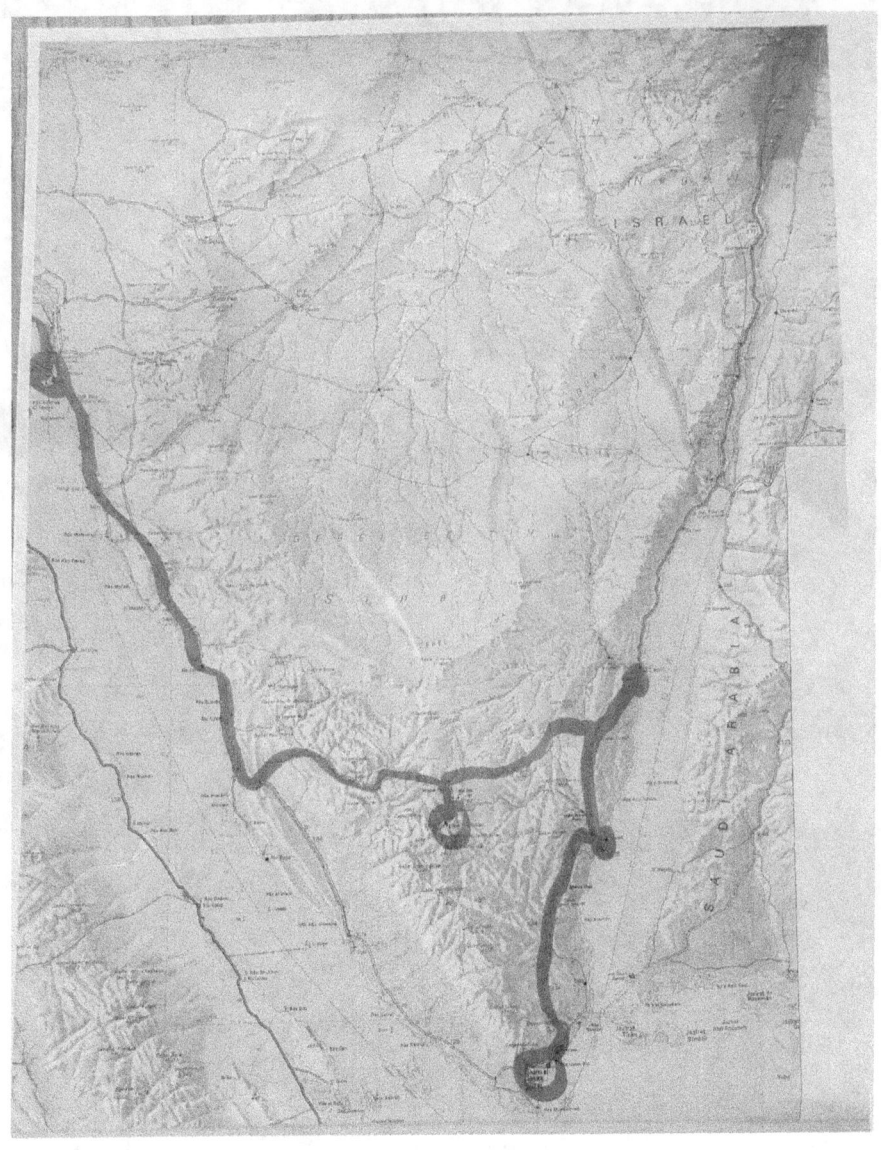

# 24 MAY 2016

## Attacks On The New Egypt Are Not Only By Terrorists But Also By Egyptian Journalists

Friday, May 13, 2016

A mirror case is that of the Saudi islands of Tiran and Sanafir. For it mirrors a malaise in Egyptian media, as they lie or obfuscate under a new cover. That is the cover of the **"freedom of expression."** Also known as **"the freedom of the press,"** born in the vortex of the two companion revolutions: **January 25, 2011** and **June 30, 2013.**

There are limits to every freedom, and frameworks for every right. The freedom context is of two layers: the lower is that of the individual; the higher is that of the community. No freedom can be without limits. And no expression is to be protected regardless of its contents. The very term **"protected speech"** indicates that there are limits to that freedom.

In regard to **Tiran and Sanafir,** that reasonable limitation on the freedom of expression has been massively breached. The perpetrators are the very journalists who are required to observe it. For the following reasons:

- **Journalism is a public trust.** Its role is to investigate, and report accurately. Because those requirements are the **bases for their licenses.**
- In return, the State has the duty to protect the public from being infected by biased national journalism. No State, especially the

New Egypt, which is transitioning from dictatorship (military from 1952-2011; then Islamist from 2012-2013), can move forward, with its media thriving on the **business of lying to the public.**

- That explains why the media, in any orderly society, try to police itself. Self-policing for that profession goes by the name of **"the code of professional honor."** Whatever exists in Egypt of today has not been manifest in the case of Tiran and Sanafir.

Without citing again the names of Egyptian writers, as I did in the prior blog posting, it is necessary to cite here the themes of the Egyptian media in regard to this critical national, regional, and international case.

**Samples of the provocative themes** adopted by a media that lacks the honor of its profession are the following:

- **"Oppression shall not create a successful regime;"**
- **"Freedoms in Egypt are in retreat following two revolutions;"**
- **"The Journalists Syndicate is subjected by the Interior Ministry to increasing violations against its members;"**
- **"Rumors regarding disaffection within the Armed Forces because of returning the islands to Saudi Arabia;"**
- **"Saudi Arabia is reembarking upon cooperation with Israel in joint projects in the whole region;"**
- **"Is there a threat to the Suez Canal resulting from returning the two islands to Saudi Arabia?;"**
- **"Has the Egyptian Saudi joint committee on the islands taken these issues into account?;"**
- **"Why has the Saudi flag been flown in many parts of Cairo on the national occasion of April 25, commemorating the liberation of Sinai?;"**
- **"Why has the Shura (consultative) Council in Saudi Arabia approved the delimitation of the Egyptian/Saudi boundaries on the very day of Egyptian commemoration of the liberation of Sinai?;"**
- **"The angry Egyptian youth shall not return from their demonstrations without getting definitive assurances that Egyptian territory has not been surrendered;"** and
- **"The purpose of demonstrations is to exercise the freedom of expression"** on the Friday called **"Land Day."**

None of the above provocative themes propagated by a dishonorable Egyptian media can be legally described as **"protected speech."** None of the above can be immunized from State sanctions against **media engaged in destabilization.** All the above is an amalgam of:

- Attacks on the legitimacy of the post-Islamist presidency and governance;

- Calls for outright mobocracy intended to undo the painful progress of Egypt towards normalcy;
- A total misunderstanding, in fact proverbial ignorance, of the meaning of freedom;
- Incitement to disaffection, **including defection in the armed forces,** the only historical cohesive national institution in Egypt;
- Impugning the motives, intent, and measures adopted by Riyadh and Cairo for some degree of economic integration, and for cooperation with the Gulf States;
- Crying **"wolf,"** in a a sordid attempt to link unlinkable elements in the rightful return of Tiran and Sanafir to their sovereign, the Kingdom of Saudi Arabia; and
- Outright, stupid, and vain interference in the internal affairs of a proud, benevolent sister State **-Saudi Arabia.**

Such shameful reporting, which in every respect lacks fact-checking, serving the public and national interest, does underline the national need for:

- Reviewing the legitimacy of those licenses issued by the State and/or the syndicate, enabling those journalists to openly become **"agents provocateurs;"**
- Upholding the recently-enacted regulations regarding public demonstrations;
- Linking between the war against terrorism in Sinai and at the Libyan borders to the internal calls for hooliganism and violence. Spewed by Egyptian media which find in the new freedom a hospitable **environment for subversion;** and
- Realization that the failed attempts by the **so-called Muslim Brotherhood** to change Egypt's DNA as a secular State might find in today's Egyptian media a **needed oxygen for their revival.**

Thus a bundle of central questions emerges out of the illegal efforts by Egyptian media to claim Saudi territory as a part of the national Egyptian patrimony. These questions are:

- Isn't it treasonous to conspire publicly against a New Egypt under a secular constitution of 2014? **No doubt!!**
- Is yelling **"Fire, Fire"** mischievously in a crowded theater, causing sta
- mpede and death, an exercise of the freedom of speech? **Of course Not!!**
- Has there been any damage to the image of a stable Egypt resulting from these hallucinating journalistic accusations of territorial surrender? **Yes, indeed!!**

- Is the State entitled, and is in fact duty bound, to put an end by legal means, to this charade of a **contrived cold war on El-Sisi administration? Absolutely!!**
- Under what human rights theories should Cairo act to bury that campaign of vilification and mob-arousal by voices which would have never found their vocal chords **under Nasser?** None, as far as I know.

*Both theories of human rights law and humanitarian law intersect when the destiny of the State is in question, as a result of foreign threat or internal dangers.* There can be no foreign tutelage over human rights -a domestic issue.

We haven't even touched upon the issue of **aid to Egypt from Saudi Arabia, Kuwait and the United Arab Emirates.** All benefactors by the billions of dollars for funding of Sinai and other projects. Those Gulf allies of the New Egypt, in March 2015 have each offered $4 billion in investments in Egypt.

Respect by Egypt of the Saudi/Egyptian agreement of 1950 for the temporary administration by Egypt of Tiran and Sanafir has nothing to do with Arab aid. The nay-sayers make that idiotic linkage.

In rebuttal, I, as a defense attorney who is still in active practise, posit this hypothetical:

If Egypt is in the practise of giving up territory for financial aid, then I must pose this question: Why not give up, say, **Marsa Matrouh,** to America's fifth fleet for the annual $1.3 Billion allocated by Washington to Cairo since the signing of the Egypt/Israel Peace Treaty of 1979?

While April witnessed the Egyptian media false campaign for the Egyptianization of the Saudi islands in the Gulf of Aqaba, **May 1st** registered more grievous stances by the same outlets.

On that day, the police pursued two journalists against whom judicial subpoenas had been issued for acts contravening the law. That hot pursuit led the pursuing officers into the headquarters of the **Journalists Syndicate** in downtown Cairo. From the circumstance, it was obvious that the fleeing suspects were under the false impression that that building afforded them, **immunity from the long arm of the law.**

Following that lawful arrest, the council of the Journalists Syndicate, issued on May 4 a collective protest against what that group characterized as **"an**

**invasion."**

It labelled that lawful police action as a dictatorial attempt by the Ministry of Interior to muzzle the press. Most of the newspapers called for the resignation of the **Interior Minister.** Some even called for an apology by President El-Sisi. And the editorials throughout the first week of May were nothing but a parade of public incitement to open revolt.

- The President of the **Supreme Council of Journalism,** Galal Aref: **"Press freedom is an inherent right for every citizen. The invasion of our Syndicate building was an attack on basic freedoms."**
- The CEO of **Dar Al-Tahrir** Establishment, Muhammed Abu-Alhadeed: **"Fabricating such provocation of the press by the regime can only mean that a big event for destabilizing Egypt shall occur on June 30 -"** (the third anniversary of the second revolution which brought about the elections leading to El-Sisi becoming President).
- The CEO of **Al-Ahali** newspaper, Nabil Zaki: **"should we expect the reinstatement of the police State which the Egyptians, through two revolutions, have demolished?"**
- The CEO of **Al-Wafd,** Wagdy Zain: **"The actions by the Interior Ministry cannot be understood except as intending to undermine the presidency."**
- The CEO of **Al-Masriyoon,** Mahmoud Sultan: **"How could the President convene a meeting with the Military High Command instead of rushing to meet with the Journalists Syndicate on the crime of invading its HQ?"**

These are not low-level press stringers. These, as well as others who spoke in the same vein, are top executives of important press outlets.

The shrill voices which have attempted to rewrite international law in claiming two Saudi islands for Egypt, are the same voices who, out of ignorance of the law of immunities, are bestowing immunity on that building **as if it were a foreign embassy.**

Immunity is generally defined as an exemption from prosecution. And **"hot pursuit"** by the State for the apprehension of two suspects fleeing from a lawful warrant is integral to the police powers of any sovereign State.

**The ugly face of ignorance with regard to the freedom of expression in the New Egypt has been unveiled.** Unveiled in early April in the issue of Tiran and Sanafir, and again unveiled in early May in the issue of the two journalists escapees. **Amr Badr and Mahmoud Al-Saqqa.** In a false pretense to immunity. And in between those fatal dates, there are numerous violations of the recently-enacted law regulatory of public demonstrations.

*Under all laws, aiding a fugitive, as happened by the Journalists Syndicate, is criminalized. This comes under the two legal theories of obstruction of justice and co-conspiracy.*

Egyptian media have encouraged those violations by depicting Tiran and Sanafir as a sell-out by El-Sisi to King Salman of Saudi Arabia. Those demonstrations, though sparsely attended, depicted the demonstrations regulation as infringing the freedom of expression.

In all countries where The Rule of Law governs, there is a basic framework for public demonstrations. In law schools in the US, we explain that framework in three words: **Time, Place and Manner.**

The licensing authority specifies the time (limited); the place to be away from access to public institutions; and the manner never to be destruction and hooliganism.

On that basis, those who advocate endless demonstrations, anywhere, and to do anything are scofflaws and anarchists.

Up till now, the real problem for the New Egypt with respect to the freedom of expression could be traced to the absence of real media. It seems that the role of the Egyptian media in the creation of an informed public opinion's gone.

*Now there is little left for the New Egypt to safeguard its gains but to fashion a Code of Honor for its indigenous media. Including the requirement to learn, think, and think again before you put pen to paper. For freedom cannot exist without limitations defined by law and practise.*

The world news headline: **"French police attack demonstrations against regressive labor law. Commented an Egyptian lady scholar, Dr. Nadia Elshazly, quoting Alex Lantier:**

*"No outcry from the world media, nor any of the human rights organizations, against the French law which regulates demonstrations."*

Truth of the matter is this: Journalism is an honorable profession. But in the New Egypt, it has become a profession devoid of honor!!

# "There Is No Virtue In Ignorance" -So Said Obama Referring to Trump

Friday, May 20, 2016

He said it on Sunday, May 15. At a commencement speech at Rutgers University, New Jersey. That is where I earned a Master's degree in 1954 in History and Political Science. A great preparation for later higher degrees in International Law and International Organization. More importantly, Rutgers taught me how to do research; how religion and politics intersect; and how to learn about American economic history, as you assist in teaching it. One of my real Alma Maters!!

**So here is a possibility for a con man like Donald Trump to assume America's presidency.** If he does, a Trump presidency **may signal total lunacy in foreign policy.** This would not collapse America. America, the home of continuous innovation, through education and selective immigration, is not collapsable. It reinvents itself. Like the generation of electricity constantly in a car by simply using it to motor it forward.

Though America is now an angry place, that anger brews on the bottom. The middle and the top keep on inventing. Thus keeping the anger without much effect on global competitiveness. Just read a book by **Robert Gordon,** professor of economics at Northwestern University. His book, titled **"The Rise and Fall of American Growth,"** has been dubbed **"the most important book on economics this year."**

I am digressing from Trump's ignorance. Ignorance in many areas, especially in foreign policy, the subject of this blog posting. In order to return back to it following couple of paragraphs. On American inventiveness, **Gordon** describes the period from 1870 to 1970 as **"the golden age."** Why?

*"It was a period when the foundation of the modern world was laid. Electricity, flush toilets, central heating, cars, planes, radio, vaccines, clean water, and antibiotics." All of which and more are innovations which transformed living and working conditions."*

Yet that brilliant author empirically did not prove the **"Fall of American Growth."** He advanced no proof that is capable of being verified by observation or experience. **Standing alone, a theory is no proof.**

359

This is a turn in this conversation at which I pivot back to Trump **as a totally ignorant voice, at most in foreign policy.** Worse than ignorant. **Dangerous.** Why?

Forget for a moment about his lack of details. **Or his flip flops!!** Just examine his few policy positions, which he keeps on reinterpreting to his hypnotized large audiences.

With his mantra **"Making America Great Again,"** he looks upon that greatness **only from the prism of brutal power.**
- **Pledging a major buildup of the military;**
- **Swift destruction of the "Islamic State;"**
- **Rejection of trade deals;**
- **Arming Japan and South Korea with nuclear weapons;**
- **Disbanding, then putting together again, NATO;**
- **Calling on allies to pay for their own defense;**
- **Announcing his intention to scuttle the Iran nuclear deal;**
- **Forcing Mexico to pay for his planned construction of a wall on its border with the US;**
- **Calling for a take-over by force of Middle Eastern oil;**
- **Insulting China daily for "ripping off America," while praising Putin's policy of force;**
- **Advocating America's renunciation of its debts to other nations, and**
- **Looking upon 1.7 billion Muslims as potential terrorists. Thus banning their entry into America** *"until we figure out what the hell is going on."*

Trump is a real estate mogul. A broker. With no experience whatsoever in foreign policy. Has never before run for any public office. Simply tapping into the **veins of rage of blue collar Americans, and left behind Americans.** Manipulating the vacuum created by the fissures in the Republican Party between **conservatives, Evangelists, America's Firsters, isolationists, and nativists.**

Tendencies now bubbling on the surface of the American vast landscape. Where each of the fifty states, especially under the administration of Obama, **the first black American President,** is prone to asserting state rights. Over federal rights. Texas of today is not the only state which threatens secession from the union. **It's constitution provides for that possibility.**

And a Congress hobbled by inaction for deep divisions between a Republican majority and a Democratic minority; a President who is obstructed in the halls of Congress from moving most legislation forward or even securing a hearing for his nominee for the Supreme Court. Plus a Supreme Court, missing its full count of 9 Justices, three conservative Justices, one **"swing"** Justice (Kennedy), and four liberal Justices.

**Throughout all these fissures, thrive the likes of Trump.** Fissures, including an electoral system where the vote of the average citizen has to go through a more politically privileged **"candidate,"** whose ultimate vote decides who shall be president.

Let us see how the outside world regards those Trump's policy positions. Positions which he now flips politically by softening them as **"suggestions."** From the country with the most enduring special relationship with America, the **UK.** Its Prime Minister, **David Cameron** calls them **"ignorant."** That is the Prime Minister of a major U.S. ally whose **House of Commons has debated preventing Trump from entering the U.K.**

**Mexico's president** had much stronger words. The **Russians** watched with amusement. **The Gulf Arabs scurried diplomatically for explanations.**

However, the **Chinese had the final laugh.** One of their intellectuals, Jiayang Fan described: **"The appeal of Trump in China."** He said: **"Mao's worldview has found curious potency in the mouth of the Republican candidate, who shares his knack for *polemical excess and xenophobic paranoia.*"**

Not to be undone, an American humorist by the name of **Aaron James** has just published **"The little book with Yuuuuge answers"** (No H in **"huge"** -a la Trump's habitual exaggeration. With a title fitting Trump's common language: **"Assholes -A Theory of Donald Trump."** In the first word of that title, the head of Donald J. Trump replaced the letter **"O."**

Aside from Trump's ignorance in foreign policy, his lying about himself goes beyond being a narcissist. **Ego centrism in the extreme.** Witness his description of himself as **"self made."**

**A patently bogus claim.** Pretending to be an **Abraham Lincoln,** the facts stare him in the face. The Donald had his business career launched by a

$100 million from his father. **Lincoln had to flee from his own slavery at the hands of his own father.** That father rented out young Abraham to rural neighbors in Indiana. (See **Sidney Blumental's** book, **A Self-Made Man: The Political Life of Abraham Lincoln**). From self-deliverance, Lincoln went on to deliverance of his nation from slavery through a brutal civil war.

Another bogus claim by Trump. On the matter of taxation, Trump unabashedly **flaunted** his **crookedness as an American citizen.** For the past 60 years, every aspirant to the presidency has released his tax returns to the public. **Reason: transparency showing that a would-be president abides by the same rules as everyone else.** But Trump refuses to divulge his tax returns. A Wall Street executive, **Steven Rattner,** has quoted Trump as saying: **"I fight like hell to pay as little as possible."** This bold admission stands out in contrast to Trump saying: **"There is nothing to learn from (tax returns)!!"**

Same bogus claim on the question of **his respect for women and gender equality.** In a seminal front page, continuing to a center-fold, the **New York Times** of Sunday, May 15, all but denuded Trump from one of his principal lies. His dealings with **Miss USA contestants** that **"he has long fixated on and evaluated women's looks."** Some other quotes and revelations gleaned from **50 interviews, conducted over 6 weeks:**
- On his public treatment of women: **"degrading;"**
- **"unwelcome romantic advances, unending commentary on the female form;"**
- **"unsettling workplace conduct;"**
- **"contradictory portrait of a wealthy, well-known and provocative man;"**
- **"Trump had the power, and the women did not;"**
- **"Mr. Trump frequently sought assurances -at times from strangers -that the women in his life were beautiful."**
- About his own daughter, **Ivanka,** he asked: **"Don't you think my daughter's hot? She's hot, right?"** At that time, **Ivanka was only 16.**

Nonetheless, Trump, as per **The New York Times,** **"sees himself as a promoter of women."** In an interview with the same newspaper, Trump **"described himself as a champion of women, someone who took pride in hiring them."**

A delusional who aspires to be America's President and Commander-in-Chief. On April 27 claiming: **"America is going to be strong again; America is going to be great again. We're going to finally have a**

362

coherent foreign policy, based on American interests and the interests of our allies." Commented the **New York Times** in one word: **"Discrepancies."**

In his forthcoming confrontation with Hillary Clinton, he again uses the feminist card. But, as usual, in a lopsided way. He proclaims: **"Frankly, if Hillary Clinton were a man, I don't think she would get 5 percent of the vote."**

For Trump, war is global, has no borders. Thus Trump has evoked a mountain of negative comments.

Summed up in the following remarks denying Trump a legitimate claim to becoming a safe Commander In Chief:

- **"When one has a hammer, everything looks like a nail;"**
- **"And when one's experience is limited to real estate deals, everything looks like a lease negotiation."**
- **"For someone who claims he is ready to lead the free world, that is inexcusable."**

All these derisive comments were not limited to mainstream American press. **They were the gist of recent testimony before the Senate's Foreign Relations Committee, headed by a Republican, Senator Corker of Tennessee.** The same party which is threatened by a Trump take-a man who was a former Democrat!!

Trump's derangement knows no end. **A distemper magnified falsely into foreign policy.** Seeking the headlines, he pays a televised visit to **Henry Kissinger -the father of foreign interventionism.** And holding an olive branch to North Korea **by declaring that he could win them over by one phone call.**

As he closes the gap in American polls with his Democratic rival, Hillary Clinton, I can imagine lots of foreign ministries closing the file on constructive discourse with Washington, D.C. Except for those who see in Trump's occupancy of the Oval Office an **opportunity to ally themselves with his lunacy.**

Nothing that Trump has said could outmatch his **idiotic buffoonery in the tragic case of the disappearance of EgyptAir flight MS 804 over the Mediterranean.** Upon its happening, he was the only voice to declare it **"an act of Islamic terrorism."** For him, it is a waste of time to await the results of expert investigation. It seems that no human event, including simultaneous and tragic death, is but an occasion for cheap political exploitation.

Judging by the **moronic conduct of Trump,** it is no surprise that the title of the best recently-published book on the America of the age of Trump is: **"The Fractured Republic,"** by **Yuval Levin.**

*An apt diagnosis of a period of bluster and saber rattling in an America where even Congress has only 16% of approval rating. "There is no virtue in ignorance." How apt!!*

# The New Religious Revolution: Countering Jihadism, Al-Azhar Strikes Back

Friday, May 27, 2016

Sharia coupled with ijtihad (reason applied to text) are of tremendous lethal power. Against jihadism: **ISIS, the Muslim Brotherhood, Al-Nusra Front, the Friends of Beit Al-Maqdis and Boko Haram.** These are the forces of evil which have for long manipulated a legitimate longing. It is the longing of 1.7 Billion Muslims to join the world caravan, moving toward technological progress **while keeping the values of faith. Every faith.**

Yet that longing needs a voice. **An institutional voice.** A voice that does not simply say that Islam is a faith of tolerance. Because Islam, though simple to understand, could be confusing to comprehend. Especially for a western mind. And we are all now living the age of rage, of the non-state actors, of Trumpism which puts force ahead of reason.

To find that voice which could effectively counter jihadism, I peer over the horizon from New York City, looking eastward for a distance of 7000 miles. Over that horizon, I could imagine seeing the **4 minarets of Al-Azhar. A mosque and a university of more than 1000 years.** That is where my late father studied, and brought up his family on the love for Al-Azhar. Why?

**It has a universal message for all.** Taught Islam in all its stripes, mainly Sunni and Shii. Has always been the focus of Egyptian nationalism and universal interaction. That is where the **idea of American Senator Fulbright originated in the 14th century when African Emperor Mansa Musa of the Mali Empire** decided on a bold course. Students studying abroad at Al-Azhar and funded by the seat of the Empire in Timbuktu. I shared that history with Senator Fulbright of Arkansas at Columbia University in 1954. He was greeting me as a Fulbright scholar. **Was enchanted by the fact that his idea originated in Africa,** and entered it in the Congressional record.

So the link between Al-Azhar and Africa is long and deep. Reason why its present **Rector, Dr. Ahmed El-Taiyeb,** a Sorbonne graduate, chose **Abuja,** the Nigerian capital, to address the **terror catastrophe of Boko Haram.** A hideous term, meaning: **"Western learning is unislamic."**

A total negation of what **Islam (faith and knowledge)** has stood for since the 7th century. Except during dark ages, not of the Crusaders (that was a passing episode); but of the Ottoman Empire. An Empire which suffered from a split personality: diversity of religions, but glorification of Turkish culture, and avoidance of modernization.

In Nigeria, El-Taiyeb's voice could reverberate through the great continent where Egyptian civilization, born 7000 years ago, was the first African civilization. And is still enduring. Threatened only by **jihadism of which Boko Haram and Al-Shabab and the ISIS franchises** are standard bearers.

The booming voice of Al-Azhar, uttered by its Grand Imam, who was hosted by Nigerian president, Buhari (A Muslim from Northern Nigeria) carried multiple messages. All of which are anti-jihadi. As his first salvo, he called jihadists **"wrong-doers,"** as he quoted from the Quran: **"And do not think that God is unaware of what the wrongdoers do. He only puts them in respite until a Day when eyes shall stare."** (Chapter 14/Verse 42).

Referring to the wayward jihadis (calling themselves Muslim extremists is giving into their high jacking of the mantle of Islam) as wrongdoers, he went on to turn the table on them. He intoned:
- **"They have placed Islam unjustly in the defendant's box; tarnishing its image; besmirching its exalted status, by blood letting, head-cutting on TV screens -a barbarism unknown before in history."**

For what end? And who is behind this anti-Islamic insanity? The Rector of Al-Azhar provided his Nigerian audience (Muslims, Christians, and others) with his hypothesis.
- **"Search for who is the beneficiary of this mischief, standing solidly behind these crimes in the name of Islam. It is those**

Dr. Yassin El-Ayouty, Esq.

who fund it, those who provide it with arms and other war material; those who help these groups in planning; and those who provide them with a false cover of legitimacy."

How about the stance of Islam from non-Muslims? After all, the Al-Azhar Rector was standing on the soil of a country of nearly 200 millions, of whom there is about 60% Muslims in the north. **An African economy measured as Number one in all of Africa, followed by Egypt, then followed by South Africa.** That is the great African triangle (Cairo/Abuja/Pretoria), rounded up in the east by a fourth historic capital Addis -Ababa (Ethiopia).

In that regard, Al-Azhar, through the voice of Dr. El-Taiyeb is heard to say: **"If we are to exit these bloody crises which inflict our world from end to end, and whose victims are largely the poor and uneducated in every faith and creed, we have to chart a new course..."**

**"A course which begins by a question: Is the relationship between Islam and other religions based on tension, suspicion, and foreboding? No!! In the Quran, Islam is not only the name of a certain faith. Islam is the name of a common faith which all believers, from whatever faith, subscribe to."**

El-Taiyeb's evidence? **"The Quran described Abraham as a Muslim. That was thousands of years before Muhammad's message. The Quran spoke of Ismail and Isaac as they raised the foundation of the first place of worship saying: Our Lord: lead us to submit to Your Will and raise from our offspring a nation which will submit to Your Will."** (Chapter 2/Verse 128).

Here the emphasis by Al-Azhar is on the connotation of the term **"Muslim." Meaning those who submit to the will of the Creator. It is not restrictive,** as the jihadis in their ignorance advocate, to the world of Islam alone. An important distinction, of an ideological nature in the ideological war on jihadism.

Now to the stance of the Quran on other holy books. El-Taiyeb provides a definitive response: Equal respect and parallel veneration. Citing the Quranic text on the Torah where it says: **"It was We who revealed the Law to Moses: therein was guidance and light. By its standard have been judged the Jews, by the Prophets who bowed, as in Islam, to God's will, by the rabbis and the doctors of law."** (Chapter V, verse 44).

Followed by Quranic continuity on the New Testament. **"And in their** footsteps we sent Jesus the son of Mary, confirming the Law that had come before him: We sent him the Gospel: therein was guidance and light, and confirmation of the Law that had come before him: a guidance and an admonition to those who fear God." (Chapter V, Verse 46).

As if in a **Heavenly Club of God's messengers, whose membership is premised on co-equality,** the Grand Imam of Al-Azhar cites **the Prophet Muhammad** as per his authenticated tradition. By that Muhammedan tradition, the Prophet of Islam has declared: **"I am the most rightful inheritor of Jesus. In this world and in the hereafter. The Messengers are brothers. Born to different Mothers. But having one faith."**

**What an apt riposte, a quick counterstrike, to the dark heart of the jihadis who claim that the only true religion for mankind is Islam.** Embellished by the wickedness and the viciousness of the ridiculous claim of **"Reserved only for Sunni Muslims."** Thus wiping out the verity that in **Islam, there is no Sunni vs. Shii.** Except in the minds of those who use faith as a mechanism for control.

In that historic speech in Abuja, the Grand Imam of Al-Azhar Al-Shareef does not limit the circle of respect and authenticity to **"the revealed religions"** (Judaism, Christianity, and Islam). For more than half of humanity abide by **Hinduism, Buddhism and Confucianism.**

El-Taiyeb goes on to clarify the reason for the Quranic silence on all these faiths. He says: **"These were religions not known to the Arabs in the Arabian peninsula nearly 1500 years ago. Yet they are included within the spacious tent of the Quran in regard to respect and equal treatment expected of every Muslim towards the adherents of these faiths."**

That inclusiveness is manifest in the Quranic instruction for justice and amity towards **"the adherents of every faith, every creed, and every philosophy which do not aggress against Muslims in Muslim lands."** The very words of Imam El-Taiyeb in Abuja. Words which he bolsters by the **primary source of Islamic Law, the Quran.**

Thus he quotes: **"God forbids you not, with regard to those who fight you not for your faith nor drive you out of your homes, from dealing kindly and justly with them, for God loveth those who are just."** (Chapter 60, Verse 8).

The above material covers only half of the Abuja speech by the Grand Imam of Al-Azhar Al-Shareef. Space limitation of this blog posting does not allow for its comprehensive coverage. So in the remaining space, let us deal with the following conclusions:

- **Jihadism is not Islam.** Calling their criminal activities **"militant Islam"** is a misnomer. The word **"Islam,"** if joined to their self-made name, would be a misconception which indirectly advances their criminal cause;
- Jihadi activity has **nothing to do whatsoever with the true Islamic meaning of jihad.** Jihad, in Islam, is of two kinds, both of which are legitimate. The first is internal: self-policing to avoid following one's base urges; the second is self-defense, permitted under all kinds of law, including international law.
- **The unity between faiths, as stressed by Imam Ahmed El-Taiyeb,** is a cardinal tenet of Islam. The principle of **"TAWHEED," "Onness,"** applies in two directions: The **"Onness"** of the Creator; and the **"Onness"** between every faith and other faiths. The first type is vertical; the second is horizontal - universal.

It is noteworthy that the fear from Islam is not only the consequence of ignorance of its precepts, and of its lingua franca, Arabic. It is also, the consequence of its criminal enemies, **"the jihadists."**

**Ironically jihadism which had inflicted on our world 9/11 and beyond, has its unwitting Muslim auxiliaries.** Here are examples:
- **In Switzerland,** students shaking the hand of their teacher upon entering or exiting the classroom is a tradition. At a school in the **small town of Therwil,** two Syrian immigrant brothers refused to shake their female teacher's hand. **Igniting a national outrage.** The cantonal board of education decided against those errant students. **The Swiss acted properly.** But the Islamic Central Council of Switzerland opposed that ruling.
- In 2009, the Swiss, in a national referendum, **voted to ban the construction of minarets.** Reason: A Saudi sued the municipality where he resided for preventing him for building there **the tallest minaret in the world.** Because of his refusal to abide by Swiss zoning laws regarding the height of any construction, a total ban was issued. Once again, the Swiss edict was correct.
- Fear from **"creeping Islamization"** in all of Europe, to which millions of Muslims, fleeing from Muslim lands, is understandably rampant. In Germany, nearly **one million migrants arrived in 2015.** The government of Angela Merkel, against all odds, proposed an integration law this week. Its purpose is to give those

immigrants **a quid pro quo:** something for something. **A path to full employment, but a requirement to learn German, and accept local laws and customs.**

- **And why not?** We all remember, how in New Year's eve, a group of Muslim hooligans went on a rampage in Frankfurt and elsewhere. **Groping German women,** in violation of every law, religious or secular, and of every custom having to do with privacy and the sanctity of the individual. Hundreds of culprits are being readied now for ejection from their hard won sanctuaries.

**The gulf between the Muslim world and the non-Muslim world remains vast.** Of course, **as Ambassador Seyed Hussein Mousavian,** the Irani scholar at Princeton is correct. In late 2015, he posited in a famous article in the American **Huffington Post** that **targeting Muslims is the real threat to peace.** Mousavian made that assertion months before the ideological anti-Islamic tsunami of Donald Trump, now the assured nominee of the Republican Party for the American presidency.

But the fact remains that **polls indicate that 7 of the top 10 countries which view America most unfavorably are Muslim countries.** It is obvious that the US/Israel strategic alliance plays a considerable role in that unfavorability. But this is not the full picture.

The issues of faith and politics cross one another at dangerous angles. **Including the misunderstanding of Islam.** By non-Muslims and those who call themselves Muslims, as in the case of the jihadis.

But at least, on the religious ramparts, there stands a **sentinel called Al-Azhar Al-Shareef.** Whose head, **Ahmed Al-Taiyeb** is now engaged in a shuttle of global efforts of enlightened clarification: **FAITH IS ONE!!**

A message which he has recently carried to **Germany,** followed by **Nigeria,** followed by the **Vatican,** and lastly to **France.**

*This is where he had internalized at this Alma Mater, the Sorbonne motto of all France: Liberte; Egalite; Fraternite. With a universal application. The most effective wooden stake being plunged in the heart of Drakula -a name which is most befitting the so-called jihadis of today.*

# 25 JUNE 2016

## Assessing An Act of Gargantuan Leadership: Saving Egypt Three Years Ago From A Seismic Civil War

Saturday, June 11, 2016

That was a one historic **act by El-Sisi,** responding to 35 million voices calling on June 30, 2013 for deliverance. From every public square in that pivotal country, called Egypt, the **chant against Morsi and the Brotherhood** to leave was thunderous. But it needed a protective mechanism. **The only mechanism was the national army.**

But the chant of **"IRHAL" (Begone!!)** had a constitutional reason. **The Islamic Constitution of 2012** was drafted by Brotherhood hands. The liberals, including the Copts, were forced out of the drafting. No provision was there in that document allowing for recalling the President. A Brotherhood overreach **meant to last,** but was **destined to collapse.**

Deposing Morsi was not planned. It was the result of **the obduracy of an ideologically-fossilized organization, the Muslim Brotherhood.** Such a group does not understand the art of political compromise. From June 30, 2013 to July 3, 2013, the national conversation begun by El-Sisi, as Minister of Defense, to have the process of choosing a President begun again, went nowhere.

371

The **Brotherhood Guidance Bureau, the actual ruler of Egypt,** was determined to fight back and keep a sham process going on. **Legitimacy (Shariyah)** for the Islamists was above practicality -a practical compromise, advocated by El-Sisi to avert civil war.

The Brotherhood's claim rang hollow. **The contest for the presidency between Morsi,** the Brotherhood's second choice for office after El-Shatter was disqualified, **and General Shafiq** produced a doubtful result. **51% for Morsi, 49% for Shafiq** was a non-verifiable statistic. And the choice of President preceded the drafting of a constitution. Talk about putting the cart before the horse!!

Prior to the plebiscite on that defective constitution, where **Coptic rights to citizenship parity** were nowhere, Morsi had declared himself to be **above the Constitution.** A determined dictatorship in the making. **Morsi was another name for Mussolini.** That fascist formula was then taken one step further. A parliament dissolved by the **Supreme Constitutional Court** on a technicality was ordered by the President to reconvene.

The agenda of that reconvened Parliament was **one item to be enacted in 20 minutes.** An enactment that delegated to the Executive (the President) legislative powers. An anomaly that alarmed a nation which since 1923 had luxuriated prior to the Nasser coup of 1952 in constitutional democracy. 80 years of practice, which anteceded the Brotherhood's birth in 1928.

With the collapse of **El-Sisi-led negotiations,** the threat of civil war loomed as a certainty. Morsi had to go; a road map in which the liberal leadership of Egypt concurred, **including the Coptic Church,** was at hand; a transitional government was formed; an interim president, **Judge Adly Mansour,** chief of the harassed Supreme Constitutional Court, was installed; and preparations for the **redrafting of a new and secular Constitution began in earnest.**

**In all of this, there was no coup by El-Sisi.** The process meant the undoing of the Brotherhood's coup which followed installing Morsi as President. The core problem of that Islamic presidency was complex: The **Brotherhood regarded Egypt as a spring board to a mythical Islamic State;** force was the first option in dealing with Ethiopia; Sinai was to be the hinterland for Hamas; The copts and the shiis were smitten into submission. Turkey and Qatar were eager funders for the new Islamic order in Cairo; and a **wahhabi-like theocracy** was seen as Egypt of the future!!

These were all realities of the one-year rule by the Brotherhood. A year which also saw in the **Islamic Republic of Iran** a role model. So parallel security forces were formed: from a replica of the Revolutionary Guards, to the militias patterned along the lines of the **Iranian Basig, created by Khomeini.** How could such developments escape the attention of the **proud non-sectarian huge Egyptian army?**

With the corrective revolution of June 30, 2013, came the physical proof of the Brotherhood's determination to collapse the national will. The occupation by unruly and gangs of street roughs trained in urban warfare occupying the Cairo squares of **Rabaa** and **Al-Nahdha.**

Weddings were performed, so was the storing of armaments. Bread was baked, and calls for soldiers and policemen to defect were issued. **Foreign intervention was urged,** and a mighty propaganda machine was put to work on a Brotherhood signal!! The two squares in the heart of Cairo were **declared Islamic emirates.**

And I was told that the Brotherhood would never leave!! Without heeding the lesson of refusing to compromise from June 30 to July 3, their tactic was that the Rabaa and Al-Nahda rebellions would spark a conflagration. **The enemy of the Islamists was, and continues to be the June 30 Revolution.** So for six weeks, the entreaties by the Government for peaceful disbanding were responded to by more violence. God was believed to be on the side of collapsing the modern secular State. It was a suicidal belief. **Spun out of the inherent hypocrisy of using faith for the ends of unjust power.**

It was not a conflict between two opponents, with each of them holding to values common to historic Egypt. **It was the onset of a conflagration of existential proportions for the very soul of Egypt.** With the Brotherhood aiming at the upending of a secular Egypt, and the majority of the population aiming at continuity. **Egypt's DNA has never carried theocratic chromosomes.** Nor has that DNA ever carried in it the germ of civil war. This has always been a cohesive and inclusive society.

For since 7000 years, the **State produced the faith, not the faith the State;** the Pyramids representing the lofty stability of the State cast their huge shadow on the temples below; even the **army was a State-creation, unlike in Israel, for example, where the army created the State.**

Thus in the fight for the soul of Egypt, the views of a noisy minority were no more than an echo chamber within the Guidance Bureau, the Islamic

Politburo. Whereas the security forces, as of July 3, 2013 were reflective of Egypt's DNA. With only the megaphones of the Brotherhood globally blaring nonsense about phony legitimacy, the **Egyptian street,** whose only protection from a fascist putsch was the national army, was asserting its sovereign primacy.

El-Sisi's assumption of the presidency was not through the armed forces. As universally witnessed, it was through the ballot boxes.

Let us now peer into the Brotherhood's ideology. In one word, their **"ideology"** translates into **"hypocrisy."** For they are not about **"faith;"** they are about **"power;"** dressed up as **"faith."** For evidence, here are examples:

- In 1947, they murdered in cold blood, Egypt's **Prime Minister, Al-Nokrashi Pasha.** An act precipitating the Government of **Abdel-Hadi** murdering their Supreme Guide and Founder, **Hassan El-Banna** in 1948 in Cairo;
- Having infiltrated the officers corps of the Egyptian armed forces, they played a crucial role in the Nasser coup of 1952. **Nasser had used them, and in return, they thought that they could use him.** With Nasser having the bigger and more disciplined guns on his side, he outfoxed the Brotherhood. Manipulated the **so-called Alexandria assassination attempt on his life in 1954.** A golden occasion, whether true or contrived, to ban them.
- **Treachery, deceit and cunning beget the same. What goes in at one end, comes out of the other end.** With the hanging of Sayed Qutb, the spiritual father of terrorism in the name of Islam, in the mid 1960s the Brotherhood laid low, focusing on social work. It was its means for grass-roots infiltration.
- But never abandoning its core values represented by its logo: **Two swords, framing the Quran, with the words "And Prepare"** (Wa Aaedou). The first Quranic words for the verse beginning with: **"And prepare for them with whatever force you can..."** (Chapter 5/Verse 60).
- In that combative logo,defining Muslims into **"we and the others,"** is a **departure from Islamic jurisprudence. A system based on Quran, Muhammad's tradition, and ijtihad** (interpretation), with the emphasis on **TAWHEED - God is One.** As the Grand Imam of Al-Azhar, **Dr. Ahmed Al-Taiyeb** had declared last May in **Germany, Nigeria and France: "A Muslim means any human being of whatever faith who makes his will subservient to God's will."**
- No wonder that the Brotherhood's celebration in June 2012 of

Morsi's taking the oath of office as President (for the third time) at Cairo University, **gave Dr. Al-Taiyeb a back seat.** Al-Taiyeb walked away from that deliberate humiliation.

- And no wonder that **Muhammad Ali,** the great boxing champion and an Afro-American, was eulogized on June 10 by an array of leaders of every faith on earth. For Ali the convert held bibles which he purchased close to his bosom. **Both Muhammad Ali and Ahmed Al-Taiyeb are on the same side of an Islam** as the expression of faith in a Creator for all of humanity. An Islam which stands on the world stage respected for tolerance, not feared for terrorism.

That is the litmus test which the Brotherhood could never pass. Claiming victim-hood at both Rabaa and Al-Nahdha in consequence of that rebellion against the Egypt of Adly Mansour as of August 14, 2013 reflects only one face. The face of hypocrisy.

From all indications, **both Rabaa and Al-Nahda represented a counter-revolution which sought self-sacrifice.** A tenet of the Brotherhood's Charter. That Charter proclaims: **"Death for the Sake of Allah is our most cherished aspiration."** Its secondary mission is an invitation for foreign intervention.

The Quran implicates the Brotherhood in bringing about that bloodshed upon itself and upon Egypt's security forces. **"Whatever good comes to you, it is from God. And whatever misfortune befalls you, it is your own doing..."** (Chapter IV, Verse 79).

Now fast forward to El-Sisi's reign, and a cursory review of its accomplishments **in a country saved by him from civil war:**

With the secular Constitution approved, then promulgated in 2014, presidential elections followed. **The result was a first for the New Egypt:** El-Sisi became the first President in the history of modern Egypt to be voted for the highest office through fair, open, and scrupulously-monitored elections. The man who is now embodying the true DNA, of his country.

The oldest nation on earth was now ready for rebuilding from the bottom up. That is in spite of an **economic decline, and two wars on terrorism going on in Sinai and at the Libyan borders.**
- A second Suez Canal;
- Rebuilding the naval forces through the purchase of French aircraft carriers. While keeping an American excess of armed vehicles flowing at no cost to combat terrorism. Armored vehicles shielding

Dr. Yassin El-Ayouty, Esq.

troops from roadside bombs; A total of 762 such vehicles called MRAP, which stands for mine-resistant, ambush-protected;

- Reclaiming 1.5 million acres from the Egyptian desert, while ensuring an adequate supply of surface and underground water;
- Returning Egypt to the African Union, and to its natural allies and sources of emergency funding in the Gulf;
- Ensuring energy sufficiency through German technology, and the return to atomic programs for peaceful purposes through Russian know-how;
- **Pursuit of the new Religious Revolution through Al-Azhar,** and the banning of the preachers of hate and anti-coptism through laws. Meaningful presidential participation in celebrations at the Coptic St. Mark's Cathedral at Abbasiya, Cairo;
- Declaring the reconstruction of a new administrative capital, east of Cairo;
- The utilization of the **"Tahiya Misr Fund"** in new zoning for roads, housing, refuse removal, bridges, and grain silos;
- Revamping the creaky educational and health systems;
- Resorting to summitry and presidential visits to newly emerging mega economies, to rebuild tourism, and to borrow from the east its new techniques for mass transfer to the 21st century;
- Refocusing on Egypt, while avoiding intervention in the affairs of sister Arab States, shunning the old interventionist propaganda line of **"Egypt knows best!!"**
- Involving the Italians and the Americans in harnessing the natural gas discoveries;
- And harnessing the huge demographics in the arduous task of national production.

Let us hear El-Sisi advocating his presidential line of thought.

In a TV interview with **Osama Kamal of the Egyptian TV,** he produces his own report card. With characteristic humility, he speaks of: **"We"** as a collective leadership: (my translation from the Arabic).

- **"Exerting before June 30 all efforts at reconciling between the Rulers and Society. Efforts emanating from fears of a rupture between the State and the people;"**
- **"The evil-doers are those who intentionally aim at hurting Egypt. Whether the Egyptian people or the Egyptian State;"**
- **"The Egyptian people know who are the practitioners of evil, internally and externally;"**
- **"For as long as the Egyptian people are united, we experience no fear. We only experience anxiety if the**

376

Egyptian public does not act as one;"
- "What goes on now is nothing more than futile attempts to destroy the State from within;"
- "I did not agonize over whether to compete for the presidency of Egypt. But there were measures which had to be in place prior to my taking that step;"
- "My goal remains to protect the State from collapse. If this shall be my only achievement, I would see in it a great mission accomplished;"
- "Today we have State institutions, a Constitution, mechanisms, and a State in the process of being restored with a renewed spirit."

This is a theory of confidence, expressed in an understated manner. **A manner that harks back to the early Arab literature which uses the diminutive as a style of describing the huge.**

Here we note:
- The Sinai terror, exaggerated in the press internally and externally as a force determining Egypt of the future. That is in spite of the fact that terror space is confined to 2% to 3% of the Sinai land mass between Gaza and El-Arish;
- That there exists in the Arab region a vacuum. Forcing Egypt to act. For what objective? El-Sisi says it best in that TV interview: **"We must be able to effect a balance, not aiming at neither hidden agendas or coveting land or wealth. Our only agenda is to repel those who aim at harming us or our neighbors."**
- That the Egyptian press of today has a zero role in public education. Its focus confuses between **"the freedom of expression,"** and **"the freedom for malicious rendering of the news."** Offering daily admonition to El-Sisi regarding their own perception of what should and should not be done. The **depth of their shame is to be measured by their calling the islands of Tiran and Sanafir a territorial Saudi grab.**

No wonder that the world press of today has pivoted in a new direction. Their main headlines are: **"Doom and Gloom Merchants Wrong Again."** So wrote Linda S. Heard of Gulf News after a recent visit to Egypt.

As Egypt enters this phase of accelerated reconstruction, confidence-building trends multiply:
- In the rejection of the neo-imperialism of foreign non-governmental organizations like **"Amnesty International."** Trying to measure the status of freedom of expression in Egypt

with the same yardstick applicable to western States which did not suffer the ravages of the Arab Spring;

- The rise of many indigenous NGOs. Examples: **"Naebat Qademat"** (women legislators in the making), headed by Dr. Nahid Shaker. And the **"Organization for Constitutional Protection,"** headed by Amre Moussa;
- The rise of the movement for local administrations, decentralized for quick response on the ground:
- The responsiveness to the Coptic Church, while calling for revamping the archaic laws impeding church construction and repairs;
- The emphasis on projects where there exists a direct relationship between cost and benefit and a time budget for completion;
- Bringing up the rear of Egypt's geographic surface, for far too long neglected, like Sinai, Nubia, and the huge western Egyptian dessert;
- The realignment of foreign relations in order to better serve the parity of sovereignty among States, the possible revision of the Charter of the League of Arab States; and
- Adherence to the laws for public demonstrations within its promulgated provisions, the respect for judicial independence, and for women empowerment.

This is a challenging process of rebirth of the oldest State on earth. A **process wearing proudly and visibly an ANKH -a key-like ancient Egyptian cross as a symbol for an enduring life and generative energy.** A country worth saving from civil war, by historic leaders like El-Sisi. **A leader for whom tomorrow starts today!!**

**On behalf of history, Thank you CC!! Your Egypt is no Syria!!**

# Lookouts On Islam: Either The Summit of Muhammad Ali, or The Gutter of Omar Mateen

Thursday, June 16, 2016

ISIS is not the only source of subversion of Islam. Of equal lethality are citizens of non-Muslim societies who act on ISIS inspiration to murder their co-citizens. In the name of Islam. A stab in the back for environments which ensured for them freedom of faith. Only, as in Orlando, or San

Bernardino, or Fort Hood, to kill in cold blood their protectors.

The choice for lookouts on Islam is immensely stark. It is either from the summit of Muhammad Ali, a world champion, or the gutter of Omar Mateen who killed and maimed more than a hundred of his neighbors at a night club in Florida.

In the world of US presidential campaigning, the choice of lookouts on Islam begins with the summit of Obama. Refusing to label such massacre **"Islamic terrorism."** And ends with the abyss of Republican presumptive presidential nominee, Trump. Clamoring for walling out all Muslims from entering the US. In the squalor of his ignorance, Trump should know that the creation of fortress America is the very hope of the evil-doers, free at the gates, gaining from American immobility for inflicting maximum harm.

Returning to the comparison between how Muhammad Ali viewed Islam, and how that Orlando thug clothed his criminality in an ISIS garb.

Let us here again recall the meaning of the term **"Muslim."** In Islamic Law, it is not restricted to the adherents of Islam. It applies to any human being, regardless of any faith, who practices what I could here term: **"the subsidiarity of will. The human will is subsidiary to the will of the Creator."** The term **"infidel"** does not mean **"non-Muslim."** It means a person who has no values. Nor is the term **"hold war"** an Islamic term. Nor is the expression **"killing for the sake of God."** Nor is **"Allahu Akbar,"** used by terrorist morons as a battle cry. It is a pledge to the **equality of all humans in the eyes of God.**

Muhammad Ali, the Afro-American convert, lived that creed of universality. At his funeral on Friday, June 10, held at Louisville, Kentucky, leaders of every faith eulogized him. In him, they had a lookout at the summit. Prayers were read from the palette of every faith which Ali had honored. As in the best traditions of Islamic Law, all of those faiths were his paths to an inner truth.

In the Quran, Ali's conduct conformed to this verse from the Quran: **"Indeed God has bought from believers their lives and their wealth, that they shall have the Gardens... a pledge from God made in the Torah, in the Bible, and in the Quran. And who is more true in fulfilling His covenant than God..." (Chapter IX, verse 111).**

By contrast, **Omar Mateen,** the Orlando mass killer, made his pledge, not to Islam, but to ISIS, the proverbial subverter of Islam. Mateen had called

**911** to proclaim his allegiance (Baiaa) to ISIS. That was before he, on June 12, stormed that night club to kill in fulfillment of their pledge.

One criminal act, in fact the worst act of mass shooting on US soil in history was soon the occasion for Donald Trump to **"appreciate the congrats for being right on radical Islamic terrorism."** Using an oxymoron expression **"Islamic terrorism."** A vicious linkage between Islam as faith, and terrorism as criminality of which the Muslim world is still the largest target. What compounds Trump's insensitivity is opportuning a massive human tragedy for sordid electioneering ends.

While Ali saw in himself a citizen of America and the world, Mateen saw himself an adherent of a mythical caliphate, soon to be thrown in the dust bin of history.

It is saddening to recall **my interviewing of Ali at the UN for the UN Radio** during my service for the world organization. His wit, his humor, his cascading torrents of adjectives, were power in action. All within the summitry of his belief in universality.

It is no wonder that Ali's widow, **Lonnie,** said that **"Muhammad indicated that when the end came for him, he wanted to use his life and his death as a teaching moment."** And it was.

As for **Noor,** Mateen's wife, she is said to have driven him to his Orlando target, armed for the kill. Purported to have pleaded with him not to harm anyone. By contrast, Muhammad Ali sought in his new faith, a connection to humanity. As for Omar, he had told his co-workers that he thought martyrdom. None of the Islamic Law standards for martyrdom applied to him.

In Islam, only self-defense is the core of permissible war. It is combat that stops at the borders of an Islamic State under attack. It is also the vehicle for negotiating peace with the adversary, once that adversary is inclined toward peace negotiations. The Quran provides for this rule of post-conflict resolution. **"But if they incline to peace, then incline to it, and trust in God. Indeed He is the All-Hearing, the All-Knowing." (Chapter VIII, verse 6).**

But for Mateen, the pretender to martyrdom, the Quran stops him far away from his goal. It says: **"We prescribed to the Children of Israel that whoever kills a soul, unless it be for retaliation or because of spreading corruption on earth, it would be as if he had killed all** mankind. And whoever saves a life, it would be as if he had saved the life of all mankind." (Chapter V, verse 32).

And where is Mateen from that gentle giant Muhammad Ali?! Mateen's former wife, **Ms. Yusufiy** had married him in a ceremony in a Florida courthouse in 2009. Following the Orlando massacre, she made revelations about him to the authorities. Referring to an incident of domestic abuse, she said: **"He almost killed me. Because he started choking me. And I somehow got out of it and I tried to tackle him."**

Where is Mateen from the tradition of the **Prophet Muhammad** who admonished: **"Do not be bad news for your household."** The moral here is that your household had nothing to do with whatever bad happened to you outside of your home. So don't even dare return home and take your anger on them.

And aside from attitudes, **Islamic Law sees only gender equality.** For it has to be read as supplemented by legislated law. Having elevated women from being a mere chattel, and decreed the abandonment of female infanticide, it made marriage a contract. A contract which ensured for the wife economic independence through an agreed dowry in arrears in case of divorce.

It is unfortunate that **wahhabism,** through enforced separation of women from male public life, had distorted those rules. By his oppressive behavior as a husband, Mateen adhered to rules which do not exist in either Islamic jurisprudence, or Islamic practices.

What a contrast between a world champion who saw in his adopted faith the common bonds between humans everywhere, and a world scumbag, who prided himself on living the gutter values of ISIS. Eulogies for Ali gushed forth on June 10 **from a priest, an imam, a rabbi, a monk, former President Clinton, and an indigenous American Indian chief, and a famous comedian.**

Through his heinous mass murder, Mateen united the whole world in his condemnation. Even the UN Security Council issued on June 14 a statement of condemnation, **proposed by the US, and joined by Russian and Egypt.**

Ali's coffin traveled through 20 miles of Louisville, cheered, saluted by thousands of people chanting his name: **Ali, Ali, Ali.** Ali had scripted his funeral as he had scripted his life. Saw in his leave-taking from this world a

**chance befitting the inclusiveness of his faith.**

From the lookout on Islam through the summit of Muhammad Ali, it is difficult to transition to the lookout on Islam from the gutter of Omar Mateen. For the latter gloried in the debauchery of mass murder in the name of ISIS. An occasion for uniting the fractured Islamophobic tendencies in the US.

As is guaranteed by the US constitution, freedom of faith is a basic precept in Islamic Law. The Quran states:**"Say, 'O people, surely there has come to you the truth from your Lord. Whoever is guided, is guided only for his own soul. And whoever goes astray, he is astray only for his soul, and I (meaning the Prophet Muhammad) am not a trustee over you.'"** (Chapter II, verse 108).

*These are the spiritual links between faith, every kind of faith, and human conduct. Epitomized at its best by Muhammad Ali whose faith was a bridge across all continents!!*

# 26 JULY 2016

## Crazy Mid-Summer Night Dreams, For An Egyptian Court On Tiran and Sanafir

Friday, July 8, 2016

This is hard to believe. An Egyptian administrative Court, within the Council of State, sitting in Cairo. Ruling on June 21, 2016 that an agreement between Egypt and Saudi Arabia, signed in Cairo in April, was null and void. Under that agreement, Egypt is to return those Red Sea islands of Tiran and Sanafir to Saudi Arabia.

That judgment is riven by so many legal errors that it resembles mid-summer night dreams. These include:

- It regards the entire Egyptian population as **"the plaintiff;"**
- **The presumed defendants are Egypt's President, its Prime Minister, and its Ministers for Defense, Foreign Affairs, and Interior;**
- Its jurisdiction cannot be established except by destruction of the separation of powers;
- Its evidence is based on hearsay produced by publicity and educational material;
- It defaults the defendant for not producing material withheld because of the Court's over-reach beyond justiciable limits;
- It appoints itself as the voice and conscience of nearly 100 million

Egyptians, none of whom has ever been consulted about the appointment of those judges.

If legal writing is an art which I teach at times in American law schools, this Court, by its writing, seems to be begging for some basic training. Aside from the offending shortcomings summed up **supra, the Court is bereft of linking between the issue and the law. In legal briefs, we call it the rule, the analysis, and the conclusion.** For short, we call it the IRAC method **(Issue, Rule, Analysis, and Conclusion).**

Thus my heaviest task in preparing this writing was not what I want to say or how I would say it. It was reading through 15 printed pages sent to me online courtesy of a friend who differs with me in this matter. That is because as I plowed through the **Court's judgment in this case (consolidated from two cases),** my task of making sense of the Court's words was made more exacting by the absence of legal common sense in that text.

From the text below, the reader may find why the Court's reasoning is circular. Meaning to say **this matter is such and such because it is such and such.**

In other words, the Court begged the central issue in dispute (who is sovereign over Tiran and Sanafir), by failure to provide proof. That is even if we overlook that the issue in this case cannot be justiciable. **Because it is an issue of sovereignty interlaced with politics.** Thus unfit for Court adjudication.

Now here is a summary of the documented facts:
- In consequence of Israel's expansion southward in the Negev, the port **Umm Rashrash** was occupied and renamed **Eilat.** Opposite the Jordanian port of Aqaba;
- With Israel now with an Aqaba Gulf seaport, **Saudi Arabia feared for the security of two of its islands (Tiran and Sanafir).** They are a part of several Saudi islands lying immediately south of the Saudi mainland, but had no military protection;
- So following a visit to Cairo by the Kingdom's founder, King Abdel-Aziz Al-Saud to Egypt in 1949, a Saudi request was addressed to Egypt in 1950 to provide protection for these outposts at the southern entrance of the Gulf of Aqaba;
- Egypt's positive response was immediate. **Its Prime Minister Nasha Pasha directed his Defense Minister, Haidar Pasha, to comply with that Saudi request.**
- An agreement was signed by the two Arab sister States in 1950.

Designating Egypt as the administrator of that sovereign territory until further notice. In that agreement, Cairo was fully cognizant of its own defense needs in the Gulf, opposite eastward of its Ras Nusrani, north east of Sharm El-Sheikh;

- Notwithstanding Israeli protestations against **"Egyptian occupation"** of those Saudi Islands, Egypt repeatedly declared at the UN that its presence on these two islands was by written agreement with the Saudi sovereign. **I was a witness to the last such assertion by Ambassador Muhammad Awad Al-Koni in May 1967. I was near where he sat in the UN Security Council chamber** as he invoked that 1950 agreement;

- Now with Egypt and Israel beholden to the 1979 Peace Treaty, and with Egypt and Saudi Arabia in military partnership fighting terrorism, and with Saudi military power in the 21st century vastly augmented, **Riyadh called on Egypt to end its administration over the islands.** Hence the agreement signed in Cairo in April 2016. It also included the construction of a land link **(King Salman bridge)** between the two countries, over the Gulf waters.

- **From the attached international Swiss map, you could see the boundary in the Gulf between Egypt and Saudi Arabia, with its eastern side enclosing Tiran and Sanafir, as Saudi territory,** and its western side tracking the shape of Sinai as Egyptian territory.

Facts are facts. There is no Egyptian territorial sell-out to Riyadh; no conspiracies engaged in by President El-Sisi and his government which symbolizes the re-establishment of **"The Strong State;"** no surprises on the Egyptian public in the process of concluding international agreements with all comers as normal business to help in the ongoing task of reconstruction; and following upon an Arab summit decision to create a **"unified Arab military force"** to keep the Arab homeland safe from terrorism.

Examining the Court judgment of June 21, 2016, in the light of the foregoing facts, it is astounding to find so many legal faults in the Court's ruling.

- The Court asserting its jurisdiction in a matter in which the April 2016 agreement belongs to another branch, called **"Parliament;"**

- The submission by plaintiffs whose standing before any Court anywhere must be predicated upon each one of them being personally injured by that agreement. Not one of them could make that assertion, and the Court did not call for the necessity of that element required for case filing;

- **The mixing by the Court between the notion of occupation by**

**agreement for defense and administrative reasons, and of the notion of sovereignty.**

- That confusion led the Court to take the introduction to the two islands of customs, police, defense support, quarantine, mail service... etc as indicators of sovereignty;

- That the refusal of the purported defendant to submit to a Court lacking subject matter jurisdiction as indication of culpability is simply a gross legal error. **The burden is on the plaintiff to prove its case; the defendant is never called upon to assist the plaintiff's allegations.**

- It is laughable to read in the Court's decision: **"The defendant government has hidden behind silence to buttress its opposition to these hearings by the Court;"**

- The faulty interpretation by Court of the law of treaties, of the Law of the Sea, and of the exclusive jurisdiction of the Executive in foreign affairs, is truly alarming.

Going beyond these litigation procedural points, we cross over to some general statements made by the Court in support of its arrogated jurisdiction:

- The call by the Court for a national plebiscite on the April 2016 agreement. Under what authority did that Court base that call?

- Invoking Article 51 of the 2014 Constitution which provides for **"respect of human dignity."** Where is the violation of **"human dignity"** in that agreement?

- The Court's ridiculous interpretation of **"sovereignty"** as **"flexible"** whereby **"its scope gets narrower in democracies and broader in dictatorships."** The Court should have known that sovereignty is non-changeable as it is inheres perpetually in the people. **"Governments"** change; **"people"** are permanent. Ironically the Court contradicts itself as it states correctly this principle in a different part of its judgment.

- The clear implication of that **"flexible definition"** of sovereignty by the Court is to characterize El-Sisi regime as less than democratic. *An indication of the politicization of the Court's decision. The role of the judiciary in civil law countries like Egypt is to apply the law, not to create judge-made law, as in countries adhering to English common law principles.*

- The Court characterizes the issue of **"Tiran and Sanafir"** as **"a national dispute."** It sees in the opposition to Saudi sovereignty on Tiran and Sanafir a matter of near civil war dispute, requiring the intervention of a low ranking administrative Court!!

- It cites Article 151 of the 2014 Constitution. **The article provides**

**for the roles of the executive and the legislature in the making of international treaties.** I fail to see how does this article help this Court in asserting its jurisdiction. Those provisions are silent on any judicial role in the process;

- The Court, as if absent-mindedly, also cites article 190 of the Constitution, stating that: **"The legality of this treaty (of April, 2016) is within the jurisdiction of this Court."** Sadly for the Court, the Article provides for issues within the competence of the Council of State, within whose structure this Court lies. **But the wording of that Article relates only to administrative disputes. It has nothing to do with the issue at hand which the Court in its own judgment characterized it as "an international treaty."**

What a wonderful mid-summer night dream for an administrative Court which, in this matter, has lost its way!! Only to wake up to the nightmare of reality of proper adjudication, anchored in a proper jurisdiction, invoked by an injured plaintiff, using probative evidence.

For those who claim those islands for Egypt should attempt to respond to the following questions:

- **Would Egypt sign an agreement in 1950 with Saudi Arabia on administering Egyptian islands?**
- Would President El-Sisi, a former Minister of Defense, and now Commander in Chief, conspire with Saudi Arabia to cede Egyptian territory regardless of his oath of office?
- Hasn't Egypt administered Gaza on behalf of a future Palestine from 1949 to 1967 to protect it from absorption by Israel -a situation parallel in purpose to the administration of Tiran and Sanafir?
- **Weren't your voices muted when Morsi, during his disastrous one-year rule as President,** gave the nod to Hamas to emigrate into Sinai, and to Sudan to claim the Egyptian triangle of **Halayeb and Shalatin** on the Red Sea?
- In your zeal for respect for the 2014 Constitution, is it legal to resort to an Egyptian Court in order to nullify the agreement on Tiran and Sanafir, a matter which qualifies for review by parliament?
- Have the plaintiffs in this case which is wrongly decided by that administrative Court, substituted for the entire Egyptian population in a **bogus claim of injury to their dignity by the agreement of April 2016?**
- Would those so-called plaintiffs have dared to launch any such challenge during the military dictatorships stretching from 1952 to

2011? Or is the new **"freedom of expression"** an abused license enabling you to dump daily on the presently constitutional and secular government?

You can scratch your head for convincing answers to these questions. **Because you should know that for winning a legal argument, you should have the law and the facts on your side.** Your deep throated screams aimed at proving treachery by El-Sisi and his government are nothing but whistling in the wind!!

Before that Egyptian Administrative Court, your cause of action should have been inadmissible. It lacked every element qualifying it for filing. It suffered from being framed as a conspiracy against Egypt's territorial integrity. **Against the very regime whose leader, El-Sisi, has saved Egypt from civil war.**

*It is with some humor that I take note of the Court resorting to primary school textbooks and related atlases which refer to Egyptian sovereignty over Tiran and Sanafir. If that is part of the evidence, the defendant should have no worry about the final outcome!!*

- An opinion writer by the name of **Abdel-Nasser Salameh** advances in the newspaper **"Al-Masri Al-Yom"** of June 30, an interesting theory. He claims, against any sane logic, that: **"There is a fact which we should admit, and of which we should be ashamed. We have, for the first time in human history, a precedent. A State goes to the judiciary to assert that its land (Tiran and Sanafir) is not Egyptian territory."**

- **How idiotic!!** That writer seeks not only to assert the truth of his conviction without advancing any evidence. He also goes to the incredible limit of **denying the defendant, the Government, the right to rebut the accusations levelled against it by those who** went to the judiciary to raise false claims.

- Calling that sort of articles **"public information"** serves as indicating the depth of ignorance of the primary principle of litigation: An adversarial claim brought before a competent Court by a proper plaintiff against a proper defendant regarding a proper cause of action.

- *All these elements are totally absent in this case. Thus one wonders whether this controversy stems from pure ignorance of the facts, or from a structural ideological bias against whatever El-Sisi presidency might do or not do. This wonderment arises from the stupid accusation by some Egyptian journalists against the Government being complicit with Parliament in perpetuating poverty!! (Ashraf El-Barbari in Al-Shorooq of June 30). How further insane can you get?!*

The Egyptian public has paid scant attention to this contrived dispute. **Its attention was on Eid Al-Fitr and the results of graduation from high school.** With the Eid Al-Fitr now over, public attention shall quickly pivot to the urgent task of institution-building. **Rebuilding a broken educational system, a dysfunctional public information system, and a national commitment to win the twin wars against terrorism and poverty.**

Faulting the judgment in the islands case is not to disparage the great Egyptian judiciary. One faulty judgment is not an adequate measure by which we measure that **third co-equal branch of the Egyptian government.** We find fault with that judgment and with those who support it, because we, as Arab students of the law, are the legal inheritors of the principle: **"The burden of proof is on the plaintiff." [Al-Bayennato Aala Mun Idaa]** A principle passed on by **Ali Ibn Abi Taleb,** 1400 years ago, to **Caliph Omar Ibn Al-Khattab. The second successor of the Prophet Muhammad.** Omar wisely integrated it in his famous judicial declaration.

**Ruling Should Have Been For the Presumed Defendant - The Government of Egypt. Through the Court's Refusal to Consider That Case For Being Nothing More Than Vexatious Litigation.**

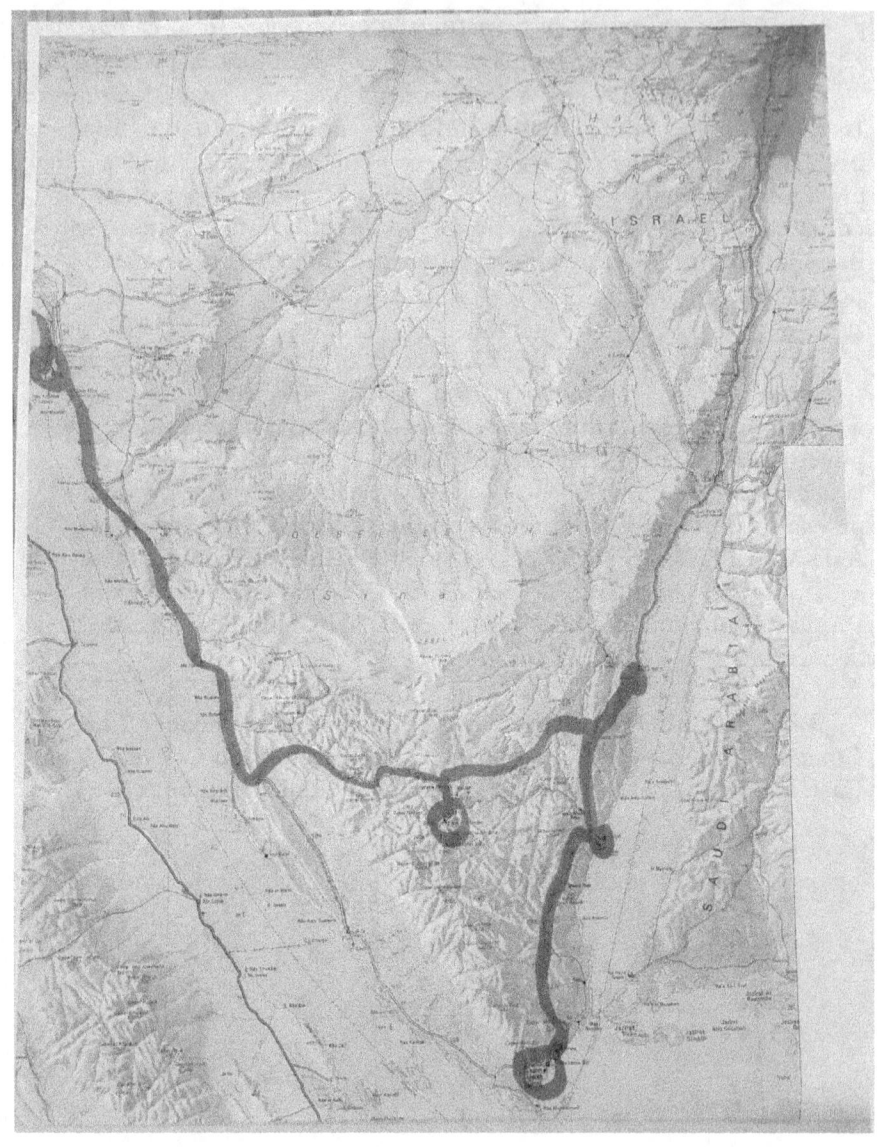

# Wahhabism Is A Crushing Burden on Islam and the Kingdom

Friday, July 15, 2016

It began in the 19th century as a reform movement in Najd, central Arabia. By the late 20th century, **Wahhabism has degenerated into a police theocracy.** A near co-ruler of the Kingdom of Saudi Arabia.

The great founder of the Kingdom, **Abdel-Aziz Al-Saud,** with an eye on legitimating his family's authority over a kingdom of 5 parts, reached an agreement with **Al El-Sheikh, the descendants of Abdel-Wahhab,** the reformist founder of Wahhabism. The Saudis would rule the new State; Al El-Sheikh would oversee religious affairs.

The Saudi family kept its bargain, including funding Wahhabism. The Wahhabis kept on interpreting Islam narrowly, and their authority expansively. What began as Islamic reform praised by **Sheikh Al-Azhar, Muhammad Abdoh,** ended up by a monstrous creature for whom Al-Azhar of today feels the jitters.

When 9/11 happened, the majority of the criminal attackers of America were Saudi nationals. Leading to intensive concern abroad about the dangers of Wahhabism. Several books reflected global unease. Including an important book by **Natana Delong-Bas,** entitled **Wahhabism Islam: From Revival and Reform to Global Jihad (Oxford University Press, 2004).**

Like other sources, this book raises a central question. **"How can contemporary extremists like Osama Bin Laden (a Saudi) use Ibn Abd al-Wahhab's ideology to justify global jihad?"** (page 227). The founder of Wahhabism, in his writings, never made jihad an individual burden. He stressed the legal justifications of who is to carry out jihad, under what circumstances, and for what purposes.

The departure of his successors from that narrow and restrictive

391

interpretation of **jihad (self-policing and the right to national self-defense within your own national borders)** created an atmosphere and circumstances contributing to world-wide Islamophobia. Wahhabism did not create ISIS. But it availed it of an incubator in which its poisonous ideology grew. **Threatening Islam and the Kingdom of Saudi Arabia itself.**

Of course, it is ridiculous for the U.S. Congress to adopt legislation enabling the families of the victims of 9/11 to sue the government of Saudi Arabia for reparations. This is a legal monstrosity. There is no way an attorney of any of these families could produce probative proof that officials of the Kingdom conspired with the criminals of 9/11 to strike. I was tempted to offer my services as a defense attorney to deflate such outrageous claims. But I curbed my enthusiasm.

This issue of official Saudi culpability is expected to go nowhere. But it does not mitigate the burden by which Wahhabism is dragging Islam and the ruling family into unpredictable directions. That is because Wahhabism is caricaturing the faith of 1.7 billion Muslims. Causing idiots like **Donald Trump** to call for a ban on the entry of Muslims to America; stimulating the rise of the European Right against immigrants; and causing all Muslims in the diaspora to always remain on the defensive.

A case in point regarding the **degenerative Wahhabi interpretation of Islam is the case against the Saudi preacher Ahmed Al-Ghamdi.** Fully exposed in a lengthy article in the **New York Times** of July 11, 2016. Authored by **Ben Hubbard,** a staff reporter (and a Christian) writing from **Jidda** under the title of **"Secrets of the Kingdom: Into the Heart of Wahhabism."**

I shall track his main findings, in order to offer a rebuttal based on Islamic Law to the responses which that fair-minded journalist has uncovered for a global audience. From the contrast between what Ben Hubbard was told, and the rules of Islamic jurisprudence which I teach as a law professor in New York City, the reader might perceive the **gulf between Sharia and Wahhabi interpretation of Sharia.**

As we embark on this comparison, let us note that Islamic Law derives from **the Quran, the authenticated traditions of the Prophet Muhammad in word and conduct, and ijtihad** (the application of common sense by Islamic experts to issues where there is no text). In addition, Islamic Law is modifiable or supplemented by legislation, man-made law.

The lack of understanding of this mix has led **38 states of the 50 American states** to ban in their State Courts the mere mention of Sharia. This legal error by these states stems directly from Wahhabi practises or advocacy through their supported Madrasas and other institutions throughout the world.

A further damage inflicted by Wahhabis had **led the US to ban the importation of copies of the Quran from abroad into the US.** A retaliation measure against Saudi ban of the importation of the Bible into the Kingdom.

Wahhabism has also led to the **banning of the construction of minarets in Switzerland,** and protests by American communities **against the construction of mosques.** They also caused infiltrating police informants in American mosques to monitor sermons, and the institution by American Congressman Peter King of congressional hearings on Muslim cooperation with the FBI and other law enforcement agents. Thus **Wahhabism is a main source for the world politics of fear from Islam.** It created a mythical linkage between Islam as a faith, and jihadism as global terror.

**Now to the Ghamdi case.** Ahmed Qassim al-Ghamdi has worked most of his adult life for the **Saudi Commission for the Promotion of Virtue and the Prevention of Vice,** a wahhabi religious police organization. Now he is in self-imposed retirement. No job, fearing the threat of torture for **daring to evolve away from Wahhabism into a thinking human being** questioning their flagrant interpretation of Islam.

A top member of the Saudi religious establishment, **Sheikh Saleh Al-Luhaidan** addressed the Ghamdi matter. As if instructing the State on how to handle Ghamdi's progressive views, he issued this threat publicly: **"There is no doubt that this man is bad. It is necessary for the State to assign someone to summon and torture him."** A Khomeini style call for violence against a Muslim scholar, Ghamdi, who, through resort to the traditions of the **Prophet Muhammad,** is perceived as an apostate.

Backing up this threat for daring to stand up for a distorted Wahhabism, another Saudi religious leader described Ghamdi as **"troubled and confused;"** and **"he is not really a Sheikh,"** though he has a doctorate in Sharia.

Yet here is a host of indicators on the fact that **it is the religious Wahhabi establishment, the State within the State, which is troubled and**

**confused:**

- The non-admission of the existence of **"Wahhabism."** For them, that term is called **"true Islam."** A form of **takfirism (apostasy) in reverse.** As if the rest of the Muslim world, which does not follow their practices is on the wrong path;
- Flowing from this draconian non-recognition of any other religious practices are consequences including the **suppression of Shiism in Saudi Arabia;** the adoption of the non-Islamic term of **"infidel"** as descriptive of the entire non-Muslim sphere of humanity; and the **unislamic attempts to proselytize world-wide;**
- **Forbidding the mixing between men and women** unless they are related by marriage or blood. The Arabic term for gender mixing in Wahhabism is **"ikhtilat." The wall between men and women** is thus built in the workplace, in schools, in restaurants, in nearly every sphere of human activity beyond the walled homes of family life;
- This form of **gender-based apartheid** has led, among other things, to **the denial of women rights.** A full black cover from head to toe, except for slits for seeing. Prohibition of car driving. Non-travel without husband's permission;
- That is not all. There are also the arranged or enforced marriages, including for girls not yet of age. **Ban on wearing make-up,** unless unseen in public. Unequal pay. Non-access to courts except through male representations. In spite of that regime of anti-female total darkness, the Wahhabis bold-facedly dispute the obvious. They deny that Saudi women are deprived from basic human rights;
- Restrictions on commercial activities. These include the enforced closure of shops during the times of prayers; the regulation of display of a panoply of women clothing in shops;
- **The awful textbooks for grade school children,** instructing them from their tender years that: **Christmas and Thanksgiving are forbidden;** celebration of birthdays is to be avoided; music, dance, and such arts are **"haram,"** meaning religiously forbidden;
- Jihad, they claim, is the calling of every Muslim; and Islam, if not observed in the Wahhabi manner, would unravel, leading to the destruction of society.

All of the above, and more, are a close-minded interpretation of Islamic Law as derived from the Quran and the Sunna. Selective and desert-bound deduction by the descendants of the family of Al-Sheikh.

Turning now to the **criminal justice system in Wahhabi-land,** requiring a direct nexus to the Quran, the Prophet's tradition, and ijtihad, we now stand on booby trapped grounds. A booby trap is an explosive device designed to be triggered when an unsuspecting victim touches or disturbs a seemingly harmless object.

**So it is with the case of public beheadings, cutting off of limbs, public flogging, and stoning for suspected adultery.** All forms of corporal punishment said to be prescribed as **Huddud Al-Allah (God's limitations, meaning criminal sanctions decreed in the Quran).** A whole construction that suffers, even when on point, from the exclusion of: **Modifiers** provided by secular legislation; a rich history of Sharia which is premised upon being pro-defendant; and the practice of the **Enlightened Caliphs (the first four successors of the Prophet Muhammad).**

Number Two of these, namely, Omar, refused to accept the admission of a malfeasant who committed theft. And the Quran itself which made proving adultery impossible. For it called for four witnesses actually perceiving the act of penetration. Then you have the all inclusive Islamic adage of **"pardon,"** or forgiveness by an authority, and even by the blood relatives of a murder victim.

The deep dungeon in which wahhabism has descended is their denial of the great label attached to Sharia since the inception of Islam. That label is: **"Sharia Is Fit For Every Time and Every Place."**

**How? Due to its adaptability to changing circumstances. Evolution is the heart of survival.** When **Amre Ibn El-As** invaded Egypt in the 7th century during the reign of Caliph Omar, he was armed with Omar's instructions **not to interfere with Christian Orthodox practices of the Coptic population,** to safeguard their churches and property, and not to force Islam upon them.

And that is **"the True Islam,"** not as defined by the wahhabis, whose **"charitable contributions" have funded jihadism,** and whose restrictive ways of life have contributed to Islamophobia world-wide.

Countering the heavy damage perpetrated by wahhabism as a cult, **the Muslim Brotherhood as a terrorist organization, and Al-Qaeda and ISIS as criminal gangs whose crimes could be last seen in Nice, France, on July 14, 2016,** the call came from Egypt for **"A Religious Revolution."** Al-Azhar was put in charge. And before El-Sisi assumed Egypt's presidency, the secular Constitution of 2014 was very vocal on these issues.

**Article 2** of that Constitution which supplanted the Islamist Constitution of 2012 of the Morsi dark era, stipulated: **"Sharia is the principal source of legislation."** It is a call for **"broad construction."** This is because it does not provide for Sharia to be the only source of legislation. And it provides for the common sense construction that **legislation cannot nullify general principles of the Quran.**

This is bolstered by **Article 3** whose language tracks that of Article 2. Article 3 states that **"the principles of legislation for Egyptian Christians and Jews regarding their personal status (i.e. family law, inheritance, and the like) and their choice of spiritual leaders derive from their own religious practices."** A constitutional recognition of the sanctity of Judaism and Christianity. You don't see the face of wahhabism in such provisions in the Constitution of **Egypt which is home to one third of all Arabs.**

Such Egyptian constitutional pillars are the foundation on which rests the Religious Revolution, now **spearheaded by the Grand Imam of Al-Azhar, Dr. Ahmed Al-Taiyeb,** a graduate of the Sorbonne.

Here follows the ideology of that Revolution which runs counter Jihadism and counter Wahhabism:

- In Abuja, Nigeria, in March 2016, he declares: **"We believe that all revealed religions are from God."** That ignoring this faith in all faiths has produced **"the poisonous fruit of hate for Islam among the adherents of other religions."** That **"Islam, in the language of the Quran, is a term which does not refer to a particular faith. It is the name common to a collective faith which has been advocated by all prophets."** That the Quran has stated: **"We gave him (Jesus) the Scripture in which was guidance and light, and confirming what was before it of the Torah, and a guidance and an admonition for the pious."** **(Chapter V, Verse 46).**

  Later in March (March 22), the Grand Imam of Al-Azhar stood before the **Bundestag in Berlin,** to press on with the ideology of **"the Religious Revolution."**

Quoting him, he declared: **"It is not true what is said about Islam as a religion of combat. The term 'sword' was not mentioned even once in the Quran."** That jihad includes **"every effort designed to serve the needs of the community."** That Muslims living in Europe **"should become a part of the European fabric."** That women in Islamic Law are **"a full partner with men in rights and obligations... Islam is not the cause for marginalization of women. Her marginalization is the result of adhering to decrepit customs having nothing to do with Islam."**

Then in May, 2016, on the eve of Ramadan, a holy month **made bloody by jihadism in Muslim countries** (Turkey, Bangladesh and Iraq), Al-Azhar Rector declared in Paris: **"It is wrong for some who pretend to speak in the name of Islam on Muslims to distance themselves from the Europeans."**

Then he advocated for **"positive integration,"** whereby Muslims in Europe should espouse their new societies. Here he cited the **Charter of Medina** issued by the **Prophet Muhammad.** Calling it **"the first constitution known to mankind,"** it advocated for equality before the law in rights and obligations for all citizens regardless of diversity of faith or ethnicity.

**Where is Wahhabism from these universal principles of Islam** advocated by the Rector of Al-Azhar which was established more than 1000 years ago? No where.

- **No where** when the religious police in Saudi Arabia knocks on doors of the homes of citizens to check upon their daily life;
- **No where** in the plethora of religious fatwas (religious opinions) calling for the death of Micky Mouse;
- **No where** in the Wahhabi opposition to **King Abdullah University of Science and Technology** because women are allowed to study with men on the same campus;
- **No where** when a fatwa is issued by a demented cleric declaring false eyelashes for women to be sinful;
- **No where** where another crazy fatwa is issued against **"all you can eat buffets;"**
- **No where** when the **"Council of Grand Islamic Scholars"** is allowed to issue anti-social decrees in Saudi Arabia making the exit of the citizens to countries abroad **a respite from a suffocating atmosphere of enforced** and retrograde conformity.

**In all of this, one has to distinguish between Saudi Arabia as a State, and Saudi Arabia as Wahhabi land.**

But Wahhabism, as a near cult, is a crushing burden, not only on Islam. But also on the Kingdom itself. For how can Saudi Arabia, with its unlimited potential for growth and prosperity, could catch up with a world, including America, which is now **exploring Jupiter?**

Ghamdi is now in the center of a tsunami for daring to discover the simple truth about Muslim society during the time of the Prophet of Islam: Namely that ikhtilat (mixing men with women) was common. Women set at the Prophet's councils and even disagreed with him at times.

Now here is an advice for Wahhabism, whose excesses are now being partially curtailed by the State. **If the form of woman's body causes you to be excited, don't get a fatwa. Get a psychiatrist. You need help.** And cancel that travel ticket to Thailand and the Philippines. You may get venereal diseases resulting from undercover search for sexual pleasure. **A false assumption of an appearance of virtue is a sin in Islam.**

But it is OK for you to travel to Cairo, where belly dancing is an integral part of public entertainment. Gyrating on the same soil where **Shajarat Al-Durr (The Tree of Pearls), a beautiful woman ruled over Egypt in the 13th century.** The Seventh Crusade ended with her diplomatic dealings as a **Muslim queen,** with her counterpart, a **Christian queen.**

In their own peculiar ways, the **Wahhabis have tribalized Islam.** Thus it is out of the question for them to understand **"The New Normal."** Meaning, in this context, what **David Brooks,** in the New York Times of July 15 eloquently posited. He said: **"Morality is not based on loyalty to people close to (you). It is based on a universal equality for all humans everywhere."**

This is the core of Islam. Its primary source, **the Quran,** begins most of its verses by addressing itself to **"the people"** (Nas). All the people. All of humanity. Not only the segment which calls itself **"Muslim."**

It explains what **Sheikh Mummad Abdoh,** the great Islamic reformer of the 19th/20th centuries told the Egyptian reporters upon his return to Alexandria from Paris. Asked **"How did you find the West?"** His iconic answer was: **"In the West, I found Islam. But here in the East, I find only Muslims."**

*For in France, now the target of several major terrorist attacks within the last 18 months, counting the massacre in Nice on Bastille Day, has been the welcoming incubator of Islamic reform. Its liberties gave it the oxygen which it sorely lacks in its birthplace.*

# Ijtihad As the Brain in the Body of Sharia

December 2015

**Note:** Numbers at the end of certain paragraphs or phrases are for footnotes consisting of the Arabic translation of Quran verses or of sayings by the Prophet Muhammad as well as of known Islamic adages.

## I.     Our Need To Change

I begin by stressing our need to change. Change to become both Muslim and Momin (Muslims and Believers). Muslim per our true faith. Momin in the oneness of God (Tawheed), the one God of every faith.

Now to change from what? From the sorry condition in which we find ourselves and Islam mired. The instances are many; so I shall offer just a few examples to show how the practice is far removed from Islamic Law (Fiqh).

- In Bahrain: credible reports are pouring in about Bahrain. Security forces torturing detainees.
- In Afghanistan: a rocket is aimed by ISIS against a mosque at the end of October. That was during the ISHA (Last daily) prayer. Killing 6, injuring 4.
- In Saudi Arabia: A court, on Nov. 17, sentenced Ashraf Fayadh, an artist and poet, to death. The charge was apostasy based on poems he published years ago. Fayadh sees art as a line of communication between Saudi society and the rest of the world.
- In Bangladesh, a secular publisher is beheaded in early November. Through stabbing him at his office in Dakka. For publishing books critical of religious extremism.
- And in Paris, Mali, the Sinai, Libya, and California terror

399

organizations hiding behind the niqab of Islam, commit atrocities on a massive genocidal scale. Creating unmerited hate for Islam, a faith of inclusiveness and tolerance. Creating anti-Islamism, which is worse than Islamophobia.

Thus Muslims need to change. Islam is a blessing, as a faith of peace. But Allah/God has preordained that we, his creatures, should initiate our own change. In Surat Al-Anfal (verse 53), the Quran says: **"This is because God would never change a favour which He has bestowed on a people unless they change what is in their souls. Indeed God is All-Hearing. All-Knowing."(1)**

- We are 1.5 Billion Muslims. For change, we need to espouse a common denominator. Sharia - Islamic Law - is our common denominator. This is because law is an equalizer. Rich and poor; male and female, Arab and non-Arab, all stand at equal footing before the Law. **"No difference between Arab and non-Arab except by piety."(2)**

## II. What is Piety:

- Piety consists of two sectors: worship and transactions (dealings). Religion or faith has been defined in simple terms. **"Faith is the Way You Deal With Others." (3)** The other is both Muslim and Non-Muslim alike. A differentiation made clear in the Quran. **"Al-Muslimoon"** and **"Al-Momenoon." (4)**
- The Muslim has also been defined. A definition complementary to the submission to the will of God. Summed up in **"Al-Muslim is a person from whom others are safe from his tongue and from his hands (action)." (5)**
- In piety, we are all aware of how we worship. How about **"transactional piety?"** Especially when we find no verse in the Quran, and no Hadith by Muhammad (PBUH). There are gaps. Yet we say: **"Sharia is applicable to every time period, and every geographical location." (6)**
- To answer this question, a question for which the answer cannot be found in the texts (revealed, as in the Quran), and non-revealed (as in the Sunna). Especially that the Quran and the Sunnah are the two great pillars of Fiqh - Islamic Law and Islamic jurisprudence.
- Here comes the beauty, the durability, the authenticity of Sharia which is applicable for all time and for every location. The space, or the gaps, left between these two pillars, have been filled by Ijtihad. Ijtihad is essentially transactional piety.

## III. What Is Ijtihad?

- Here we begin by a definition. Ijtihad is essentially the application of reason and common sense to find a sound justification for an act where neither the Quran nor the Sunna has resolved it. It's the Arabic word for **"striving"** - Meaning do your best thinking to find a basis for your action.

- During the Muhammadan period, the bases for fiqh (jurisprudence) was the revelation. In a book by Yousef Qasim, entitled **"Principles of Islamic Jurisprudence,"** published in Cairo in 1997, we find the author correctly states that there are two types of revelation: The stated word of God in the Quran. And the non-stated, meaning the Sunna. The Sunna in its wider context is what the Prophet said, did, or acted upon. Putting the term Sunna in modern phraseology, one may say: **"It is the annotated agenda explaining the Quran."**

- But the issue of jurisprudence in regard to life events where there was no text was also acted upon by the Prophet himself. In preparation for the end of revelation and the Prophet's passing, Muhammad also permitted his Companions (Al-Sahabah) to resort to ijtihad.

- This is demonstrated in a famous dialogue, between the Prophet and an Ansari by the name Moaz Ibn Jabal.

- The Prophet had wished to assign Moaz to a judgeship in Yemen. Here is the translation of that job interview by the Prophet.
  - Question - **"If a case is brought to you, on what basis shall you judge?"**
  - Response - **"On the basis of the Quran - God's Book."**
  - Question - **"Suppose you did not find the answer for what you are looking for?"**
  - Response - **"Then by the Sunna of God's Messenger."**
  - Question - **"But suppose you could not find the law determining the case, in either the Quran or the Sunna. How would you decide?"**
  - Response - **"Then by Ijtihad without any hesitation."**

The comment by the Prophet at the end of that interview was emblematic. Muhammad put his hands on his chest and uttered these words:

**"Thanks be to God for having guided his Messenger to what is very satisfying for his Messenger." (7)**

- We conclude from the above: (1) That ijtihad in Islamic jurisprudence is a legitimate source for Sharia (The Quran, the Sunna, and ijtihad); (2) That because justice is a main pillar of Islam, the judge has to be conversant in the jurisdiction of matters on which there is no text; (3) That ijtihad is like a flowing river whose waters keep Sharia forever green, forever evolving, and forever relevant. From all the above, the Fatwa in Islam has to be anchored in those 3 sources.

## IV. **The Linkages Between Ijtihad and the Faith:**

There are several linkages between ijtihad and the faith.

1. We begin with the Quran. In Surah 2 (Al-Baqara), Ayah verse 129, it says in the name of Abraham in an appeal to God about the Prophet: **"Our Lord send to them a Messenger from among them who shall recite Your Revelations to them and teach them the Book (Quran) and the Wisdom and purify them. Surely You are Almighty, All-wise." (8)**

Here we have to note that Al-Hekmah (Wisdom) which is mentioned in the Quran 21 times, does not mean the Sunna, as Imam Al-Shafie had thought. And that Al-Hekmah is the use by Al-Mujtahid (the professionally-qualified person to engage in Al-Ijtihad) of the various tools of ijtihad to extrapolate the correct basis for a Sharia Law.

No wonder that the term Al-Hekmah, the mechanism for Al-Ijtihad when we find no text on any matter, has occurred 20 times in the Quran.

2) Following up on the Sunnah, namely the Prophet's instruction to Moaz upon appointing him as a judge in Yemen, the four Enlightened Caliphas (Al-Kholafa Al-Rashidoon) have followed the same bath. Abu-Bakr followed Omar's advice to get the Quran written; Omar's advice was simple. **"Collecting the Quran in one compendium was "a good deed;"** Osman organized the words of God by chapters and Ayahs in what became known as **"Moshaf Osman - the Book as gathered by Osman."** And Ali made his priority to ensure that not one Ayah was missing. All the four acted on Ijtihad after the passing of the Prophet who left no tradition in that regard.

3) That deliberate process of legitimating ijtihad was bolstered by many Quranic ayas about **"Al-tafkeer"** (Thinking). The Quran reports **"Don't they think?" (9)**

Why? Because in ijtihad there is a continuous renewal of Sharia to be applicable to continuously changing circumstances.

3) With that in mind, Omar in his famous legal instruction to his judge Shuraih demanded:

**"Judge on the basis of the Quran. If you find no text on point, then judge by the Sunnah of God's Messenger (Rasool Illah). And if you find non applicable text, then follow the precedents of good judges preceeding you. (This in Latin is called Stare Decisis: The Rule of the Precedent). And still if you do not find what you are seeking, then strive to find the rule of law by your own thinking - your ijtihad."**

5) Ijtihad reflects the commitment of Islam to seeking knowledge. Knowledge from every discipline, from every source. The Prophet has said: **"Seek knowledge even from as far as China."** The first word in the Quran is **"IQRA."** It does not only mean **"Read."** Its broadest meaning is **"learn."** To acquire knowledge from diverse sources, requires discipline, continuity, perseverance, openness, recording, propagation, and assimilation of diverse sources. The mosque is Jamee - meaning **"all inclusive"** - worship; schooling; social interaction; growing your mind. For both men and women. This is the soul of ijtihad.

6) That flexibility in Islam through ijtihad, which is a duty, **"Fareedha,"** is a present not only in transactions. But also in worship. Muhammad said: **"Pray as you see me pray."** Then in connection with the Hajj ritual, the Prophet opened the door of variation wide. As he said: **"Do with no impediments." (10)** This is because Islamic Law is based on making of religious practices an easy endeavor. This is completely the opposite of what Wahhabi Islam is all about.

### V. <u>Types of Ijtihad</u>
From the foregoing, you see that Sharia, Islamic Law, has three sources: The Quran, the Sunna, and ijtihad.

As a reminder, ijtihad is Al-Hekmah (Wisdom; application of the mind to solving issues where we find no text to guide us in their resolution. Neither in the Quran, nor in the Sunnah.) For additional reinforcement of the legitimacy in Sharia of ijtihad is in the Quranic chapter of Al-Nahl (The Bee). **"Invite all, to the way of thy Lord with wisdom and beautiful preaching; and argue with them in ways that are best and most gracious"** (Chapter 16; Ayah 125). **(11)**

So ijtihad (Al-Hekmah) has two primary pillars: Ijmaa (unanimity) and Qiyas (analogy). In both of these, as well as in the Quran and the Sunnah, the main principle is **"Whatever is good for society." (12)**

This principle is dealt with extensively in a mountain of Islamic sources which deal with **"Fiqh Al-Massalah"** - The jurisdiction of Societal Benefit. In chapter Al-Raad (The Thunder), the Quran says:
**"Thus doth God by parables show forth truth and vanity. For the scum disappears like froth cast out; while that which is for the good of mankind remains on the earth"** (Chapter 13, Ayah 17) **(13)**

The jurisdiction of **"Societal Interest"** (Fiqh Al-Masslaha) has been lauded by iconic Islamic reformers, like the late Gamal El-Banna. In his seminal book, entitled **"The Case For the New Fiqh"** he regarded it as the basis for reaching correct judgement. Any conflict between this jurisdiction and the text. Calls for interpretation of the text through ijtihad. It should be noted that this jurisdiction applies fully to Muslims and non-Muslims alike.

As to ijmaa, it is the consensus amongst qualified Muslim scholars in regard to the rule in an event occurring after the passing of the Prophet. In this regard, the Quran says:

**"O ye who believe! Obey God, and obey the Apostle, and those charged with authority among you."** (Chapter 4/Ayah 59). **(14)**

**"Those charged with authority"** are those scholars, fuqaha who are engaged in ijtihad.

The ijmaa means the ruling reached by consensus amongst qualified Muslim scholars. Obviously this cannot, by any stretch of imagination, include the murderous gangs of terrorism, starting with Bin Laden, and ending now with that insane Al-Baghdadi who claims to be the Caliphah of the so-called Islamic State. They are not Muslim scholars, regardless of what they claim themselves to be. They are cut off the faith of Islam, an Islam based on inclusiveness, acceptance of all religions, tolerance, and engagement in whatever advances the interest of the world community. They do not abide by the Quranic high standards of the Islamic principle of **"faith is how you treat others."(15)**

We see the reference to ijmaa in Al-Sunnah. The Prophet has said: **"My Umma (Nation) does not coalesce (meaning unite) on a consensus (ijmaa) based on evil." (16)**

The other pillar of ijtihad is Qiyas (analogy). It means that issues on which no text can be found for guidance, could be settled in sharia by analogy. Thus a Mujtahid tries to extrapolate from a text the intention of the judgment (the reasoning) in that text.

As an example: The question of alcoholic beverages. In the Quran, it is stated: **"O ye who believe! Intoxicants and gambling, dedication of stones and divination by arrows are an abomination of Satan's handiwork: eschew (meaning avoid) such abomination that you may prosper."** (Chapter 5, Ayah 90). **(17)**

By use of Al-Qiyas (analogy), Al-Mujtahid deduces the application of that rule to all matter, drinks or drugs, whether liquid or in pills or plants as

**"Khamr" (intoxicant).** The reasoning here is that partaking of such substances affects the brain, and leads to irrationality. This is in addition to their deleterious effects on good judgement, and the taking care of oneself, one's family, one's community.

Aside from ijmaa and Qiyas, there are other types of ijtihad. These less prominent types of ijtihad end their list by including **"the legal methodology of other faiths which preceded Islam." (18)**

On that unity in faith, but diversity in practice, the Quran says: **"He has ordained for you the Religion which He commanded to Noah, and that We have revealed to you, and that which We commanded to Abraham, and Moses, and Jesus: "Establish the Religion, and be not divided therein."** (Chapter 42 (As Shura); Ayah 13) **(19)**

## VI. Conclusion

- In conclusion, we should note that Islam is a faith and a community organizer within cooperative relationship with all others. Ijtihad is a basic pillar of Islamic law. The term **"umma"** means **"a community,"** not **"a State."**

- Islam provides for a balance between ritual/or worship, and secular transactions governed by whatever is good for the community. That community is not the tribe. It is the human collectivity in which you reside. The Quran states: **"But seek, with the wealth which God has bestowed on thee, the home of the hereafter, nor forget thy portion in this world. But do thou good, as God has been good to thee. And seek not occasion for mischief in the land. For God loves not those who do mischief."** (Chapter 28; Ayah 77). **(20)**

- The most abhorrent type of fasad (mischief) is to assume by yourself the heinous tasks of declaring the others as apostate. Or worse still kill them in the name of Islam. 9/11 or the Paris massacres, or the Beirut butchery, or the death sentences issued by some Islamic courts against so-called blasphemers, are acts of aggression against Islam and the broader humanity.

- The jurisdiction of public good is at the heart of the dynamism of Islam. And is a primary source of its continuous renewal to make it accord with changing circumstances.

- Note that the Quran advises not only the Muslims, but the humans in general. Al-Insan means the human being regardless of their faith - The Quran addresses those humans, as human. **"O people" (21)**

- Al-Tawheed, the oneness of God, is the eternal tie between Islam and all other faiths, including Christianity and Judaism. **"Allahu Akbar"** - **"God is Great,"** is not, as ISIS or Al-Qaida or Boka

Haram claims, a battle cry. It means that we are all equal before God. He is the final judge; not a so-called Calipha or a muallim, or a faqih, or anyone of these sectarian titles. Your link to your creator is a 24/7 hotline, direct, with no static; a constant dial tone; without a broker between you and Allah.

- Ijtihad is essential for a pertinent Fatwa (an opinion based on Sharia).
- Islamophobia, now turned **"anti-Islamism"** is the outcome of ignorance about Sharia. Sharia is perceived to be the crazy rules sputtering from the mouth of actors who know very little about Islam as a faith whose values are universal.
- Finally it is incumbent upon all Muslims who reside outside of the lands of Islam to harmonize between their being Muslims and also being good citizens abiding by the legislated laws of their host States. That is the beauty of our Hijrah to America and other lands. That is the great lesson of the Hijrah. (immigration).
- Those who call for the return of Islamic law and practice of more than 1400 years ago contribute to that anti-Islamism whereby 38 American States have unconstitutionally banned the mere mention of the word **"Sharia"** in their State courts. Their perspective is faulty. They look with apprehension at the brutal practices in certain Muslim countries. In those countries discrimination on the basis of gender, oppression of, spouses and daughters, and other females, floggings, cutting of human limbs, stoning for adultery, killing of secularists, and waging terrorism in the name of Islam have caused a revulsion against Islam and Muslims. These are all horrendous practices which are patently illegal under Islamic jurisprudence.
- In Islamic law, Sharia, both the text and ijtihad open the doors daily to whatever is reasonable, balanced, based on the good of society. That is the essence of Sharia - a constantly renewed system of laws with 80% commonality with the US Constitution.
- So let us live it, study it, understand it, and find in it a solid bridge to world peace and universalism.
- Ending by a quote from the Quran: **"Those who disbelieve in Allah and His Messengers, and seek to make distinction between Allah and His Messengers, and say: We believe in some and disbelieve in others, and seek to close a way in between. Such are disbelievers in truth; and for disbelievers we prepare a shameful doom."** (Chapter 4, Ayahs 150 and 151) **(22)**

Before closing, I would like to address America, our land of adoption or birth:

**America:** Your fear of terrorism is understandable. But don't understand Islam through the criminality of the few who call themselves Muslims. Terror organizations falsely hiding behind the term "Islamic" are nothing but the viporous snakes in the great green grass of Islam.

- Our American Constitution says that "Congress shall make no law respecting an establishment of religion, or prohibiting the free exercise thereof."
- This basic law, we American Muslims uphold, support and defend. Yet anti-Islamism is on the rise in this great land. Isn't this a sinister intimidation of the free exercise of Islam in America?
- Just witness the attacks on a sitting US President by calling him "a closet Muslim." As if Islam was Ebola or HIV!!
- Just witness the Nazi move by Donald Trump, a Republican aspiring to the Oval Office, calling for registering all American Muslims in a database. Another manifestation that he, and Ben Carson, need to have heads examined;
- Just witness the Congressional hearings organized by Congressman Peter King of Nassau County asking Muslims about their degree of cooperation with US security forces. How would you legally measure "a degree of cooperation?" And why single out Muslims in this land of immigrants?
- Just witness the lionization of a Somali woman by the name of Ayaan Hirsi Ali who is calling for the re-writing of the Quran. Such crazy advocacy is the oxygen which ISIS craves for recruiting more misguided adherents.
- America: The problem of your security is not Islam. Nor is it the huge majority of Muslims in America who are peaceful and law-abiding.
- America: The problem is your near total ignorance of Islam as a universal faith of peace; of SALAM. Learn about Islam before you rush to all those faulty judgements; to that Islamophobia; to that dangerous espousal of anti-Islamism.

# ABOUT THE AUTHOR

Dr. Yassin El-Ayouty, Esq. has a Ph.D. from New York University in international law and international organization (1966); and J.D. from Cardozo School of Law (1994). A U.S. Fulbright Scholar (1952-1954); assisted Raphael Lemkin in genocide issues (1955); recipient of N.Y.U. Founders Day Award, and Cardozo Faculty Award for Best Legal Writing. University professor since 1966; and Distinguished Visiting Professor, Nova Law Center, Fort Lauderdale, Florida. Member of American bars and Federation of Arab Bars. Practising litigation in America and abroad. Served the UN for 32 years, retiring as Political Director. Co-founded UNITAR; drafted its Statute for UN General Assembly (1965). Established SUNSGLOW - Global Training in the Rule of Law in 1998, now a not-for-profit. Presently, Professor at Fordham University School of Law, teaching "Islamic Law and Global Security;" St. Francis College (New York City); Cairo University Law; Focal point in North America for Al-Azhar University (Cairo); and Emeritus at Stony Brook University, New York. Present focus: Islamic Law; the New Egypt; US/Arab strategic relations. Author of 12 books; the most recent: "The Transformation of Egypt Through Revolution" (Amazon, 2015).

www.ingramcontent.com/pod-product-compliance
Lightning Source LLC
Chambersburg PA
CBHW060612290526
45793CB00001B/3